AEROTROPOLIS
THE WAY WE'LL LIVE NEXT

JOHN D. KASARDA | GREG LINDSAY

ALLEN LANE
an imprint of
PENGUIN BOOKS

LIBRARIES NI

C700585913		
RONDO	02/03/2011	
307	£ 14.99	
LSBNCL		

ALLEN LANE

Published by the Penguin Group
Penguin Books Ltd, 80 Strand, London wc2r 0rl, England
Penguin Group (USA) Inc., 375 Hudson Street, New York, New York 10014, USA
Penguin Group (Canada), 90 Eglinton Avenue East, Suite 700, Toronto, Ontario,
Canada m4p 2y3 (a division of Pearson Penguin Canada Inc.)
Penguin Ireland, 25 St Stephen's Green, Dublin 2, Ireland
(a division of Penguin Books Ltd)
Penguin Group (Australia), 250 Camberwell Road, Camberwell, Victoria 3124,
Australia (a division of Pearson Australia Group Pty Ltd)
Penguin Books India Pvt Ltd, 11 Community Centre,
Panchsheel Park, New Delhi – 110 017, India
Penguin Group (NZ), 67 Apollo Drive, Rosedale, Auckland 0632, New Zealand
(a division of Pearson New Zealand Ltd)
Penguin Books (South Africa) (Pty) Ltd, 24 Sturdee Avenue,
Rosebank, Johannesburg 2196, South Africa

Penguin Books Ltd, Registered Offices: 80 Strand, London wc2r 0rl, England

www.penguin.com

First published in the United States of America by Farrar, Straus and Giroux 2011
First published in Great Britain by Allen Lane 2011
1

Copyright © John D. Kasarda and Greg Lindsay, 2011

The moral right of the authors has been asserted

Portions of this book originally appeared in *Fast Company*.
Grateful acknowledgment is made for permission to reprint the following material:
Quotation from "Airports: The Cities of the Future" by J. G. Ballard, originally
published in *Blueprint: Architecture, Design & Contemporary Culture*. Copyright ©
1997 by J. G. Ballard, used with permission of the Wylie Agency, LLC.
Image on page 100 from *Flying Smart, Thinking Big: Global Market Forecast 2009–
2028* courtesy of Airbus.

All rights reserved
Without limiting the rights under copyright
reserved above, no part of this publication may be
reproduced, stored in or introduced into a retrieval system,
or transmitted, in any form or by any means (electronic, mechanical,
photocopying, recording or otherwise), without the prior
written permission of both the copyright owner and
the above publisher of this book

Printed in Great Britain by Clays Ltd, St Ives plc

A CIP catalogue record for this book is available from the British Library

isbn: 978–1–846–14100–3

www.greenpenguin.co.uk

MIX
Paper from
responsible sources
FSC
www.fsc.org FSC® C018179

Penguin Books is committed to a sustainable
future for our business, our readers and our
planet. This book is made from paper certified
by the Forest Stewardship Council.

For Mary Ann, my foundation while I'm in the air
—JDK

For Sophie, who was always waiting in arrivals
—GL

I suspect that the airport will be the true city of the 21st century. The great airports are already the suburbs of an invisible world capital, a virtual metropolis whose fauborgs are named Heathrow, Kennedy, Charles de Gaulle, Nagoya, a centripetal city whose population forever circles its notional centre, and will never need to gain access to its dark heart. —J. G. Ballard

A city made for speed is made for success. —Le Corbusier

CONTENTS

AEROTROPOLIS

INTRODUCTION

The shapes and fates of cities have always been defined by transportation. Today, this means air travel.

Stan Gale was exultant. The chairman of Gale International yanked off his tie, hitched up his pants, and mopped the sweat and floppy hair from his brow. He beamed like a proud new papa, sprung from the waiting room and handing out cigars to whoever happens by. Beckoning me to follow, he sauntered across eight lanes of traffic toward his baby, New Songdo City, delivered prematurely days before.

Ten years ago, Gale was a builder and flipper of New Jersey office parks. But his fate began to change in 2001 with a phone call from South Korea. The Korean government had found his firm on the Internet and made an offer everyone else had refused. The brief: Gale would borrow $35 billion from Korea's banks, partner with its biggest steel company, and use the money to build from scratch a city the size of downtown Boston, only taller and denser, on a muddy man-made island in the Yellow Sea. When Gale arrived to see the site, it was miles of open water. He signed anyway.

New Songdo won't be finished until 2015 at least, but in August 2009, Gale cut the ribbon on its hundred-acre Central Park modeled, like so much of the city, on Manhattan's. Climbing on all sides is a mix of low-rises and sleek spires—condos, offices, even South Korea's tallest building, the 1,001-foot Northeast Asia Trade Tower. Strolling along the park's canal, we heard cicadas buzzing, saws whining, and pile drivers pounding down to bedrock. I asked whether he'd stocked the canal with fish yet. "It's four days old!" he spluttered, forgetting he wasn't supposed to rest until the seventh.

As far as playing God (or SimCity) goes, New Songdo is the most ambitious instant city since Brasília appeared fifty years ago. Brasília, of course, was an instant disaster: grandiose, monstrously overscale, and immediately encircled by slums. New Songdo has to be much better, because there's a lot more riding on it than whether Gale can repay his loans. It has been hailed since conception as the experimental prototype community of tomorrow. A green city, it was LEED certified from the get-go, designed to emit a third of the greenhouse gases of a typical metropolis its size. It's supposed to be a "smart city" studded with chips talking to one another, running the place by remote control. Its architects borrowed blueprints from Paris, Sydney, Venice, and London, sketching what might become the prettiest square mile in Korea. (Nearby Seoul is a forest of colossally ugly apartment blocks.)

New Songdo isn't so much a Korean city as a Western one floating offshore. Smart, green credentials aside, it was chartered as an "international business district"—a hub for companies working in China. Worried about being squeezed by its neighbors, New Songdo is Korea's earnest attempt to build an answer to Hong Kong. To make expatriates feel at home, its malls are modeled on Beverly Hills', and Jack Nicklaus designed the golf course. But its most salient feature is shrouded in perpetual haze opposite a twelve-mile-long bridge that is one of the world's longest. On the far side is Incheon International Airport, which opened in 2001 on another man-made island and instantly became one of the world's busiest hubs.

"They tracked us down, wanted us to build a city in the ocean, and no one else was interested? *What was going on here?*" Gale told me, still dazed. "Their vision scared everyone else away. It wasn't until I saw the airport that I understood where they wanted to go with this." China. His sales pitch to prospective tenants is simple: move here, and you're only a two-hour flight away from Shanghai or Beijing, and four hours away at most from cities you've never heard of, like Changsha. Chairman Mao's hometown happens to be larger than Atlanta or Singapore. Nearly a billion people are a day trip away. When Stan Gale looks at a departure board, he sees a treasure map. And when he gazes upon his creation, he sees potentially dozens of new cities, each next to a dot on that map.

"There's a pattern here, repeatable," he said that summer, stunning his partners with plans to roll out cities across China, using New Songdo as his template. Each will be built faster, better, and more cheaply than the ones that came before. "It's going to be a cool city, a smart city!" he promised. "We start from here and then we are going to build twenty new cities like this one, using this blueprint. Green! Growth! Export!" Their jaws dropped. "China alone needs five hundred cities the size of New Songdo," Gale told me, and he is planning to break ground on the next two. How many will be umbilically connected to the nearest airport? "All of them."

To the jaundiced American eye, New Songdo and its clones might appear to be fantasies left over from the Bubble. But dismissing them as the product of Asia's infatuation with all things mega misses the carefully calibrated machinery underneath. It's a machine the rest of us ignore at our peril as we enter the next phase of globalization—one marked by the shift from West to East and the trade routes up for grabs in between. It even has a name, which Stan Gale pronounced for me with a flourish: "It's an *aerotropolis*."

It isn't his word. The man who taught it to him is John Kasarda, a professor at the University of North Carolina who has made a name for himself with his radical (and some might say bone-chilling) vision of the future: rather than banish airports to the edge of town and then do our best to avoid them, we will build this century's cities around them. Why? Because people once chose to live in cities for the wealth of connections they offered socially, financially, intellectually, and so forth. But in the era of globalization, we choose cities drawing closer together themselves, linked by fiber-optic cables and jet aircraft. Stan Gale is simply taking this idea to its conclusion, building a network of instant ones joined by their airports.

Many aerotropoli will evolve out of the cities we already call home—only their highways and byways will lead us to terminals instead of downtown. For instant ones like New Songdo, Kasarda has drafted a set of blueprints replete with air trains and "aerolanes" connecting prefab neighborhoods and business districts. They range in size from a few thousand residents to a few million. Aerotropoli designed according to his principles are under way across China, India, the Middle East, and Africa, and on the fringes of cities as desperate as Detroit and as old as Amsterdam. In Kasarda's opinion, any city can be one. And every city should be.

The aerotropolis represents the logic of globalization made flesh in the form of cities. Whether we consider it to be good or simply inevitable, the global village holds these truths to be self-evident: that customers on the far side of the world may matter more than those next door; that costs must continually be wrung from every piece of every business in a market-share war of all against all; that the pace of business, and of life, will always move faster and cover more ground; and that we must pledge our allegiance if we want our iPhones, Amazon orders, fatty tuna, Lipitor, and Valentine's Day roses at our doors tomorrow morning. If the airport is the mechanism making all of these things possible, Kasarda reasons, then everything else—our factories, offices, homes, schools—will be built accordingly. The aerotropolis, he promises, will be a new kind of city, one native to our era of instant gratification—call it the Instant Age.

The Man with the Plan

If, thirty years ago, John Kasarda had tried telling a mayor to build his city around the nearest airport, the mayor would have told Kasarda he was crazy, and he would have been right, judging by the available evidence. Looking back now, however, the aerotropolis seems inevitable, at least when we stop to consider what a city is, what we want from it, and what we gain from living in one.

I first met him in his office, surrounded by model planes received as gifts from one foreign delegation or another. The only other place I've ever seen him is in an airport. You have too, I bet, floating in your peripheral vision: delayed in Hong Kong's, laying over in London's, or maybe wending his way through customs at New York's JFK, back from Bangkok or one of his conferences in Beijing. He's the one in the noniron shirt and wrinkle-free suit, jet lag stamped on his face. He's flown more than three million miles in the last quarter century—farther than any of the men who set foot on the moon. He's up in the air two months a year, flying far enough to circle the globe a half-dozen times. But his numbers are barely half of his peers'. He blends in with all the middle-aged men in first class whom you pass on your way to coach, because he's one of them—the traveling salesmen recognize him, academic posting or no, as one of their own. They're his tribe.

Kasarda's mother tongue is academic jargon leavened by the argot of business bestsellers. Chat him up at the gate and he'll spit out long strings of professorial verbiage about "spatial friction," "sustainable competitiveness," and "the physical Internet." Listen closely enough, however, and the technobabble crystallizes into themes that have obsessed him since his teens: our lot in life is shaped by circumstance; our fates are not necessarily ours to choose.

He knew this instinctively growing up in Wilkes-Barre, Pennsylvania, near the end of King Coal's reign in the 1950s. He was thirteen when the miners dug upward into the Susquehanna's riverbed, which then collapsed. A dozen died, sixty-nine others escaped, and he watched the survivors fail to plug the ensuing whirlpool. "We knew this was the end," Kasarda recalled. "They couldn't change that, no matter what they did." Their fate was sealed long before the flood.

At Cornell, where he studied economics as an undergraduate and simultaneously earned an M.B.A., he clashed with professors more interested in defining deviancy than in divining the order of things. One instructor sneered at his apostasy, comparing him to Amos Hawley, the dissident who developed the field of "human ecology" to ask the big-picture questions his colleagues wouldn't touch. How do we adapt to our environments? How does this shape the way we start families, build cities, launch companies, found institutions? And how do these, in turn, determine how we see the world? So Kasarda followed Hawley to the University of North Carolina and set to work disassembling the machinery of everyday life. He became a professor himself at the University of Chicago in 1971.

He hadn't seen any hints of the aerotropolis yet. It would be another two years before Frederick W. Smith moved home to Memphis with his start-up Federal Express in tow. Its airport was typical of the time, with two stubby runways too short for the new 747s, and its most frequent fliers belonging to the Tennessee Air National Guard. If an airline wanted to fly to Chicago, it needed permission from the government; if you wanted to, you called your travel agent, because the Internet was then still just a science experiment.

Twenty years later, by now a professor at North Carolina's Kenan-Flagler Business School, Kasarda had seen enough of NAFTA to know that factories were headed overseas, and call centers, branch offices, and even headquarters would soon follow. They would all need to link up again somehow, and faster than before. "The Global Air Cargo–Industrial Complexes" was his first stab at explaining it in 1991, imagining factories lining the runways someday. FedEx saw these schematics and called seeking his help—it was grappling with something called e-commerce. Amazon.com and its ilk didn't exist at the start of the nineties, but by the end they had transformed both FedEx and Memphis. New business models begat new companies, new jobs, and a new way of life for the quarter of the city's one million residents now in orbit around the airport.

Plans for the aerotropolis sprang from Kasarda's head fully formed at the millennium as a way to explain this, control it, plan for it . . . and maximize it. Suddenly, he held the plans to build an airport that was more than just an airport, and the world beat a path to his door. Memphis called, wanting to double down and remake itself as "America's Aerotropolis." Detroit, searching for life after the Big Three, wondered if its airport held the answer. Kasarda's brainchild first made him a regular on the Chamber of Commerce luncheon circuit, then attracted offers to chair conferences, and then meetings with foreign ministers. Soon, he was being summoned to China, India, Taiwan, and Thailand, where he emerged from closed-door meetings with "aerotropolis" dripping from bureaucrats' lips. He is the rare scholar whose ideas have consequences, for whose ideas governments have staked billions of dollars on his instant cities and strategy. His vision draws on decades' worth of data showing the trend lines creeping steadily upward.

There is still a bull market for business gurus, and Kasarda's stock has steadily climbed as "competitiveness" became the idée fixe of not just CEOs but also mayors and presidents. The Econ 101 approach of "I'm a Mac" vs. "I'm a PC" doesn't hold water anymore. Half the battle in any market is now fought by invisible armies of suppliers, any of which might be arming both sides. "Individual companies don't compete," Kasarda told me. "Supply chains compete. Networks and systems compete." And so, it follows, do the cities and countries they call (for the moment) home.

Kasarda is probably shuttling between Taipei and Bangalore right now, following the herd whose paths he's already traced. Not that he's enjoying it. The man hailed by trade ministers as the prophet of living our lives aloft is disinclined to fly, if only because he does so much of it. There's no irony in this. His finding isn't that we *should* take to the skies in a perverse reprise of the Jet Age, but that we must, or else this flat world we've gotten used to will remember its former shape.

You don't need to see New Songdo for a vision of this future. Visit Kasarda at home in Chapel Hill, which forms one side of the urban triangle that lends its name to Research Triangle Park. The park opened in 1959 as a magnet for high-tech talent, which was then in short supply. A few years later, IBM arrived with the first group of some eleven thousand employees. Monsanto, GlaxoSmithKline, and dozens of other companies followed, sloughing off pieces of themselves to Tobacco Road, a five-hour drive from Washington, six hours from Atlanta, but only an hour's flight from Manhattan. When Lenovo bought IBM's ThinkPad line six years ago, it moved its headquarters there from China. The CEO's office is exactly three minutes from the airport (I've timed it), and needs to be, considering how often he flies to Singapore and Beijing.

"Despite all the talk of the service economy, of health care and software as our national industries, ours is still a goods economy," Kasarda once explained to me. "Even most services are concerned with paying for goods. And the people performing those services need iPods and computers, which create manufacturing jobs somewhere—today, in China. Aside from education, entertainment, and health care, we consume very little in the way of pure services. And health care is increasingly about the goods given to the patients.

"A large and growing proportion of these goods moves internationally, as a consequence of trade and modern supply chains. Components are made in a dozen different countries and assembled in a thirteenth. They move by air either because there's an emergency, because it's too valuable to sit in a warehouse, or because it's perishable, like flowers, fish, and pharmaceuticals. All of this passes through a physical Internet, the network of hubs and planes for trading and transporting goods—and people—almost as quickly as the Internet itself. And it's arguably more important—the Web can't move your box from Amazon.

"The aerotropolis is the urban incarnation of this physical Internet; the primacy of air transport makes airports and their hinterlands the places to see how it functions—and to observe the consequences. The three rules of real estate have changed from location, location, location, to *accessibility, accessibility, accessibility*. There's a new metric. It's no longer space; it's time and cost. And if you look closely at the aerotropolis, what appears to be sprawl is slowly evolving into a system reducing both. It's here where we can see how globalization will reshape our cities, lives, and culture."

Cities and Speed

"Don't tell anyone," the bomb-throwing architect Rem Koolhaas once said, "but the 20th-century city is over. It has nothing new to teach us anymore. Our job is simply to maintain it." He's right, but his secret didn't get out in time. New cities began climbing fast and furiously in Shanghai, Mumbai, and Dubai at precisely the moment we in the developed West lost faith in our ability to build one.

Humanity is officially an urban species—at this moment, more than half of us live in cities. The percentage is even higher in the developed world, but Africa and Asia are catching up. The number of city dwellers is expected to double by 2050 to more than six billion people—the number alive on earth right now. The number of megacities (those with a population of ten million or more) will increase from three in 1950 to twenty-seven by 2025, housing 450 million people among them. Stan Gale wasn't exaggerating: China really does need five hundred new cities the size of New Songdo, and another hundred cities of a million residents or more.

Who will pay for all this? The world's governments are poised to spend a staggering $35 *trillion* on infrastructure in the next two decades, the majority on transport and urbanism. The biggest build-out in human history will reset the global pecking order, as new flows of people and goods displace financial churn. Before the rise of the rest resumes in earnest, we must find cities' new form before their skylines are locked in place for another hundred years . . . or subsumed by slums.

We have always chosen to live in cities for the wealth of networks they create—the elaborate webs of kinship and commerce delivering sustenance and security. That promise hasn't changed since the agora and acropolis, but the size and scope of cities have. Cities grew by shrinking the distances within and between them, using technology to expand their grids and cover more ground.

Lewis Mumford, cities' foremost historian, recognized them by their elements, many of which were in place by the time of the ancient Greeks and are still in use today: "the walled enclosure, the street, the house-block, the market," even the office. But Mumford confused the lobster with its shell. Cities molt and outgrow their shapes, regularly exploding into new ones when the opportunity arises, typically when a new form of transport arrives on the scene.

There will never be enough time in the day, but space is fungible; it can be overcome with speed. Karl Marx called it the "annihilation of space by time." Distance is less of an obstacle to daily life than it is a persistent friction on our ability to get things done, which we can measure by the time and effort involved in commuting from Point A to Point B. The sociologist Melvin Webber dubbed this idea "the elastic mile," because our perception of just how far a mile is shrinks as we move faster, leading Amos Hawley to note that we tend to live our lives within a sixty-minute radius from home. While that once meant a life maybe six miles wide, today it means a commute between Barcelona and London. And e-mail bound for customer service or colleagues in India is returned instantly.

Edge City author Joel Garreau declared, "Cities are always created around whatever the state-of-the-art transportation device is at the time." When the state of the art is shoe leather and donkeys, the result is the hilly paths of Jerusalem. When it's men on horseback and sailing ships, it's the ports of Lisbon, Hong Kong, or Boston, and the canals of Venice and Amsterdam. The birth of the railroad produced Kansas City, Omaha, and the stockyards of Chicago. And the mass production of the Model T led first to Los Angeles and later to Levittown. Today, the modern combination on the ground is the automobile and Internet, yielding Garreau's exurban "edge cities," which are everywhere and nowhere within America, and have since cropped up in Bangalore and beyond. Soaring above them all are jet aircraft—first put into service sixty years ago, at the onset of the Jet Age—collapsing the distance between Dallas and Dubai as effortlessly as the Internet nodes connecting them. "Because of the airport," Garreau says, "it's possible to imagine a world capital in a place that was once an absolute backwater—a Los Angeles or a Dallas appearing in an utterly improbable location, [like] Bangkok."

The capitals of each era were cities native to them. Venetian ships ruled the Mediterranean and Dutch ships the oceans, briefly, from their home harbors, making their docks the centers of Western civilization. Chicago broke all records for urbanization during the back half of the nineteenth century, absorbing two million residents drawn to the factories surrounding its railroad stations, the de facto gateways to the American West. Los Angeles and its highways became the template for the suburban good life, while Silicon Valley's bandwidth enabled the Internet boom and the largest legal accumulation of wealth in history. Each one was a function of the fuel that fed it, whether wind or peat or coal or oil. *Especially* oil. The gravest threat to cities is the prospect of their pipelines of cheap oil running dry. Without oil, or a substitute that burns cleaner and just as brightly, the next form of cities may depend on the oxcart.

In every case, as the friction posed by space has decreased, cities have become less dense and contiguous and grown more dispersed, networked, and fluid. In the Net Age, this fluidity promised (or threatened) to become extreme—in theory, those of us who make our living with computers could live anywhere. No one has preached this vision more fervently than the technologist George Gilder, whose utopia of the "telecosm" and infinite bandwidth has us scattering back into the countryside to live like Jeffersonian gentlemen-farmers, with Facebook serving as the village green.

But total dispersion hasn't come to pass, and it won't, no matter how much bandwidth we're able to route through our iPhones. In fact, the same technologies that were supposed to disaggregate us have only made concentration more useful. We're becoming more urban at precisely the moment our outlook is growing more global. We keep an eye on the street and a cell phone to our ears, somehow managing to be in both places at once. The same thing is happening at a macro level too. The hinterlands of Los Angeles, for example, aren't California's Central Valley or the high Mojave Desert but the outlands of Seoul, Hong Kong, and Mexico City. Webber's elastic mile has stretched so far we're now turning ourselves inside out, crowding closer together so we can scatter across continents on a moment's notice. The product of the Jet Age and the Net Age is our current Instant one, simultaneously favoring aggregation *and* dispersal.

This is where John Kasarda comes in. With the aerotropolis, he attempts to answer the question of what the cities of this age should look like. What will their shape and purpose be when the state of the art at the time of their birth is ubiquitous WiFi and jumbo jets shuttling from New York and London to them? Implicit in his thinking is a coming world of exponential population increase and cutthroat competition for resources and profits. His vision may evoke everything Americans find terrifying about globalization—a civilization cast in quick-drying cement, packed with worker drones—but even if you accept Kasarda's seemingly implacable logic, you have to ask: Who are these cities for? The companies that profit from marginally leaner operations? The leaders, each one a little more ruthless than the last, jockeying to land them? Or the planners, architects, and sages given carte blanche to raise islands from oceans and plant tarmac in desert—all in the name, when pressed, of "competitiveness"?

Cities have always sprouted at the junctions of commerce and industry, coalescing over time as we followed our callings to them. No one has ever succeeded in building one from scratch out of pure anticipation, following a logic that makes perfect sense on paper but falls apart in practice. What makes Kasarda and his fellow travelers think the aerotropolis will be any different, and will we—its potential residents—fare the worse for it if they fail—or if they succeed?

This book aims to answer such questions and to ask whether we will consciously choose to live in cities built in globalization's image—machines for living linked in great chains and tasked with specific functions: factories, farms, headquarters, hospitals, and hubs. Kasarda believes that we will, that we should, and that we'll suffer the consequences if we don't, because these debates have already been settled (one way or another) in places like China and Dubai, which have staked everything on the global triumphing over the local. The rest of us are not so sure.

The Heathrow Hassle: "Our Prosperity Depends on It"

There's a video on YouTube of London Heathrow titled *The World's Unofficial Longest Line*. Set to the Proclaimers song "500 Miles," the clip starts at the head of a line waiting to enter a security checkpoint and pans back, *waaaaay* back, for several minutes—through the concourse, down a flight of stairs, along twisting corridors, up another flight of stairs, and emerging in an entirely different terminal before stopping at the end of the line. This bravura sequence, worthy of Orson Welles, is just one entry in an entire genre online. Each snippet bears the same warning: Abandon all hope, ye who enter here . . .

Heathrow was voted the worst airport in the world by passengers in 1982, and still was in 2009. In the meantime, the ground beneath the pair of runways became the world's most valuable piece of real estate. Owning rights to land there is worth incalculable billions to the airlines, which horse-trade a hard and fast number of slots among themselves for millions of pounds each. They have no choice but to pay up—Heathrow is the closest thing we have to a truly global hub. And it's falling apart.

Like most cities, London has an airport problem—it's a victim of its own success. Heathrow's terminals aren't crumbling from neglect but buckling under once unimaginable growth. Almost seventy million passengers endure its lines annually, twenty-five million more than the airport was made for. The sparkling Terminal 5 has since relieved some of the stress, twenty years after it was first suggested.

The "Heathrow hassle" has long been a painful fact of life for Britons, but in 2007 the most damning criticism of all came from an unlikely quarter: Kitty Ussher, a member of Parliament and City minister, London's equivalent to the mayor of Wall Street. In her first day on the job, Ussher warned that the Heathrow hassle was not only intolerable; *it was also a threat to the entire U.K. economy.* The bankers who had made London a world financial capital would rather pack up and leave, she intimated, than suffer a horrid airport. And after the bust, they quit flying—and started leaving—in droves.

"Heathrow does shame London," scolded Ken Livingstone, then the city's mayor. "It's typical of the English disease of short-termism with a lack of planning and lack of investment." Livingstone dreamed of London as a multicultural capital of the world, a virtual city-state within Britain. "A Singapore of the West," he called it. Ironic, considering the former British colony—the air hub of Southeast Asia—is poised to supplant it as a financial center.

He should have directed some of his scorn beyond the terminals, to the clogged motorways and suburban sprawl hemming Heathrow in. The real threat to London's competitiveness wasn't the world's unofficial longest line at security but irreparable harm to the "Heathrow phenomenon" that has made west London and the Thames River Valley an economic engine in their own right comparable in output to Sydney. "A landscape which most people affect to loathe but which I regard as the most advanced and admirable in the British Isles, and a paradigm of the best that the future offers us," wrote the science-fiction author J. G. Ballard, a resident of the valley for forty-nine years. "I welcome its transience, alienation and discontinuities, and its unashamed response to the pressures of speed, disposability and the instant impulse."

The growth of that engine has created problems of its own. The airport's slow suffocation is visible—the number of destinations served has fallen by 20 percent over the last two decades, and no European airport hemorrhaged more routes during the recession. The multinationals based there have hinted they are looking to leave. In 2008, the British government announced plans to build a third runway, evoking screams of protest. Prime Minister Gordon Brown was unmoved. "We have to respond to a clear business imperative and increase capacity at our airports," he said. "Our prosperity depends on it: Britain as a world financial centre must be readily accessible from around the world." The idea that its preeminent international gateway could muddle through with just two runways was as absurd as digging the Chunnel wide enough for only one set of tracks.

In January 2009, Brown's transport secretary gave his final approval. The entire neighboring village of Sipson would vanish beneath a mile of tarmac, joining its twin hamlet Heath's Row, which was entombed in 1944. "I got married in the local church. My children were born here. Our family home is here," one resident lamented. "All of my family history will be buried under concrete."

Vowing no surrender, Greenpeace bought a patch of land in the middle of the proposed runway. "I don't understand how any government remotely serious about committing to reversing climate change can even consider these ridiculous plans," sniped the actress Emma Thompson, one of several celebrities who supplied the money. Brown's supporters wondered the same thing; a sizable fraction of his party opposed expansion on environmental grounds. The day of the announcement, the MP representing Sipson was dragged out of Parliament shouting, "It's a disgrace to the democracy of this country!"

Sipson received a stay of execution a year later, when Britain's High Court declared the plan "untenable" in light of climate change. The town's final deliverance came in the May 2010 general elections, which deposed Gordon Brown's Labour Party in favor of a coalition of Conservatives and Liberal Democrats. The new prime minister, David Cameron, scrapped the third runway within days, while ruling out expansion at London's other airports, Gatwick and Stansted. His government vowed to curb "binge flying" with new taxes, promising to build a new high-speed rail network across Britain instead. Meanwhile, London mayor Boris Johnson, the disheveled Tory toff who ousted the Socialist Livingstone, has talked up plans for an $80 billion replacement on a man-made island in the Thames estuary—unlikely considering the new government's intransigence.

The nonpartisan Town and Country Planning Association pleaded with Tony Blair's government to "retire" the airport altogether and plan a successor somewhere far beyond the suburbs. "Heathrow's history is a series of minor planning disasters that together make up one of the country's truly great planning catastrophes," the group declared. It had been a victim of the law of unintended consequences from the moment it opened out of an army surplus tent in 1946.

That was all in hindsight. Decades passed with Heathrow up and running before anyone—airline, architect, mayor, or prime minister—realized that while cities grow organically, airports cannot. They would learn their lesson through trial and error. The airports we have learned to live with (and despise) are stuck serving 747s that weren't even on the drawing board when their runways were laid. Imagine trying to run our wireless world through Ma Bell's original copper wires, and you'll get a sense as to the degree of difficulty.

Heathrow's intractability is one of the reasons British Airways agreed to merge with Spain's national carrier, Iberia—because although Heathrow has only two runways, Iberia's home in Madrid has four. If BA can't connect passengers through its London hub, it will reroute them through its partner's hub instead. Blocking expansion wouldn't put a stop to growth or cut carbon emissions, argued Willie Walsh, the airline's chief executive, but simply divert flights and opportunities to the Continent's competing hubs. "We shouldn't take Heathrow for granted," he pleaded, but his opponents were unimpressed.

The day after Heathrow's third runway was tentatively approved, Frankfurt's airport announced plans for a fourth, to little fanfare or protest. "The expansion keeps Fraport on course for staying competitive in the future," its chairman explained. "Globalization will not only continue but will gather momentum as soon as the crisis has bottomed out." And then we will be forced to choose: Do we retrofit our cities to become aerotropoli in the future, or save people's homes? The consequences of each choice are equally stark: either we risk weaving a competitive disadvantage into the very fabric of our cities, or we begin unwinding the fabric itself.

The Shape of Things to Come

There is no question that the fruits of globalization—literally, the mangosteens, lychees, and passion fruit on your grocer's shelves that weren't there a decade ago—are delivered through the air. In the thirty years between 1975 and 2005, global GDP rose 154 percent, while world trade grew 355 percent. Meanwhile, the value of air cargo climbed an astonishing 1,395 percent. More than a third of all the goods traded in the world, some $3 trillion worth—but barely 1 percent of its weight!—travels via air freight. Air passengers and cargo had recovered their recessionary losses by the summer of 2010 and were accelerating ahead of the global economy. More and more pieces of the latter are living aloft and landing in some pretty strange places. Planes carry the products of the Instant Age—what we want, right now, and typically our most ingenious creations. Wanting the world right this instant has created incalculable wealth, completely reconfigured how many companies and even industries operate, and is now willing entire cities into being. It's just that we tend to notice only when our choices are taken away from us.

When the Icelandic volcano Eyjafjallajökull erupted violently in April 2010, ash carried into the upper atmosphere drifted southward, forcing a shutdown of European airspace. For more than a week, tens of thousands of flights were canceled daily. Six million travelers were trapped, and millions of others were grounded at home. Everyone seemed to have a friend on Facebook who was stuck. Thousands rediscovered trains. Professional wrestlers, opera singers, and musicians missed performances;

long-distance runners missed marathons. The actor John Cleese hired a taxi to drive him from Oslo to Brussels—the fare came to $5,000. President Obama, Gordon Brown, Nicolas Sarkozy, and Angela Merkel all missed the funeral of Polish president Lech Kaczynski, who had died the weekend before in a plane crash.

As the week dragged on, fresh produce disappeared from supermarket shelves—pineapple from Ghana, basil from Cyprus, beans and chilies from Egypt, asparagus from California—but was not replenished. In Britain, Tesco ran low on Thai orchids and Kenyan roses. In Kenya, three thousand tons of roses rotted after being picked. Thousands of farmers were sent home without wages. They lost $2 million a day; the world's airlines collectively lost $450 million daily.

No one knew how long the eruption would last—days, weeks, months? As the crisis dragged on, the scope of what we'd come to take for granted kept expanding. Even the notion of European integration turned out to be one of air travel's inventions. As the *Washington Post* columnist Anne Applebaum noted, "Over the last two decades—almost without anyone really noticing it—Europeans have begun, in at least this narrow sense, to live like Americans: They move abroad for work, live for a while in one country, and then move to another, eventually going home or maybe not. They do business in countries where they don't know the language, go on vacation in the Mediterranean and in the Baltic, visit their mothers on the weekends. Skeptics who thought the European single market would never function because there would be no labor mobility in Europe have been proved wrong."

But is the opposite also true? Do we really need to rearrange our lives to better serve these slices of our self-interest? John Kasarda's answer is an emphatic yes. "I see organized competition, strategy, and structure as the major forces shaping human life, not individual actions," he professed. "I don't believe in 'agency,'" sociology-speak for free will. "Agency is inevitably trumped by structure." Most of us are shaped by the family and community we are born into. Taken on its face, it's a reductionist worldview, but his underlying point is that our slightest whims, multiplied several billion times and duly noted by the marketplace, have already had the effect of conjuring aerotropoli where you'd least expect them, transforming everything and everyone they touch.

It's no wonder, then, that developing nations such as China and

India have been the aerotropolis's most eager adopters. They see it as an indispensable weapon for hijacking the world's trade routes. China's grand plans are perhaps more ambitious than anyone realizes—it intends to keep adding factories, corner the market on green energy technologies, double down on its export-driven growth strategy, and chart a New Silk Road to markets in Africa and the Middle East. The goal is to keep a lid on dissent by lifting another six hundred million citizens out of absolute poverty. The plan is to pack up the factory towns along the coast and move them inland. And the key is a network of a hundred new airports under construction in the hinterlands, which will connect these provincial cities to each other and to customers overseas. Twenty thousand factories have already closed, while a city eight hundred miles west of Shanghai named Chongqing has been chosen as China's answer to Chicago. Chongqing is currently growing at eight times the speed of the Windy City during the Gilded Age, adding three hundred thousand new residents a year. But it has never had a window on the world until now.

More than cheap laptops are at stake. The United Nations expects 115 million tourists a year to leave the Middle Kingdom by 2020. The most closed society in history is poised to make its presence felt outside its factories—in our cities, on our beaches, and waiting in line at the Magic Kingdom. They're signing up for "foreclosure tours" to buy the homes we can no longer afford.

The pace and scale of such urbanization threaten to overrun every model for building cities we've ever had. Architects and urban planners are in crisis about what to do with cities like Chongqing—or just about any city in China, India, and even established but sprawling capitals like Bangkok and Seoul. Rem Koolhaas coined the phrase "generic city" to describe megalopolises that throw tentacles in all directions, following neither form nor function. Kasarda believes the aerotropolis offers an antidote, imposing a hierarchy of needs on cities so that they openly and honestly express their true purpose: creating work for their inhabitants and competitiveness for their nations.

For Bangkok, he drafted plans to transform the swampy sprawl east of the city into an ideal aerotropolis surrounding its new airport, Suvarnabhumi. In his sketches, the outermost rings extend nearly twenty miles into the countryside from the runways. There, giant clusters of apartment towers and bungalows would take shape, the former for housing

Thais working the assembly lines and cargo hubs in the inner rings, the
latter for the expatriate armies imported by the various multinationals
expected to set up shop around the airport. (Golf courses would keep the
expats happy, as would shopping malls, movie theaters, and schools that
seem airlifted straight from Southern California.)

Moving in from the residential rings, the next layer was slated for the
manicured campuses of those same multinationals—the back offices,
R & D labs, and regional headquarters of the Toyotas and Nokias per-
suaded to relocate. Here, one would also find hotels, shopping malls,
convention centers—anything and everything to sustain the knowledge
workers laboring in the shadow of the airport. In the innermost rings,
essentially abutting the runway fences, were the free-trade zones, factories, warehouses, and logistics hubs designed for the FedEx/UPS/DHL
combine—the just-in-time manufacturers and suppliers for whom time
and distance from the belly of a 747 equals, quite literally, cost. New six-
lane highways would link the inner and outer rings, with semitrailers
barreling down dedicated aerolanes while residents stroll along boulevards lining canals.

It didn't happen. A high-speed rail link costing more than a half a
billion dollars connects Suvarnabhumi to Bangkok, but the rest of Kasarda's plans were scuttled by not one, but two coups deposing supportive
prime ministers, dropping his project into limbo. The riotous sprawl of
Bangkok, meanwhile, keeps creeping toward the site like kudzu.

In Amsterdam, home to the world's first aerotropolis-by-design,
Dutch planners have a saying:

The airport leaves the city.
The city follows the airport.
The airport becomes a city.

Although Kasarda's models are more elaborate, the fact remains: the
aerotropolis is a city with a center. As such, it represents a return to the
way our cities were built and how they produced some of our greatest
monuments. We have not built high-rise cities in Manhattan's mold since
the turn of the previous century, when the owners of the New York Central railroad oversaw the construction of a shining "Terminal City" above
Grand Central's tracks buried beneath Park Avenue—thirty square blocks
of midtown Manhattan and some of the most prestigious real estate in the

world. Cities since then have followed the galactic model of greater Los Angeles and its sclerotic freeways. The aerotropolis offers a new transportation paradigm powerful and compelling enough to assert itself as the bustling center of commerce within a city whose hinterlands lie a continent away. "Look for yesterday's busiest train terminals and you will find today's great urban centers. Look for today's busiest airports and you will find the great urban centers of tomorrow. This is the union of urban planning, airport planning, and business strategy," Kasarda told me. "And the whole will be something altogether different than the sum of its parts."

But what if the center cannot hold? What if globalism falls apart? There is a growing Greek chorus warning us the age of air travel is over, undone by the twin calamities of peak oil and climate change. They point to oil prices tripling over the last decade, while noting that a flight from New York to London releases more greenhouse gases into the upper reaches of the stratosphere than the thirstiest Hummer when driven for a year. They find it impossible to reconcile our urgent wish to go green with jaunts across the country or continent—the reason why Britain has elected to rein in airport expansion. Fortunately, their thinking goes, the imminent exhaustion of cheap oil will take care of the problem for us.

Then again, Judgment Day has been repeatedly postponed. For one thing, airliners are more virtuous and resilient than you might expect. China's airports aren't the source of its noxious air; its coal-burning power plants are. (China burns more coal than the United States, Europe, and Japan combined.) In the United States, as many as half of our own emissions emanate from "the built environment," the energy consumed to build and service sprawl. We emit more carbon living in McMansions.

For another, air travel's actual share of our carbon footprints is currently 3 percent and *falling* (at least in the United States), thanks to a bounty of incremental and potentially revolutionary advances meant to slow and hopefully end its carbon contributions. The next generation of airliners, headlined by Boeing's 787 Dreamliner, is lighter and more fuel efficient than last century's models, complemented by new engines that burn quietly and clean. Airlines thirsty for fuel that's both sustainably cheap *and* green are looking to high-octane biofuels refined from algae. Virgin Atlantic's grandstanding chairman Sir Richard Branson has pledged all of his airline's profits through 2016 (an estimated $3 billion) on R & D toward this end. Green crude might reliably cost $80 a barrel, enough to save the industry as we know it, and not a moment too soon. "Drastically curtailing flights or even closing airports outright for the sake of climate change—the prescription of the most fervent environmentalists—is social and economic suicide," Kasarda argues. "It's a cure for cancer that cleaves healthy muscle, flesh, bone, and arteries in its desperation to kill the disease."

Despite a decade's worth of high oil prices, terrorism fears, and the airlines' endless nickel-and-diming, we have never flown as far or in greater numbers than we do right now. As recently as 1999 (when gas still cost a dollar a gallon), JetBlue had yet to start flying, Ryanair had no website, and starting your own airline was illegal in both China and India. No one west of Jerusalem had even heard of Dubai, and it was impossible to take a nonstop flight from New York to New Delhi or Beijing. The world may or may not have flattened since then, but there's a lot less changing planes.

In the end, we won't stop flying for the simple reason that quitting now would run counter to our human impulse to roam. Will you be the one to tell a hundred million Chinese tourists (and another hundred million Indians) they'll have to stay home?

I live in one of the oldest sections of Brooklyn, blocks of leafy streets and brownstones I like to think Jane Jacobs would have recognized as her own. The park where I read the newspaper most mornings is a small one—a few tables and benches, a patch of grass, a playground—but it sits on the site of a fort defended by George Washington's troops, one that gave the neighborhood its name: Cobble Hill.

Most mornings, the only patrons at 7:30 a.m. are a few bleary-eyed dog owners or the parents of overeager toddlers. But already I can hear the planes. They wheel overhead on final approach to LaGuardia, five miles distant, with a dull roar that is distinct but not distressing—certainly not loud enough to wake the children, of which there are many. But it's too much for my neighbors in Park Slope, another patch of brownstones down the hill to the east, where the typical approaching plane swoops so low you can clearly read the "Delta" painted on its sides. The brownstoners have lobbied unsuccessfully to have the flight paths moved over some less fortunate neighborhood. They're much like my neighbors here—lawyers, writers, and financiers. "Knowledge workers" is what they would call them in New Songdo, where the item at the top of Stan Gale's to-do list is to woo more of them there.

A few blocks west are the docks of Red Hook, where a faint few ships unload containers by day and blow foghorns by night. It's a rumble as startling as jet wash, though several degrees more romantic because their era seems farther removed. Walt Whitman lived here, hopping ferries to the city and back in the mornings and evenings, confronted each time with the simple, joyous fact that the city's lifeblood was commerce. He wrote:

> Look'd toward the lower bay to notice the vessels arriving,
> Saw their approach, saw aboard those that were near me,
> Saw the white sails of schooners and sloops, saw the ships at anchor,
> The sailors at work in the rigging or out astride the spars,
> The round masts, the swinging motion of the hulls, the slender
>   serpentine pennants,
> The large and small steamers in motion, the pilots in their
>   pilot-houses,

. . . the jetliners and captains of a distant epoch. That was 150 years ago, but longshoremen walked these streets from dawn to dusk for another hundred years, before the first Wall Street families arrived and gentrification followed. This was a neighborhood created by commerce, for commerce—as joined to those docks as surely as the fate of New Songdo and its offspring are tied to runways.

One morning, while a Delta Shuttle spluttered across the sky, I thought of the newborn city and its twelve-mile bridge across the Yellow Sea. New Songdo is farther from its airport than I am from LaGuardia. Perhaps the biggest difference, then, between my idyllic nabe and the aerotropolis of Kasarda's dreams is philosophical rather than material. What does it mean to live everyday life in relation to the airport? And are we mentally prepared to do it?

These are urgent questions for all of us. The age of suburbia is passing, just as the economy that drove it—cheap cars, cheaper gas, still-cheaper mortgages, and free highways—is passing with it. What's replaced it is the Instant Age, with its global economy of ideas—of people, really—and the lightweight, infinitely configurable expressions of those ideas: iPhones, solar panels, and the human capital in the Shanghai office. These are the things that can't wait, the things we pay dear prices for and need right this second—even though they're being minted on the far side of the world.

John Kasarda sees the history of cities as a rising tide of breaking waves. Ocean harbors were swept away by river ports, which yielded to railroad terminals that were in turn exploded by highways and suburbia. Transportation is destiny. The fifth wave is here, and while we won't commute to work George Jetson–style anytime soon (though rest assured there are dreamers working on this), how we measure and meter our personal velocity has already begun this shift.

On a bench in Brooklyn, I can feel the tug of LaGuardia whenever a FedEx truck rumbles by, or when I spy a neighbor—suited up, wheelie suitcase in tow—emerging from a brownstone, obviously setting out on a business trip. I spent the better part of a year living out of a suitcase myself, following such tugs back to their sources in the warehouses of Memphis, the greenhouses of Amsterdam, and the factory towns outside Hong Kong. I even slept on terrazzo floors for weeks to meet the "road warriors" who congregate there—and it was there that I found John Kasarda, whose grand unified theory of their existence produced the aerotropolis. By then, I implicitly knew what he was saying to be true, even if we as Americans refuse to acknowledge the consequences. After profiling him for *Fast Company*, I agreed to partner with him on this book. The words are mine—I'm Greg Lindsay—but it's Kasarda who provides the framework for the apparently unrelated phenomena commonly lumped under the term "globalization."

As I shuttled between terminals, it struck me that they offer a map of the last half century, from the dawning of the Jet Age through the Net Age to our Instant one born in Asia. I traced a path from Sun Belt cities such as Los Angeles and Dallas (where the layover was invented) through Louisville and Memphis—decaying river towns reinvigorated by e-commerce—and onward to meet Kasarda in North Carolina. By then, he'd convinced Detroit's leaders that an aerotropolis was their city's best chance at a future. In Amsterdam, I learned how flowers portended the airborne future of food, and while connecting through India, China, and Dubai, I met the traders who traverse the New Silk Road. The aim of this book is to tell the story of how these things went from being impossible to inevitable.

A TALE OF THREE CITIES

Los Angeles, Washington, and Chicago are the sum of their airports. Without room to expand them, they face limits to growth.

Los Angeles: Neighbors, Noise, and NIMBY

In 1926, a year before Charles Lindbergh flew solo across the Atlantic and two years before the first Academy Awards, the burghers of Los Angeles were worried they didn't have an airport. In fact, they had too many. There were fifty-two landing strips in LA County that year—mostly dirt, with a windsock and maybe a barn doubling as a hangar. But forty-seven were in private hands, and there was no municipal field open to all comers. The Chamber of Commerce began lobbying the city to build one, and to speed things along, it hired the meteorologist Ford A. Carpenter to examine twenty-six sites of varying potential.

One of them was a one-mile-square patch of land known as Mines Field. In his report, Carpenter described what he dubbed the "Inglewood Site" as "an ideal location as far as level unobstructed space is concerned . . . No hangars, markings, phone, oil, or other supplies." In the photograph accompanying his summary judgment, a Model T has come to rest in the middle of a wide, muddy road with empty bean fields on either side. This was the future site of LAX.

There were other practical considerations. In deference to the urgency of airmail, Carpenter observed that Mines Field was fourteen miles from the Los Angeles central post office. Evangelizing a bit, he also included a map of the country, comparing the relative speeds and distances traversable by air and rail. Denver was as far as a train could make it in the time it would take to fly to Maine. And New York was now only twenty-eight hours away. "There is no reason why Southern California should not be to the aircraft industry what Detroit is to the automobile business," he noted in the margin. "The first essential is an air-harbor in which to accommodate aircraft."

LAX is a case study for how airports are incubators for trade and the cities that spring up to seize it. And then there are the side effects. Before air travel, for instance, the Brooklyn Dodgers would have never left Ebbets Field for Dodger Stadium; baseball's westernmost outpost until 1958 was St. Louis, the last convenient stop by train. Absent transcontinental and transpacific flights, it's impossible to imagine Los Angeles as a culture capital rivaling New York, Hong Kong, and Tokyo. Without them, it would have remained a dry, dusty city of farming and industry—a Fresno or a Sacramento, minus the Hollywood.

Airports' triumph over time, space, and the drag their hosts impose on them is so easily overlooked that awe soon gives way to familiarity, and then contempt. This was the case in Los Angeles, Washington, D.C., and Chicago, to name just a few. In America, we built our airports before we knew what they were for. We planned them for biplanes and barnstorming tours instead of shuttle runs to New York every hour on the hour or nightly flights to China. No one could have foreseen a 185,266 percent increase in passengers transiting Chicago—skyrocketing from forty-one thousand in 1928 to seventy-six million eighty years later. But despite their constraints and growing pains, airports transformed the look and character of each of these cities. In Los Angeles and Chicago, they became the pawns of city politics, while Washington's would be the beneficiary of benign neglect. None of them qualifies as an aerotropolis in John Kasarda's eyes, because they were not planned in tandem with their cities. They are prototypes hampered by residents who gradually became suspicious of the very things that made the modern urban way of life possible.

Angelenos' long and difficult marriage with theirs was consummated in 1928, when Mines Field beat out two other finalists to become Los Angeles Municipal Airport. Supporters of the losing sites complained bitterly (and ironically) that it was much too far from downtown to be much of use, and they were right for twenty years. The airlines of the time preferred to stay in Burbank, the favorite of Hollywood. The military took control of the airfield during World War II, prompting Hughes Aircraft to open a plant a mile north for building the wooden prototype of its H-4 Hercules military transport, the infamous "Spruce Goose." Hughes wasn't alone. Donald Douglas, cofounder of McDonnell Douglas, had begun making planes in Santa Monica in 1920. One of his engineers was Jack Northrop, who ran a division of Douglas Aircraft just south of the airport in El Segundo, before leaving to start his own eponymous firm next door. Two brothers named Allan and Malcolm Loughead founded Lockheed out of their Hollywood garage a few years later. Their successors would go on to build the ocean-crossing Constellation, the first modern airliner, at Hughes's behest for TWA.

Together with the real estate developer Harry Culver, these were the men who successfully pressed the city to build them an airfield at the taxpayers' expense. In doing so, they laid the pavement on which California's postwar prosperity was built. Los Angeles's defining characteristic in these formative years wasn't Hollywood or the automobile, but aerospace. Disneyland and McDonald's took backseats to the bottomless number of contracts procured by Hughes, Douglas, Northrop, and Lockheed to supply fighters, bombers, tankers, and transports. These upstarts collectively employed 13,000 skilled technicians in 1939; only four years later, the figure was 190,000. Hughes Aircraft began the war with four full-time employees; it finished with 80,000.

Their fortunes dipped after the war, but the resumption of hostilities via the Cold War proved to be an even bigger boon. Every commission for supersonic interceptors or mammoth airlifters spawned civilian uses and customers. When Boeing ushered in the Jet Age in 1959 with the 707 airliner, the air force was first in line to buy one. The situation was reversed a decade later, when the blueprints of the 747 emerged from a failed Boeing bid at the Pentagon. With the very large exception of Boeing, every major airliner until the formation of Airbus was manufactured around Los Angeles and might as well have had "Made in California" stamped on the side. McDonnell Douglas built DC-8s, -9s, and -10s—and more recently, MD-80s—at its factory in Long Beach. If you've flown on American Airlines anytime in the last thirty years, odds are that your plane was born there. Lakewood, the "Levittown of the West," was a Douglas factory town. Lockheed assembled its wide-body TriStar in Burbank, once it had finished the U-2 and SR-71 spy planes.

The aerospace industry pollinated everything it touched. CalTech didn't emerge as a rival to MIT until the army endowed its Jet Propulsion Laboratory. Over in Santa Monica, the Dr. Strangeloves of RAND plotted to win thermonuclear war in between rounds of margaritas. By 1960, Ford A. Carpenter's prediction of a Detroit-of-the-air had come to fruition, as a full third of Southern California's jobs were directly or indirectly related to aerospace, earning it the nickname the "Warfare State."

Aerospace's reach extended three hundred miles north to Palo Alto, where transistors made of silicon had just been perfected. A decade before Intel and before there was any Silicon Valley to speak of, the aerospace cartel arranged to buy integrated circuits as fast as their makers could etch them. In 1967, for example, seven out of every ten microchips were slated for Minuteman missiles and lunar landers, not mainframe computers. Based on this evidence, a few economists have persuasively argued that computing would have been set back for decades if the military hadn't been there to hold its hand during those baby steps. Not until the end of the Cold War and the adolescence of the Internet (yet another Department of Defense project) were we able to get our hands on the coolest gadgets ahead of the generals.

By then, firms that had gotten started building aircraft had long since moved on to missiles, spy satellites, and spaceships. George Lucas's *Star Wars* had less of an impact on California's fortunes than did Ronald Reagan's real-world remake a few years later. You can see their legacy along the southern border of LAX, where blue-collar suburb El Segundo boasts installations of Hughes, Boeing, Raytheon, Lockheed, and the headquarters of DirecTV (a Hughes spin-off).

The first neighborhood adjacent to the airport, Westchester, was built during the war years to house Hughes employees. Westchester's population was just 353 in 1940; ten years later, it was 33,000. Fields and hog pastures were built out overnight, with one developer tossing up prefab homes at a rate of four per day, earning a comparison from California historian Carey McWilliams to the camps of the original gold rush. Not long thereafter, Westchester also became the first neighborhood in America to seriously suffer from engine noise. By the early 1960s, when the low-frequency *thrum* of piston-powered propellers had given way to the piercing screams of early jet engines, local homeowners began to mobilize. The Greater Westchester Homeowners Association was soon joined by fellow NIMBY (Not in My Back Yard) groups to the east, south, and west in Inglewood, El Segundo, and Playa del Rey. The first noise-related lawsuit, *Aaron v. City of Los Angeles*, was filed in 1964 on behalf of 765 property owners claiming $2.8 million in damages. It took nine years to settle, and by that time the airport faced $3 billion in additional lawsuits filed by everyone from the local school districts to the Catholic church.

LAX, which would swell to five times the size of the original Mines Field, paid nearly $150 million just to cover litigation costs from expanding its runways, and another $20 million went to pay for residents' soundproofing. In response, the airport began buying homes outright and knocking them down—some thirty-five hundred to date. Westchester has begun to disappear, street by street and block by block.

The original fears that LAX would be too far from downtown proved unfounded, as downtown came out to meet it. The sprawl encircling it has calcified, and traffic on its interstate arteries—especially the 405—is the most sclerotic in the region. However orderly Westchester may have seemed at the time, no one planned for the strip malls and fast-food alleys of Inglewood, or the defining features of El Segundo: an enormous Chevron oil refinery and the accompanying 250-million-gallon oil spill beneath it.

Despite its handicaps, LAX has been the catalyst for the city's metamorphosis into America's premier trade entrepôt over the last thirty years. It was during those decades that the industrial fulcrum of California first shifted north—out of the hangars of Hughes Aircraft and into Silicon Valley—and then west, all the way to China. We have LAX to thank for our iPhones and iPods being "designed by Apple in California, assembled in China," as they advertise on their backs. Not just Apple, but every Valley company that began life combining transistors there—think Intel, Hewlett Packard, Sun, and Cisco—long ago began outsourcing work from its messy, depreciating factories to ones across the Pacific. Now they wait for airborne freighters to land in Los Angeles with the first samples of their latest holiday smash in the hold.

The airports on each edge of the Rim, in Hong Kong and Los Angeles, are able to perch in the corners of the so-called smiley curve, named for the U-shaped smile of the seventies cartoon happy face. Devised by Chinese manufacturers, the curve depicts where all the value is added and profits are made in a gadget like the iPod. In the upper left end of the smile—the product's conception—are the idea, design, and branding. At the right end are distribution, marketing, retail sales, and customer support. In between, at the bottom of the curve, is where the grunt work of manufacturing, final assembly, and shipping happens. The corners are where the money is, which explains why farming out the entire industry to China has been win-win so far for all involved, especially on California's side of the ledger. In the case of a $299 iPod, for example, Apple's brains, branding, and stores produce $155 in gross profits. The parts, made by Toshiba, Samsung, and a host of unknowns, amount to only $144, and their profits are marginal—which is what happens when you build something instead of invent it.

Apple's heirs apparent don't even pretend to be interested in making things. One such start-up is chumby, which makes a $99 device that might best be described as a clock radio crossed with an iPod. Based in San Diego, chumby has thirty-seven employees, of whom "maybe two and a half are focused on hardware," admits its CEO, Steve Tomlin. He isn't one of them, having apprenticed at AOL and Disney. "To the outside world, we look like a consumer electronics company, but we're not," he explains. They intend to get rich selling purely digital "widgets." Chumby's device is meant only to prove what they're capable of. Facing a chicken-and-egg dilemma—how do you sell widgets when there's nothing to play them on?—they sat down and hatched one.

Not that they own a factory. Nor did they let the fact that (in Tomlin's words) "we didn't have anybody who had ever worked in China before" stop them. They found a factory near Hong Kong to make a few hundred prototypes, and eventually found another ready to stamp out a few million, if necessary. Their shipments are landing at LAX too—making good on its original promise for airmail—and where would they be without it? For that reason, it's almost impossible to quantify what the airport means to California. But even a pre-Internet-era estimate pegged its contributions to Los Angeles at $61 billion a year and four hundred thousand jobs in 1995, starting from a mere $3.3 billion in 1970.

Escape from LAX

Complicating any attempts at a fix has been a decades-long debate over whether the city should focus solely on LAX expansion (and the wrath of litigious neighbors) or build up regional airports to pick up the slack. Faced with the prospect of LAX hitting a hundred million passengers a year around 2015, the airport authority looked into both options. The most audacious mid-nineties proposal was to build straight into Santa Monica Bay, adding new runways as far as two miles out into the ocean. Supporters argued that an unfettered airport would pump another $60 billion into the economy as it grew, adding the equivalent of a Hamburg or a Dublin. California state senator Tom Hayden spoke for the environmentalist opposition when he labeled it "insane." LAX officials scuttled the plan.

They had scrapped thirty others by 2001, when a vortex of mayoral politics, community pressure, and 9/11 conspired to end any grand expansion plans. The NIMBYs and wannabes in favor of a regional approach appeared to have won. While Long Beach, Burbank, and John Wayne in Orange County had already reached their limits, Ontario, lying east of LA in the Inland Empire, had room to grow, and there was hope of building a new Orange County International airport at the former Marine Corps airfield of El Toro. Perhaps the city could even resurrect Palmdale, the Ghost of LAX Future.

Sprawled across the high Mojave Desert fifty miles north of the city, on the far side of the San Gabriel Mountains, Palmdale is home to both Air Force Plant 42 and Edwards Air Force Base. The former is where the space shuttles were assembled, and the latter where they glided back to earth. Inspired by the brave new world they heralded, the city bought seventeen thousand acres of Joshua trees and sand adjoining Plant 42 at the start of the seventies. This would someday be LAX II. Its creators imagined a future, now past, that included jets ascending straight up, like helicopters; Mach 12 cruising speeds; bullet trains to transfer between LAX and Palmdale; and even "interplanetary travel," presumably aboard the Pan Am space planes last seen in *2001: A Space Odyssey*. None of it was ever built, of course—not after an earthquake ruled out any bullet trains through the mountains.

No replacements or successors or supplements to LAX are in the cards, even as the original is showing visible signs of strain. The airport's metaphorical crumbling became real a few years ago, when the spidery legs of its iconic Theme Building began shedding concrete, exposing decades of rust beneath. While they were stripped down to the steel, sanded, and reclad, there's nothing to suggest that the same can be done for LAX itself. I could see the scaffolding over the shoulder of Mike DiGirolamo, who invited me into his wood-paneled office atop the old control tower to expound on the sad state of airports in the LA basin. DiGirolamo is in charge of operations for LAX, placing him in the cross-fire of airlines, neighbors, and City Hall. He has a complete grasp of the absurdity of his situation: he's the one procuring the Southern California dream for millions—the iPhones, the It handbags, the Prozac prescriptions—and they despise him for it. "Can we change the infra-structure? I don't know," he told me. "It's a political issue. We had the de-sire to do it, but we lost it. We empowered the community so much here that they think they're running the airport, and that's the problem."

Not that the Los Angeles City Council has done a better job of it, or even understood what it was dealing with. "Cities got into the airport business through a mind-set of, 'Well, we have a train station; why wouldn't we operate the airport?' That's a fallacy," he offered by way of introduction to the mess he's in. "Imagine someone from Ralph's," a local supermarket chain, "going to the city and saying, 'We'd like you to build a supermarket to our specifications. We'll sell groceries and give you a return on your investment over the next sixty years. You're going to get hammered on the environmental front and the noise, and we're going to come bitch at you because you're driving prices up, and because there's not enough checkout lanes, and would you like to sign up for this?' And the mayor says, 'Absolutely! We already have an airport like that, so why not get into the grocery business!'"

We laughed, but it wasn't that funny. America's airports are a joke to its citizens, while foreign visitors see them as symptoms of some deeper malaise. LAX is bad enough, but New York's airports are even worse. "Fly from Zurich's ultramodern airport to La Guardia's dump," Thomas L. Fried-man challenged his readers in *The New York Times*. "It is like flying from the Jetsons to the Flintstones." The *Financial Times*'s John Gapper sin-gled out New York's other airport: "If anyone doubts the problems of U.S. infrastructure, I suggest he or she take a flight to John F. Kennedy airport (braving the landing delay), ride a taxi on the pot-holed and congested Brooklyn-Queens Expressway and try to make a mobile phone call en route."

It's scary how much not just Los Angeles but the entire West—and to some extent, the entire country—depends on an airport as dysfunctional as LAX. "Eighty percent of all iPods sold at Christmas last year came through here," DiGirolamo told me: around fifty million, most arriving via a single route on a single airline—straight from Hong Kong in the bellies of Cathay Pacific's 747s.

"Almost fifty percent of all consumption of all products in the ten western states is through Southern California," when you lump in the ports with the airport, he said. "We're the intake for Las Vegas, Tucson, Phoenix . . . all the way to Albuquerque. When you look at the total tonnage that comes through LAX versus the total tonnage that goes through harbors, we have about ten percent, and they have ninety percent. When you look at the value of the cargo, though, we have eighty percent."

Piling up on the docks are cars (LA's number 2 import), clothes (number 4), oil (5), and toys (7). Landing at LAX, meanwhile, are miscellaneous electronics (1); MP3, CD, and DVD players (3); and just about anything else electric (6 and 8), along with medications, cameras, and textiles. But the statistical abstracts reveal nothing about the contents.

Anyone lucky enough to have hitched a ride aboard a freighter or been taken under the wing of the "freight dogs" who pilot them could tell you enough stories to pass the eighteen hours to LA from Singapore. At any given moment, there are aloft "incomprehensible quantities of the mundane," in the words of one such witness: 160,000 pounds of roses leaving Amsterdam, 25,000 wiring harnesses bound for auto plants around Detroit, or 5,000 pounds of Grand Theft Auto games inbound for LAX. Another writer babysat a stableful of horses in transit between O'Hare and Tokyo, including a dozen Appaloosas bound for a Hokkaido ranch. One pilot recounted the tale of a mysterious ice chest, insured for millions, which he later learned was the vessel for the first HIV drug cocktail.

It's the freight dogs' job to be on time, just in time, every time with whatever they're carrying, especially when it's close to Christmastime. "If you're Joe Shmo, who cares if your flight leaves or not?" griped a 747 freighter captain named Tony Baca. "Grab another flight—it doesn't really matter. But when I'm hauling one hundred tons of Nintendo Wiis, it starts mattering. That's millions of dollars of revenue. You have people waiting at Target for that. One time I ended up hauling one hundred thirty tons of Happy Meal toys. And the reason was, a container ship sank in the middle of the Pacific. If a huge shipment has just sunk, you can't dispatch another ship. So you start hauling Happy Meal toys on a 747."

A ship doesn't have to sink for squadrons of jumbo jets to scramble. DiGirolamo has his own war stories of supply chain snafus that were no fault of his own. "We had a major problem with the ports—we couldn't get the ships offloaded and they couldn't get goods into the stores" because a ten-day strike in 2002 had left more than one hundred ships arriving from China anchored helplessly offshore, just two months before Christmas. "A lot of people had figured how to do it just in time," using aerial shipments, "but a lot hadn't. Distributors were calling stores to say, 'I can't get it to you because it's stuck on a boat in the North Pacific.' And their customers answered, 'Well, you had *better figure out* how to get it to me.'"

Companies dependent on the holiday crush, like Hasbro, raced to implement contingency plans for airlifting millions of dollars in backup merchandise to the stores. They would need them again two years later, when an October oceanic traffic jam left another fifty ships parked offshore for weeks. Somehow the ports had become even more clogged than the tarmac at LAX.

Those caught in the pinch had gambled on the wrong time/cost equation—they'd sacrificed months of the former to save a few pennies per item on the latter. That's typically how it works in hair-thin-margin industries, but it's also increasingly a luxury in the Instant Age, when customers' patience isn't salved by the costs manufacturers have managed to wring from their supply chains.

"We're seeing more just-in-time these days," DiGirolamo said, implying they've learned their lesson and are putting it on planes instead. Or maybe the crises just keep mounting—according to one survey, "emergencies" stemming from ocean delays accounted for more than a third of all air shipments from China. The most common reasons, however, had to do with the high value of the products in question, coping with volatile consumer demand, and an outright need for speed in production.

The last one is also why LA has begun a slow descent into flyover country as far as cargo is concerned. Asian airlines in particular have learned to skip its tangle of runways and freeways in favor of direct flights to Dallas to drop off their laptops. It's Yogi Berra logic: nobody lands there anymore; it's too crowded.

Orange County: The Battle of El Toro

"Airports come in two sizes," Rem Koolhaas wrote, "too big and too small." But John Wayne Airport, nestled snugly in Orange County, was just right. Big enough for locals to enjoy the connections it offered but too small to really annoy anyone, it was a perfect fit for the O.C.

Then not one, but three cities sprang up around the airport in the 1980s—Newport Beach, Costa Mesa, and Irvine—and none possessed the clout to enlarge the airport's footprint, which is smaller than that of the original Mines Field. By 1985, local NIMBY groups had extracted an ironclad promise from the county to cap the number of flights, so as not to disturb the nighttime rituals of Newport Beach. To this day, takeoffs from John Wayne have more in common with those at Baghdad International than O'Hare: pilots must lock the brakes, power up the engines to full throttle, and then release, hurtling down the short runway at top speed before climbing as steeply as possible. Then, just five hundred feet in the air, they all but kill the power so as not to wake the neighbors. Not until after they've floated out over the Pacific do they resume their ascent.

John Wayne was ideal for short flights to Las Vegas or hubs around the country. If you needed to hop one to Tokyo, you just drove up the 405 to LAX. Orange County's three million residents were the proverbial free riders, content to overload the neighbors' airport instead of shoring up the one at home.

In 1993, the Pentagon announced it was closing the El Toro Marine Corps Air Station and handing over the keys to the county. The gesture was meant as a "peace dividend" to make up for the end of the Cold War and the tens of thousands of jobs the Warfare State subsequently lost. What it did was touch off Orange County's civil war, once again pitting north against south. Proponents of a new airport floated an Orange County

International as busy as New York's LaGuardia or Washington's Dulles. The advantages of their plan were obvious—El Toro would replace John Wayne and had room to grow where LAX didn't. It would cost far less to start anew than expand the existing airport, where costs of the resulting lawsuits would inevitably add up. Over the long haul, it would make the county even more of a high-tech mecca, attracting overseas companies to complement the ones already there. The downsides were no less apparent: noise, pollution, traffic, and the one thing homeowners cannot abide—lower property values. The ensuing Battle of El Toro exposed Orange County's existential dilemma: become the new Silicon Valley or preserve the gilded country club America imagined as the O.C.

The battle lines were drawn: nine cities in the north in favor of the new airport arrayed against seven in the south stridently against it. (The dividing line was real estate prices.) Each side attracted a strange mélange of allies. Supporters comprised a mix of Hispanic immigrants, the salivating Orange County Business Council, and the haute bourgeoisie of Newport Beach, who saw their chance to do away with John Wayne forever. Opposing them was an uneasy coalition of entrenched NIMBY interests along the coast and alarmed environmentalists. As it dragged on, the fight over El Toro turned into a referendum on Los Angeles's own airport strategy. The city's mayor saw an opening to defuse the LAX crisis and exploited it accordingly.

John Kasarda entered the debate by writing a series of reports that became the Federalist Papers for pro-airport forces. After running the numbers, he concluded that Orange County International would elevate the county to a full-fledged rival of Los Angeles itself. "To the extent Orange County depends upon [LAX]," he wrote in one report, "its economic future is uncertain and remains in the hands of Los Angeles decision makers. Yet there is an alternative—independence."

Both sides drafted armies of lawyers, consultants, and pollsters to craft ballot measures, canvas support, and file lawsuits. The legal struggle lasted eight years, costing $90 million in taxpayers' money spent on voter initiatives and environmental reviews. Then the World Trade Center was destroyed, and a new airport suddenly seemed like a big bull's-eye. Its opponents took a new tack—rather than ask residents to vote for or against it, they had a choice between an airport and a "Great Park" covering its forty-five hundred acres. Relieved to have an alternative, the people chose the park. El Toro was auctioned off to developers a year later.

In doing so, residents turned their backs on history and the origins of their own prosperity. Orange County was a modest bedroom community until the two dozen towers of the Irvine Business Complex rose beside John Wayne in the 1980s. Now there are more blue-chip firms around it than in downtown San Diego, and close to half the county's office space. The luxury megamall on its far side, South Coast Plaza, moves more merchandise every day than all of the shops in downtown San Francisco.

The failure of Orange County International was an especially tough blow to companies like Western Digital, the world's second-largest maker of hard drives. The discs that end up in your PC or DVR are made of components stamped in its Asian factories, sent by plane to Orange County for final assembly, and then flown out again. Western Digital's output is typical of American exports and manufacturing in the Instant Age. Our exports are airborne to an even greater extent than our imports—at last count around $554 billion worth, or more than half the total.

As America's intangible assets have cratered—$12 trillion in household wealth has simply evaporated—its exports of goods and services have arguably been the only thing keeping the economy afloat. (That, and government stimulus.) President Barack Obama's prescription for a "new economic foundation" amounts to "export more and consume less"—a goal made explicit in his first State of the Union address, in which he called for a doubling of exports within five years. "We've got to go back to making things," he said last spring, while visiting a California solar panel factory. "We've got to go back to exports." Whatever we learn to make and sell abroad will command prices high enough to go by air—to say nothing of the contracts needing to be negotiated. More exports will require more runways.

Orange County International would have been a start, but Orange County itself was the problem. Or rather, the *idea* of Orange County: the shining cities on *The Hills* built on a rising tide of home equity made possible by the rogues' gallery of subprime lenders chartered in the county. When America tried to follow its lead, the result was calamity—especially on the fringes of Los Angeles, where homeowners drowning in their underwater mortgages still cling stubbornly to the dream.

Their defeat left Southern California's urban planners with no real alternatives—unless you count a floating airport off the coast of San

Diego. The brainchild of a local lawyer, Oceansworks Offshore Airport would be moored a dozen miles out to sea, with runways on the roof and an aerotropolis larger than San Diego itself stowed below. All its creator needs is a permit and someone to lend him $20 billion.

No matter what happens, LAX will get busier. Its many missteps will be mitigated but never rectified, and the crush on its crumbling infrastructure will worsen until—from a competitive perspective—it finally implodes. Qantas and Singapore Airlines have both threatened to reroute their daily A380 flights unless something is done about the condition of the airfield. Trying to preempt this, the Los Angeles City Council pushed through a $1.3 billion face-lift in October 2009. The largest sum ever awarded by the city for a single project will be financed entirely with bonds. Obama's plan to spend $50 billion on infrastructure— including a pledge to pave 150 miles' worth of runways—came too late.

Renovations and expansion of the terminals should be finished by 2013. By then, San Francisco, Phoenix, and Las Vegas will all have new or improved airports. Will it be too late to prevent Los Angeles from descending into flyover country? "These aircraft don't have to stop at LAX," a city councilwoman explained. "People in the airline industry were telling me they could just pass us over. LAX was not getting its fair share of the future."

Dulles: America's Wealthiest Invisible City

President Dwight D. Eisenhower dropped his finger on a map of the rolling Virginia countryside and chose the site of his second great invasion. As was the case with Normandy, his choice of battleground was deceptively remote: a field in the middle of nowhere, eleven thousand wooded acres twenty-five miles due west of the White House, with no highways to connect them. There, in 1958, thirty years after the original bean field strips of Los Angeles Municipal Airport, Dulles International was built using the same template.

Opened on the cusp of the Jet Age, it sat all but empty for twenty years, as Beltway drivers stuck with the more convenient Washington National (now Reagan) airport on the west bank of the Potomac River. In the afternoons, passengers could hear their own footfalls echoing off the vaulted ceiling of Eero Saarinen's main terminal. And still no one had thought to make any provisions for what should and what shouldn't be built beyond the perimeter, because even in the year following Sputnik, no one could foresee what would happen next: Ronald Reagan's blank checks for Star Wars and the contractors who cashed them would conspire to plow under the hillsides and erect the prototypical edge cities that redefined our urban landscapes. Dulles would be the anchor.

The airport's saving grace was its size, nearly four times the landmass of LAX, and more than all of greater LA's airports combined. No one could build horse farms or McMansions close enough to complain about the noise, leaving the airport to operate in peace and (relative) quiet. It wouldn't emerge from its torpor until Reagan took office in 1981. His plan for winning the Cold War—to outspend the Soviets into oblivion—opened a gusher of defense contracts that poured out of the Pentagon and spilled across Virginia in the 1980s. After a pause during the New World Order, a second flood of federal procurement funds never subsided, and kept rising in the post-9/11 reshuffling of dollars and duties to the likes of Homeland Security, Halliburton, and, once again, Boeing. The bill for federal outsourcing came to $4.2 billion in 1980; in 2006, it was $54 billion. Half a trillion dollars has flowed out the doors of the Pentagon since Reagan was inaugurated, and half of that figure, in turn—some $223 billion—has found its way to the bottom lines of the companies that pitched their tents between it and Dulles, in neighboring Fairfax County.

The bulk of those contracts now have less to do with military applications than the software kind. Beginning with the technical specs for Star Wars, the Department of Defense has leaned on high-tech purveyors for help in buying, building, configuring, and integrating the fully networked battlefield. The so-called Beltway Bandits were paid handsomely for it; in the largest contracts to date, EDS (now part of HP) was promised $10 billion for running the navy's IT department.

Buried in the voluminous paperwork accompanying these deals was a clause requiring the winning bidder to dwell within thirty miles or thirty minutes of the Pentagon for impromptu meetings with the brass. In exchange for its cash, the Pentagon made itself the impatient center of their universe. The typical outfit had only two choices: pack up headquarters and move to Fairfax, or transfer their contractors there and shuttle the CEO in and out for meetings. Either way, the ability to hop a flight to Washington on a moment's notice became an absolute necessity. Baltimore's airport wouldn't cut it (too far) and neither would National, which lies barely a mile from the Pentagon but can't handle transcontinental flights. That made it useless to Boeing execs flying from Seattle, for example, or a Lockheed team leaving LAX.

So Dulles was where you went to extract cash from the federal government. Soon whole companies moved in down the street from the Pentagon, with the Joint Chiefs on one side and a portal home on the other. Scouting the surrounding terrain, they discovered good schools, cheap land, relaxed zoning, and ever-so-slightly-lower taxes than Maryland or the District of Columbia. It wasn't long before they were convincing zoning boards to condemn the horse and dairy farms and toss up smoked glass cubes within spitting distance of the runways.

The Pentagon and its affiliates have kept funneling some $16 billion a year into their neighbors ever since, more than they send to the entirety of California. A few of the largest contractors, like the San Diego–based SAIC, have more staff kicking around Dulles than back at headquarters. (Bowing to this reality, Northrop Grumman moved its headquarters to Virginia last year.) Government outsourcing spawned one hundred thousand private-sector white-collar jobs in Fairfax County between 1990 and 2005, more than triple the number created in the District itself. By then, the number of residents had topped a million (nearly twice as many as Washington) and had been recognized as the nation's wealthiest, with the median household income climbing above $100,000 for the first time in history. Fairfax was the birthplace of the original edge cities, Tysons Corner chief among them. It's the second-richest county in the country; neighboring Loudon County, which shares the airport, is first. Fairfax isn't officially a city—it doesn't even have its own zip code—but if its size was measured in mall and office space, it would be the sixth-largest in the country.

Fairfax today is wealthier than either Bangkok or New Delhi, and it hasn't plateaued yet. While America grapples with double-digit unemployment, the Obama administration has added hundreds of thousands of jobs around Washington.

What you make of this depends on your politics. Armchair sociologists with a local's bias and conservative bent—like Joel Garreau or the *New York Times* columnist David Brooks—see a shining, privately owned and publicly financed city on a hill. A liberal polemicist like Thomas Frank, on the other hand, finds a starched-and-pressed Sodom:

> When you drive among these wonders, northern Virginia appears as a kind of technicolor vision of prosperity, American-style; a distillation of all that is mighty and righteous about the American imperium: the airport designed by Eero Saarinen; the shopping mall so vast it dwarfs other cities' downtowns; the finely tuned high-performance cars zooming along an immaculate private highway; the masses of flowers in perfectly edged beds; the gas stations with Colonial Williamsburg cupolas; the street names, even, recalling our cherished American values: Freedom, Market, Democracy, Tradition, and Signature drives; Heritage Lane; Founders Way; Enterprise, Prosperity, and Executive Park avenues; and a Chivalry Road that leads, of course, to Valor Court.

All well and good, except for the fact it's corporate welfare. Dulles is also crucial to the county's plans for its next act. First, Fairfax hopes to wean itself from the Pentagon so as not to suffer the fate someday of another company town, Detroit. Then it aims to use the taxpayers' money as bait to attract the next generation of high-tech entrepreneurs looking to consult for the consultants.

It almost worked once before. The all-time greatest instance of the military's power to spin its science projects into gold runs like a river directly beneath Dulles and most of Fairfax County. MAE-East, a buried stream of fiber optics, is the first and largest of the Internet's trunk routes. Built by government mandate in 1992, it was the single most potent node of digital connectivity in existence. By the time Netscape went public in 1995 and dot-com mania had begun, one could make the case that Dulles, not Palo Alto, was the de facto capital of the Internet. A third of all Net traffic ran through it, drawing bandwidth-thirsty companies from far and wide to drink from its torrent.

Two titans from the era planted their headquarters here: MCI and America Online. It's no coincidence they sound like government agencies.

When the former announced its $37 billion merger with WorldCom in 1997, it was the largest in U.S. history. By then, AOL had already moved from crowded digs in Fairfax to a spacious headquarters in "Dulles, Virginia," a piece of Loudon that not only lacks a zip code but doesn't technically exist. "Dulles" is an alternative name for the town of Sterling, which has been summarily dumped in favor of all that "Dulles" implies— proximity to the only landmark that matters, the mechanism that made it possible for AOL's chiefs to practice shuttle diplomacy in their failed attempt to manage the world's mightiest media conglomerate in the heady days of 2000. Within a couple of years, they had been ousted over a plummeting stock price in a palace coup, while MCI imploded even more spectacularly amid an Enron-style accounting scandal. But by then they had proved what county boosters already knew—Fairfax was the capital now, and D.C. its suburb.

The companies headed there today look more like Netezza than AOL or Netscape. Netezza sells "appliances"—a server-software combo that crunches millions of records ten times faster than the competition. The patterns it finds buried deep in the data are invisible to the naked eye or spreadsheet. Amazon would like to see where its customers are clicking on its site; Neiman Marcus wants to know not only what its shoppers are buying but also why. IBM liked it so much that it bought the company in the fall of 2010. Netezza began life in Boston in 2002, salvaging customers and talent from the dot-com rubble. It grew in every direction at once, opening offices in Tokyo, Sydney, Toronto, and outside London. A few years later it landed in Tysons Corner, opening a "federal division" that Netezza's chairman, Jit Saxena, can't really talk about.

All I wanted to know was how a start-up with fewer than a hundred employees could become a real multinational overnight. "The physical barriers, in terms of connectivity and travel, are gone," he told me. "We invest in a new geography based solely on the opportunities there, and that's decided by the size of the market. If we were a Web 2.0 company, then geography wouldn't be that important. But in the business we're in, you're dealing with customers face-to-face, and that's something you cannot do over e-mail. You still need presence, and since the market in the Fairfax area is huge, we need to be here." Netezza has a major presence in India as well, where much of its R & D work is done. That can't be performed over e-mail, either. Why not? Saxena sounded bemused by the idea that a company trafficking so heavily in the virtual should depend on air traffic to keep up.

"The Internet doesn't make any of that obsolete," he said. "It even encourages more travel, because it emphasizes how tightly costs and communication are bound together. When we build R and D centers or a new sales office, we ask, 'Are these places easy to get to? Or do we have to change planes to get there?' And for that, Fairfax is perfect."

The man most responsible for luring Saxena here is Gerry Gordon, president of the Fairfax County Economic Development Authority and its foremost corporate headhunter. Receiving me in his office in Tysons Corner—just around the block from Netezza's—Gordon had the self-satisfied glow of a man who knows just how lucky he is to be the captain of a perpetually winning team. His adopted hometown was blessed before he arrived with this century's answer to a deep-water harbor or rich veins of iron ore: a hub with plenty of room. "With a fast-growing international airport on one side and the federal government on the other, you'd have to try to fuck that up," he said, laughing.

He also has as many foreign bureaus as Netezza—in London, Frankfurt, Tel Aviv, Seoul, and Bangalore. "We have more overseas offices than most cities," he explained. "Actually, we have more than most states." The reasons go beyond simple economics. While the county's outposts search for new recruits that match up well with its strengths—the Tel Aviv staff, for instance, are on the lookout for transplant candidates in software, security, and biotech—there's a deep cosmopolitan yearning at play here as well. The fields where the Civil War was once fought have become diverse suburbs filled with upwardly mobile immigrants. More than a third of all the children born in Fairfax have at least one parent from overseas, and that percentage is rising; its one million inhabitants already include forty thousand foreign-born Indians and fifty thousand Koreans. Fairfax is also home to some 358 foreign-owned companies, and the key to finding life after the Beltway Bandits is to lure more of them here. Thanks to its connections, the future of Fairfax is bound up more tightly with Beijing or Bangalore than with Washington, D.C., next door.

Gordon began to have an inkling of the airport's power in the early 1990s, when the United States and Canada hammered out an Open Skies agreement that finally allowed nonstop flights between Canadian cities and Dulles. Until then, "to get to Toronto or Montreal, you had to fly through Detroit, Boston, or Pittsburgh. I never thought that businesses that could make a buck by coming would find that sufficient to curtail their presence. Really? One stop?" Once nonstop flights started, however, "you could immediately—*immediately!*—see the Canadian companies start streaming in. So the growth of the airport and the ability to get places . . . golly, the impact is enormous."

You can see just how much it means to them by looking more closely at a single daily flight, between Dulles and Beijing. The first nonstop between the G2's capitals didn't start until March 2007, and it's been flying full ever since. Each leg carries a mix of diplomats, businessmen, and tourists, but the suits are the ones Gordon's after. They're worth as much as $250 million a year to the greater D.C. economy, according to research conducted at George Mason University. Just this one route will create 1,760 new jobs, with a median salary of $81,000, or about $140 million in wages. The rest will come when they spread that wealth around, generating another $100 million in trickle-down effects. That will stem from Chinese companies on the prowl for the programmers and consultants who can bring them up to speed in the Instant Age.

"China is a developing nation that is experiencing very rapid growth and is an importer of information and high technology products," the George Mason report noted. "Workers in this sector are heavy users of air transportation making on average 60% more trips than workers in traditional industries." They haven't landed in Fairfax yet, at least not in large numbers.

"China Telecom has its North American headquarters here in Fairfax County," Gordon told me. "That's the only Chinese company to date worth going after, and it's already here. So we haven't been as active in China as we will one day be." This struck me as a stunning development—that Dulles will be the means for Chinese companies to move to Virginia and outsource their own needs to Americans. We've gotten so used to the idea of our factories vanishing overseas, never to be seen or heard from again (except for postcards in the form of our digital cameras), that the prospect of China handing over the keys to its software industry is nothing short of astounding. "It's interesting for us," he added, "because we don't make things. We only deal with services and thoughts."

The new arrivals have an easier time than the locals seeing Dulles and Fairfax County for what they are: a full-blown (if accidental) aero-tropolis. There's plenty of anecdotal evidence to suggest that they don't even know, or care, that there's a city with a big obelisk at the other end of the Dulles Toll Road. Near the end of our chat, Gordon offered proof of this: "When we talk to people in places like Seoul or Bangalore, we ask, 'How many of you have been in Fairfax County?' And two or three hands to go up. 'How many of you have been to McLean?' There's a few more. 'How many of you have been to Dulles?' Every hand in the room goes up. 'How many of you have gone from Dulles to Washington, driving down that Toll Road?' And everyone says, 'Sure, sure, it's a big technology park.' To them, that's Fairfax, and it's why every company wants its name on the Dulles Toll Road. I've seen people writing down a list of who they saw there."

A few hours later, I balanced my notebook on the steering wheel and tried desperately to take in the galaxy of logos swirling by on either side: Northrop Grumman, Cybertrust, Booz Allen Hamilton, ITT, Verizon, Symantec, and RCN. Farther along, there was Unisys, Oracle, Sprint, and XO Communications. Just about every Internet, cable, and telecom company in the land adorned some piece of real estate. The Dulles Toll Road was, in effect, the template for the high-tech avenues I would see later in Dubai, Doha, Guangzhou, and even Dallas.

In the middle distance, I spotted a cluster of condo high-rises. Was that the Washington skyline already? Where was I? After pointing my rental car in their general direction, I ended up cruising through a pocket of oversize London row houses as warm and fresh as a sheet of ready-bake cookies straight from the oven. I'd stumbled into the outskirts of Reston Town Center, "What downtown was meant to be," or so its signs proclaimed. At its center, sheltered by office blocks containing Accenture and Sallie Mae, is the eminently walkable Freedom Square and its centerpiece, the faux Beaux Arts Mercury Fountain. It was as if someone had broken off a piece of gentrified Washington and carried it out here, twenty miles west of city limits, and attempted to transplant it in fresh dirt where people really wanted to live and work: next door to the airport.

The tidal wave of growth that rolled across Fairfax over the last two decades finally crested here before crashing on the rock of Dulles and breaking to either side. The overflow of new homes and mixed-use, master-planned landscapes like Reston's is spilling north into Loudoun County now, where the reception of Dulles's amoebalike aerotropolis has been decidedly mixed. Despite Loudoun's jockeying with Fairfax to be the wealthiest county in the nation, its residents are inclined to keep their horse farms and rolling estates at home while commuting to their day jobs in the next county over.

But the developers who built out Reston and Tysons Corner are having none of that. Having reached the end of developable land heading west, they're now determined to lock up every piece of open ground between the airport and the Potomac. The de facto aerotropolis is maturing; the communities being built now are so far from Washington's orbit that it's a stretch even to consider them part of greater D.C.—they belong only to Dulles. At the same time, they're denser and more recognizably urban—closer in form to Reston than to the nameless suburbs covering the fields like clover. Last spring, Fairfax County passed a forty-year plan to double Tysons in both size and density, adding two hundred thousand jobs and half as many residents in a bid to transform the sprawling edge city into a vertical, walkable one above an extension of the D.C. Metro out to the airport. Dulles offers hope that given room to breathe, aerotropoli make so much sense that they can and will be born by the invisible hand of market forces alone. But it also demonstrates the hard limits of what unplanned, unintended, and purely private growth can do.

Chicago: Bulldozing the Airport in Order to Save It

Chicago mayor Richard J. Daley was the last of the big-city bosses, the mayor-for-life who delivered the city—and thus the state of Illinois and the nation—for John F. Kennedy in the 1960 presidential election. Only a few years earlier, he'd delivered the suburban footprint of O'Hare Airport to the city of Chicago in a brilliant bit of gerrymandering. He annexed a five-mile-long tether to the airport, strong-arming the swampy village of Rosemont to cede him the final few hundred feet. In exchange, Rosemont became O'Hare's front door. Today it has more hotel rooms than residents, and more office towers than downtown Kansas City. The highway leading from the Loop to the terminals is a dead ringer for the Dulles Toll Road.

O'Hare, the world's busiest airport for nearly the entirety of the Jet Age, succeeded as Dulles did in reversing the polarity between downtown and its suburbs. "Richard the First" accepted this, so long as he controlled the airport, its revenues, and its opportunities for patronage. But a proto-aerotropolis was busily forming outside city limits, in the "Golden Corridor" running through the northwest suburbs. As early as 1972, more than half the business travelers arriving at O'Hare never strayed beyond meetings at the adjacent Hyatts and Hiltons. (Why fight traffic?) They settled in instead, encouraging local companies with a global footprint—Motorola, Sears, McDonald's—to do the same, vacating downtown for a headquarters nearby. In 1991, Sears abandoned its namesake—the 110-story Sears Tower, the world's tallest building when it opened in 1974—in favor of a low-slung campus along the toll road that begins and ends at O'Hare. Management looked far and wide when they gave up on their aerie, until they realized they could just as easily roam far and wide themselves by setting up shop in Hoffman Estates, thirty miles away. Allstate, ACNielsen, and U.S. Cellular have all followed to the mirrored office corridor larger than downtown Detroit, Miami, or Tampa—larger, in fact, than any downtown in the entire Midwest, with the sole exception of the Loop.

O'Hare was its linchpin, but it was not *of* it. With only the airport in his grasp, Daley was at loggerheads with his neighbors in Des Plaines, Elk Grove Village, and Bensenville, who, like the locals around LAX, despised the pollution and noise. But unlike his counterparts in Los Angeles, Daley had no political incentive to kowtow to residents or rein in O'Hare as it annually shattered passenger records—the fallout wasn't technically Chicago's problem. The nonstop connectivity it offered was just as vital to the commodity traders shouting orders in the pits of the Chicago Board of Trade as it is to the thousands of McDonald's managers making the trek to the eighty-acre campus of Hamburger University in Oak Brook.

The natural solution to O'Hare's mounting congestion was to add another airport somewhere. This line of thinking had led to O'Hare after Chicago's original airfield on the city's South Side, Midway, had become hopelessly boxed in. But Richard the First had no intention of building anything he couldn't control. He'd actually been first to propose a third airport in his 1967 inaugural address, floating the idea of runways built five miles offshore in Lake Michigan (presumably on territory annexed by the city). He dismissed it shortly thereafter, claiming O'Hare would suffice "until the year 2000."

The next push for a new airport came in the mid-1980s, during the interregnum between the father and son Mayor Daleys, when Illinois state officials explored more conventional sites in the farmland south of the city. Their favorite was a stretch of soybean fields forty-five miles from the Loop, near a small town named Peotone. The Peotone site was championed by the suburbs bordering O'Hare, which dreaded the airport's otherwise inevitable expansion. But they failed to rally enough support in the legislature and Congress to pay for the new one's multibillion-dollar construction.

When Richard M. Daley (Richard the Second) was elected in 1989, within months he announced his own plan for an airport on the city's southeast side, atop abandoned steel mills and landfills full of toxic waste. Before the full costs of displacing sixty thousand residents and condemning thousands of acres could be calculated, his downstate opponents—led by Governor James "Big Jim" Thompson, Daley's only real rival—killed funding for it, setting a pattern of reprisals for the next decade. The *Chicago Tribune* won a Pulitzer Prize in 2001 for probing Daley's ruthlessness in protecting the city's hold on O'Hare, revealing an impenetrable web of patronage and political contributions.

Among the highlights were his unholy alliance with United and American Airlines—O'Hare's largest tenants and two of the largest airlines in the world—to head off the competition a Peotone airport could mount. (United went so far as to hire Daley's younger brother and his former chief of staff as lobbyists; American settled for former governor Thompson.) Daley and his aides hired more than a thousand new employees in the city's Department of Aviation, including the sons, wives, and nephews of their allies. Some were later planted within the FAA, where they did their best to frustrate Peotone plans. Then there were the $356 million in contracts handed out to twenty-nine architectural and engineering firms, including $12 million a year for the aviation consultants Landrum & Brown. They were the ones the *Tribune* accused of doctoring growth projections in a misguided effort to dissuade all involved that a third airport was necessary, or that O'Hare needed expansion. ("Forecasts are generally made to order," said Daley's first—and subsequently ousted—aviation commissioner.) The real numbers never stopped climbing.

Los Angeles's NIMBY-derived paralysis was about fear; Chicago's was the willful denial of reality. Daley was willing to hamstring the entire region rather than commit the political and financial capital for Chicagoland to grow in directions that might not benefit him and the city directly. A leaked memo revealed Daley had no intention of building a third airport, describing his feint on the South Side as "successful guerrilla warfare." The impasse attracted national attention. "I say pox on all of them," Senator John McCain declared in 2000. "Chicago is one of the most gridlocked places in America and a critical transportation hub. We can't get O'Hare expanded, and we can't build another airport. And those are the only two options."

There was a third: federal intervention. Tired of watching delays at O'Hare gum up flights from coast to coast, the FAA cracked down in 2004 with a cap on the number of arrivals per hour. Prevented from stuffing more flights in and out, the airport would languish; a year later, it relinquished its title as the world's busiest to Atlanta, ending a forty-year run at the top. (It has since fallen to fourth place, behind Heathrow and Beijing.) The crisis gave Daley just the opening he needed to fast-track his new plan for overhauling O'Hare. This plot twist led one of Illinois's own senators to smell a conspiracy, accusing the mayor of forcing the FAA's hand.

The O'Hare Modernization Program (OMP) is a $15 billion, twenty-year effort to build a new airport atop the current one without canceling any flights. The centerpiece is a scheme to realign its runways while adding new ones, allowing more planes to take off and land simultaneously. When finished, the airport will look a lot like the one in Dallas–Ft. Worth, which laid down most of its seven runways in 1972. The price tag is staggering and the benefits modest—the biggest dig in American history will increase capacity by only 20 percent. While that's enough to retake the title and reduce delays, the cost-effectiveness of the endeavor seems a bit skewed. Much of the time, energy, and money will be spent on the contortions necessary to solve the airport's layout like a Rubik's Cube. The taxpayers won't foot the bill—not the local ones, anyway. Daley vowed to pay for it all with a mixture of bonds, fees, federal funds, and checks from the airlines, which were crying poverty even before $150 oil and the recession.

With the first $3 billion in hand, work began on the runways in summer 2007, nearly a year behind schedule and already a billion dollars over budget. I paid a visit to the OMP's headquarters that spring and discovered a warren of bright and earnest engineers wrestling with manuals a foot thick and spilling over every available surface. Pinned to the walls were maps I needed 3-D, or maybe 4-D, glasses to interpret, as each color-coded phase of the project was overlaid atop the next. Contractors from dozens of firms handling grading, paving, and planning stalked the halls.

One consultant I met belonged to the team that helped develop the OMP and was now waist-deep in the (very) long-term planning. What would happen when it was finished, I asked, when another 195,000 jobs had poured into the region, as Daley had promised? What would the cities around O'Hare look like then, and had anyone drawn up plans for those? Did the airport create an aerotropolis, or had the northwest suburbs effectively created the airport?

"There's no question the airport created this region," he answered, "but what do you do with it now that it's there? That's what we're grappling with: What role should the city play in the development of the surrounding area? Should Chicago do that, the airport, or the region? And how do you plan for it?" Left unspoken was the question of whether anyone could, and what will happen if no one does.

The OMP's executive director is Rosemarie Andolino, a relentlessly perky Daley protégé who doubles as the city's aviation commissioner. However else the program fits into Chicago's business as usual, Andolino understands the stakes. "The airport is stagnant," she said over coffee in her office. "It's capped and there's no more growth. What happens then? Businesses have choices. They can come here—for the workforce, the cultural activities, and the location—or they can go someplace else more efficient." She shot me a helpless look that said lakefront parks and top-tier universities mattered less to Chicago's bottom line.

She grew up on the west side of O'Hare, in what is now the cargo village of Elk Grove Village. "I moved there when I was in first grade, thirty-three years ago," she said. "Our subdivision was one of the new ones, and all around us were farms. [O'Hare] was originally Orchard Field not because it was a cute name, but because this was once apple orchards. Now there's Walmart, Kmart, Home Depot, and not one piece of farmland left in Elk Grove Village."

And now she finds herself bulldozing the village in order to save it. To accommodate half a dozen new and extended runways, the OMP will annex an additional 433 acres to the airport's footprint. O'Hare's feud with its neighbors is lurching toward a climax of condemnation, invasion, and eventually demolition. Andolino fills her days catching flak from enraged suburban mayors. The one bearing the brunt of condemnation, with more than six hundred homes slated to vanish beneath tarmac, took to issuing communiqués such as "Judge halts Chicago's hell-bent effort to destroy a good part of Bensenville for O'Hare Airport expansion." The injunction was overturned; they always were. When airport workers arrived one day to clear a few trees ahead of the inevitable, the village president sicced his police on them. (They settled out of court.)

The city intends to evict both the living and the dead. The latter reside in a pair of cemeteries tucked within the new footprint. St. Johannes and Rest Haven preceded O'Hare by more than a hundred years— among the first to be buried there were Civil War vets. Plans call for St. Johannes to be paved over; Rest Haven will survive as an island of green sitting well behind the fence, where maps show a taxiway running right alongside it. Late in the day I went to pay my respects. St. Johannes is the larger of the two, with obelisks and monuments standing tall beside some thirteen hundred graves. Its parishioners have dug in deep, vowing to appeal all the way to the Supreme Court. "Frankly, it's nothing less than the immortal souls of their relatives that are at stake" is how one of their attorneys framed it. "Is it morally correct to move graves?" asked another. "We'll find out on Judgment Day."

But who wants to spend eternity wedged between a FedEx hangar and one of the world's busiest runways? Those interred at Rest Haven just down the road would discover how the screams of a Pratt & Whitney engine sounded soon enough. Jet wash drowned out the birdcalls at dusk. There were fresh bouquets on the headstones of family plots dating back a dozen generations. Past the graves, bulldozers were busy excavating a mountain of mud ahead of an eleven-thousand-foot runway. Earlier that day local archaeologists had gently probed Rest Haven's edges for traces of unmarked graves, lest they be carried away and reburied in the muck.

Twenty years and $15 billion later (or quite a few billion more, depending on delays, overruns, and inflation), O'Hare will be the world's busiest airport again (or not, depending on Beijing), and yet the streams of arriving 787s will be forced to pirouette around a graveyard upon landing. In its sad attempt to be a good neighbor, the OMP unwittingly underscored the impossibility of ever truly "modernizing" O'Hare, not while the Union dead still hold a place of honor in the infield.

One could make the case (and Peotone's proponents had) that the program was the sunk cost fallacy run amok for all sorts of reasons: historical, political, and the utterly irrational. Daley and the airlines were throwing good money after bad, and the latter have threatened to stop writing checks. Fifteen billion dollars can buy you a lot of airport—building Richard the First's island airfield in Lake Michigan would probably cost less today—but it cannot completely undo the mistakes the planners of O'Hare (or LAX or Dulles) had unknowingly made during construction. Not that it matters; the inertia around O'Hare dictated that it remain Chicago's primary node. If the OMP cements O'Hare's hub status for another generation, it will have been worth it for the city, no matter how mind-boggling the price tag. But drifting among the graves at twilight I wondered: Just what was so crazy about Peotone, again?

Conventional wisdom says the rural airport is dead, extinguished once and for all by Daley. And yet those in power kept sending mixed signals: the state bought half the land and then stopped; the governor who made a big show of his support flip-flopped; and officials swearing, "It is coming . . . it's only a matter of when and how," were incommunicado afterward for months or even years.

I didn't think it would ever be built, either, but I wanted to see those soybeans anyway. As it happens, I grew up less than ten miles away, in the next town down the interstate. My parents shivered when the first plans were unveiled in 1984, and I distinctly remember, when I was seven years old, my father threatening to move away if it were ever built. He reassured me, after I'd bleated in horror, that "it'll take them twenty years to build anything." Twenty-five have passed since then, and he's still there. My uncles farmed the land in between, and even now, you can spot a few weathered signs with the once-familiar icon of a plane's silhouette set inside a red circle, with a slash running through it—the symbol of the resistance.

The airport's last true believer in the wake of Daley's fait accompli was Jesse Jackson, Jr., the congressional representative from Illinois's Second District, just north of the site. His plan, which the FAA promised to take seriously, outlined an "Abraham Lincoln National Airport" run by a coalition of suburbs. Tellingly, the list of charter members contained neither Peotone nor any town from Will County (Chicago and his district both lie in neighboring Cook), while his most ardent supporters were the familiar pair of O'Hare foils, Bensenville and Elk Grove Village. (As Kasarda discovered in Orange County, everyone is for an airport in Illinois, so long as it's somewhere else.)

Curious as to what Jackson had in mind, I arranged a tour of the phantom airport with Rick Bryant, its executive director. We met one morning at a truck stop along I-57, where he had apparently spent the night. Disheveled and wearing a black polo faded to the same shade as his shaggy hair, Bryant doubled as Jackson's press secretary, a former newspaperman who threw in his lot with the congressman and took the title of airport director as an unpaid volunteer. Bryant also played a bit part in Illinois's most mesmerizing scandal to date: the indictment of Governor Rod Blagojevich, who was subsequently impeached for allegedly auctioning President Obama's vacated Senate seat.

The FBI's sworn affidavit revealed Jackson as "Senate Candidate 5," whom Blagojevich considered a serious bidder, according to wiretap transcripts. Federal investigators requested an interview, while Jackson claimed to have been an informant all along, ever since Bryant had publicly leaked details of a secret meeting about Peotone in 2006. The pair had arrived at a Chicago hotel prepared to negotiate with the governor's aide, only to be greeted by Tony Rezko—a Blagojevich fund-raiser later convicted for collecting bribes. Rezko promised the governor's support in Peotone in exchange for handpicking its board. Jackson stalked out. Rezko himself was indicted shortly thereafter, and the long fuse leading to Blago's arrest was lit.

Heading off in his truck, Bryant ran me through their latest plan. Abraham Lincoln will open (someday) with one runway, a few gates, and a handful of low-fare carriers like Southwest or JetBlue. The bill from groundbreaking to opening day is pegged at $1 billion, and no taxpayers will be harmed during the making of this airport. Jackson and Co. will have sold it off before it even opens, having already struck a public-private partnership with the developer LCOR and the Canadian construction giant SNC-Lavalin to buy, build, and operate it. (Both have run terminals before but never an entire airport.) Bryant's job will be cashing

royalty checks and passing on the proceeds to the townships lucky enough
to be on board. And no matter what, they'll hoard the land, because if
all goes according to plan, Lincoln will someday sit on twenty-four thousand acres of pavement and soybean fields, three times the size of
O'Hare. "That's so we won't end up with businesses at the end of the
runway or communities sitting out there you someday need to bulldoze,"
he said.

We turned off the highway onto Eagle Lake Road, one of the strips
of two-lane blacktop that slice and dice fields into grids. Ahead of us was
freshly planted dirt, its nakedness allowing us to see the subtle lay of the
land. On either side were farmhouses set back from the road and accessorized with barns, combines, and silos. Pulling over to the side of the
road, Bryant reached into a folder balanced on the seat, producing a single sheet of paper. Anyone puzzled as to why he and his boss kept cham-
pioning their airport in the face of superior political firepower needed
only to see this page to understand—it explained the ultimate payoff of
Jackson's dream to build an aerotropolis anew on Chicago's South Side.

The page contained a map, sketched five times, depicting the counties
in orbit around Chicago. Drawn on each one were colored squares indicat-
ing where the jobs were and in what density. Pinks giving way to crimson
and finally to deep blue stood in for office parks and skyscrapers. Also included were the three airports: O'Hare, Midway, and Lincoln. The map
labeled "1960" described a city where downtown was the center of the
universe, except for the steel mills of Gary, Indiana, teetering on the brink
of decline. O'Hare is the faintest pink; Midway and Lincoln are moribund.

Fast-forward twenty years to the second map, "1980." The Loop has
lost half its jobs, and Gary is bleeding white. O'Hare, by contrast, is a
vibrant and spreading red. Skip to "1990" and the red has deepened to
the point where O'Hare is the beating heart of the city both in life and
on the page. "These are census numbers," Bryant explained. "There are
now more jobs in the O'Hare corridor than there are in downtown Chicago, five hundred thousand up here versus four hundred thousand
downtown. They ain't hurting out there. Our folks down here," in Jackson's district, which is china white in every map so far, "all drive up to
O'Hare or else head into Chicago. We have the longest average commute
time in the country, because all of the jobs that used to be here are now
around O'Hare."

Then he pointed to the last two maps, labeled "2020 Build" and "2020 No-Build." They referred to Abraham Lincoln. On the one marked "Build," the blood has begun returning to the city's South Side. There's a crimson spot centered on Lincoln itself, spilling out into the countryside. On the "No-Build" map, there's none of this. Either way, O'Hare is unchanged.

His model was almost heartbreaking in its simplicity, but his maps barely began to tell the whole story. Downtown hadn't stagnated; just the opposite. O'Hare also played a pivotal role in elevating Chicago to the ranks of "global cities"—the half-dozen or so financial capitals that are the wealthiest in the world. Over the last twenty years, the per capita incomes of 465,000 people living in and around downtown rose anywhere between 62 and 640 percent. "Those are the lawyers, consultants, traders, media mavens and the like who work downtown," wrote *Crain's Chicago Business*, "providing the brainpower needed by big companies that could locate just about anywhere in the world." They could locate in Chicago because of O'Hare, which explains why Daley is so committed to expanding it. The city no longer sees itself in competition with its suburbs or St. Louis and Milwaukee, but with megacities half a world away—Mumbai and São Paulo.

But Jackson's district is historically the poorest, blackest, and highest taxed in Chicago—even its suburbs are wilted specimens compared to the boomtowns north by northwest. "Chicago is a tale of two cities," Jackson once said. "There is a growing downtown Chicago—it's expanding. But there are some communities where there are sixty people for every one job . . . We're losing tourism. We're losing industries. We're losing dollars." The gleam of the Golden Corridor just over the horizon had sold him. There would at last be jobs next door—"restaurants and hotels to car rentals to gas stations to new warehouses to new companies and ambitious technology guys deciding they want to get out here in greenfields," Bryant chanted like a mantra—greenfields turned fields of gold. And best of all, if the airport was parked next door in Will County, Jackson's constituents would reap all of that gold while suffering none of the noise (and electoral consequences).

What would happen to Beecher? I asked, pointing on my map to the small town lying just east of us, up the road from my grandparents' farm. "Beecher is the next Rosemont!" he exclaimed. "They'll have so many businesses there they won't know what to do with them. That'll create its

own problems, I suppose, but sometimes that's a good problem to have."
This became a common refrain during the bust, although I doubted
whether the good people of Beecher—the children of farmers, like my
mother, or suburban refugees—would feel quite the same way.

Driving along, I spied the silhouette-and-slash logo reappearing on
trees and telephone poles while Bryant yammered obliviously about the
genius of his plan and the lunacy of O'Hare. "By the time you figure in
the graft factor, it's going to be thirty billion dollars. And what that thirty
billion buys you is one hundred fifty thousand new flights. Our cost for
adding the same number of flights is one billion. It'd be a no-brainer if it
weren't for all the corruption and graft . . ."

He reminded me of something Mike DiGirolamo had said in Los
Angeles: "Airlines don't serve airports. They serve markets." Meaning they
didn't care how crowded O'Hare or LAX got; that's where the market
was, and that's where they wanted to be. Dulles sat more or less empty
until the airlines detected at least the faint whiff of customers, and
then . . . *boom!* Southwest or JetBlue weren't about to give up their slots
elsewhere just because Abe Lincoln had room. The proof was Gary's
airport across the state line. Despite $50 million in federal funding and
plenty of vacancy, it had no service. The last regularly scheduled tenant
had been the short-lived Hooters Air, a misbegotten spin-off of the tacky
restaurant chain.

So what was the endgame? "The missing link for us is the land." The
farmers refused to sell, and the governor had refused to invoke eminent
domain. But the real threat, as always, was Daley, who had bought off
the city's construction firms with the promise of work at O'Hare. "Can
you imagine handing out thirty billion dollars' worth of contracts? How
long will that keep you in office? I swear, if Jesse Jr. was part of the Chicago political machine, this thing would already be under construction,
because graft is the underlying premise for everything. I don't know if it
will be us who builds it, but I promise you, it will happen."

The Airfield of Dreams

The next morning I set out with my mother to retrace my steps. We
found my uncle Chuck in his tractor, tilling the fields. He'd been making

some calls on my behalf, searching for one of the ringleaders of STAND: Shut This Airport Nightmare Down! The silhouette and slash was their insignia. He urged me to find Jim Berdyne, a gentleman farmer who still had a convert's zeal for the land.

Berdyne was working in his yard when we pulled in the drive, and while my mother and uncle waited in the car, I joined him for a glass of lemonade. He was well acquainted with Rick Bryant, he growled, and wasn't having any of his arguments. A new airport would never work, he claimed, because the airlines would never stand for it, let alone serve it. They hadn't sunk billions of their own into O'Hare only to watch Peotone be built now. He had been in the room at the state capitol in Springfield when Daley's brother and Big Jim Thompson had all but whispered in the governor's ear on behalf of United and American. "The ones that run the show have got just what they want at O'Hare," he told me. "In fifty years, they may need this airport, but by then the suburbs will have moved on."

He had his own guess as to how this long, tortured story would end: "I think Jesse believes he's going to be the next mayor of Chicago. And if Daley has a heart attack and quits, he will be." He would have his chance. Daley shocked everyone in the fall of 2010 when he announced he would not seek reelection. He was leaving the city with a $655 million budget deficit and had failed in his bid to win the 2016 Summer Olympics. ("The Olympics decided not to come to the city of Chicago for a reason," Jackson had said.) Scandal or not, Jackson was considered one of the frontrunners to replace him. By the time you read this, Chicago will likely have a new mayor, the first in more than twenty years. "If he does that, he owns O'Hare. Will he want Peotone? No. Will he walk away? Yes."

Bryant had been right about one thing: all they needed was the land. The state had made it halfway there before Blagojevich self-destructed. His successor surprised everyone by allotting another $100 million for buying out farmers, despite staring down the barrel of an $11.5 billion budget deficit. In response, Berdyne built a coalition of farms piece by piece, grid square by square. "Ain't none of them can sell. I've got 'em locked up." He grinned wolfishly.

As I stood to leave, he shot me a last piece of advice, one that seemed especially pertinent considering the airfield of dreams set to be paved through his yard: "'If you build it, they will come.' It works for baseball, but it doesn't work for airports." Illinois farmers knew from experience. Lying several hundred miles southwest of here is Peotone's abandoned twin. MidAmerica St. Louis Airport opened east of the Mississippi River amid cornfields in 1997 to relieve pressure on the city's hub—pressure that disappeared when TWA went bankrupt shortly thereafter. The self-styled "Gateway to the World" cost $313 million to build but has never seen steady passenger service. Tom Brokaw once derided it as the "Gateway to Nowhere" in his "Fleecing of America" segments on *NBC Nightly News.*

Berdyne had a point: paving tarmac was never enough. There needed to be some kind of catalyst present, whether it's the Warfare State, the Pentagon, the Internet's trunk routes, or the guaranteed connections of a monster hub like O'Hare, which handled more people back in 1960 than Ellis Island did in its entire existence. We built our airports before we knew what they were for, and we had gotten lucky—we left them with just enough wiggle room to find their true purpose. But the costs have been enormous and have grown to the point where they are almost more than we are willing to bear. LAX, O'Hare, and Dulles succeeded in spite of the cities they ostensibly serve, not because of them. Our refusal to make peace with the airports we already have carries its own price.

2

JUST IN TIME

How FedEx and UPS reinvented commerce and rescued two dying river towns. Memphis and Louisville now straddle an Amazon's worth of goods.

Memphis: From King Cotton to Cargo King

The trading floor of the Memphis Cotton Exchange sits at the corner of South Front Street and Union Avenue, overlooking the bank of the Mississippi River and the docks that once lined it. Plantation owners and their salesmen guided skiffs up and down the delta to those piers before dragging their bales across the road to the base of the exchange. There, beneath its vaulted windows, traders broke pieces off the soft piles and twisted them into ropes called snakes. They would hold these up to sunlight, judging the cotton's color, quality, and seediness on the spot. "Spot trading" was their métier, buying bales already picked and packed, unlike their counterparts at the Chicago or New Orleans exchanges, who traded in futures—essentially contracts to deliver a later harvest at a set price.

Front Street was both the geographic and the spiritual center of Memphis's cotton trade, and the center of the world's until the 1970s—a strip of warehouses, dry-goods stores, barbecue joints, and diners populated by traders, bankers, Teamsters, and hangers-on all swapping gossip with discarded snakes underfoot. The exchange's dues-paying members, fearing they had drifted too far from the street in their headquarters just a few blocks inland, decided in 1922 to move the trading floor back onto "Cotton Row," into the base of an Art Deco tower built to house it.

Today, the Memphis Cotton Exchange is the Memphis Cotton

Museum, the trading floor frozen in time and reconstituted as an average day in 1939. On the spring afternoon of my visit not too long ago, the exchange was empty of traders and visitors alike. Under brass ceiling fans and above the glass display cases was the original Big Board—a chalkboard fifty feet long and ten feet high, spanning an entire wall and rising to the ceiling. Chalkers, usually young men with deft hands, stalked back and forth along an elevated walkway, continually rewriting prices sent over the ticker from New York and Liverpool to the Western Union office below. When exchange members spotted an opening for arbitrage or an untenable position, they strode to one of the four phone booths lining the far wall.

Mounted in each booth today is a small screen displaying a lineup of talking heads reciting the history of King Cotton in Memphis. One of them is a Southern gentleman well past retirement age named William B. "Billy" Dunavant, dubbed "the Michael Jordan of cotton" by his peers.

"We used to consume eleven million bales of cotton each year," he says through a molasses-thick drawl. "Now it's six million. China used to consume fifteen million bales a year. Now it's forty million."

Dunavant liquidated his own firm's physical position on Front Street in the early 1970s, moving to one of the broad, squat warehouses that had already begun sprouting like toadstools along the access roads just east of Memphis International Airport. He dismissed the rivals he left behind as "a bunch of old men gossiping." A few members stayed in the exchange tower for sentimental reasons. Many others followed Dunavant's trail to East Memphis, where the airport, highways, and rail yards had given birth to an entire forest of white, multistory warehouses adorned with the stubs of truck-loading docks instead of Art Deco flourishes. These were the spawn of a twenty-seven-year-old former marine pilot named Fred Smith, who moved home from Little Rock with his new company in tow, Federal Express.

While still at Yale in 1966, Smith had written a paper he claims was subpar in every respect except for its premise. The Information Age then dawning wouldn't happen, he argued, unless IBM could convince skittish customers that it would fix their mainframes immediately when they tilted. No company would replace its flesh-and-blood employees with several acres of temperamental circuit boards if it didn't.

So he outlined the ultimate backup plan—a fleet of jets carrying spare parts (and whatever else he could charge for), operating only at night, all flying through a single hub where payloads could be mixed and matched in time to deliver packages before noon. For that, he supposedly earned a gentleman's C.

Six years later, he opened his brainchild for business in a hangar at Memphis International. There's another story that he first asked the airport in Little Rock to make room for him but was rebuffed. If true, in light of everything that was to follow, it would be one of the biggest economic blunders a city has ever made.

"I never approached them," Smith told me warily, eager to debunk a myth. "It's too far west! If you want a system that connects every point in the U.S. to every other point, the hub has to sit somewhere in a trapezoid between Memphis in the Southwest, to Champaign, Illinois, in the Northwest, over to Dayton, Ohio, and down to Chattanooga. It has to sit in that footprint."

Why? Aerial geography. Just as sitting at the center of the delta had made Memphis a nexus for the exchange and the barges and railroads carrying away cotton, so did sitting in a sweet spot of climate and time zones make the city irresistible to Smith, whose small, French-built Falcon jets could sprint from the coasts and back by daybreak.

I heard differing dimensions for what some called "Cargo Alley"—referring to the thin longitudinal strip it formed—but the gist was always the same. There are only so many airfields from which one can serve the entire United States overnight. The most valuable commodity Memphis has to offer is not cotton but speed, which isn't measured in bales or tonnage but in the bonus hours of productivity that can be wrung from the day. "Yet, a generation ago, it was far from obvious speed pays," James Gleick noted in *Faster*. "When Federal Express entered the marketplace, the older parcel-delivery services were baffled by the high prices it proposed to charge. The traditional pricing models were based on just two variables: weight and size. Speed, anyone?" What Fred Smith understood and his professors didn't is that he could charge more if he guaranteed speed. Today, FedEx and its overnight rivals carry 75 percent of all U.S. air cargo, despite prices three or four times higher than the incumbents.

After an aborted launch yielded just six packages (and was promptly relabeled a "system test" by panicked staff), Federal Express held its first official sort the night of April 17, 1973. Six Falcons brought 185 packages back to Memphis, where workers scattered the envelopes and boxes across a table and sorted them by hand into sacks. Early shipments included microchips, government documents—hence the name Federal Express—even a bear in a cage. (Where's *he* going? one of Smith's investors asked. "Wherever he wants to go.") The planes were reloaded and dispatched to their final destinations, as they have been every night since. Now three hundred planes nose up to its gates nightly, and 3.3 million packages pass through its labyrinth of belts on any given day. Memphis International has been the busiest cargo airport in the world for eighteen years running—since the rankings began—and 95 percent of its title is due to FedEx.

The city's iconic export now is a white box barely larger than a laptop, or a man's shirt, or a stack of DVDs, all of which arrive here along with stacks of overnight envelopes and then leave again on flights costing thousands of dollars per hour in flight time and fuel. Regardless of their contents' retail price, these packages are priceless to their owners, and they pour from the bellies of wide-body planes here by the millions each and every night.

Its trucks, planes, and trailers—not to mention its purple logo—permeate Memphis, which for all intents and purposes is a FedEx company town. In 2008, University of Memphis researchers sought to measure the airport's impact on the city. They discovered that it was indirectly responsible for nearly half of the local economy, worth $28.6 billion, and for 220,154 jobs—one out of every three in the region. Not only is it the largest private employer in a metropolitan area of more than a million people, it sits at the center of an ecosystem of warehouses, trucking firms, factories, and office parks with roots that stretch back to its not-so-far-gone cotton days.

More telling are the companies that have moved to town since then just to take shelter in the shadow of FedEx. The airport, built on the edges in the days when even Graceland was still a country home (now it sits only a few miles from the fence), has turned the city inside out. It is the de facto center of Memphis as well, with the hub at its core. It transformed what was formerly one of the South's sleepiest cities into "America's Aerotropolis," as the Greater Memphis Chamber of Commerce has dubbed it. It is the Pittsburgh or Detroit of the Instant Age. Truth be told, it is what Detroit wishes it could be next.

Historically, cities exist to exchange goods between each other from their hinterlands—in Memphis's case, that meant Mississippi cotton. FedEx exploded this notion with a hub capable of serving every city in the United States overnight, every night, turning the entire country into one big hinterland. Rivers, railroads, and highways were suddenly obsolete; the airport and FedEx's jets were all any city needed to trade with anyone. Memphis became the crossroads for potentially all of America's goods, not just cotton. Boosters still crow about the city's rail lines and trucking fleets, but they're only a piece of a larger network. FedEx was revolutionary because it *was* the network, limited only by the size and reach of its planes. By those measures, Memphis's hinterland now covers most of earth, while FedEx is seen on Wall Street as the ultimate bellwether of our economy.

"Not every great city will be an aerotropolis, but those cities which are an aerotropolis will be great ones," Fred Smith told me, although Memphis still has a long way to go. "New York is long past being a great port city, but it won't stop being a great financial center. There are lots of factors that can create great cities, but those that happen to be aerial ports will have a significant amount of economic activity they wouldn't otherwise. It's the difference between Memphis and Birmingham."

Once dubbed the "Pittsburgh of the South" during its steelmaking boomtown phase, Birmingham's postindustrial fortunes withered while Memphis's revived after FedEx came to town. The latter has become an inland port for goods arriving from Asia; more than a hundred foreign companies have set up shop around the hub. As FedEx evolved from a boutique airline into Richard Scarry's *Cars and Trucks and Things That Go* sprung to life, its corporate customers doubled down, relocating and expanding enough here to add tens of thousands of jobs over the past two decades.

Nine years after the first FedEx sort, UPS landed in the opposite corner of the trapezoid with its own hub at Louisville. In the intervening years, the government had deregulated American aviation, allowing any airline (passenger and cargo alike) to fly wherever it wanted whenever it wanted, using whatever aircraft it liked. With FedEx already staked to a huge lead in airfreight, UPS—many times bigger on the ground—took its time preparing for battle.

After outsourcing its early efforts, it went on a spending spree, acquiring several hundred planes, including a dozen of its very own 747s. By the 1990s, UPS put the "International" in Louisville International Airport with its nightly sorties to Europe. Even more than Memphis revolves around FedEx, Louisville and its airport depend on UPS. So does Kentucky—UPS is the state's largest private employer, with more than twenty thousand workers.

This might explain why local officials were willing to tear apart the airfield, replacing its cruciform runways from World War II with a long set of parallel ones allowing jumbo jets to land simultaneously. They left 550 prime acres empty between them, earmarked for UPS. Using a mixture of cash and eminent domain, they also condemned more than 1,500 homes, closed 150 businesses, and relocated more than 4,000 residents along the airport's fringes, all because of aircraft noise and construction. Entire neighborhoods vanished, although one was resurrected in an open field on the edge of town—the aerotropolis's first accidental suburb, Heritage Creek.

Repaying the favor, UPS opened its Worldport there in 2002 to duel with FedEx. Two cities rooted in the steamboat era have been refashioned into the most important hubs of our era. Over thirty years, each carrier has lured a galaxy of e-tailers, tech-repair geeks, orthopedic surgeons, and even drug kingpins into a slow rotation around their respective primary hubs. Their CEOs will tell you that they are not there because of Churchill Downs or Beale Street or even for the quality of life and the schools. They moved there to nestle against UPS and FedEx, and if either were to leave, they would follow.

Louisville: Lost in the Sort

The midnight skies over both cities are filled with stars bearing down on you. Wait on the tarmac long enough and they gradually come into focus—727s, 747s, 757s, 767s, 777s, A-300s, and MD-11s, blinking steadily as they approach in parallel, landing every ninety seconds on each airport's twin runways. The biggest difference, to my eye, was that FedEx's fleet approached like a buzzing swarm in the northern sky, all seemingly trying to land at once, while in Louisville the incoming "browntails" landed from the south, veering wide around the airfield one by one. They line up single file, bunched as tightly together as pearls on a necklace, at least from the controllers' point of view.

I found the UPS Worldport the more interesting of the two. The hub at Memphis is larger, but being stuck at number two had spurred UPS to try harder, and its outsize role in Louisville meant the mechanics of the aerotropolis were easier to see. I spotted it in the spooky clearings along the airport fence where homes had been demolished and trees clear-cut to the stumps in anticipation of some future use that UPS planners hadn't imagined yet.

I paid a visit one spring before its expansion, which has added another million square feet to its footprint. There were four million square feet within its giant white box already, roughly half the size of downtown Louisville. It actually consumes more electricity than the entire waterfront at night, even though vast stretches are dimly lit and unoccupied.

Seeing the sort demands pulling an all-nighter. The Worldport handles more than a million packages daily, most of them between 11:00 p.m. and 4:00 a.m. In Memphis, FedEx computers estimate nightly when the sort should be finished, and the approaching zero hour (and minute) blinks red on screens posted throughout the hub. There is no less a sense of urgency in Louisville, even if the countdown isn't so obvious.

By half past midnight, the string of pearls is thinning out and the ground thickening with aircraft taxiing to gates or remote stands for unloading. It may take as long as forty-five minutes before their packages are added to the sort, which is why—in an operation where every minute is weighed and measured—there is a definite hierarchy to the jockeying planes. Those bound to and from the West Coast are given the best spots, as they arrive last and must depart first due to the distances traveled. (Second-day-air packages are typically absent altogether, routed through the hub during the more relaxed daytime sort.) All of this is calculated by the UPS hive mind of intelligent software more adept at sorting planes and packages than any harried human planner.

What emerges from the planes is not a loose stream of boxes but a sequence of aluminum canisters, abbreviated by the ramp workers to "cans." Pie-sliced and semicircular, cans are to air cargo what the container is to shipping and trucking. Depending on the shape, they're roughly the size of a U-Haul truck or van. You'll find scarred and battered ones stamped with airline logos in cargo depots scattered around the world. Their shapes reflect the cylindroid interiors of empty cargo jets—unlike passengers, they can be squeezed against the walls and require no overhead bins. Cans might weigh as much as two tons each, but they are easily moved by staff working solo or in tandem, thanks to miles of inverted casters and ball bearings studded in the Worldport's floors and at gates. The cans need only a solid push to glide across them into the hub or onto the caravans of waiting tugs.

If all goes well, each package inside will be touched only twice by a pair of hands—once exiting its can upon arrival, and then again as it's placed into a second can for departure. The progress of each parcel is guided by the "smart label" affixed to it at pickup. The labels contain a zip code and what was described to me as "a string of characters that is proprietary to UPS." In other words, a tracking number. My guide was delicate in his phrasing because tracking numbers happen to have been invented in Memphis.

They are descended from an older and more fundamental technology, one that undergirds not only overnight delivery and e-commerce but also those stacks of Victoria's Secret catalogs in your recycling pile: the bar code. Having humbly begun life as the Universal Product Codes found in your grocery store since the seventies, the bar code has since matured into the fastest, cheapest, and most ubiquitous method to convert a package from an inert box into a bundle of bits parsable by a computer. It is the electronic foundation of any warehouse that expects to handle a fair bit of volume. I saw scanners in action the next morning down the highway in the cavernous home of Zappos.com, and I kept seeing them until I was halfway around the world in the electronics factories of Shenzhen. But FedEx reinvented them, UPS helped perfect them, and here the latter was pushing the technology to its practical limit.

Workers unloading cans have only two tasks: place each package on the proper belt, and place it label-side up. It's actually harder to fix a mistake in the second case than the first, as the Worldport's computers are able to re-sort a box traveling on the wrong belt by themselves. Flipping the box demands human intervention, however, as the software is helpless until it can see the label. Every package entering the sort passes under a camera and infrared sensor capable of reading characters and correctly estimating dimensions and weight. In the future, even that won't be necessary once radio frequency identification chips are embedded in their sides, broadcasting the vital signs of what's within. For now, these RFID tags still cost more money than they save, and until that flips around, any labels missing a key piece of information—a scrawled digit in the zip code, perhaps—have their pictures flashed to a room full of PCs where human operators are required to fill in the blanks.

At two in the morning, it is typically filled with college-age men and women slumped in silence, iPod earbuds firmly in place, clicking and dragging over and over as they zoom in to see what's the matter. They have thirty seconds to key in whatever is necessary, as the parcels have never stopped moving on the belts. If they blow the deadline, it's rerouted to the "Exceptions Area," where it will literally become someone else's problem.

I could see all of this from a perch on the top floor, after picking my way through the thickets of columns and struts supporting just a few of the seventeen thousand belts coiled inside the hub. Traversing it while the sort is in progress is like roaming through the trestles of an antique wooden roller coaster, except that the intermittent bursts of screams and motion are replaced with a waterfall of white noise.

At the center of the sort is an abyss cleaving a cross section of its many levels straight down to the bottom. From here, you can take in the entire lattice at a glance: a three-story matrix of belt loops and chutes that runs sixteen belts across and is sixteen levels deep. Each belt, in turn, has 364 positions for packages, easily producing more combinatorial multiplicities for a given package than UPS has worldwide outposts. At any moment, a package will pause just long enough for "hockey pucks" of thick black rubber to emerge from one side of the belt and knock it down a long loop on the other. The timing and force of the blow are the product of that first infrared scan—the tracking number determines which sequence of belts and loops it will travel down to the planes, while the dimensional and weight data decide how hard the pucks will strike it.

The physical structure of the sort mirrors the logic embedded in the Worldport's silicon, an endless string of if . . . then decisions that methodically moves parcels to their proper can or sack, processed faster than my or any other brain could manage. None of this would be possible without the billions spent on technology. That pays for not only tracking-and-tracing packages but also the GPS transceivers mounted in every aircraft, package car, and eighteen-wheeler, along with the systems that drive the hubs, the phone-book-size PDAs their drivers carry, and many experiments. UPS is test-driving what the FAA hopes will be the next generation of air traffic control, while its drivers are assigned routes daily by arcane algorithms that minimize their left turns, thus saving twenty-eight million miles a year and roughly three million gallons of fuel across its trucking fleet. Another program, named VOLCANO (short for volume, location, and aircraft network optimizer), simultaneously solves for the best flight plans six months out, the best mix of aircraft and equipment ten years out, and how to tackle the perennial Christmas rush the next time around.

The majority of this software resides within the Worldport itself, making twice as many calculations in an hour as the New York Stock Exchange does in a heavy day of trading. UPS is justifiably proud of the machine intelligence now embedded in every belt, puck, and package, which corresponds with its desire to strip as much human intelligence as possible out of the hub, in the name of efficiency. The company's term for it is "de-skilling," a tradition that dates back to Henry Ford's first assembly lines for the Model T. The difference now is that there is a greater fortune to be made in moving goods than in making them.

It also means that while UPS employs ten thousand people nightly in the sort, most are part-time. FedEx, with fifteen thousand in Memphis and thousands more scattered across its domestic hubs, pays the same, and not even the offers of generous benefits and free tuition hide the fact that what they are looking for is a pool of loyal but unskilled labor.

UPS has so thoroughly de-skilled the Worldport that even desert nomads could work there now, and they do. Several hundred members of Somalia's Bantu tribe have resettled in Louisville in recent years, working mostly in and around the hub. They're part of a larger influx of immigrants recruited to meet the needs of the companies drawn here. The Bantu's lack of English (or any form of written language) hasn't deterred UPS from hiring them.

The Bantu are busy loading cans back onto planes when I emerge from the hub a little before 3:00 a.m. It's late, and flight dispatchers are already clearing the decks, ordering MD-11s and other West Coast–bound heavies to take off in tandem to the north. Climbing sharply, they soon vanish and take their place among the stars.

The Cities That Shipping and Handling Built

Two miles south of the runways is another cluster of windowless white buildings containing more floor space than the Worldport's vast expanse. This is the forward position of UPS Supply Chain Solutions, the arm that burrows inside and straightens out kinks in its customers' operations. This immaculately groomed campus, hidden behind barbed wire and blank façades, is the closest anyone can come to setting up shop inside the hub itself, and UPS charges accordingly for it. How much, it won't say. It doesn't say much at all about the campus, actually, either to outsiders or its own clients, because their archrival is likely camped a building or two away. But everyone's here for the proximity and instant access to the hub at virtually any hour of the day.

By now it's an open secret that if your Toshiba laptop needs repairs, UPS technicians are the ones standing by to fix it. The same goes for your missing MasterCard—its replacement will be printed here and rushed overnight into the sort. If the Worldport is the vortex of the Louisville aerotropolis, then the SCS complex is the most clearly marked piece of the first ring surrounding it. The value proposition for the seventy or so UPS customers who have relocated here has little to do with the facilities (the same are available elsewhere) and even less to do with its location vis-à-vis Louisville proper. Being next to the hub is a safety blanket for CEOs; what it's worth to them to be here is clearly delineated by the figures next to their signatures on the contracts.

The ones who aren't willing to pay to sit on top of the hub can elect a second, less expensive warehouse half an hour down the interstate in Elizabethtown, Kentucky. Bentley and Rolls-Royce both stock engines there, although Bentley's are for coupes and Rolls's are for jet engines. I didn't make it that far, turning off I-65 a few exits early in Shepherdsville to find the mammoth warehouse of Zappos.com. With eight million customers, Zappos is the Amazon.com of shoes, competing with Amazon itself for the unofficial title of the logo most frequently seen bobbing in the sort. Theirs is an intramural rivalry—Amazon bought Zappos in July 2009 for $850 million, its largest purchase ever. Curious to see what it could learn from its younger, more nimble counterpart, Amazon has kept the company separate thus far.

Zappos has also been described as the "long tail" of footwear, borrowing a term typically applied to purely digital retailers like eBay or Apple's iTunes Store, which offers a potentially infinite selection of music and sells more obscurities than hits. When Zappos opened in 1999, it relied on the long tail to find its customers—women wearing a size thirteen, for instance—who were frustrated by the selection at shoe stores. Zappos made its mark early by always being in stock. I once called Converse about a pair of Jack Purcells. "We're out," the operator said, "but you might want to try Zappos."

Since then, Zappos has rebranded itself around customer service, which it has elevated to an almost saintly ideal. It famously pays new employees to quit—as much as $2,000—if they are insufficiently committed to the cause. The ones who stick it out receive free, comprehensive health insurance and full indoctrination into a cult. The first item on Zappos' list of core values is "Deliver 'wow' through service," and the last is "Be humble." In between is "Build open and honest relationships with communication." Tony Hsieh, its CEO, has taken this to heart, Facebooking and Twittering constantly to a half-million followers. After the acquisition was announced, he displayed seller's remorse on Zappos' blog.

This philosophy has made Hsieh a guru of the middle-management set, and Zappos one of America's most enlightened companies. But its gold standard of customer service is based on something more prosaic: free overnight shipping and returns. This was overkill by any standard. Amazon, for instance, is often faster than its shipping guidelines suggest but is loath to offer any guarantees. "We don't compete with online retailers," Craig Adkins informed me when I arrived in Shepherdsville. Adkins is Zappos' director of fulfillment operations. "We compete with shoe stores. The only way to do that, to match their experience, is to get them the item as quickly as possible. So if somebody places an order at eight o'clock at night, and it's on their doorstep at nine the next morning, that's as close to going to the store and getting it immediately that you can possibly get."

Which is why it offers free, unlimited returns. Zappos wants you to treat your living room as the store, trying on as many pairs in as many colors and sizes as you like, guilt-free, before sending back what you don't keep. Customers love it. In the first half of 2009—dark days for retailing—buyers of fashion footwear spent almost 20 percent more online than they had the previous year, while sales at brick-and-mortar stores fell 11 percent. "In the long term," Tony Hsieh told me, "we want our brand to be about the best service. And we deliver the best brand experience with overnight delivery and free returns. We just happened to start with shoes the same way Amazon just happened to start with books."

In the short term it's worked, albeit too well. Zappos' best customers also have the most returns. In 2008, Zappos surpassed $1 billion in gross sales for the first time, a year ahead of schedule. But because of the lenient return policy, revenues were only $635 million. And once operating and shipping costs were taken into account—including UPS bills of more than $100 million a year—net profits were a measly $10.8 million. This might be why Zappos' investors were motivated to sell, and is almost certainly why the company has quietly dropped its free overnight guarantee for all except "VIP" customers, who have been granted free shipping for life. Despite what the name implies, anyone can become a VIP simply by asking, but the enrollment window opens and closes on Hsieh's whims. (Although it did stay open for four days—from Black Friday to Cyber Monday—to kick off the holiday shopping season in 2009.)

Zappos moved to Louisville in 2002, graduating from UPS Supply Chain Solutions to a series of ever-larger warehouses. The current one has a footprint of 835,000 square feet, one of the biggest in the state. Once it's full, Adkins said on our tour, "we'll build another building."

Amazon's tail may be longer than Zappos', but Zappos is pure tail. Amazon has fulfillment centers in fifteen American cities, including one in Louisville and five in Kentucky. Zappos has one, with four million items on hand and an average of only four of everything in stock. Its owner regards its warehouse as a Petri dish and intends to stock some of its bestselling goods there.

What happens inside depends on your purchase. Say you're browsing Zappos' clearance sale and come across an irresistibly priced pair of Ugg boots. In one corner of its warehouse are racks stacked several stories tall, filled with the more obscure items and slow sellers. Human "pickers" guided by computer-generated lists troop up and down stairs, manually picking half-forgotten pairs from the shelves.

Or say you're me, placing an order for Jack Purcells—a perennial bestseller. Items "with a higher sales velocity," in Adkins's terminology, are kept in what's known as a carousel picker. Its cages circle and spin like rotating dry cleaner's racks, with shoe boxes stacked in one of a half-dozen compartments. Zappos' computers dictate which pair is next and send the appropriate one spinning the human picker's way. An LCD mounted on the carousel lists the rack and compartment number where the pair can be found, reducing the task to hunting and pecking while speeding it up considerably. When the pickers find the pair in question—whether Converse or Crocs or Doc Martens—they scan a bar code on its label for the computer's confirmation. Once the system is convinced, the box is set on a conveyor belt and ferried downstairs for shipping.

Or maybe you haven't come to the site for shoes at all, but for sunglasses, jeans, handbags, or pajamas. Just as Amazon outgrew the book business, Zappos has begun branching out of shoes. Apparel is the largest niche in e-tailing—bigger than electronics, bigger than books—surging from zero to $23 billion in sales in barely a decade. The company plans to double its apparel sales this year and predicts clothing will surpass shoes to become its largest category within the next five.

If you happen to be in the market for a Michael Kors dress, your order vanishes behind a wall running the height and width of the warehouse, carried by a robot. There are seventy in all—orange cubes three feet tall, resembling oversize Roombas—zooming between the shelves, which they slide under and haul to pickers on their heads. Seen from above, the warehouse itself appears to be moving, as racks shudder and glide to the front, seemingly of their own volition. The organizational principle of the warehouse has been inverted—pickers no longer search into the stacks; the stacks now come to them.

The robots are supplied by Kiva Systems, a company started by a band of MIT engineers whose other customers include Staples and the Gap, which employ them by the hundreds. At Zappos, the robots touch only inventory that doesn't fit in a shoe rack, or about a half-million items. As its offerings expand, so will its fleet, which is twice as efficient, requires half as much energy, and has resulted in a 40 percent reduction in human labor.

Regardless of who picks your order, all conveyors lead to the same place. Unlike the Worldport, the belts here stand naked in the open air, rising on steel struts to the upper reaches of the warehouse. Craig Adkins and I climbed down a gantry from the carousel picker, watching a few boxes lazily wend their way down. They would be packed and in the back of a truck in less than an hour, bound for tonight's sort. "We're always trying to process orders in real time," he said.

Before the boxes enter the packing and shipping area, they pass under a bar code scanner mounted above the belt. Every item entering the warehouse passes under an identical one on a second belt. Each of the three scans (including one when it's picked) has a purpose. In chronological order, they are to tell the Zappos database what it is and where it is in the warehouse, to confirm it's been picked for an order, and to double-check which order it's been assigned to. No one could find my Jack Purcells without them, because no one else knows how.

There is no Dewey decimal system. Arriving inventory is simply dropped in the next available space (increasingly by robot) and stocked randomly on the shelves. Its location is noted by Zappos' omniscient inventory system, named Genghis, and forgotten by everyone else. Random pick, as it's called, has been used off and on for twenty years. It was already installed at Zappos when Adkins arrived from a competing retailer still struggling to pinpoint the most logical approach. How did Tony Hsieh figure it out? By imagining his warehouse as Genghis would—as if it were a giant computer. Hard drives store bits of information randomly, wherever there happen to be free electrons. The machine keeps track of each bit's location, retrieving it only when necessary. Genghis simply does the same with shoes. The robots nominally under its command follow their own rules, subtly rearranging the shelves to make their own lives easier. The best sellers end up in front, around the edges, while the worst are gradually buried in the stacks.

These innovations, not one-click, are the real miracles of e-commerce. Fulfillment software is harder to install than any virtual storefront like Apple's. Zappos' competitive edge isn't its website, but the twelve minutes it takes for one of Kiva's robots to pick, pack, and have your order waiting on the shipping dock.

Malcolm Gladwell made a similar point during the original dot-com madness by dropping in on the warehouse of Lands' End. The catalog merchant was then the world's largest e-tailer. Gladwell found that the Internet revolution, as far as it had progressed, hadn't transformed its business. But it was one of three fundamental shifts. "The first was the introduction of an 800 number, in 1978," he wrote. "The second was express delivery, in 1994; and the third was the introduction of a Web site, in 1995. The first two innovations cut the average transaction time—the time between the moment of ordering and the moment the goods are received—from three weeks to four days. The third innovation has cut the transaction time from four days to, well, four days."

"E-commerce *is* express mail," Gladwell concluded. The real revolution had taken place twenty years before, with the widespread adoption of bar codes. Lands' End could retire hunt-and-peck picking methods and switch to more efficient methods, quadrupling productivity from 175 items picked per hour to 600 or 700. Zappos' carousel picker tripled their pace; Kiva's robots doubled it again. Kasarda believes the next doubling will come when RFID chips replace bar codes, and then again when "intelligent agents" embedded in those chips guide packages, robots, and belts to their final destinations, with no humans necessary.

The Internet arm of Zappos could physically be located anywhere, and Tony Hsieh knows it. He moved his headquarters from San Francisco to Las Vegas several years ago in pursuit of cheaper labor. But he wouldn't dream of touching the warehouse, because "we're within a fifteen-minute drive from the hub. If we were an hour away, I would be concerned about traffic. I wouldn't necessarily want a warehouse inside of UPS, either, but we need to stay close." Close means filling orders after midnight and delivering them by 9:00 a.m. Zappos has longer hours and a better selection than any shoe store between Louisville and the Atlantic coast. And that's why it's growing 20 percent a year.

"We shipped ground until we reached a scale where we could afford it [next-day delivery], but the goal was always next-day," Hsieh explained. "Back in 1999, I read an article about South Korea, where at the time, thirty percent of retail was already online." The Internet was ubiquitous there even then. American retailers saw this and decided they needed better websites. Hsieh saw something else. "Everyone lived in one of four major cities, so overnight distribution was fairly simple. I thought that was the model for the future here as well." It was and it wasn't. Memphis and Louisville stand the Korean model on its head, consolidating goods in blimp hangars instead of customers in sixty-story apartment blocks.

The management guru Peter Drucker surveyed the dot-com landscape around the time Hsieh experienced his epiphany. Drucker was unimpressed by the New Economy's supposed revolutions, save one. "E-commerce is to the Information Revolution what the railroad was to the Industrial Revolution—a totally new, totally unprecedented, totally unexpected development," he wrote in *The Atlantic*.

In the new mental geography created by the railroad, humanity mastered distance. In the mental geography of e-commerce, distance has been eliminated. There is only one economy and only one market. One consequence of this is that every business must become globally competitive, even if it manufactures or sells only within a local or regional market. The competition is not local anymore—in fact, it knows no boundaries. Every company has to become transnational in the way it is run. Yet the traditional multinational may well become obsolete. It manufactures and distributes in a number of distinct geographies, in which it is a *local* company. But in e-commerce there are neither local companies nor distinct geographies. Where to manufacture, where to sell, and how to sell will remain important business decisions. But in another twenty years they may no longer determine what a company does, how it does it, and where it does it.

In other words, they will all look like Amazon. Recently, it's become trendy to think of the world's biggest bookseller as a technology or even a media company. There's Kindle, digital music competing with Apple's, and an entirely separate business leasing spare storage and computing cycles on its servers. But retailing remains the core of its $25 billion business, a fact underscored by the Zappos deal. Which is why the shoe seller's eight million customers have been cherry-picked for Amazon's own loyalty program, Amazon Prime.

Introduced in 2005 to universal skepticism, Prime subscribers pay $79 a year for free second-day shipping on most items, or overnight shipping for just $3.99. Much like Zappos' VIPs, Prime members tend to shed their remaining inhibitions once they sign on. *Slate*'s Farhad Manjoo is one: "These days, whenever I become cognizant of some need that would ordinarily require an unplanned trip to the store—when I want a bathroom hook, a shelving system for my closet, a new wireless router, or a discount pack of kitchen sponges—I check Amazon first. It's usually faster to order the item there and get it shipped for free than to add the thing to my shopping list. With Prime, you don't really need a shopping list."

Amazon won't disclose how many members Prime has, or how much all of this free shipping is costing it. In 2009, the Piper Jaffray analyst

Gene Munster pegged their numbers at two million out of ninety-one million customers, growing at a 24 percent clip. Their purchases tended to double in value their first year in the program, rising from an average of $400 to $900, while renewal rates hovered around 90 percent. The experience hadn't changed, and the prices were still the same, but free shipping triggered a Pavlovian response. Munster estimated that simply converting a quarter of its customers to Prime members would add $9 billion in revenue—growth of nearly 50 percent. The key to Amazon's continued success may not be adding more customers but convincing its current ones to buy more items, and more expensive ones at that. (The average Zappos order is six times greater than Amazon's.) And the best lever for doing so would appear to be free shipping. What's driving the growth of Amazon Prime, founder and CEO Jeff Bezos has told analysts, is the company's third-party fulfillment service, which offers the same shipping options to its online partners and their customers. Or as one of his investors put it, "Amazon's logistics is its secret sauce."

Prime's higher sales velocity represents a significant shift in how Amazon does business. What drew Bezos to books was the long tail. Selection was his original selling proposition, not selection *and* speed, as with Zappos. Amazon was the poster child of a Net Age company—Bezos was *Time*'s Man of the Year in 1999—but with Prime, it has evolved into a retailer tailor-made for the Instant Age. Like Zappos, its velocity of shipping blurs the line between online and offline, erasing the last advantage of retail stores—that you can walk out with the merchandise.

Speed has put the squeeze on retailers. E-commerce didn't exist in 1995, but the first wave of e-tailers collectively racked up $7 billion in sales four years later. It was $155 billion in 2009, and it may top $250 billion a few years from now. An entire galaxy of one-click shopping has been summoned into existence, with Amazon poised to become the next-generation Walmart in the eyes of Wall Street. A recent study by four economists at the University of Chicago found that Amazon and e-commerce have crushed small and midsize booksellers (along with travel agents and auto dealerships) as prices fell and bigger, more efficient retailers got even bigger.

Two billion boxes land on our doorsteps each year, three-fourths of which have been sent either overnight or second-day air. E-commerce (and why call it that? Isn't it just "commerce" by now?) at present accounts for 7 percent of all retail spending. Half of all Americans are online shoppers, spending an average of $1,006 per year. Jeff Bezos's original prediction that it would eventually account for 15 percent of a multitrillion-dollar industry is well within reach.

What the Internet added to the retail equation wasn't long tails and thoughtful comparison shopping, but the acceleration of impulse. Our increasing comfort with our digital selves—composed of Google searches, Facebook friends, YouTube clips, and tweets—awoke a belief in us that physical atoms should always move at the same light speed as our digital bits. The real breakthrough was our collective acclimation to this new degree of speed. Having settled into the fast lane, slowing down for even a second is viscerally painful, no matter what our speedometer actually says. As counterintuitive as it sounds, the best thing that ever happened to overnight mail was being made halfway obsolescent by e-mail. Our desperate struggle to accelerate everything else to the same velocity has only made us more dependent on its fastest physical analogue. And so our impulse purchases are increasingly accompanied by the equally impulsive selection of next-day air for just a few dollars more. And if our impulse was wrong we return the item on the seller's dime.

The aerotropoli around Memphis and Louisville were created by those dollars. These are the cities "shipping and handling" built. In the business, those dollars are referred to as "value added," an accounting term describing the money to be made from touching goods and improving them at the right time in the right place. Memphis and Louisville are where, in the United States at least, goods are tenderly massaged. These are cities made of hubs, one for each industry, or maybe more.

Just up the road from Zappos is "Geek Squad City," population six hundred. It's a Kentucky-fried slice of Silicon Valley, filled with locally trained techies in short sleeves and skinny ties cracking open and snapping back together broken laptops on behalf of Best Buy customers. What started as an elite unit in Minneapolis more than a decade ago has since blossomed into a twelve-thousand-strong Geek Corps that moved its overnight repair operation here a few years ago for many of the same reasons Zappos did. It's the hub of computer repairs.

"All we knew is that we had to be at the end of the runway, because it gives you seven extra hours in the day," said Wes Snyder, the "mayor" of Geek Squad City. "That's all it is. Take our Chicago service center, which receives shipments at eleven a.m. and has a final drop-off at seven p.m. Here it's five a.m. and ten p.m., so I have that many more hours to fix something." That extra time is invaluable when you oversee a few hundred geeks scrambling to repair a few thousand computers a day. All of the dot-com-era perks inside—Ping-Pong tables, video games, and couches for power napping—are a means to an end: ruthless efficiency.

Everyone's eyes watch the clock, although not always because they need more time here on the ground. Some are anxious their cargo doesn't spoil. Across town from the Worldport, nestled amid a few hundred acres of white boxes hugging the Ohio River, is a warehouse for the biotechnology firm Genentech. This is the hub of cancer drugs. The company keeps thousands of doses of its cutting-edge, time- and temperature-sensitive treatments for lung, pancreatic, colon, rectal, and breast cancer here, storing them in a refrigerated warehouse the size of a lecture hall and packing them with frozen bricks cooled to $-9°$. While most companies worry about supply chains, Genentech is obsessed with what's been dubbed the "cool chain," the seamless network of freezers guaranteeing the safety and efficacy of a breast cancer drug bound that night for someone's mother in South Dakota.

It reminded me of the National Eyebank Center, which is tucked next to a dentist's office in Memphis. It's the hub of eyeballs—a way station for thirty-five hundred human corneas in transit each year from deceased donors to blinded recipients. The logic is the same as always: it's faster and easier to set up the lab here and fly the eyeballs in and out. I held one between my thumb and forefinger—floating in a vial, of course—and thought it most closely resembled a Life Saver, which in some sense, it is.

What eyeballs and cancer drugs have in common with laptops and assembly lines is that they are all just-in-time. The aerotropolis is a machine designed to process the perishable in any form, and in the need-it-right-this-second economy, that might be this year's model iPhone a month before its planned obsolescence, or a tailored wonder drug unraveling one molecule at a time. Anyone selling anything with a sell-by date can save time and money by moving here, because the reigning presumption in the hubs is that they are one and the same.

Corridors of white boxes line all the highways of America, but what sets these hubs apart is the possibility that behind the loading bay doors is Willie Wonka's factory full of surreal and precious merchandise—like a lifetime supply of morphine and OxyContin.

That particular stockpile hides in plain sight somewhere in Memphis (I wasn't allowed to remember where) in an unmarked building guarded by off-duty police. In back, locked in steel cages, are enough pills, drips, and miscellaneous narcotics to put all the cartels out of business; this is the largest legal cache in the world. It's all owned by excelleRx, a specialist in hospice care. Nurses tending to dying patients call in sixty-five thousand prescriptions daily for these industrial-strength painkillers, and while a missed flight is not necessarily a matter of life and death, it might mean someone spending his last hours in teeth-grinding agony. The temptation posed by the pills is so great that robots are on hand to fill bottles, count their contents, and then count them again before they're sealed in FedEx envelopes.

The FedEx executive who found this base for them, Jo Ferreira, was as visibly proud as any ace real estate agent as she tagged along with me on a quick tour. She's the managing director of hub-area business development, meaning that at any given moment she's juggling the requests of as many as forty or fifty companies jockeying for space around Memphis and regional hubs in Indianapolis, Oakland, Fort Worth, and Greensboro. "Proximity matters more and more to them," she said, "but the biggest driver for this happening now is the growing urge that when we want something, we want it now. And as soon as one company relocates here or to any of our hubs, the next thing that happens is that three or four of its competitors come calling."

She was one of my first clues as to why Memphis and Louisville qualify as true aerotropoli, and New York and Chicago do not: the aerotropolis isn't born, it's made. It doesn't occur naturally or simply emerge from the urban cores it's supplanting. When that happens, you're either stuck with messes like LAX or happy accidents like the Dulles Toll Road. What sets these hub cities apart is the belated realization that their airports are their edge against competing cities, states, and regions. The largest pair of overnight carriers made this possible, if not obvious at first.

Memphis, for example, didn't know it was "America's Aerotropolis" until John Kasarda told it as much in 2006. He was no stranger to the city after an earlier stint advising FedEx's Fred Smith on where to put new hubs overseas and how to better run them. A decade later, the regional Chamber of Commerce welcomed his suggestions for revamping the entire city along similar lines. An Aerotropolis Steering Committee was drafted within months to implement them, chaired by a FedEx executive. Fast-forward to last year, when the city's congressional representative Steve Cohen drafted legislation calling for a Council on Aerotropolis Development within the U.S. Department of Transportation. Besides awarding federal grants to the most promising examples, the council would be in charge of disseminating Kasarda's principles nationwide.

In the meantime, the responsibility for remaking Memphis into a full-fledged aerotropolis has fallen to the public servants and private consultants charged with the care and feeding of companies thinking of moving there. Jo Ferreira is one, but she is hardly alone. Urban planners, corporate headhunters, chambers of commerce, mayors, governors, and even congressmen such as Representative Cohen provide the public sector support system (and tax dollars) that is pointedly never mentioned in any of the *Forbes* or *Fortune* profiles.

It's incorrect to describe these men and women as the "architects" of the aerotropolis or as planners in any conventional sense, because their particular craft has little to do with any traditional notions of centralized planning. Besides, they're too hamstrung by zoning laws and the intransigence of developers to do anything other than park their clients where they want to be—next to the nearest on-ramp. This approach has its obvious flaws, the worst of which is the hideous, unsustainable sprawl barely held in check by the hub's gravity well.

All the same, Louisville and Memphis both languished until they deliberately embraced the overnight carriers calling each one home. It's striking how their past, present, and future so closely mirror each other, just as FedEx and UPS are reflections of their futile attempts to outflank each other.

Whereas Memphis had once been the seat of King Cotton, Louisville was a tobacco depot on the south bank of the Ohio, sitting above the rapids that forced steamboat captains to lug their shipments ashore and past them. Warehouses, wholesalers, and freight haulers sprang up to take advantage, supplemented by shipyards and foundries after the steamboat's arrival in the 1830s.

Like Memphis, Louisville stuck to its agrarian roots right through the Great Depression, but even before their respective cash crops bottomed out, both cities remade themselves into blue-collar burgs. Memphis made tires for Firestone and cotton pickers (what else?) for International Harvester. Louisville built appliances for GE, cars for Ford, and bottled bourbon for Brown-Forman. Almost all of those jobs left in the 1970s and 1980s. Even the cities' tales of woe are similar.

In Louisville: "Bourbon, tobacco, aluminum, agriculture, manufacturing, hardware, and tools—all the things that built this economy, today are really irrelevant. UPS will have as great an impact on Louisville this century as the railroads did last century and the river before that."

In Memphis: "When Firestone and International Harvester left, taking with them good blue-collar, union jobs, there was a question in the air: 'Well, now what are we going to be?'"

The one asking that question is Dexter Muller, whose office at the Greater Memphis Chamber of Commerce is only a few doors down from the Cotton Exchange on Front Street. The view from his window is a snapshot of the city's transportation history: Cotton Row below, the muddy Mississippi beyond, and, in the distance, the long span of the Hernando de Soto Bridge bearing six lanes of truck traffic to and from points west.

His unrepentant drawl and modest pompadour mark him as a native who grew up in the Age of Elvis. He is a third-generation Memphian; his grandfather was a cotton trader, and mother a local belle, while his father moved here from New York in 1937 to build a paper plant for Kimberly-Clark, only to see it promptly swept away in a flood.

Dexter has been on the economic development beat for more than thirty years, so he remembers the day in 1979 when the city essentially decided to go back to the land. Not all the way back to cotton or timber (another discarded mainstay) but to the river and the railroads that had sprung up to support them, to the trucking lines that called the tangle of interstates around Memphis home, and suddenly to the airport, where FedEx was finally beginning to gain some altitude.

"There was a huge swing back to the city's roots, which were geography and logistics," he said. "About that time, you had Indianapolis, Louisville, Atlanta, and Memphis, in that middle swath all seeing this big opportunity taking place, and we were the first to say 'We want it.'

"At the time, it wasn't that popular. 'Distribution,' as it was referred to, had lower-paying jobs, less investment, and not as much personal property, so it didn't build your tax base. And so cities like Nashville and others said, 'Well, if you guys want that, it's fine. We don't care.'"

Why should they? Although clean and quiet—more so, at least, than steel mills and oil refineries—warehouses were still sprawling, empty, unpopulated, inert real estate. Clustered together, they swallowed landscapes, defeated density, and were a poor substitute in both absolute numbers and wages for the union jobs they replaced.

"Our strategy was, you bring that in, and then you build the next piece, which is their headquarters," Muller continued. "Pfizer is a good example. They started with distribution and said, 'This is a good place for us to operate—low cost, good location, we can hire good people'— and so they brought backroom operations for finance here, and there it is. You just keep building off the distribution into other industries and other segments of these companies." And it's worked . . . to a point.

While driving through the rusting industrial parks clinging like barnacles to the airport's west side, Muller explained how warehousing had evolved into distribution as companies eager to cut costs replaced dozens of warehouses with a handful of distribution centers serving entire regions instead of cities or states. The phrase carried connotations of movement and turnover as speed and reach replaced pure geography as the critical factor, and with FedEx promising to move anything anywhere overnight, it wasn't long before its customers consolidated again into a single, gargantuan distribution center capable of holding everything and moving it anyplace, one preferably next door to the hub.

The shape of the Memphis aerotropolis tells this story in much the same way a redwood encodes a lifetime of rains and droughts into its rings. It's the urban embodiment of an evolution from warehousing to distribution to logistics that took less than twenty years and saw it rise from a necessary evil to the front lines in an eternal war on costs and the competition. You can trace the shift in this thinking through title inflation, a local consultant explained. "When I started in the mid-eighties it was the 'warehouse manager,'" he said. "Then it was the 'assistant manager of logistics.' Today, it's the 'SVP for global supply chain,' and he might sit on the board of directors." He or she likely sits on the boards of companies that decided they were better at logistics than anything else, such as Walmart, which achieves "everyday low prices" with a pythonlike squeeze on its suppliers. Everyone else, it seems, moved to Memphis or Louisville to let FedEx and UPS handle it for them.

But the flowering of the distribution center carried unforeseen consequences for both cities. In Memphis especially, large swaths of land around the hub that had been paved over just a few years before were rendered obsolete by the end of the 1980s. And with land being cheap to the south and east, newcomers and incumbents alike preferred to set up shop on the periphery rather than get entangled in the mess. They exchanged physical proximity for fast access via highway and byway, as Zappos and the Geek Squad have done in Louisville. The shapes of both aerotropoli sprawl along the splines of I-65 in Kentucky and I-55, I-40, U.S. 72, and U.S. 78 through Tennessee and Mississippi. They have lapsed into what Robert Lang of the Brookings Institution has dubbed "edgeless cities"—fuzzy patches of urbanity dispersed across hundreds of square miles and barely knit together by roads. The phrase is a play off Joel Garreau's notion of edge cities, and he has no confidence in the civilizing properties of warehouse space, either. "Industrial and warehouse workers rarely demand specialty retail, high-end services, cloth-napkin restaurants, hotels, and bookstores," he wrote.

The ascendency of distribution has sparked a philosophical debate in Memphis: Is the city content to be a hub where goods are moved and sorted instead of created or invented? Kasarda and his allies say yes; local members of the "creative class" say no. Their champion is Richard Florida, author of *The Rise of the Creative Class*, whose prescription for economic growth boils down to the "three Ts" of technology, talent, and tolerance. If Memphis can attract the designers, musicians, and biomedical researchers who crave Whole Foods and gentrified juke joints, he argues, then companies desirous of their talents will soon follow. The city's future lies in brains, not boxes.

Cargo doesn't need quality of life. It doesn't need density, or neighborhoods, or even surface streets. All it needs is a highway with a straight shot and no gridlock. This has made the Memphis aerotropolis sprawl from day one, from the ghost parks on the west side to Billy Dunavant's turf on the east, to the rolling fields south of the airport, where it has jumped the fence and keeps plowing deeper into Mississippi, unconstrained by anything except on-ramps to I-55. Its core atrophies while vitality flows to the outermost rings, applying still more pressure to keep moving.

There is a price for this, and one community that has paid it is Elvis Presley's own, Whitehaven. Hanging on to the western edge of the airport, the former pastureland surrounding Graceland has devolved due to white flight and sprawl from an affluent neighborhood to a fraying, predominantly African-American one ("Blackhaven") within two generations. The local foreclosure rate is twice the national average; residents have seen two decades of wage gains disappear with their homes. The previous tenants fled first to the city's eastern suburbs and later across the border. The city followed, incorporating bits and pieces of the outlying county to preserve both its integrity and its tax base, but has hit a political wall at the state line of DeSoto County, Mississippi. (Louisville took this strategy a step further, and better, by merging with its county outright in 2003.)

I drove south on I-55 to see for myself the fresh subdivisions bursting from former cotton fields, next door to the hulking distribution centers slapped together in less than six months. DeSoto is one of the fastest-growing counties in the nation, having more than doubled in population since 1990, to the point where it is nearly a quarter the size of Memphis itself. More than half of its residents commute to the city but choose to live here, in part because Mississippi has no personal income tax.

The rest work, I imagine, in the bright and shiny barns lining the access roads, painted with names like Hillwood, Future Electronics, Emerson Motors, and ConAir. The county seat of Hernando is still an equal mix of Faulkner and Mayberry, but only a few miles away is the DeSoto Trade Center, the only foreign free-trade zone in the region, ten miles south of the hub.

Driving back to Memphis, it was as if a film had started running backward—the distribution centers shrank, corroded, and lapsed into being warehouses again, while the signs touting lots "starting in the 100s!" disappeared, replaced by actual homes that lost second stories, then yards, and finally much of their value—as I drove progressively north. At the border, skin tones flipped from light to dark again with no transition.

I pulled off the interstate at the intersection of Brooks Road and Elvis Presley Boulevard to find what should be the center and was instead the ground zero of the Memphis aerotropolis: an empty industrial park, a vacant lot, and a homeless man standing on the median, holding a sign that read "Please Help. Homeless Vet." "He's our welcome wagon," sighed Jack Soden, president of Elvis Presley Enterprises, whose office is down the street. "It's an unwritten rule that he stand there, because if he leaves, someone else takes his place."

Later, I ran the film forward again, this time riding shotgun with Brian Pecon, a FedEx executive of the old school who moved on to run economic development efforts around Memphis for more than a decade. Now retired, he had once been in charge of aircraft maintenance, a life-or-death practice that had instilled a gruff tell-it-like-it-is concision I found refreshing after so much cheerleading.

Touring the warehouse district just south of the airport, we passed a gray box with the Technicolor sign out front—"They move millions of DVDs out that door each year," he explained, and in fact, nearly half the discs sold in America, some 1.2 million daily, are shipped from there— and hung a right at Memphis Oaks, a massive tan building with an empty parking lot and a tiny white "Now Leasing" banner waving in front. A sign at the intersection advertised "200 acres: 3,700,000 sq. ft." for development. He shook his head and said, "Now I've got a question for you: What do you do with all of this"—"this" being the sprawl—"now that you have it?" And the unspoken question: How do you prevent this from happening over and over again?

You can't, not when three states, two counties, and a city keep ante-ing up with lower taxes and more land, with no plan for managing the sprawl, or even an entity capable of drafting one—the Aerotropolis Steering Committee lacks special powers. Instead, its members have banded together to clean up the worst excesses along the airport's approaches, starting with the most scarred artery of them all, Brooks Road.

When the employees of the medical device maker Smith & Nephew look up from molding ceramic hip replacements and glance out the windows, their view of Brooks Road is of barbed wire, strip clubs, streetwalkers, and their johns. One executive shared a few surveillance snapshots of a recent transaction: "It wasn't hard; I only had to wait ten minutes," he deadpanned. Down the block was Black Tail, a club made locally infamous by its entrance, a two-story plywood depiction of a woman's thighs.

Brooks Road undercuts Kasarda's axiom that "the airport area is the calling card and the handshake. It's the first thing people see when they enter a region and it's the last thing they see when they leave." The city's answer is to spend millions planting trees.

Six hundred thousand tourists a year drive along this stretch from the rental car lot to Graceland. Soden, whose company owns the King's estate and controls his posthumous cash flow, has spent $40 million acquiring small parcels around the mansion, slowly accumulating about a hundred acres of strip malls and housing just begging to be condemned. His dream is to convert the typical three-hour tour into a three-day all-inclusive vacation at a Graceland resort complex that so far exists only in the minds of the former Disney Imagineers consulting on the project. "On a worldwide basis, Elvis may be better recognized than Disney except in the far corners, but not by much," he told me. But unlike Walt's disappointment with the urban decomposition around Disneyland, Presley didn't live to see his neighborhood go to seed. "It's eight-tenths of a mile of pure ugliness," Soden said.

Heritage Creek: Life in the Shadow of the Hub

Unlike Los Angeles, Memphis has suffered the noise from its airport in silence. There have never been any serious complaints—let alone lawsuits—despite thirty-five years of round-the-clock takeoffs and landings. While I was driving along the airfield's edge one night with Brian Pecon, the familiar scream of a 727 split the air. Pecon, who was present at the carrier's creation, confessed, "If there had been any kind of revolt about noise at two thirty, three, three thirty in the morning, we would have gone back to Little Rock." There wasn't. For thirty years, it's been a company town. "I think people in Memphis understand because we employ so many people here," Fred Smith tersely explained.

UPS wanted more in Louisville. On Good Friday in 1987, one of its executives called the office of Jerry Abramson, Louisville's mayor. "They said, 'We're leaving.' They never told me where they were going; they wouldn't tell me *why* they were going. But they were going," he recalled. "They said, 'Don't say anything, we'll announce it in a week,' and hung up. I closed the door to my office and cried.

"They swore it was nothing we had done," he added, but it likely had everything to do with what Louisville hadn't done with its airport, which was built during World War II with crisscrossing runways too short for 747s. "Three days later," Abramson continues, "I got a call from Jack Rogers," then the CEO of UPS. "He said, 'Mayor, I've changed my mind. We're staying.' What happened, I have no idea. To this day, no one will tell me." What if UPS had made good on the threat? "We would have had twenty-one thousand less UPS jobs, and probably another twenty thousand less jobs that are here as a result of UPS," he replied. This is what Kasarda means when he says that cities exist to create jobs.

Barely a year later, on June 22, 1988, the city and state announced a $700 million plan to essentially build a new airport atop the existing one, with long parallel runways, a sweet spot in between for the hub, and room to grow on either side. The next day, local officials announced what they dubbed the Louisville Airport Improvement Program: the condemnation, under "urban renewal" statutes, of the homes of 3,760 families in a half-dozen communities. Looking at a before-and-after mural hanging in the offices of the airport authority, one can see that entire neighborhoods have been wiped off the map. No one left empty-handed, at least—nearly $400 million was set aside to pay for buyouts of homes and businesses, including Minors Lane Heights, now the site of a "Renaissance Zone."

The city did it to make UPS happy. No one ever fooled themselves otherwise. The hub giveth, and the hub can taketh away. Twenty years later, the residents of Wilmington, Ohio, found this out the hard way. In 2003, Deutsche Post, the owner of DHL (and Germany's post office) bought Airborne Express in a multibillion-dollar deal. DHL folded America's also-ran common carrier into its own brand to battle the heavyweights on their home turf. It spent another $1.3 billion to buy Airborne's hub in Wilmington—not the sort, but the entire airport. The state of Ohio chipped in another half billion in incentives. Overnight, DHL became one of the state's largest employers. And then it began hemorrhaging losses. Five years later, facing another billion-dollar loss (and this was before the recession), DHL's brain trust in Bonn pulled the plug. In May 2008, it announced it was shutting down its American operations, outsourcing what was left to UPS. It was obvious that everyone at what was Airborne would lose his or her job—as many as ten thousand employees in a town of twelve thousand. Wilmington faced total ruin.

The unions vowed to fight; so did the governor, on antitrust grounds. It even became a presidential campaign issue. At one town meeting, a tearful woman begged Senator McCain for help. He called it a "terrible blow" but admitted he didn't have the power to stop it. DHL laid off nine thousand employees nationwide a week after Election Day—seven thousand were in Wilmington. "If you stay, there's no place for you to work, but if you go, how can you sell your home?" asked one of the victims, a forklift driver who had lived there since the age of four. "Lots of small businesses have closed. I can see signs for rent all over, but nobody's buy-ing or renting. It is so sad." A year later, the unemployment rate had dou-bled to 15 percent, homes had lost half their value, and foreclosures had risen 30 percent. Wilmington's middle class had been destroyed.

Reconstruction was the price Louisville paid to avoid a similar fate, and that was fine with everyone. Well, not quite everyone. While in Lou-isville, I was introduced to Burt Deutsch and Linda Solley-Kanipe, the city's point pair on the resettlement program. Burt had been Abramson's deputy mayor at the time of the Good Friday call, and he had spent al-most two decades since then working with Linda to clear the last hold-outs. They had worked so hard and so closely together under occasionally harrowing circumstances—Linda had had more than one gun waved in her face when she knocked on residents' doors—that their manner sug-gested not just a married couple, but a married vaudeville couple, with Burt playing the polished magician and Linda his frazzled assistant.

Exasperation still leaks into Burt's voice when he describes the home-owners' gut reaction to the improvement program: howling and lawsuits. Part of the problem was the "urban renewal" clauses in their foreclosures. Although he had tried to convince them that the payouts would be greater, a little extra cash had meant nothing to their pride—their homes were *not blighted*. They sued, took the relevant agencies to the Supreme Court, and won. Burt and Linda sighed and found another statute that would get the job done.

Twenty years on, neighborhoods like Edgewood and Highland Park—wedged between highways on one side and the airport on the other—have turned feral, as if civilization had vanished and the land was returning to wilderness. In a sense, that is exactly what happened. While we cruised through a limbo filled with abandoned churches and the shotgun shacks of the last stragglers, Burt explained the rationale behind the wholesale depopulation. "We kept ahead of UPS, realizing that UPS itself didn't know what it needed." Resettlement has begun, with UPS moving its global operations center and several thousand parking spaces to these weedy lots.

By the early 1990s, the airport had begun offering to buy out anyone afflicted by noise. More than two thousand families qualified, flooding the market with buyers and driving prices skyward, out of reach. At the time, the citizens of Minor Lane Heights were considering a lawsuit, as they now lived under the new runways' final approach path. They hadn't gotten used to UPS browntails hurtling overhead, nor did they want to.

They issued an ultimatum instead: We'll go quietly, but only if we can all go *together*. That meant everyone and everything: lifelong friends and neighbors, the mayor, the nine-person police department, even the Weenie Wagon, a truck the town had bought to sell hot dogs at picnics, all airlifted to new culs-de-sac somewhere on the edge of town. Burt, Linda, and Co. quickly agreed to terms, and the airport closed on 287 acres of farmland ten miles to the southeast that it had already been eyeing. This became the core of what is today called Heritage Creek, the aerotropolis's first purpose-built suburb.

The setting is bucolic. We wended our way down country roads, past Erector-set subdivisions with names like Woodridge Crossing and Cedar Brook ("New homes from the 150s!") until we reached a white picket fence bearing "HC" heraldry. "They designed the city the way they wanted it," Burt said. "The chairman of the planning commission said, 'This looks like it came out of a 1950s subdivision!' Well, duh! These people came out of a 1950s subdivision; it's all they know!"

And sure enough, it was. They had used their walkaway money to buy lots and choose homes from a handful of specs. The houses were handsome by Midwest standards—faux colonials and brick homes garnished with tiny colonnades and porches. It could have been another wing to the anonymous Illinois suburb I grew up in, only cut from whole cloth with government money.

Beyond the homes themselves, several hundred of which have been built, there isn't much to Heritage Creek as far as being a town goes. It hasn't acquired enough mass yet to earn a strip mall, and so the only other building so far is the Community Center—its town hall, police department, and village green all in one.

A wake was in progress when we arrived. Someone's twenty-year-old son had died in a car crash, and one room was filled with neighbors somberly picking at ice cream and chocolate cake. Waiting for us in back was the mayor of Heritage Creek, and former mayor of Minor Lane Heights, Fred Williams. Permanently tan, wearing both sunglasses and a grandfatherly red sweater indoors, he could have passed for Retired Elvis.

"When the airport announced it was going to buy us out, we started getting calls upon calls," he said. "'What am I going to do? I've lived next door to Susie for years,' and blah, blah, blah. So we surveyed whether people wanted to stick together if we could actually do something about it. Eighty-five percent said, 'Yeah, we want to stay a city,' and it just went from there. But it was a tough road, and it's never been done before.

"I lived in Minor Lane for thirty-seven years," he went on. "I bought my house for nine thousand and thirty dollars in 1966 and sold it for ninety-five thousand to the airport when I left. I think people are just tickled to come out here." Today his house sits across from the first to break ground here in 1999. A race car sits in his driveway as testament to his prowess on the circuit for twenty years, in between stints as his town's mechanic. Several hundred homes surround his now, bounded by a state park on one side and a creek on the other.

Did he ever think much about the airport before moving here? "I know plenty of people who work for UPS. It wasn't no problem at all until they shifted the runways, and that's when all hell broke loose. You'd look up and there's a plane sitting above your head. I ain't ever been on a plane at all until next week." Really? Where are you going? "Vegas. Never been there before." And it's too far to drive, even for him.

"I've never understood, and I'm a mechanic, how those suckers stay up there. I've driven cars faster than those airplanes go, and they don't go off the ground. I have to think that something that goes up must sometimes go down, and if it happens over there, it'll be rough."

He reminded me of a bit of wisdom passed along in Los Angeles: "People may complain about the noise, but it's the fear of falling aircraft that gets to them. All seven hundred thousand pounds of it."

Standing in the parking lot afterward, I spotted a UPS browntail overhead, far above us. It didn't make a sound.

3

UP IN THE AIR

Before goods move, people do. It no longer matters where your business is based, so long as it's a few minutes from a major airport. No wonder the exurbs of Dallas are thriving: sprawl comes from the sky.

How Tonga Landed in Texas

The loud, clear tone of a conch shell echoed across the Texas prairie, hushing the packed stands of Euless Trinity High School's football stadium. Hearing his cue, seventeen-year-old Alex Kautai threw off his helmet, freeing his mane of curly black hair. As he waved his arms and barked in a foreign tongue, nearly a hundred of his teammates milled about behind him. At his command, they dropped into a crouch, rhythmically slapping their thighs, arms, and chests. They stomped back and forth, thrusting and jabbing at an invisible enemy, all while chanting: "*Ka mate! Ka mate!*" (I may die! I may die!) "*Ka ora! Ka ora!*" (I may live! I may live!)

Across the field, the visiting team stared stonily at their backs. The Odessa Permian Panthers had been lionized in print, on film, and on television as the embodiment of *Friday Night Lights,* and they did not look kindly on Polynesian war dances performed at their expense.

Euless Trinity's stars are Tongans, children of the world's most far-flung and yet tightly knit diaspora, making regular pilgrimages to their namesake South Pacific islands hugging the international date line. Euless is a suburb of fifty-four thousand in the center of the Dallas–Ft. Worth Metroplex. Four thousand Tongans call it home. That may not sound like many, until you consider there are only a hundred thousand

Tongans in Tonga. Tall, fast, and massive, they've pulverized the quarter-backs of traditional powers like Odessa, a boom-and-bust oil town, and Southlake Carroll—a football factory just north of Euless in what *Forbes* anointed the "most affluent neighborhood in the country." Trinity has done much more with less, winning two state championships and star-ring in their own Gatorade commercial. Their war dance, the *haka,* has since become a staple of big-time football.

How did several thousand descendants of the world's most intrepid sailors wind up in the Metroplex—the largest metropolis in America that is nowhere near a body of water?

By plane. That's the simple answer. A more complex one lies within Euless city limits on the vast apron of Dallas–Ft. Worth International Airport, one of the largest and busiest passenger hubs in the world. Their parents began settling here thirty years ago, lured by the jobs and flights promised by the brand-new airfield. They left Tongan enclaves in Salt Lake City and Los Angeles and took jobs as baggage handlers and sky chefs for American Airlines, not so much for the pay as for the free and discounted airfares offered to employees and their families. Their remit-tances, sent home to aunts and cousins, keep the country afloat, while custom dictates they be ready to return on a moment's notice—and eigh-teen hours in the air—for funerals and formal ceremonies lasting days or even weeks. So they landed here at DFW, each family taking care to have at least one member on American's payroll.

"Throughout history, Polynesians have always valued connections," says Ilaiasi Ofa, host of the local cable show *Voice of Tonga.* "And they have always valued family and extended family. Wherever they go, they always find a gateway home."

The American hub at DFW was the world's first. Its opening in 1981 was to the modern era of aviation what the interstate highway system was to the postwar car culture: the innovation that made everything else possible. The hub-and-spoke system, with its waves of flights to anywhere and everywhere, created a critical mass of connectivity—so much that the laws of nature governing how we live, how we work, and how far we'll travel to do either on any given day were seemingly repealed. One unin-tended consequence was several thousand Tongans appearing on its door-step; another was a six-foot-two, 297-pound tackle screaming *"Mate ma'a Tonga!"* (I will die for Tonga!) each time he knocked some fair-haired linebacker on his back. They were the first, but by no means the last, road warriors to find refuge in their neighbor's long shadow.

The Invention of Nowhere

DFW represents a turning point in how we build airports and how we think of them. Finished in 1974, it was the last new big-city airport in America for a generation, and easily the most monumental. Its eighteen thousand acres of prairie scrubland is five times the footprint of LAX and twice as large as a revamped O'Hare. Its architects were the first to grapple successfully with the bulk of a 747 and the torrents of passengers spilling from it. Their best asset was sheer size, now de rigueur for any new airport, with room for seven runways, ten semicircular terminals (if necessary)—each more than a mile in circumference—and a thirty-six-hole golf course tucked inside.

To help prepare them for the immensity of their undertaking, they drafted the landscape artist Robert Smithson, who learned more about art from them than they were able to glean from him. The scale of DFW astonished him. Used to thinking in terms of gallery space, here he was confronted with gargantuan landing strips fourteen thousand feet long, "or about the length of Central Park," he noted; the entire site was larger than Manhattan. At that size, he surmised, any project—whether airport or artwork—is too vast to stay fixed forever. It couldn't help but expand infinitesimally and irreversibly, like a glacier cutting across the plains.

His personal contribution would have been an equally immense work of art, a whirling progression of concrete triangles that "could be built as large as the site would allow, and could be seen from approaching and departing aircraft." But he repurposed the idea for his most famous work, *Spiral Jetty*, a black basalt sculpture submerged in the Great Salt Lake, its dimensions appreciable only from the air. Its shape deliberately echoes the terminals and twisting ramps of DFW.

Smithson didn't live to see the airport reach fruition; he died a year earlier in a plane crash. But he had already proved prescient. Before DFW was even finished, the fringes of Dallas and Ft. Worth began creeping toward it and each other. The adversarial cities had been compelled by the FAA to think regionally for once, after it refused to fund separate airports for each city. DFW was their compromise. Seizing the opportunity, the airport's executive director rounded up a band of ambitious CEOs and civic leaders to form the North Texas Commission in 1971, determined to end the cities' rivalry once and for all. They coined the word "Metroplex" as a replacement for the greater agglomeration, now a sprawling city of six million. DFW sits at the middle of the Metroplex and occasionally lends its name to it. More than one official swore to me the airport had created it, a de facto aerotropolis. No American city grew faster during the decade just ended, and none grew faster during the recession.

DFW was the pivot between the overmatched airport of the Jet Age and the megalithic ones at the heart of most aerotropoli. Not entirely modern, in some respects it was obsolete by the time it opened. The layout of its terminals had been inspired by a Hertz Rent a Car commercial in which a businessman literally floats from his plane to a convertible. The airport director commanded his architects to do something similar, designing DFW with no barriers between plane and car. They obliged, stringing the semicircular terminals along a central highway. You would park next to your gate and slip through the terminal with minimal fuss. "No crowds, no confusion, no pain," they promised.

They reneged after Congress demanded luggage-screening and security checkpoints for all airports, starting in 1973. For the first fifty years of commercial flight and the first decade of the Jet Age, anyone could board packing anything they liked, and many came heavily armed. Between 1969 and 1978, there were more than four hundred international hijackings involving seventy-five thousand passengers as hostages. In the United States alone, there were 154 attempted hijackings to Cuba in a four-year stretch. (As one hijacker explained, it was the easiest way to get there.) The solution was X-ray machines and magnetometers, leading to the choke points we all know and despise. DFW's in-and-out, "park-and-fly" concept never got off the ground.

What they could not have foreseen was President Jimmy Carter signing the Airline Deregulation Act into law on October 24, 1978. The airlines' business model changed overnight. The government would no longer set fares or assign routes, and had removed all legal barriers to competition. The immediate effect was to drive down prices as new entrants forced the incumbents to match their discounts. Even today, after oil spikes, baggage fees, and hundreds of grounded planes, the cost of flying on a per-mile basis is barely half of what it had been, adjusted for inflation. Estimates of passengers' annual savings range as high as $20 billion. The airlines' massive losses have been our personal gain.

Deregulation made the triumph of the plane over all other means of long-distance travel inevitable. The price of air travel compared to trains and driving has declined steadily since 1960, when it cost twice as much as either. By 2000, however, air travel had thoroughly beaten both on a per-mile basis. Our travel preferences had been erased and were being rewritten: the shortest distance between any two points in America was the path to the nearest airport.

Competition proved fatal for Braniff, Dallas's hometown airline since 1928 and one of the fastest growing in America until deregulation. Four years later it was defunct, followed by Eastern and Pan Am within a decade and more than a hundred others in their wake. The surviving majors scrambled to be more efficient in the face of the industry's first perfect storm. (There would be so many others in the years to come.)

Suddenly able and expected to fly to and from every city, they found it impossible to do so profitably. American Airlines was the first to stop trying and to switch to a hub-and-spoke system instead. The advantage was mathematical: Routes increased exponentially as the number of cities served increased arithmetically. Thirty aircraft flying through a hub could run five hundred different routes. Given enough planes and enough runways, an airline could conceivably link every city in the country— some fifty thousand city pairs—from a centrally located one like Dallas. For cities, hubs meant dozens of new destinations and frequent service to them—more flights than they could have justified on their own. The airlines were learning about "network effects" and "first-mover advantage" long before the Internet escaped from the lab. American moved its headquarters to Dallas immediately after deregulation and opened its hub there two years later, filling the void left by Braniff. With concentration came immense economies of scale. Today, American is the largest private employer in the Metroplex, bigger than Walmart.

Competing hubs opened at O'Hare, in Atlanta, Detroit, and Denver. The layover was their first unintended consequence. Travelers were used to delays and congestion, but it wasn't until American's hub at DFW that compulsory downtime was included in the price of the ticket. Hubbing placed unimagined strains on terminals. Rather than flowing in and out like the tides, transiting passengers swirled and eddied from gate to gate. DFW's were perversely unsuited to this task, requiring arrivals to trace mile-long parabolas or hop a poky "air train" between them. Built for the Jet Age just ended, its park-and-fly layout needed a serious retrofit for the new era.

Layovers induced altered states as they stretched for hours inside concrete sensory deprivation tanks, augmented by jet lag—a condition first diagnosed in 1959. Hubs offered an environment to match: a limbo in which physics and human experience no longer applied. They're amnesiac places with no future and no past, only a continual present offering the same choices—flights, duty-free, and fast food—day after day after day. They make for perfect shopping malls, outfitted with Brooks Brothers, Brookstone, Borders, and kiosks hawking souvenirs to a captive audience. Sales per square foot in the busiest hubs are on par with the highest-grossing malls in the country.

They are in the business of killing time. *Generation X* author Douglas Coupland distilled their essence in a rant undoubtedly written during a delay at O'Hare:

> It is a pit stop, an in-between place, a "nowhere," a technicality—
> a grudging intrusion into the seamless dream of teleportation
> that is transcontinental jet flight . . . The hub is essentially an
> anti-experience born of technological necessity and the impera-
> tives of petroleum, flight schedules, the curvature of the planet,
> and geographic accident. Hubs are nowheres . . . Connection to
> the world is what happens at your destination, not at your hub.
> O'Hare is like what happens to you just after you die and before
> you get shipped off to wherever you're going, what happens to
> you while your final destination is being determined. It is not
> judgment; it is transit distilled—like crack—pure neutrality
> made concrete—extreme.

The invention of "nowhere" offered a rich seam of metaphor for pop philosophers and academics to mine. After 9/11, hubs became the domestic front in the war on terror and the nexus of all our anxieties about mobility, anonymity, globalization, and the latter's discontents. Airports have replaced the road itself as the signifier of the open road and the restlessness inherent in our national character. We don't even bother to call a moving van after the eviction notice; all we need for the next life is a carry-on.

But if flight represents freedom, reinvention, and self-renewal—and barring all of that, *escape*—then the terminal itself has evolved into something resembling a destination. Hubs wouldn't stay barren forever. The combination of money + boredom + "dwell time" + sheer numbers = Alice's Wonderland: a through-the-looking-glass world of encapsulated theme parks, malls, and hotels. Once through security, you need never leave. Or be allowed to. That's the predicament of Tom Hanks's character in *The Terminal*, a man without a country stuck in a bureaucratic "nowhere."

Or you can serenely float between them, like George Clooney's Ryan Bingham in *Up in the Air*. Bingham is a corporate hyperflier who has gone native in the terrariums of first-class cabins, airline clubs, suite hotels, car rental counters, and fast casual restaurants that permeate the sprawl surrounding hubs. In Walter Kirn's original novel, Bingham claims them as his personal domain:

> I call it Airworld; the scene, the place, the style. My hometown papers are *USA Today* and the *Wall Street Journal*. The big-screen Panasonics in the club rooms broadcast all the news I need, with an emphasis on the markets and the weather. My literature— yours, too, I see—is the bestseller or the near-bestseller, heavy on themes of espionage, high finance, and the goodness of people in small towns. In Airworld, I've found, the passions and enthusiasms of the outlying society are concentrated and whisked to a stiff froth. When a new celebrity is minted in the movie theaters or ballparks, this is where the story breaks—on the vast magazine racks that form a sort of trading floor for public reputations and pretty faces. I find it possible here, as nowhere else, to think of myself as part of the collective that prices the long bond and governs necktie widths. Airworld is a nation within a nation, with its own language, architecture, mood, and even its own currency—the token economy of airline bonus miles that I've come to value more than dollars. Inflation doesn't degrade

them. They're not taxed. They're private property in its purest form.

Airworld has its own populace too, with their own customs, migrations, and tribes. It has a GDP bigger than Thailand's or Turkey's. It is worldwide and "nowhere," hermetically sealed and connected only to itself someplace else. If the aerotropolis refers to the cities crystallized around these hubs, then Airworld exists within what Kasarda considers their new downtowns, the increasingly urbane terminals at their core.

I once mounted an expedition to explore them, spending the better part of a month living inside, leaping from airport to airport, and flying around the world without a breath of fresh air. I found "Sir, Alfred" Mehran Nasseri waiting for me in the basement of Charles de Gaulle. This lost soul in transit was Steven Spielberg's inspiration for *The Terminal*. At the time, he had been sitting on a bench there for seventeen years, a refugee from the world.

Airworld, Population Two Billion

Who calls Airworld home? No one lives here in any conventional sense, not even Sir, Alfred, who was finally dragged away a few years ago. We spend only slivers of our lives there—typically two hours at a stretch—and so it's impossible to take an accurate census.

By any measure, the totals are astounding. The world's airlines carried more than two billion passengers in 2009, setting yet another record. That figure is equal to the populations of China, America, and the EU combined. It doubled in only twenty years, and doubled before that in ten. (Then the crash and the law of large numbers kicked in.)

The number of passengers in the United States this year is expected to hover around seven hundred million, 10 percent off its peak but still triple what it was in 1980. It's grown five times faster than population since then. In thirty years, the number of miles flown by Americans dipped only once before our current crisis, in the wake of 9/11. Neither the early eighties oil shocks nor the first Gulf War slowed us down. Air travel follows the money. It's a leading indicator of economic health, flying higher when times are good and falling faster when they turn bad. As it is, six hundred thousand Americans hopped a flight last week, more than the population of Milwaukee.

Hubs are easily the world's most central places, concentrating us like nowhere else. DFW annually handles some sixty million passengers, equal to one in five Americans. Heathrow sees more traffic than Britain has citizens. The world's busiest hub, Atlanta's Hartsfield-Jackson, has a day-time population larger than Orlando's and an annual one that would rank it as the twelfth most populous nation on earth. (It's also the state of Georgia's largest employer.)

All of these figures have a sky-high fudge factor, failing to account for fliers counted twice or more. The media research firm Arbitron made a better measurement a few years ago. It estimated ninety-two million Americans—nearly one in three—had flown at least once in the past twelve months. A clear and bright line separates those of us who fly and those of us who don't. The former are almost twice as likely to make more than $100,000 a year, and more than half have incomes of $50,000 and up, compared to barely a third of the latter. Frequent fliers (defined as those who make four trips or more a year) are three times likelier to earn six figures. The study confirms a rule of thumb also seen among nations: the richer you are, the more you fly. The Israeli economist Yakov Zahavi noted in the 1970s that people tend to spend about 13 percent of their disposable income on traveling. The percentage is the same in dif-ferent countries and different eras. When you plot our proclivity to travel on a GDP per capita basis, it looks like the chart on the following page.

The rapid rise of a global middle class suggests that the countries on the left will ascend smoothly toward the right, just as the United States did in the twenty years between 1980 and 2000, when our dispos-able income grew 21 percent and our mileage doubled. The reason: time equals money. The wealthier we become, the more we value our time, and the more we value our time, the more likely we are to fly. This is why, even with higher oil prices, passenger numbers continue to increase in growing economies. A bump in airfares leads to an equal decline in de-mand. But a bump in GDP growth causes demand to rise twice as fast. By this standard, the average American (and Dane, Swiss, and Irishman) is already a frequent flier, not that four trips a year is enough to establish residency in Airworld. Its constituents are the real-life Ryan Binghams making forty trips a year, a caste better known as road warriors.

Large potential to increase propensity to travel

Trips* per capita - 2008

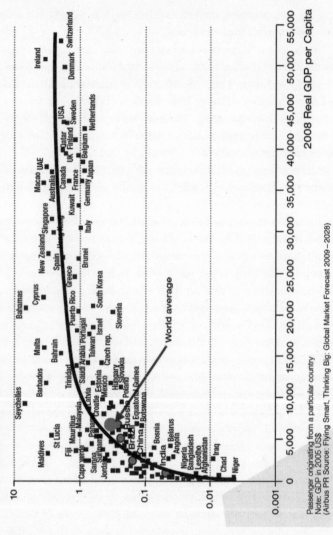

2008 Real GDP per Capita

Passenger originating from a particular country
Note: GDP in 2005 US$
(Airbus PR Source: Flying Smart, Thinking Big: Global Market Forecast 2009–2028)

They fly to work instead of drive on Monday mornings, casually overturning ten thousand years of civilization before breakfast. Prior to flight, humans always balanced mobility with domesticity, venturing farther and farther afield while picking up speed, although never straying too far from home. The size and shape of cities evolved in turn, but our daily lives stayed rooted in them. Road warriors said goodbye to all that, commuting halfway across the country for lunch and back in time for dinner. This rupture of time and space was shocking at first, leading the sociologist Alvin Toffler to pronounce that "never in history has distance meant less. Never has man's relationship with place been more numerous, fragile, and temporary . . . We are breeding a new race of nomads."

They're a tribe of mostly middle-aged men, married without children and earning a median salary of $78,700. Their time, as calculated by Brookings, is worth an inflation-adjusted $67 an hour. Not bad. More live around DFW than any other American city besides New York or Los Angeles, and their time is worth more—$88 an hour. An estimated three hundred thousand have flown a million miles or more in their lifetimes, equal to a pair of round-trips to the moon. They are the red blood cells of globalization, coursing through Airworld's arteries. They clot the world one handshake at a time, constantly inventing new communities that materialize just in time to schmooze. Road warriors' destinations may differ, but their attraction to hubs is the same.

A few, like *Up in the Air*'s Ryan Bingham, have achieved escape velocity, leaving families and worldly possessions behind. The ne plus ultra example is management guru Ram Charan. Best known as the coauthor of *Execution*, his job is to be Jiminy Cricket for clients like Jack Welch of GE and former Citigroup chairman John Reed. Although his fee can top $20,000 a day, Charan is homeless. He sleeps every night in a hotel or aloft in first class, spending holidays with clients' families. He sends his dirty laundry to an office here in Dallas manned by assistants he's never met. Three days a week they stuff a FedEx box with clean shirts and suits and ship it a few stops ahead on his itinerary. It sounds crazy, but CEOs pay for his presence. Between his books and the bulk of his clients (DuPont, GE, Verizon) there's a decent chance his whispered advice has had something to do with your hiring or firing. (Tagging along for a week, *Fortune* dubbed him "the most influential consultant alive.") His only

regret is turning down an offer from American Airlines thirty years ago
for a $100,000 lifetime first-class upgrade.

Anyone who lives aloft like Charan quickly becomes obsessed, à la
Bingham, with airlines' loyalty programs. Since American Airlines signed
up its first frequent fliers practically on a whim, it has added upward of
sixty million members. Airline miles are now a currency like any other,
legal tender not just in Airworld but in the economy of flat-screen TVs,
washing machines, and even diamond rings. There are an estimated seventeen trillion miles in circulation right now, which would get you two-
thirds of the way to Alpha Centauri. At their nominal exchange rate of a
penny per mile, that's still $170 billion—more than the foreign currency
reserves of either the United States or Germany. Only a fraction are ever
redeemed, for some forty million free trips a year. The most frequent fliers earn elite status, upgrading them to first-class cabins and business
lounges. Over time, planes and terminals have evolved into a series of
gated communities, each more exclusive than the last, not unlike the
chain hotels and rental-car companies the fliers frequent beyond the gates.
They serve to distract these budding Ryan Binghams from the fact that
they are living, even reveling, in an ultimately sterile environment. Strip
away the logos, and they would find themselves flying in metal tubes,
striding through steel corridors, driving cars that are not their own, and
sleeping in rooms just vacated by others. No wonder they cling to brands
in such places, because otherwise it's too crushingly impersonal.

Road warriors once embodied connectivity. They were emissaries
from the home office sent to do its dirty work closing deals, kowtowing,
and cleaning house. They carried information until technology caught
up with them, and now their atoms struggle to keep up with their bits.
Most of us are too young to remember when the jet itself was a touchstone for all things modern, streamlined, and in motion. The Jet Age
ended when we acclimated to the new pace of things—when adventure
gave way to business and leisure, and finally to being a cog in the finely
meshed gears of a global machine. Whereas *Time* magazine once grandly
estimated that the advent of jets had shrunk the world by precisely
40 percent, today, it is said, the world is flat. And where air travel itself was
once dizzyingly fast, now it's too slow for our always-on selves. Ironically,
aircraft cabins became the last refuge from our BlackBerrys before finally succumbing to in-flight WiFi last year. The reason we mourn that

vanished era so is that the Jet Age was the all-too-brief flowering of our romance with speed. Later, we fell for seamlessness instead, spurning the freedom to go anywhere anytime for the ability to be nowhere all the time. We traded the clouds for the cloud, and we're living in an Instant Age.

Matthew Kelly's commute is a weekly routine. A married thirty-something consultant for AlixPartners—the ones tasked with disposing of General Motors' spare parts—Kelly awakens each Monday at 4:00 a.m. in his Brooklyn apartment, showers, dresses, and slides into a waiting taxi at four thirty, arriving at LaGuardia by five. He slips through security and boards a flight at five thirty, landing in Atlanta or Wichita by eight thirty and gliding into the client's office an hour later. He travels light, packing only his laptop, not stopping to pick up fresh laundry from the dry cleaner until he's on his way to the hotel. Three days later, he catches a four forty flight home. Thursday night flights are known as "consultant expresses," and there are never enough seats to check everyone's egos into first. Barring delays, he's on the ground by seven and home (if you can still call it that) in thirty minutes. Fridays he works from Manhattan; he spends weekends on the couch.

Most Mondays, the Delta terminal at LaGuardia has the ambience of the train platform in Greenwich, circa *Revolutionary Road*. After bumping into the competition at the coffee machine, he will nod and say hello to his colleagues, while their bosses "just bury their heads in *The Wall Street Journal* or the *Times*," Kelly told me. "They've been doing this for who knows how long. There's a senior GM guy here who's been doing this for ten years, commuting with the rest of us," including the head of his firm's restructuring team. "Detroit is where consultants go to die," and where everyone else flies to pick over its bones. The condemned nicknamed their 7:29 a.m. flight the "Distress Bus," filled with the same cast of bankers, consultants, and bankruptcy lawyers week after week. (Every meltdown has its commuting patterns: for a while, the shuttle was packed with bankers pleading their case in Washington.) Wherever the scene, "It's a bunch of guys who look thirty or forty years old, all wearing blue shirts and gray pants, with short, clean-looking haircuts and the look of vague unhealthiness from traveling and working too much." Home life is an afterthought; if they weren't on the road all the time, they'd be in the office.

Consultants are the consummate road warriors. They are talent incarnate, with nothing to offer but their expertise (or its opposite, a fresh set of eyes and "best practices") rendered actionable as a deck of Power-Point slides. These are presented personally to the CEO. Work is a series of "engagements" at the client's office, lasting months or sometimes years. Their job is to fix what the company cannot, and take off. They're not paid to have a stake in the status quo. As Clark Gable once said of the prostitutes he frequented, "I don't pay them for sex; I pay them to leave."

Kelly started in London six years ago, ranging as far afield as Poland and Romania bringing Soviet-era steel plants up to speed. From there he was on to Dusseldorf and Munich, then home to Detroit and Indianapolis, and finally to his standing engagements in Dallas and Atlanta.

"The idea of sitting at a desk and going to the same office day after day and making good money is history," he called to tell me before a flight. "Even the guys I work with in corporate jobs will be in Europe for a week, then Brazil. If you have any responsibility at all, from the midlevel on up, and the company you work for is global—which it almost certainly is—then you'll be traveling. Or you will be if you're ambitious, and your ambition is to make money. You'll have to become global in your outlook and responsibilities." His thoughts were seconded by two thousand road warriors polled last summer by *Harvard Business Review*. CEOs, small-business owners, and salesmen all expect to fly more often in the coming months, budgets be damned.

"And if your boss or your client wants to see you in the office, you might counter with, 'I work from Moline, and it's all about what I accomplish,'" Kelly added. "That's all very nice, but they want to see what they're paying for. And what they want to see is you sitting there working hard." He found it impossible to manage from afar without first establishing trust and authority. "You have to be there, nagging them. A lot of the time, the only way to accomplish something is to stand behind them and ask, 'Is it done yet? Is it done yet?' A lot of what I do is nagging them until they do it themselves."

Jim Tam spent sixteen years nagging colleagues remotely as an executive at Citigroup in Manhattan. Assigned to one of the financial giant's many far-flung acquisitions, he commuted between Dallas and New Jersey until "it eventually opened my eyes to a better way of life," he told me. He untethered himself, leaving for Dallas and a new life up in the air. Tuesdays and Thursdays he commutes to and from his job at Kastle Systems in Houston, selling building security. "It's almost like taking the LIRR. When I was living on Long Island, I would just wait on the platform; here we wait at Chili's or Subway and grab a sandwich before boarding the plane. Half my time I'm in Dallas, half my time I'm somewhere else," in New Orleans or Albuquerque—wherever the client happens to be. "You can't sell our product online."

Tam and his wife live in Southlake, which she discovered after searching the Web. America's most affluent suburb rests on the south shore of Grapevine Lake, less than a mile from the nearest runway. The Town Square (an outdoor mall wrapped around City Hall) lies under the approach path, as does Dragon Stadium—the $15 million home field advantage of Southlake Carroll Senior High, the archrival of Euless Trinity's Tongans.

They are the children of DFW too. Fifty years ago, this was cattle pasture. Southlake hired its first police chief the year planning began on the new airport. Today, twenty-five thousand people live here; since 1990, its population has exploded by 257 percent; Euless's has nearly tripled. They are models of New South strivers. Not long ago, *D* magazine offered reasons "why you should hate Southlake: because the kids are stronger, smarter, and better looking than yours." While parents in Euless toil as baggage handlers, the largest employer here is Sabre Holdings, owner of the original airline reservations system and the website Travelocity.com.

"People in New York still think it's the Wild West out here, but nine out of ten people on my block aren't from Texas," Tam said. One of his neighbors would fly back to town from business trips for his son's baseball games and fly back out again. Owning three jets helped. Another is a developer named Ron Peddicord, who moved his family back to the States from Toronto. He and his wife, an executive coach, searched high and low for a suitable city to call home, grading them on schools, climate, housing stock, and the nearest airport—how far away it was, how many flights, and how often they're on time. The winner and the runners-up were all hubs (Cincinnati, Atlanta, and Charlotte). The reason: Peddicord still commutes weekly to his job in Canada, flying home to Texas on Thursday nights in time to coach his son's basketball team.

"You would think that the fact that I live in Dallas and work in Toronto would be big cocktail conversation," Peddicord told a reporter from

BusinessWeek. "In Dallas, not so much. One dad on my son's team works for a company based in Massachusetts and spends most of his time in France. It's not normal, but it's not weird anymore."

Not around here. Southlake is a textbook "Reloville," one of the master-planned subdivisions populated by "relos," the organization men and women regularly reassigned and moved by their employers. Relos belong to the privileged sliver of the middle class who still have faith in their upward trajectory. Their chronicler, Peter T. Kilborn, describes them as "the shock troops of national and world commerce, the conscripts who stalk and collect markets . . . American foreign trade leaped from $374 billion in 1970 to $3.3 trillion in 2007," he adds. "*Someone* knocked on those doors to buy and sell all those goods and services, negotiate contracts, run marketing and advertising campaigns, and balance companies' books."

Modern relos are descended from the rank and file of IBM, for whom the initials once stood for "I've Been Moved." But relos are a more itinerant breed than their ancestors in the gray flannel suits. Like Tam and Ron Peddicord, they frequently find themselves moving to one place and wind up commuting to another—often on their own initiative. The one thing they have in common is that they are all from someplace else. "Relos don't have accents," Kilborn writes. "Wherever they go, they don't belong. Their kids don't know where they are from." They compensate with six-figure salaries and low-interest mortgages. They went to Big Ten and Big 12 schools instead of Ivies, and vote two to one Republican. Like the road warriors with whom they overlap, "the vast majority of relo breadwinners are white men aged thirty to fifty." Kilborn estimates there are as many as ten million relos on the move, and of the top twenty-five Relovilles in America, six are in the Metroplex—more than any other city.

Relovilles such as Southlake are assemblages of gated communities in which the homes are twice as large and cost twice as much as the national average. Like the leased cars relos drive, they're to be traded in for even bigger ones down the road. While Jim Tam sees himself chasing the American dream between Dallas and Houston, the downside is a slackening of the bonds in corporate, community, and family life. Homes, subdivisions, office parks, and even cities become disposable assets. Life in Reloville has about as much permanence as a plane ticket. In the aerotropolis, that's not weird, it's normal.

What *is* weird is commuting to nowhere in particular, which David Topus does whenever he needs new clients. A one-man "consultant, trainer, and coach" who lists "personal branding" among his services, Topus does his best work canvassing first-class cabins to drum up business. "I could spend $15,000 and put it into an online marketing strategy, or I can spend $1,000 and take an airplane trip with multiple stops, and come home with a dozen business cards and contacts," he explained to *The New York Times.*

Meetings, Marts, and Markets

Less strange is never leaving Airworld during your trip. The airport hotels catering to lost souls caught between flights have reinvented themselves as slick conference centers and convention sites. It made too much sense not to—320 million people fly to business meetings each year, more than the population of the United States. Business travel is a $261 billion business in the United States and an almost trillion-dollar one worldwide. During my weeklong stay in Dallas at the Grand Hyatt DFW—a black onyx slab sticking out of the new International Terminal—the conference rooms were booked by the likes of Advanced Bionics, the American Heart Association, AT&T, and Atrion. And those were just the A's.

Taking my coffee in the lobby each morning, I eavesdropped on job interviews—the inquisitor jotting notes on a legal pad while the candidate confessed her weaknesses ("If anything, I work too hard"). It was unclear which one, or whether both had alighted here expressly for this purpose, and for only an hour or two. The setting is pure node—white space—the incarnation of an Internet chat room.

"The hotel is a meeting planner's dream," my mother informed me, and she would know, having planned meetings there herself. She's the events director for CCIM Institute, an association of commercial realtors—the men (indubitably men), she said, who "buy and sell office buildings, golf courses, shopping centers, and strip malls" that are built, flipped, refinanced, and foreclosed upon in Sun Belt cities like Dallas. The Grand Hyatt is perfect for a twenty-four-hour budget committee summit. Members fly in around two in the afternoon, work through dinner, bond over drinks, hash out the details during breakfast the next morning, and wrap up by lunch, adjourning in time to catch an early afternoon flight. (These are the kind of closed-door meetings you might overhear in the halls. I snuck a peek inside one in Denver in which the squad leader stood snarling in shirtsleeves, exhorting his troops: "We got killed last year!")

Why bother meeting in person at all? I asked. Why not schedule a conference call? "That's a valid question," she replied, "but most of these committees consist of twenty-five people, and it's hard to get them all on the line. The most efficient thing is to put them all in the same room."

She had just flown home from a reconnaissance mission in Dallas. The spring meetings were approaching, when three or four hundred members would land here for a week's worth of seminars, open bars, and banquets. She chose the Metroplex for its hub, but the Grand Hyatt wouldn't work; the delegates would grow restless. They feel primal needs to golf, to sightsee, to offset business hours with pure boondogglery. (It's all-inclusive in the registration fee.) So they would fill a new Omni in downtown Ft. Worth, within reach of enough bars and brisket to keep everyone happy.

"The biggest reason these people need to get together is to network," she told me. CCIM has nineteen thousand members in thirty-three countries and all fifty states. "They want to see each other face-to-face. Honestly, the sessions themselves don't seem to matter all that much. They're checking e-mails, taking calls—they're busy doing business back home. They're not paying much attention. To them, the most important thing is just being there."

The Omni was still a hole in the ground when she signed the contract. Taking precautions, she had looked at backups on the periphery of DFW, starting with the Gaylord Texan, which arriving guests might mistake for a domed stadium. Hugging the airport's fence along its northern edge, the Texan is one of the world's largest and most expensive hotels, finished in 2004 at a cost of just under half a billion dollars. Inside is a theme park of Tex-arcana under glass skylights, replete with replicas of the Alamo and the Panhandle's Palo Duro Canyon. Bars, ballrooms, and breakout rooms are scattered throughout, as the Texan caters almost exclusively to the conventions crowd; they fill twelve hundred of its fifteen hundred rooms. On a typical weekday, you might find a few thousand employees belonging to Henry Schein (a *Fortune* 500 wholesaler of dental supplies) sporting badges emblazoned with "007 Bond-ing Together."

Gaylord Entertainment owns equally gargantuan resorts outside Nashville, Orlando, and Washington. Its long-term strategy is to sprinkle enough of them across the country for companies to rotate conferences among them in a closed loop. To that end, a fifth billion-dollar hotel will be the centerpiece of an aerotropolis slated for Mesa, Arizona, on the fringes of Phoenix. It will be the largest in the state and the Sun Belt, with the exception of Las Vegas. This seems appropriate considering Gaylord has borrowed the casinos' business model.

It isn't gambling; Sin City's dirtiest secret is that it's slowly scrubbing the sin from its name. "Gaming" is less and less relevant in Las Vegas, contributing less than half the Strip's revenues last year. Wynn, MGM Grand, and Sands cashed out of slot machines to stuff their pleasure domes with luxury brands: Armani in the mall, Wolfgang Puck in the kitchen, Cirque du Soleil in residence, and Canyon Ranch in the spa. To please shareholders, they became a volume business dependent on filling 140,000 hotel rooms seven days a week. Naturally, they turned to conventioneering.

Since the opening of the first megaresort twenty years ago, the number of visitors has doubled in lockstep with air passengers, while conventioneers have quadrupled and the number of meetings has risen sevenfold. Las Vegas hosts nearly a quarter of America's two hundred largest trade shows, generating $8 billion a year—more than all of the Strip's casinos. (Kasarda looks at the Strip itself and sees a paved extension of the neighboring airport's runways.) It's not uncommon for entire industries to gather there for a few frantic days of deal making. One of the biggest draws is the Wireless I.T. show, religiously attended by forty thousand of the same cell phone–toting visionaries who swear location no longer matters. They come because even the most random encounter might yield a potential ally, investor, or acquirer, and these connections must be made face-to-face. Deals depend on trust, and you must be in the same room to have it; Las Vegas has plenty of rooms.

Its most significant civic monument isn't the obsidian pyramid of the Luxor or the bronze crescent of the Wynn, but the Howard Hughes–era Convention Center, in the midst of its fourteenth expansion. This one will cost $890 million, the price of staying ahead of New York, Chicago, and Orlando. The airport's future is next on the list. McCarran International is hemmed in by the Strip; a second is planned to complement it. Las Vegas may have built its reputation as an oasis, but its future depends wholly on its role as a hub.

Dallas has its own attractions. Looming off the Stemmons Freeway between DFW and downtown is the upside-down wedding cake of the World Trade Center; the inside is honeycombed like a hive. Each cell is packed with furniture, fabrics, tableware, tchotchkes, toys, jewelry, bed, bath, and beyond. One sells only scented candles; another, men's moisturizers; another, the Art of Tea. The upper floors are reserved for boutiques carrying the latest fashions for every occasion, from bridal gowns to bolo ties to bedazzled denim. Stacked on fifteen levels are twenty-three hundred showrooms in all, stocking thirty-five thousand product lines. Dwarfing the Mall of America, it sits locked and empty four out of five days a year, coming alive only when fifty thousand professional shoppers from across the country descend en masse like crazed sparrows in Hitchcock's *The Birds*.

The World Trade Center is the centerpiece of the Dallas Market Center, the largest wholesale market in the world. Like the Merchandise Mart in Chicago (which it surpassed in size and importance), the complex is closed to the public, opening only for trade shows drawing buyers from retail chains around the world. Unlike in Paris or New York, the clothes sent down its runways are the kind people actually wear. The buyers, fittingly, are not from Barneys, Harrods, or Takashimaya, but Sam's Club, JCPenney, and Dillard's. Instead of jostling for front-row seats, they're more likely to glance up while scarfing down lunch between appointments. Catwalks wind between the tables in the adjoining Grand Atrium, where President Kennedy's motorcade was headed for a luncheon on November 22, 1963.

Besides the World Trade Center, there is the International Floral and Gift Center, home to the "world's largest collection of permanent botanicals." Spread over nearly half a million square feet is a boreal forest behind plate glass, guarded by animatronic Santas. "Where do Christmas trees come from?" my tour guide asked rhetorically. "They come from here." So do lamps. The self-described "international home of lighting" shelters yet another industry under one roof. Customers drop in during the seasonal Total Home & Gift Markets, when Walmart, Home Depot, Amazon, and Whole Foods decide what to stock on their shelves.

Before goods are made in China and moved through Memphis or Louisville, the decisions of what to make and how many are made here in Dallas. The agents who slip in and out of town unnoticed are an invisible but vital link in the global chain of designers, marketers, manufacturers, wholesalers, and retail chains that dictate how and what and why we buy. The Market Center is where our stuff comes from: our daily bric-a-brac of cellophane-wrapped silk roses, a stuffed and mounted singing bass, prom dresses—the stuff that surrounds us. Four hundred thousand visitors pass through its halls in a typical year, ordering $8 billion in merchandise, booking 300,000 plane tickets, and sleeping 720,000 nights in neighboring hotels. Before goods move, people do. Both fly.

High Point, North Carolina, was the "Furniture Capital of the World" until its factories left for China. The semiannual High Point Market still attracts one hundred thousand visitors, but the fair nearly decamped for Dallas. The Market Center offered what High Point could not: a faster, more efficient combination of size, concentration, and accessibility—a hub.

That's what the city's decorators and wholesalers had in mind in 1953 when they approached a local developer named Trammel Crow to build an answer to High Point and the Merchandise Mart—ordered by Marshall Field & Co. a generation earlier on the site of a train station. Crow resurfaced two days later with the blueprints for the Dallas Decorative Center, the first plank in his complex. Together with his partner, John M. Stemmons (whose family owned the land beneath the freeway), Crow spent the next thirty years building ten million square feet of exhibition space, along with the largest hotel in the Metroplex—the Gaylord Texan of its era.

Crow's great insight, predating both FedEx and today's Las Vegas, was that people could be sorted, routed, and stored around hubs as easily as packages. And in the interests of saving time and money, they would. The core of his portfolio were warehouses and wholesale marts—each type a bare-bones node for doing business. Crow treated property as a commodity, becoming the first big developer to build on spec, tossing up buildings before he had tenants. He was also the first to build globally. At his peak in the early 1970s, he commanded a staggering 550 million square feet of airport hotels, office blocks, plazas, and shopping malls to go with his more prosaic holdings—an empire larger than every square inch of commercial space in Manhattan. He bought out his partner in 1974 when Stemmons balked at the price of the World Trade Center—the final piece in Market Center's puzzle. Undeterred, Crow staked his career on the catalytic effects of DFW opening that year, and won.

"As much as any single person, he made Dallas what it is," *The Dallas Morning News* gushed upon his death in 2009. But his greatest legacy lies in Atlanta, where his later partner, John C. Portman, Jr., unveiled the world's first atrium hotel as the first Hyatt Regency. (Chain founder Jay Pritzker bought the original Hyatt next door to LAX while waiting in its coffee shop to catch a flight.) Portman's innovation was paid the ultimate compliment by his colleagues: it became a cliché. You know the type—the yawning voids ringed by rooms along the edges, decorated with hanging gardens and glass elevators. They're still building them that way; the Grand Hyatt Shanghai soars for thirty stories at the top of the Jin Mao Tower in Pudong, until recently the highest hotel in the world.

With Trammel Crow's money backing him, Portman rebuilt block after block of downtown Atlanta as a series of hollow hotels, convention centers, an "AmericasMart," and office cubicles, all connected via skywalks and air-conditioned atria. When he finished Peachtree Center in 1976, the result was a hermetically sealed "Center" central to nothing except its clones elsewhere. He had built the urban equivalent of a hub, profitable and infinitely repeatable anywhere. And with that, his LEGO-block approach became the reigning vernacular in Airworld's peculiar geography of nowhere.

Kasarda's Law and Marchetti's Constant

It wasn't supposed to be this way. Technology was going to ground us by linking and shrinking the world, and in doing so set us free. The world would flatten. Road warriors would beat their platinum medallions into plowshares. It hasn't happened.

For twenty years, we've heard how e-mail and videoconferencing—relabeled "telepresence"—would eliminate the need for cross-country meetings. AT&T once promised us we could attend them from the beach. "You Will," it assured us. We don't. More recently, Cisco has run ads depicting telepresence as a looking glass with China waving to us from the other side. It's a seductive vision, especially with travel budgets slashed and expense accounts frozen. But new technologies are part of the problem, not the solution.

There's a paradox at the heart of our enduring need to connect. Call it Kasarda's Law of Connectivity: every technology meant to circumvent distances electronically, starting with the telegraph—the original "nervous system of commerce"—will only stoke our desire to traverse it ourselves. The Internet is the ultimate example. If the first decade of its growth was fueled by e-commerce—which put more goods in the air than anyone could have imagined—then the second has been driven by the social networking of Web 2.0. Its flag bearer, Facebook, added 500 million friends in just five years—one-third of everyone on the Internet—who collectively spend twenty-three billion minutes a day on the site (that's about forty-four thousand years). When you add up the Wall posts, status updates, and news bulletins exchanged daily, the number of connections quickly spirals into the trillions. Only a few years ago these weak ties didn't exist, or at least you couldn't tug on them.

Facebook is the first (and possibly last) tool for keeping tabs on practically everyone you've ever met. As far as free-and-easy telepresence goes, it's unsurpassed. And yet our wanderlust has deepened. The number of air passengers worldwide has risen 83 percent during the Internet years, leveling off only briefly in the face of terror and again under the threat of global financial ruin. Since the invention of the Web, another billion people have taken to the skies each year. This isn't a coincidence, but a correlation. Technology is only a starting point for long-distance relationships; it piques our curiosity but doesn't satisfy it. It actually makes us more inclined to fly.

Kasarda's Law has a corollary: for every message we send—whether by phone or e-mail or some handheld fusion of the two—there's a chance it will lead us to meet face-to-face. Facebook friends drop in and become real ones; stray tweets on Twitter breed followers, contacts, and business trips. Ergo, trillions of connections yield billions aloft. The more wired we are, the more we fly. Not less. At the current rate, the Internet will render business travel obsolete at about the same time it replaces paper.

While no one has calculated the precise odds, the highest doubtless belong to the road warriors. The Internet made it possible for us to do business anywhere, but you must still clinch the deal in person—and truth be told, you *want* to. "I've gotten a lot of work because I'm willing to take the last-minute ten-hour trip," says Peter Shankman, a serial entrepreneur and social networking evangelist. He's maxed out on Facebook friends and has eighty-eight thousand followers on Twitter (and count-ing). He could stay home and start a cult if he wanted, but "I'm willing to go because you asked me; it separates the men from the boys." He ex-pects to crack four hundred thousand miles aloft this year upholding a code best expressed by one of John Kasarda's old professors at Cornell: "Never consummate a deal until you can look them in the eye. Only then will you know if you're doing the right thing."

No one knows Kasarda's Law better than the technology executives themselves; in the irony of ironies, they're some of the most itinerant com-muters of all. His studies have shown high-tech workers flying 400 per-cent more often than civilians, especially between industry hotbeds like Silicon Valley, Austin, Boston, and Raleigh-Durham. American Airlines started running "Nerd Birds" in the early nineties after Cypress Semi-conductor's founder, T. J. Rodgers, complained about connecting through DFW week after week. He led the Valley's lobby for nonstop flights be-tween San Jose and Austin. Reluctantly, the airline gave him one. When it sold out, it quickly gave him another. Before long, his competitors at Advanced Micro Devices (Intel's closest competitor) were logging twenty thousand trips a year on the route. In one poll of passengers, a third con-fessed to being "nerds"; another third conceded they might be nerds in denial.

Airlines didn't hesitate to launch others to New York, Seattle, and Dulles. Considering how much time they spend aloft, you'd think nerds would be amenable to relocating around a hub. And they are. Studies by the transportation analysts Kenneth Button and Roger Stough found that the presence of a hub in fifty-six American cities increased their high-tech workforce by an average of twelve thousand employees. All things being equal, their connectivity added the equivalent of an extra Yahoo! or eBay or AMD to the local talent pool. Some hubs are bigger than others, like Dallas, which has a nerd surplus closer to twenty thousand, equal to an extra Google or Amazon dropped on top of what was here before DFW opened, namely, Texas Instruments, the inventor of the silicon tran-sistors that later gave the Valley its name.

Why do nerds fly so much? Because they toil in perpetually nascent industries. By definition, high tech implies the bleeding edge, where fleeting breakthroughs appear and then vanish into obsolescence along with their creators. Even nerds can't keep track of it all over e-mail. Innovation depends on collaboration; high tech relies on a high degree of touch and face-to-face consultation. At the same time, fierce competition demands they go global to chase the best talent, the best price, or both. The tools that have made worldwide operations feasible have also made it necessary to jump on a plane to manage them.

I bumped into one such executive in New Songdo, the aerotropolis rising from the Yellow Sea off the coast of Korea. Wim Elfrink is Cisco's chief globalization officer, charged with unearthing new markets and new customers from his campus in Bangalore. The Dutchman conducts most of his meetings at home via his company's own telepresence screens. One of his maxims is "Don't commute to compute." And yet there he was on the outskirts of Seoul, in town to meet and greet for a week. What happened to telepresence killing the business trip?

"The volume of travel won't decrease," he conceded cheerfully, "but it will become more efficient. My weekly meetings to go over numbers and projects are conducted via telepresence—why should I fly my folks in for that? But if we're having a strategy meeting, we have to have dinner, go for walks, take breaks, and be creative. People say that telepresence is killing travel, but it's not killing it. It adds and it replaces."

The software business is just one example of what the urban planner Melvin Webber called "community without propinquity," or one without a sense of place. In a series of papers published in the early 1960s, during the first flush of the Jet Age, he made a case for rethinking the definition of "community." Teaching at Berkeley at the time, he had seen firsthand how freeways, long-distance phone calls, and flights underwritten by "gratuitous expense accounts" had undermined the density and historical raison d'être of cities, paving the way for sprawl. This was a *good* thing, he argued.

Mobility gave us choices, including the chance to decide our communities for ourselves—a choice that may have little or nothing to do with geography. These communities without propinquity are formed by professional, familial, and recreational ties, bound by avocation instead of location. Webber's reference point was jet-setting academics like himself, who even then were ricocheting across the country from one conference to the next. Today, the obvious examples are omnipresent ones like Facebook.

He was one of the first to realize that telecommunications and the jet had expanded the scope of communities worldwide. People could scatter, float, and re-form as necessary simply by hopping on a flight. He discovered flyover country:

> When people can interact with others across great distances and when they can readily move themselves into face-to-face positions as the need to do so arises, it scarcely matters whether a greenbelt intervenes or whether the space between them and their associates is used for houses and factories. Surely Los Angeles is an integral part of the national urban system, despite its 2,500-mile-wide greenbelt that separates it from New York . . . Surely the researchers in Los Alamos are as much a part of the world-wide community of atomic physicists as if they happened to be at Brookhaven or Berkeley or Argonne.

In fact, theirs was the same fraternity that invented the World Wide Web a few decades later. By then accustomed to working closely from wherever they happened to be, they could no longer bear to wait until conferences to share data and discoveries. They built one of the first online communities atop their widely scattered one.

Webber's point about such communities is that they are more vivid, more intense—more authentically *who we are*—than the ones composed of neighbors we've never met. In this sense, wholesalers, mall developers, Vegas visitors, and nerds all compose their own communities too, and it wasn't until the jet brought them together that they could function as one.

In light of this, Webber wanted to throw out the old models of urban planning and start over. A city's space-time continuum was relative, he asserted, but planners acted as if it were absolute. He meant to correct them with his notion of the "elastic mile," a more pliable way of thinking about space. Where you are matters less than how far you move; location is trumped by access, as the latter expands the scope and opportunities of daily life. The first step to addressing inequality, therefore, was increasing mobility, preferably in the form of cars and wide-open freeways. Sprawl was a sign of progress.

At least he was right about the elastic mile. His theory was buttressed several decades later by the Italian physicist Cesare Marchetti, who offered a one-hour rule of human movement. When walking was our only option, a person could cover three miles per hour on foot. This, he noted excitedly, was *precisely* the diameter of cities in antiquity—they were just wide enough to walk from the edge to the center and back in an hour's time. Drawing on the empirical work of the economist Yakov Zahavi, he demonstrated that this pattern is fixed in history. The time we spend commuting has never changed, only our modes of transportation have. The Berlin of 1800 was a compact, walkable city. But as horse trams came along, followed by electric trams, then subways, and finally cars, the city's periphery raced away from its Enlightenment-era core. Berlin's diameter was effectively ten times wider in 1950 than it was 150 years earlier, yet it still took only an hour to traverse. The rule has since been dubbed Marchetti's Constant.

Marchetti contended that transportation, not communications, was the "unifying principle of the world." Ratifying Kasarda's Law, he attested that the "so-called explosion in communication during the last 20 years did not dent transportation expansion; on the other hand, they tend to move together." In France, for example, the volume of messages sent and miles traveled annually since the Napoleonic Wars have grown together in a tight correlation.

There appeared to be no upper limit on the size cities could attain if they obeyed his constant. Mexico City is a galactic megalopolis of fifty million people living at the density of Hadrian's Rome. As a thought experiment, Marchetti imagined a maglev Shinkansen train connecting Tokyo and Osaka in under an hour each way, comparable to a New Yorker's typical commute. Functionally speaking, it would create a single city of one hundred million people. (Greater Tokyo is halfway there already.) Applying this principle hyperbolically to Europe: "Operating a Maglev between Casablanca and Paris . . . would cover the distance in about 20 minutes. In other words a woman in Casablanca could go to work in Paris, and cook dinner for her children in the evening . . . Incidentally, businessmen who can afford the extraordinary cost of air travel in Europe do exactly that. They take the plane because it permits them to come back at night to sleep in their beloved cave, with family, cultural, and status symbols in place."

The "extraordinary costs" of air travel fell nearly to zero a year later, when easyJet launched in 1995 to tangle with the Irish upstart Ryanair.

It wasn't long before flights across the Continent cost as little as a penny or a pound (plus taxes), once they were joined by a fleet of copycats flying under the colors of Baboo and Wizz Air. Free to move about a landmass only a few hours wide, a hundred million passengers take advantage every year. They treat Ryanair and its rivals as buses, and strange migrations have emerged. Roving bands of Danes pack the stands of soccer matches in England, Estonia is the stag party capital of Britain, and Polish surgeons commute weekly on nonstops between Wroclaw and Nottingham. "It takes about three hours, and I'm eating lunch at my house," one doctor said. A group called the Future Forum predicted there will be 1.5 million people working in the U.K. but living overseas by 2016, commuting daily or weekly between London and Barcelona, Marrakech, Dubrovnik, Verona, Palma, Pula, and Valencia.

Dallas residents know the drill. Started here in 1973, Southwest Airlines was the template for Ryanair and every low-fare carrier since. The combination of deregulation, cheap tickets, and gratuitous expense accounts has brought air travel well within range of Marchetti's Constant, hence consultant expresses and Jim Tam's perambulating across Texas.

Consider Angela Kim, who commutes from Houston to Dallas every Tuesday to babysit her grandson for a few days while her daughter the physician pulls back-to-back shifts for her residency. Occasionally she lands, scoops him up at the curb, and boards the next 250-mile, fifty-five-minute flight back to Dallas. A Johns Hopkins sociologist asked to make sense of this arrangement didn't bat an eye. "In low-income families, it may be the grandmother down the street who helps out," he said. "In high-income families, it is the grandmother in a neighboring city who helps out."

Kim's commute has made all the difference for her family. Her daughter was ready to quit medicine rather than put her son into day care, and she wasn't about to uproot herself for a permanent move to Dallas. It turns out buying tickets in bulk is more cost-effective than either.

The mobility offered by aerial commuting may be one reason why, in terms of changing cities and homes, we are a society increasingly staying put. The sociologist Claude Fischer has shown that, relos aside, and despite the demographic tilt from the Rust Belt to the Sun Belt and the fallout from the housing bust, Americans are less itinerant than they were half a century ago—before the Internet, the Jet Age, and interstate highways. Home ownership hasn't been a factor, and neither has age, race, or (with the exception of the lowest) class. The reasons "must be deep and pervasive," Fischer wrote, namely, "increasing longevity, greater affluence and security, and the widening range of daily mobility."

It's impossible, of course, to commute to Houston and points beyond from anywhere in the Metroplex. Try it from Allen or Frisco and you'll spend more time on the ground than in the air, fuming at traffic in one of the most congested cities in America. What's the point of cruising between cities at five hundred knots per hour if you're at a standstill once you're there? It's no accident that Jim Tam and his carry-on-carrying neighbors live next door to the airport in Southlake. Measured in the time saved each week or each morning, it is clearly worth more to them to live near DFW than somewhere else. As for how much more, it depends.

Maybe the best estimation is derived from Kasarda's formula calculating a hub's worth to its surrounding city. It's not an exact science. A simple version might read *size × air connectivity × local accessibility,* and the result can be measured in all kinds of ways, all of them having to do with money. It might be reflected in property values around the hub, or in rents and occupancy rates for office and warehouse space. It can even be seen in the average household incomes of local residents—$172,945 in Southlake, compared to $105,000 in Virginia's Loudon and Fairfax counties, which share Dulles.

The aerotropolis represents what Kasarda describes as a new economic geography, which takes the relationship of location and connectivity into account and prices their true worth accordingly. He didn't have a chance to apply his theorem to DFW; someone beat him to it.

The Aerotropolis on the Hills

A few of the glittering towers featured in the opening credits of *Dallas* are found not downtown but on DFW's eastern flank, opposite Southlake and Euless. They occupy the remnants of El Ranchito de las Colinas, the Little Ranch of the Hills. Its onetime owner John W. Carpenter made TV oilman J. R. Ewing look like a small-time conniver, and his roots made Trammel Crow feel like an arriviste.

Carpenter left his family's farm at age nineteen to provide for his widowed mother and sisters, and by middle age he owned the state's largest insurance firm. The ranch started as his weekend retreat, but he aggressively added acreage to keep sprawl in check for some higher purpose. On his death in 1959, he bequeathed his station and twelve thousand acres to his son. DFW was chosen to be his neighbor less than a decade later, following a lifetime of lobbying for it.

As his father's understudy, it fell to Ben Carpenter to implement their dream of a wholly owned and operated city carved from the mesquite-shrouded hills. In 1973, Carpenter unveiled his master plan for Las Colinas after five years of research. It was the largest urban development in the country. Before a single plot of land was sold, he ordered the dredging of lakes and canals, stocked them with gondolas, and ran a monorail overhead. His aesthetic was the Old World meets World's Fair, with an ersatz campanile offsetting the on-spec office spires. For years, passengers driving to and from the airport along State Highway 114—the John W. Carpenter Freeway—passed through a Hieronymous Bosch landscape of leveling, paving, burrowing, and planting.

Carpenter sank a billion dollars into building the Emerald City of company towns. Not a blade of grass is out of place on either the unnaturally verdant lawns or the Four Seasons putting greens, which Tiger Woods stalks each spring. The neighborhoods studded with million-dollar manses have gates within gates within gates. "It's not what you see; it's what you don't see" was how Carpenter deduced its appeal. What you don't see is any trash, signage, or signs of life. Las Colinas is ruled by draconian covenants enforcing his tastes. "It is Disney World for the affluent," *Texas Monthly* reported. "In fact, when executives from Disney World visited the development a few years ago, one of them commented that it was a shame ol' Walt couldn't have lived to see the real thing."

The quality Carpenter prized above all else was control. He lost it in the eighties real estate crash, costing him everything. Control passed to his corporate tenants, who preferred it that way. Las Colinas is the city you get when it's designed by CEOs. Two thousand companies now call it home, as do thirty-five thousand of their employees. (Their numbers triple during business hours.) The hillsides bristle with logos of the usual suspects—Microsoft, Nokia, Verizon, and AT&T. The BlackBerry maker Research in Motion has its American headquarters here, as does the Japanese computing giant NEC.

The most forbidding resident is ExxonMobil—the most profitable company in the history of the world. The slate pagoda of its worldwide headquarters barely peeks above the trees; the rest is hidden behind an electric fence. Inquiries as to what goes on within yielded only a brief, abruptly terminated phone call with its real estate manager, Randy Raudabaugh. There's no one here, he confided, except the CEO and his closest lieutenants, who are holed up in an executive wing nicknamed the "God Pod." Drilling is run from Houston and refining from Fairfax, Virginia. The dirty work of siphoning four million barrels of crude daily is scattered across deserts and deep-water derricks. Survival in the oil business entails taking the long view of boom-and-bust cycles while delegating the day to day. The CEO's only here so he can fly anywhere as needed, Raudabaugh explained, and so he can summon subordinates on a whim.

It's a similar story at Fluor's campus up the street. The engineering firm best known for laying the Trans-Alaskan pipeline moved its top two hundred executives to Dallas after a century in California. The reason: to scoot a little closer to their clients in Washington. They considered Dulles, but settled for Dallas—you can day-trip to both coasts from here. The head of Fluor's Government Group spends 80 percent of his time on the road (in Russia, lately). His colleagues average between fifty and a hundred flights a year on their own.

Las Colinas started slow. Timed to the airport instead of the market, it debuted amid an oil embargo and stagflation. Three years passed before anyone broke ground. Carpenter's investors demanded answers: Who in their right mind would move their headquarters next to an *airport*? Nobody had heard of such a thing in 1973. His advisers urged him to build warehouses instead. (Trammel Crow was waiting in the wings.) But he was adamant that Las Colinas become the white-collar capital of the Metroplex. If he built it, they would come—not in spite of DFW, but because of it. He was right, of course. Modern Las Colinas and the freeways running along its edges possess more office space, higher rents, and a higher residential density than downtown Dallas *and* Ft. Worth. It's the largest business district from here to Chicago.

Carpenter intuitively understood Kasarda's Law, and so do his disciples at the local Chamber of Commerce. "We sell three things," its executive director told me, "location, accessibility, and speed." As sterile as it sounds, Las Colinas is proof of this new economic geography. Fluor's peripatetic executives turn out to be the exception, not the rule. The majority of inhabitants shuttle only between their cubicles and home. What's changed is the premium tenants pay for the *potential* connectivity of the airport. It's ten minutes away if they need it, and often they do—more and more, in fact. For this reason, airports and their aerotropoli are supplanting downtowns and competing edge cities as the nexus of white-collar work throughout the world.

A case in point: according to Kasarda's research, one in six Americans works within a short driving distance of the twenty-five busiest hubs. DFW has four hundred thousand jobs lying within a five-mile radius of its terminals, O'Hare has half a million, and Dulles two hundred thousand. None are near traditional downtowns. DFW lies twelve miles distant from Dallas proper; O'Hare sits seventeen miles from the Loop; Dulles is twenty miles west of the District. Draw a five-mile-radius circle around each airport and another around downtown—or around each in Philadelphia, Charlotte, or San Francisco—and you'll find that these budding aerotropoli are three-quarters the size of the old cores already. At ten miles out, they're almost identical. And the aerotropoli are growing much, much faster. The upshot, Kasarda notes, "is that distant travelers and locals alike can now shop, meet, exchange knowledge, conduct business, eat, sleep, and be entertained without going more than fifteen minutes from the airport."

Crunching U.S. Census data from 2002, Kasarda discovered that aerotropoli were adding jobs in their nuclei at seven times the pace of America's downtowns, and one and a half times faster on the fringes. These jobs are the white-collar kind you're more likely to find in Las Colinas than in the big-box badlands south of Memphis. Twenty-five aerotropoli are home to a fifth of all IT, finance, insurance, consulting, management, scientific, and technical work nationwide, as broadly defined by the census. Amid the galaxies of edge cities appearing on the urban periphery in the last thirty years, aerotropoli are the closest thing we have to a burgeoning center.

Even before the hubs, the airlines picked winners and losers among American cities. Examining route networks from 1950 to 1980—from the dawn of aerial mass transit to the end of regulation—Kasarda found they had led the way from the Rust Belt to the Sun Belt. They enabled the rise of Dallas and Los Angeles by shifting routes at Detroit's and

Cleveland's expense. Adding flights added jobs to the Sun Belt, especially the types easily able to just pick up and move—the white-collar functions abandoning Manhattan blocks for bucolic parks like Las Colinas. His research shows that a metropolitan area's position in the airline network determined its employment growth and not, as commonly supposed, the other way around.

After deregulation changed the rules, Kasarda suggested that international routes would become the new catalyst for jobs and investments. His hypothesis has since been confirmed by others' research. A recent study of international routes converging on LAX concluded that each flight to Europe or across the Pacific created 3,126 jobs paying $156 million in wages, with ripple effects of $623 million. Another study of flights between the United States and Japan revealed that Japanese firms were more likely to set up shop in American cities served by their native carriers. Why? Because it meant they were more plugged in to opportunities arising in Chicago or Los Angeles than in Houston. The money followed the flights.

Transportation analyst Kenneth Button confirmed as much in another study published during the dot-com bubble. Analyzing the catalytic effects of European flights from forty-one American cities, he discovered that simply increasing the number of flights to the Continent from three to four daily would create almost three thousand "new economy" jobs. (Picture the khaki-clad visionaries behind Pets.com.) Overall, he calculated that every thousand passengers crossing the Atlantic created somewhere between forty-four and seventy-three new jobs around the hubs.

A similar formula applies to all air traffic. When the economist Jan Brueckner ran the numbers for ninety-one airports from Albuquerque to Wichita, he found that a 10 percent increase in passengers led to a 1 percent bump in employment. For a hub on the order of O'Hare and a city the size of Chicago, the impact could be massive. Supposing a 50 percent jump in passengers following its current expansion (a decidedly optimistic assumption), the corresponding 5 percent rise in employment would yield about 185,000 jobs—more than the population of Little Rock or Salt Lake City. Working backward, he estimated that O'Hare creates twenty-two jobs for every thousand passengers it adds, and it doesn't matter whether they're going to Toledo or Tokyo. Interestingly, all appear to be the white- or pink-collar kind. They range from CEOs and insurance salesmen to real estate agents and teenagers manning fast-food counters.

What sets Las Colinas apart from Chicago and every other city in America is that its boosters won't settle for anything less than luring a headquarters here. They woo executives at the apex of the org chart, the ones whose time is worth whatever the stock price closes at that day. The hub is at the heart of their pitch. This is "where your airline gate is just as close as your front gate," and where three-hour flights to anyplace in the lower forty-eight states trump Plano commutes. Las Colinas is all about "convenience," defined as such in its brochures: "Fast response: There's no substitute for it. The company that gets its products and people where they need to be first is the winner. Strong relationships: You've got to have them. And they can't be forged through email. They demand a sincere smile, a hearty handshake and a personal promise. In other words, you need to go where your customers are, to be there in person and on time. And that's a big advantage of being based in Las Colinas."

Fluor thought so; it was the last *Fortune* 500 headliner to land here. All of Las Colinas's other advantages can be copied—"business-friendly" tax codes, country clubs, bottomless incentives—but no one in America will build another hub like DFW in our lifetimes. "We can recruit them, but we can just as easily lose them," lamented Leanne Weymouth, its top saleswoman. "Without the airport, we might as well just pack up and go home."

Companies Without Propinquity

Las Colinas just might lose them to the airport itself, because we're not about to slow down. Don't be fooled by the recession's pause—if anything, we're still picking up speed, propelled by the hubs' centrifugal force and our tireless pursuit of a competitive edge. First, road warriors joined companies to customers and the home office to the field office. Then, more and more of us became junior road warriors too, as electronic correspondence goaded us to move. Sensing this shift, companies settled around hubs seeking economies of connectivity to match their economies of scale. The trend is to keep going, flinging ourselves ever farther into space, until we scatter completely, forming what Melvin Webber might have called *companies without propinquity*—maybe the next step in corporate evolution.

Corporations have struggled with how and where to best arrange themselves since Henry Ford built the world's biggest factory outside Detroit, then changed his mind and started taking it apart. In 1937, the economist Ronald Coase wrote "The Nature of the Firm," exploring just how big a vertically integrated one like Ford's might get. Not much bigger, he argued, because beyond a certain point, the drag of managing huge organizations over long distances would offset any advantages of scale. Size mattered, however, if advances in transportation, communication, and management techniques could shrink these distances and diminish the drag. This is exactly what happened.

Emboldened by the Jet Age, companies broke themselves into pieces and spread them around searching for comparative advantage. Given enough telephones, flights, and mainframes, they could put their headquarters in one place, their factories in another, their R & D labs in a third, their back-office file cabinets in a fourth, and their call centers in a fifth. Once they added FedEx to the equation and swapped out their mainframes for PCs, factories left for Mexico (then China), call centers for India, and R & D for Beijing. The puzzle keeps rearranging itself, and the pieces keep moving farther away. The next thing to go is the notion of having a headquarters, and the idea that a global enterprise can and should be run by one person from one place.

In this regard, Lenovo is ahead of the game. Its purchase of IBM's entire PC business six years ago produced the world's third-largest computer company, along with the strangest management structure anyone had ever seen. The chairman left China for Raleigh, North Carolina, while the American CEO split his time between Singapore and Beijing. "Lenovo has forgone the notion of a corporate headquarters, so essentially I am flying around the world most of the time," former CEO Bill Amelio explained.

Neither a Chinese nor an American company, Lenovo is managed by tag teams of executives dispersed throughout the world. No one has ever tried to run a $16 billion company on Skype calls, e-mail, and the occasional Paris rendezvous until now. The company calls this "worldsourcing." "It's about leveraging the best people, processes, and costs, no matter where they're located," says Gerry Smith, the American running its global supply chain from Singapore. "I have staff in Shenzhen, Raleigh, Baddi [India], and Brazil. I'm a lonely figure in Singapore. I'm here because I have the best airport in the world; we don't need a brick-and-mortar headquarters to make decisions."

Neither does anyone else. Consultancies like McKinsey and Accenture have long since jettisoned theirs, and scores of multinationals act like they already have. For example, SAP is the largest software company no one's ever heard of (it's number 2 after Microsoft). Its business is running your business, automating the daily grind of fulfillment, billing, and payroll. Theoretically, it should know a lot about locating one. Headquarters is in Walldorf, Germany, a small town forty minutes' drive from Lufthansa's hub in Frankfurt. SAP America lies outside Philadelphia—an impossible choice until the start of nonstop flights between the two in 2003. Global marketing is in New York, and SAP Labs are in Palo Alto, Israel, Shanghai, and Bangalore, to name a few.

Then there are the outliers like Scott Lutz, who runs global marketing for small and midsize businesses as a one-man show from Denver. He was already there when SAP poached him, and he simply refused to leave. "I'm looking out my window at Pikes Peak right now," he told me on the phone. "I'm an hour and a half from the best skiing on the planet, and my four-thousand-square-foot house cost me $80 per square foot. So which part of that would I want to give up? I'm literally twenty-eight minutes from Denver International and can be anywhere in the world in twenty-fours hours. Even if I moved to Frankfurt or Paris, I would still spend all of my time on a plane."

When the recession hit, SAP's accountants pulled back on the reins. Internal meetings were canceled and travel budgets slashed; training sessions and team briefings were all moved onto the Web. "This is an industry in flux right now," Lutz said. "It's been a license to print money for thirty-five years, a real embarrassment of riches. If you can afford to invest in face-to-face meetings and travel, then by all means do it. There's no way to avoid human contact, especially when you're in a bleeding-edge industry—you can't even explain this stuff on the phone. Having said that, the software industry is going through a major restructuring. It's becoming commoditized. And although we still concentrate in Walldorf, Paris, and Palo Alto, at some point even those locations are going to start affecting the bottom line. All of the software companies have major, major physical plants around the world. And I think those are going to start going away," Las Colinas included.

He suspects the entire industry will effervesce into a cloud of software, reconnecting in person by air only when necessary. This is consistent with Kasarda's Law, which predicts that Lutz and his colleagues will end up aloft more than ever. If Skype, Twitter, netbooks, and smart phones erode the need for daily physical contact, then air travel will pick up the slack, bringing together the ad hoc teams tasked with catching lightning in a bottle. The upstarts nipping at their heels do so already.

The original companies without propinquity were start-ups, because the economics made too much sense. Bandwidth is cheap and getting cheaper, and talent is bountiful, if you know where and how far to look. In light of this, plane tickets can be a smarter investment than an office lease. One of SAP's fledgling competitors is Ultimus, located in the Research Triangle Park near Raleigh. When it came time to hire a new CEO, the company found one in Boston, although he wasn't willing to move. Like Lutz, he didn't need to.

Ultimus isn't a virtual company—it has eleven offices staffed by some 240 employees—and Richard Davis isn't an aerial commuter. He runs the company from the road, cycling through company outposts in Germany, Pakistan, and Taiwan between meetings. His living in Boston is best for all involved, he explained, because its airport has more overseas flights than Raleigh-Durham's. It's why his CFO also lives nearby. Only three of his ten direct reports work from headquarters. Davis spent his first month on the job in North Carolina, but "after that, I only needed to be here six to eight days a month," he said. "The rest of the time, I'm traveling."

In that case, he might as well move his office into the terminals—not that it hasn't been tried. Sage Software is another of SAP's adversaries, the billion-dollar outcome of Scott Lutz's bleak vision of the industry: a crazy quilt made from dozens of scattered acquisitions during a decade-long spree. Most had little to do with each other and many still don't, making Sage one of the purest examples of a company without propinquity. Once a month, its eight-member executive team would fly from wherever they were—Tampa, Irvine, Atlanta, Vancouver—to DFW, where they would check into the Grand Hyatt for two days. Pressed to explain this arrangement, former CEO Ron Verni replied, "Business is no longer about location, it's about talent. If you want the right people, you have to be flexible." Headquarters, when he needed one, was an airport hotel.

Most companies would prefer something a little more concrete, and DFW has plenty of room. As big as Las Colinas is, the airport dwarfs it—it is bigger than Manhattan. Very little of its eighteen thousand acres has been paved over for runways; much of it is still covered by noise-buffering woods. If the *Fortune* 500 are willing to settle just over the fence, then why shouldn't the airport invite them inside?

The answer will determine whether the hub deserves a say in its own aerotropolis. Having enriched the surrounding region, is it entitled to build on its own success? As the airport's CEO, Jeff Fegan, phrased it, "It's a public-policy concern. Should an airport be allowed to pursue tenants who could exist outside it?" In other words, is it in the aviation business, the real estate business, or the urban planning business? The answer is all three.

Ben Carpenter and Trammel Crow weren't alone in grasping the implications of DFW. The announcement of its location in 1965 touched off a frenzy of speculation in the pastureland of Southlake, Euless, Grapevine, Irving, and half a dozen other farm towns. Today these communities have a population of a million. The remaining acreage at Las Colinas has been sold; the Metroplex has run out of room. The last place to build is within DFW itself. The airport is planning its own strip malls, big-box stores, and convention hotels to pair with a miniature Las Colinas tucked against the fairways of its twin golf courses.

Fearing this day would come, the communities surrounding DFW sued twenty years ago to stop its expansion, refusing to let it build on what was technically their land. Euless, Grapevine, Coppell, and Irving took their case to the Supreme Court, and lost. These days, DFW gives each a cut from whatever happens to land on their property. Euless receives the rental car fees, for example. Fegan believes they should be thankful for what they've got: "These are all dollars they get for no investment." Or maybe they pay in different ways.

The residents of Euless will learn the price when the University of North Texas finishes its five-year study of the benzene collecting in their blood. Joe Hennig, their retired city manager, mentioned it offhandedly while we were chatting in his office. A highly toxic carcinogen, "benzene's found in all sorts of things," he drawled, "from Styrofoam cups to toothpaste, soft drinks, cigarettes . . . and jet fuel. Kerosene." He chuckled wryly, joined by Ilaiasi Ofa, seated next to him.

The *Voice of Tonga* told me what happened after they left their islands and landed here to haul luggage and Cryovac in-flight meals. It was the classic immigrant's story, with the twist being they could go back to the old country anytime they pleased: they had scrimped and saved, working menial jobs and manual labor for the free flights and a pension. The second generation grew up flattening local quarterbacks on their way to college. When they returned home—*if* they returned, having grown up thoroughly American—they were more likely to work in the cubicles of Las Colinas than on the ramp with their parents. Now, when they fly, it's to see family and friends in Salt Lake City and Los Angeles. Or for work. Free seats to Tonga are getting harder to come by.

A few years ago, not long after the Tongan players began to lead their teammates at Euless Trinity in the *haka* before games, Ofa screened one such performance for his elders. They were transfixed by the white players in the front row, dancing alongside their kinsmen's children. They told him afterward, with tears in their eyes, "After seeing that, we know that our future generations will be accepted here."

That much is obvious seeing Ofa and Hennig sit side by side, the jowly Texan and the Polynesian, leaders of communities thrown together by the airport. "I cannot imagine a day when I'm not living close to one," Hennig said at one point. "I can sit on my back patio and watch the planes take off, and there is some noise, sure. But when I'm ready to go, I can get up from my chair and be there in ten minutes. And when I get back, in ten minutes, I'm home."

4

WELCOME HOME
TO THE AIRPORT

Denver's Stapleton Airport strangled on its own success. Our protests to the contrary, it's happening again—new arrivals want to live in the airport's shadow. What kind of fix do we need to accommodate both?

Stapleton: Strangling on Success

When Brian Tellinghuisen was ten years old, his family moved into a tan brick house across the street from Stapleton International Airport. The house sat perpendicular to a runway barely a quarter of a mile away, separated by a patch of dry grass. Beginning around six every evening, they could watch from their windows as a starting line of 727s and DC-8s took their marks, set, and started their departure rolls. The full-throated screams of their engines were enough to rattle every pane of glass in the house, shattering Brian's concentration while he watched *Star Trek*. This would go on for hours, takeoff after takeoff, until curfew descended. By then, he would have given up on TV to lie in fields beneath the flight paths, waving at descending jets with his brothers and sisters. Sometimes passengers would wave back. Sure, it was noisy, but forty years later he could honestly say, "It didn't bother us. It was our backyard. It was a different kind of childhood. I was a kid and I loved it."

And in this he was alone. By 1984, fifteen years after the Tellinghuisens had moved in next door, Stapleton was one of the busiest airports in the country—home to hubs for three airlines—and also one of the noisiest. Stapleton fit the old airport model to a T: a municipal field, opened in 1929 on the edge of the city with more land than it knew what to do with (at the time, at least) and no clue as to its destiny. As with

LAX, its story is one of nearly continuous piecemeal expansion until it was straitjacketed by its footprint. Each improvement made things worse by tapping ever-deeper reservoirs of latent demand.

It's no coincidence the suburban fringe of Denver underwent its own transformation during the same period. Aurora, the township adjacent to the airport on the city's eastern flank, was one of America's fastest-growing municipalities at Stapleton's peak. Its population doubled in the preceding decade, and would do so again by the millennium, booming from 75,000 to 276,000 in thirty years. (Denver proper grew 8 percent in that span.) Aurora was suburban sprawl par excellence, a prefab land-scape of culs-de-sac and tract houses built with less sense than the prairie dog towns they displaced. The airport was soon hemmed in by suburbia on three sides and by neighbors who resented the jumbo jets careening overhead. On the fourth side was a chemical weapons plant turned Su-perfund site, the Rocky Mountain Arsenal.

And Stapleton, naturally, needed desperately to expand. The triple whammy of a stuffed-to-capacity hub, narrowly spaced runways, and mountain weather meant delays early and often, gumming up airspace and connections nationwide. It was a joke—literally a bit in the late-night asides of Johnny Carson—that if you had to change planes in At-lanta to get to heaven, then purgatory was Stapleton.

Brian Tellinghuisen's neighbors felt the same. While his mother made her peace with the noise, they filed lawsuits. Then the neighboring county threatened to do the same to keep Stapleton's runways from encroaching on the arsenal's toxic turf. With the airport beset on all sides—by congestion, sprawl, lawyers, and ridicule—Denver's mayor and the state legislature hammered out a deal in 1985 to do what Los Ange-les or Chicago never had the guts to: clear the slate and start over.

Stapleton had strangled on its own success. The answer was obvious: close the airport and build a new one bigger and beyond the urban fringe, as cities have always done. In Denver, this formula produced the airport to end all airports—in America, at least. Stapleton's replacement, the tented Denver International Airport (DIA), was the United States' first greenfield hub in twenty years when it opened in 1995 and will likely be the last. It is perched on the high plains twenty-five miles northeast of downtown, a good twenty miles past Stapleton and seven times larger. With fifty square miles of land banked for future runways, terminals, and anything else it needs, DIA can float serenely behind its fences forever. Even if, in some perverse twist, the city spent another half century unfurling itself to its doorstep—and who would move a dozen miles past city limits just to butt heads again with an airport?—it could never draw close enough to choke it.

DIA and Stapleton prove the lie that no one in his right mind would move next door to an airport. The Tellinghuisens did exactly that; families did it at Stapleton for more than thirty years. They do it at DIA now. No one could have conceived of a better experiment than shuttering the old airport and opening a new one in the middle of nowhere. Would families flock there too, or stay away, as they swore up and down they would? They flocked, creating a new quarter of the city where there had been only dirt.

But the challenge—in America, at least—isn't where to put new airports but how to clean up the messes surrounding the ones we have. How do we undo the metastatic sprawl consuming Memphis, or create neighborhoods more organic than Las Colinas? This only raises more questions that have yet to be satisfactorily answered in a foreclosed America: Where should we live? In cities? In suburbs? Not "spurbs," the exurban bubbles abandoned during the bust—some believe they're destined to become slums. In fact, there are signs the decades-long outflow from cities to suburbs may be beginning to reverse, or at least subside. What if, by choice or necessity, the tide begins rolling back into cities? America's population has doubled since people began leaving in the 1950s; there aren't enough *Sesame Street*–ready brownstones to house them all. We'll have to choose which pieces of cities to redevelop, and if John Kasarda's theories are correct, then the badlands around our airports may be the best place to start. Improbably, Stapleton's new incarnation as the largest "New Urbanist" community in America hints at a solution.

Denver isn't a mountain town so much as a railroad one, resting at the foot of the Rockies where the pioneers ran out of plains. It was a mining town too, a terminus where gold and silver riches collected before heading east by train. It wasn't an obvious hub. When the Golden Spike linked the Transcontinental Railroad's tracks in 1869, they bypassed the city completely. The Union Pacific's president pronounced Denver "too dead to bury," but desperate boosters sprinted to build a new line connecting them, ensuring its place as capital of the Rockies.

This time around, the taxpayers were more skeptical. They greeted the new airport's aloofness with exasperation instead of relief. Once too close for comfort, it was now too far away. Noise complaints rose instead of fell as a new set of neighbors inveighed against the giant. But they couldn't sue DIA out of existence, seeing as they fell well outside the "noise contours" the FAA had sketched. Noise contours form the invisible sonic fence where the din of jet wash soars to deafening. They demarcate the outer limits where developers can build, and young families priced out of Aurora might drive until they qualify.

The airport's splendid isolation amid the buffalo grass—planned for half a century—lasted barely five years. In the spring of 2001, a local real estate scion named Cal Fulenwider, whose family owned much of the land on which DIA was built, announced plans to build Reunion, a three-thousand-acre, master-planned community home to some forty thousand residents.

Since then, Reunion has been joined by more than a dozen exurbs-in-a-box in various stages of construction, foreclosure, or both. Denver's northeast quadrant, a former backwater—"the last part of town to do anything," as one developer put it—is now the fastest-growing quadrant of the city. Comprising pieces of Aurora, the suburbs, and the eastern tip of Denver (including the once and future Stapleton), the "Aeropolitan" (as local boosters once called it) has a population of around 350,000 at about the density of suburban New Jersey. It is expected to add jobs at twice the rate of metropolitan Denver, and add another two hundred thousand residents by 2030. By then its population should be nearing the size of Denver's itself. The passion play of Stapleton is being staged again with an expanded cast and twist ending—the airport doesn't die for our sins this time. It can be the good neighbor Stapleton never could.

The life cycle of Denver's airports—attraction, congestion, strangulation, death, rebirth, and attraction—follows this simple principle: "The airport leaves the city, the city follows the airport, the airport becomes a city." This has happened in Dulles and Dallas, and in Denver too—flouting the express wishes of all involved that the city honor its restraining order.

More remarkable than its messy breakup with the city is that Denver's aerotropolis is purely residential. There is no cargo hub or Las Colinas. The suburban growth around DIA isn't preordained by the city's development patterns. It didn't exist before the airport opened, and Denver's favored quarter, where its growth was historically clustered, is on the opposite side of town. DIA's suburban bloom flies in the face of developers' conventional wisdom, which brands airports as the ultimate LULUs, "locally undesirable land uses," on par with strip mines and prisons as places where you wouldn't like to raise a family. Building the largest one in the country there should have been the ultimate deterrent to growth, not its catalyst.

"It's going to take a long time, but the land will only become more valuable. The history of every airport in the United States will tell you this will happen," promised a developer who spent two years wrangling with the FAA for the right to build closer to the fence. "Are there really people who want to live close to an airport? Yeah, there are. That's been proven around the country too. They travel a lot on business, or whatever it is they do, but they're connected to the airport in some way, shape, or form. Somehow."

Clearly, cognitive dissonance is at work. We loudly decry the noise, pollution, and congestion of airports, and yet our fundamental quality-of-life decision—*where and how to live*—seems predicated on having one close at hand, even if we rarely fly. It helps that especially massive ones like DIA and DFW double as enormous publicly financed infrastructure investments galvanizing private developers—much like what I-70 and I-225 had done for Aurora in its 1970s and 1980s heyday. With the terminal and runways came eighteen miles of gas lines and sewer mains, more highways—including a slice of the city's new outer beltway—and even a trunk line of the $7 billion FasTracks light rail service that will run, among other places, directly from downtown to the airport.

But just because we truly, madly, deeply desire to be near one—no matter how much we protest otherwise, heliotropic growth patterns around any decently trafficked airport bear this out—there's no point trying to choke them with the same low-density sprawl choking our economy. DIA can withstand any wave of single-family faux Colonials headed its way, but its open range offers Denver a chance to build something better than the paved wastes of Aurora.

Every urban epoch has its own geography, a function of the state of the art in transportation at the time. The shape of cities is determined by how they're used and how we move around in them. Riverboats + cotton

trading = nineteenth-century Memphis. Just-in-time cargo + 777s = aerotropolis Memphis. The geographer David Harvey calls this the "spatial
fix" of each era, with "fix" having multiple meanings. For one, cities are
fixed in space and time—once they take shape they're difficult to alter,
as we've seen in the sprawl around Memphis. They also fix problems, like
moving bales of cotton down the Mississippi or a box across the country.

Each fix creates a landscape suited to its era. Suburbs were the spatial fix of the Industrial Age, when there were cars to be made and sold,
and workers wanted to put some distance between their families and the
factory. Edge cities like Las Colinas sprouted the moment work shifted
to the office, when most of us began trafficking in ideas and didn't mind
living closer to our workplace. Our Instant Age is the product of the Jet
Age and the Net Age, of global reach and always-on connectivity, of aggregation and dispersal. As Richard Florida and others have asserted, we
need both *velocity* and *density* in our daily lives, for the production and
transmission of ideas as well as goods. Postrecession, we need a new
spatial fix that is locally dense and globally connected.

Kasarda believes he holds the blueprints to a fix that is beautiful, efficient, and ultimately sustainable—a far cry from the hideous, haphaz-
ard, and polluted messes most cities have inherited. He has made it his
mission to imbue Airworld's geography of nowhere with a sense of place.
There is no better place to start building this New Urbanism than in
Denver, whose hub is the cleanest slate. What will these cities look like,
and where should we look for a model? The answer, I discovered, would
be Stapleton's redemption.

Would You Be Mine, Could You Be Mine, Won't You Be My Neighbor?

The deal struck to shutter Stapleton and erect its successor depended on
a decade of city, county, and state approvals, followed by voter referen-
dums, bond issues, cost overruns, and a voracious robotic baggage system craving Samsonites. Before any of this could come to pass, a more
basic question needed answering: Where to put it? A vague consensus
wasn't enough—land needed to be bought and condemned before serious planning could begin.

Six plans were under consideration, and five landed squarely on the holdings of L. C. Fulenwider, Denver's original land baron. His grandson Cal Fulenwider III tends to the remnants of his Box Elder Farms, which at one time totaled forty thousand acres, much of it purchased for a dollar an acre in the depths of the Depression. His specialty was irrigation, a skill that proved useful in growing both winter wheat and subdivisions. His descendants evolved from farmers into moguls, and his grandson blends the mannerisms of his forefathers' homespun bluntness with the ease and impatience of a man who's made too much money to suffer fools gladly.

The godfather of Denver's aerotropolis was busy building downtown condos when the airport pact was sealed. One belonged to a fellow developer named Robert O'Donnell, who was a fixture at the Urban Land Institute, a think tank for developers and their enablers. (Fifteen years later, John Kasarda would unveil the aerotropolis in the pages of its magazine, *Urban Land*.) An anxious Fulenwider asked O'Donnell to help him come to grips with the looming catastrophe (ten thousand of his acres would eventually be condemned) and the opportunity it presented. O'Donnell offered to assemble a blue-ribbon panel of experts under ULI's umbrella. Before the powers that be selected a plan already on the table, he promised, Fulenwider would scuttle them with his own alternative.

He spent the next two years picking the brains of every major airport, beltway, and megadevelopment expert, beginning with Las Colinas's Ben Carpenter, whose brainchild became an idée fixe for Fulenwider. There were meetings with Donald Bren, the multibillionaire who bought the Irvine Co. and single-handedly developed the half of Orange County around John Wayne. He also huddled with the Arvida Corporation, Disney's wholly owned designer of gated golf course communities. A decade later, it would have a hand in building the company's experimental prototype community of yesteryear, Celebration.

Fulenwider's job was to bring the squabbling local governments to the table, "which sounds like a monumental undertaking, but it was a piece of cake because no one knew where it was going, and no one wanted to be left out. They all said, 'Absolutely, we're on board,'" he told me one morning over coffee in an office overlooking what remains of Stapleton.

The plan he spent two years refining plopped the airport east of the arsenal (relabeled a "wildlife refuge" once cleanup began) with the E-470 tollway/beltway running between them, along the edge of his property. Fulenwider had cast himself as a local, less malevolent answer to John Huston's megalomaniacal tycoon in *Chinatown*, except rather than diverting reservoirs to turn his prairie green (or aquifers, as his grandfather had done), he would tap the airport. The possibilities entranced him. One example that stuck fast was the presence of Japanese companies in Atlanta pre– and post–airport expansion. Before Delta's hub opened in 1980, they occupied roughly half a million square feet of office space. Their presence expanded exponentially within a decade. "Just because of the airport," Fulenwider concluded. "Boom! That was the reason."

His dream wasn't to build a new San Fernando Valley à la William Mulholland, but his very own Las Colinas on the prairie. When he squints into the sun, he sees mosaics of parking lots, manicured lawns, and smoked-glass hexahedrons with bronze plaques in front. "We came up with a master plan for that twenty-seven square miles," he explained, referring to the developable land surrounding the airport property, "based on a .25 FAR, which stands for floor-to-area ratio. Basically, for every acre of ground, you'll develop twenty-five percent of it, whether it's residential, commercial, whatever. And the balance counts toward open space, roads, utilities, and so on. That's a pretty reasonable FAR, and [when] we took all the uses we had seen in Dallas and Atlanta and plugged them into our theoretical plan—based not only on the airport but also the beltway—we came up with two hundred seventy million square feet of land uses. That's just mind-boggling!"

It's enough, in fact, to absorb every square inch of office space in Chicagoland, and the result would be equally suburban—the Magnificent Mile diluted to strip mall consistency. A more modest plan left 90 percent of the land fallow and still produced ninety million square feet of usable ground, larger than Denver itself, counting only corporate occupants. When he finally presented his findings to the assembled stakeholders, "They didn't believe we were going to be able to build the airport or the highway," he said. "They really just laughed at us. They said, 'You know, those Texans have high aspirations, but you Coloradoans make the Texans pale in comparison.'"

He had the last laugh as to the airport's location, which landed right where he wanted it. "That was just sheer dumb luck," he said, his lobbying efforts having proved futile. Undeterred, he set about building Denver anew anyway. To clone Las Colinas, he needed tenants, and to lure those tenants, he needed a guaranteed supply of "executive housing," the multimillion-dollar estates where CEOs can envision themselves living. "If you're going to create this commercial mecca," Fulenwider said, "it will never succeed unless you have a state-of-the-art, master-planned community in close proximity. When *Fortune* 500 types visit DIA and take the CEO of Life around," i.e., Mrs. CEO, "the key decision maker is when she sees where she could live, because this is her way of life too. Don't kid yourself—if she doesn't like it, they ain't coming."

The urban anthropologist William H. Whyte made a similar point in 1988 by plotting a map depicting the final destinations of thirty-eight companies that moved out of New York "to better meet quality-of-life needs of their employees." Thirty-one moved to Connecticut, circling around Greenwich. On Whyte's map, black circles show where the CEO already lived when the move was planned; white circles show where the new headquarters was subsequently located. The average distance from the CEO's home was eight miles. The bull's-eye, Whyte reported, was "a circle about four miles in diameter, bounded on the east by the Burning Tree Country Club and on the west by the Fairfield Country Club." The deciding factor, he surmised, was "research" conducted by the CEO after a round of golf.

Fulenwider learned his lesson. The first piece in his twenty-year plan to create his own aerotropolis was a neighborhood where the CEO of Life could see herself living. In exchange for an easily kept promise not to julienne his holdings into matchstick-size lots, he was awarded an interchange on the beltway, the aerotropolis's automotive aorta. A short time later, he invited Arvida's chairman to tour his windswept territory. Accustomed to terraforming the Everglades into putting greens, "he said, 'The first thing you need to anchor yourself out there is a championship-caliber golf course,'" Cal recalled. "And I said, 'Well, that makes sense to me.'" Buffalo Run opened in 1997, a Pebble Beach hugging an ocean of wheat. With that, he had reached the limits of his expertise; it was time to find a bigger partner more experienced at wholesale city planning and construction. He didn't have to look very far.

Shea Homes landed in Denver that year with the acquisition of Highlands Ranch, a Reloville past the city's southern edge, spread across twenty-four square miles. It's one of the largest unincorporated communities in the United States with seventy-one thousand residents, ironic considering it was conceived, bought, and sold by a succession of corporations. Shea Homes is a division of J. F. Shea, the oldest and largest privately owned developer in the country, a builder of the Golden Gate Bridge and Hoover Dam. What Fulenwider liked was its privacy—it could ignore the vicissitudes of Wall Street and the inevitable bingeing and purging publicly traded builders suffer during a housing bust as bad as the current one. And Shea needed a second act in Denver.

In June 2001, the partners broke ground on Reunion, "a new hometown for the age-old pursuit of happiness," according to its logo—a nicked and weathered sign seemingly pried from the roadside of Route 66. Although its three thousand acres have provisions for hosting some future Microsoft campus, Reunion is unambiguously a suburb. The first residents arrived in 2002, just as mortgage rates began falling to historic lows, and just in time to qualify for new breeds of increasingly exotic and toxic loans.

It didn't take long before the achingly empty landscape was cluttered with signs, some more subtle than others. The plains surrounding Reunion were stripped bare, graded, and paved for plug-and-play subdivisions; in a few others, the hulls of future homes materialized. And if that wasn't clear enough, they spelled it out for you: "Wildhorse Ridge Sales Center; From the $140s" and "Oakwood Homes at Juniper Ridge; Up to 3,819 sq. ft. From the High $200s."

When Reunion was announced, it was an island of intention floating on a lake of open land between DIA, the arsenal, and an actual lake to the north. Since then, this loamy isle has become an archipelago and might someday be a continent of Colonials as pilot fish developers backfill the gaps. These are me-too suburbs with names like Potomac Farms, Fronterra Village, and Buffalo Mesa, the last one picking up where Reunion's sidewalks end. South by southeast of here is another cluster of development, centered on a project named High Point, next to another eight hundred acres owned and code-named Aurora 800 by Fulenwider. Perhaps that's where he'll end up building his Crystal City of the plains.

The entrance to Reunion trumps them all: red picket fences flanking the road and a weather-beaten sign cooing "Welcome Home to Reunion." The red of the fences (rather than an even more idyllic white) is meant to echo its centerpiece: an enormous red barn, set beside a man-made, eight-acre lake. Inside is the town's (if I may call it that) camouflaged recreation center, a compound of gyms, courts, swimming pools, and even a water slide.

Reunion woos visitors with nods to a rustic, bygone era no one here remembers (save for Cal, who drove tractors through here in his teens), but the locals thrill to it anyway. "The Big Idea," as stated succinctly in the brochures: "The name Reunion was chosen to represent a deep appreciation for the past, a sense of wonder about the future, and a commitment to living every present moment to the fullest. Over time, Reunion will connect people through lasting friendships and, in the process, create a place where each resident will pursue happiness in his or her own way. Which makes Reunion something entirely new, a community specifically created for the pursuit of happiness." Which turned out to be the problem.

The accompanying manifesto touts four precepts. The first and most important is the "New Suburbanism," a deliberate echo (and subversion) of the New Urbanism first practiced by the architects Andres Duany and Elizabeth Plater-Zyberk. They built cities you could walk in—neighborhoods with schools and shops, parks and offices, homes and apartments all mixed together and connected by leafy streets and boulevards instead of access roads and parking lots. Doing this in a prefab, spec-built, single-use zoning universe required writing their own manual, SmartCode, containing not only guidelines for densities but also prescriptions for everything from street widths to rooflines, porches, stoop heights, and even the style of streetlights.

In practice, the results were startlingly good—so good they seemed unreal. Their first and most famous experiment was Seaside, Florida. Its invocation of the Panhandle's beach cottages was made famous by *The Truman Show* as a town too halcyon to be true. But New Urbanism has succeeded in building entire communities from scratch and rehabbing sick ones. Any Mayberryness is just salesmanship, a shortcut for convincing a skeptical generation of suburbanites why living in a freshly reconstituted urban village might actually be safe, humane, and *fun*.

Shea Homes had taken the opposite tack with their patented New Suburbanism: they had wriggled free of the commitment to build cities instead of culs-de-sac, while dialing the nostalgia knob to eleven. On the streets lining the lake, homes still sport two- and three-car garages as their defining features, overshadowing the nods to Frank Lloyd Wright and the yards landscaped with native grasses and decorative wheat. More than a thousand had been built by the time I arrived, only a fraction of the ten, twelve, or as many as fifteen thousand expected eventually.

A sign at the Welcome Center informed me that "Happily Ever After Starts Here." The interiors were reminiscent of your grandmother's house, provided your grandmother was Cal Fulenwider's. Waiting for me were the stewards of Reunion, Terri Kershisnik and Marty Zemcik. Terri was Shea's point woman in Denver, having been in charge of Highlands Ranch for twenty-three years. She combined a motherly air with the steely resolve of someone used to dealing with the implacable demands of children (or adults acting like them). Marty was Reunion's community development manager, in charge of fostering the intangible sense of community so integral to the sales pitch.

Surrounded by the iconography of the West, I asked why they'd chosen to traffic so heavily in a vanished era. Because it worked. "It's trying to come back to the history," Terri began, "so people feel that this history is part of what we did here, and therefore that it's not brand-new, and not something they have to create or we had to create, and that it wasn't something totally out of the ordinary for the area," as if the aerotropolis had been waiting out there all along. "This isn't Dubai or Hong Kong—or Disneyland, for that matter—because it's part of the history here," Fulenwider's family history repackaged and exaggerated.

"We created a bit of a backstory about a ranch here, and a farm," Marty explained, "and as you drive in the entrance of Reunion, you're supposed to be going through a historic farmstead. The walls are supposed to represent the foundations of farmhouses no longer here, the tree plantings represent an orchard, and even the streetlights have a gooseneck that harkens back to the galvanized fixtures that were on every farmhouse in northern Colorado. We did it really because this is a blank slate." A slate that is filling up quickly with people both real and anticipated, and little time to acclimate them to what's really coming. The best way to prepare people for the future, it turns out, is to convince them they're living in the past.

Municipally speaking, Reunion belongs to Commerce City, a 'burb named for its lunch pail roots. A few months before, a longtime resident and Reunion transplant had petitioned to rename the city Reunion, in a transparent bid to bolster both civic pride and property values. The measure landed on the ballot but was handily defeated. As the aerotropolis fills up, it's not hard to imagine a second referendum in ten or twenty years. By then, Reunion should possess its own schools—it has plots set aside for separate elementary, middle, and high schools—and it already pays for maintaining its own parks and road infrastructure. All that Reunion—and the aerotropolis in general—is missing is the downtown Fulenwider promised.

"As far as Cal's vision goes," Marty said, "we've reserved seventy-five acres for a whole office campus, and it's there, forever, waiting for him." Truth be told, less than half of Reunion's acreage is devoted to houses. Twenty percent is slated for parks, while more than a third is assigned as business and commercial, a category that includes a Walmart by the highway and a "town center" supposed to be its answer to Main Street. It's what urban planners have in mind when they talk about New Urbanism—"urban villages," in Reunion's own description, fusing "commercial, educational, civic, cultural, and entertainment uses." In other words, it's a place to mail a package, grab an iced coffee, pick up the kids, and bump into a neighbor along the way.

When I asked why Shea had opted for the New Suburbanism instead, Marty demurred. "Our zoning's flexible enough so we could do a full-on New Urbanist plan, but we're kind of admitting this is an automotive, suburban neighborhood," he said. One of the pearls of wisdom dropped by his boss early in the planning process was, "Nobody rides his bike to Home Depot and takes home a sheet of plywood." It was implicit that Reunion would attract people for whom trips to Home Depot are an inviolable right.

The New Suburbanism is preferable to the old, but is it compact enough to accommodate two hundred thousand new residents at any density other than sprawl? Probably not. Even though Reunion is three times as dense as Fulenwider's original estimate, it doesn't take into account that this strip of prairie is busy being transfigured from God's country to a city the size of Madison, Wisconsin, or Augusta, Georgia. Denver itself is five times as dense as Reunion. The view only gets worse when your gaze shifts to its cookie-cutter neighbors. "The reality is that there aren't enough large blocks out there for people to really make a difference, and that will lead to sprawl" is Fulenwider's own pessimistic conclusion.

"The city's worried about residential development south and east of here, even though it's beyond the noise contours," Marty told me. "They'd like to preserve more of this land for future commercial development. I'm sure someone has done a study on what the perfect ratio of residential and commercial development is, and most developers prefer commercial, because it's simpler—"

"Easier," Terri interrupted. "And you make more money. But they need the residential base to get 'em here."

"And unfortunately," Marty continued, "there's so much commercially zoned ground in Colorado already that residential is the immediate opportunity, and that's coloring what's happening in these other master plans." He waved a hand over a map displaying the locations of his competitors. "I don't think it's the zoning map that creates community. One thing I've learned from Reunion is you hold—you don't put in everything you could do. You have to hold back and not just take the easiest deal, the low-hanging fruit." Except they did. And that's when the trouble began.

Because the airport occupies Denver's neglected quarter, land costs were lower here than anywhere else in the metropolitan area. This simple fact triggered a pattern of development all too common in the era of easy money. Reunion's relatively modest land costs allowed Shea and its handpicked list of builders to offer homes for about $70,000 less than similar ones closer to town. And this, in turn, attracted a class of buyers priced out of other areas. They were ripe targets for predatory lenders underwriting inconceivable loans.

One was Shea's own mortgage arm. "We should have walked away sooner and quit selling to some of them," its president said. "But it's just so hard." The builder of Reunion's pièce de résistance, a $2.2 million Tuscan-style farmhouse named La Grande Cannoli, refused to sell to speculators with neither a down payment nor any visible source of income. Reunion and its copycats were some of the earliest and the hardest hit by the financial crisis, with one of the highest foreclosure rates in the region. The New Suburbanism was tailor-made for the bubble.

In the end, demography will save Reunion and finish what it started. The airport is the hub not only of Denver but also of a swath of cities and towns running the entire eastern slope of the Rockies through Colorado. Stretching for about 175 miles along I-25—from Fort Collins in the north to Pueblo in the south, with Denver and Colorado Springs in between— this twenty-five-mile-wide strip is known as the Front Range, and it contains some 80 percent of the state's residents, or about four million people. Belying its mountains and open skies, Colorado is one of the most densely urbanized states in the union.

It also has one of the highest net migrations of any region in the country. Since 1990, the Front Range has added almost 1.3 million people, concentrated in Denver's suburbs. A Pew study conducted in October 2008—the darkest hours of the Great Recession—revealed Denver as the city Americans most wanted to live in. The Front Range is expected to add another two million residents by 2040—an increase of 50 percent—and demographers are inventing new vocabularies to describe the seismic shift under way.

Brookings's Robert Lang has dubbed it a "megapolitan," one of a handful of "mountain megas" including Arizona's Sun Corridor, Nevada's Greater Las Vegas, and northern New Mexico. Holding them back, Lang found, is a lack of global connectivity frustrating their attempts to diversify beyond tourism and real estate. While the start of nonstop jet service from the coasts had led to the elevation of onetime mining towns such as Vail, Aspen, Telluride, and Park City into internationally famous ski resorts beginning in the 1960s, Denver, Albuquerque, and Phoenix had not achieved their full potential. "If the Western megapolitan areas are to become world cities," he wrote in his report, "they need international connections" at least on par with DFW's or Atlanta's. Instead, they seemed content to funnel passengers through LAX, adding to the airport's strain. The sole exception is Las Vegas, "a unique world city" as the capital of conventions, with its own flights to Asia and Europe.

As the prime examples of cities appearing in places they have no business being—the arid high plains or deserts—all of these regions rely heavily on air travel to connect them to the coasts and each other. In 1950, Phoenix had a population of roughly one hundred thousand while Las Vegas had half of that; each has grown fortyfold since then. The mountain megas' airports have added forty million passengers in just the last twenty years, which is why Denver was forced to build DIA and why Las Vegas and Phoenix are both planning second airports.

While Lang worries about a lack of nonstop flights, the greater threat to Denver is the tide of migration. Even in the depths of the recession, the aerotropolis was filling faster than expected, was sparser than it should be, and was top-heavy with starter McMansions. Reunion and the surrounding boomburbs have been zoned for forty-four thousand homes and roughly 150,000 people. The nascent aerotropolis is making the same, albeit less fatal, mistakes of a Schaumburg or Fairfax at warp speed, spreading across so many cities, counties, and assorted municipal entities that no one is in a position to fill in everyone on the bigger picture, which is how Cal Fulenwider was able to sell his own in the first place.

Denver may be squandering its best chance to avoid a repeat of the urban planning (or lack thereof) on the city's south side. "We don't even have words to describe these places," David Brooks wrote. "Over the past few decades, dozens of scholars have studied places like Arapahoe County," where exurban Cherry Hills, Centennial, and much of Aurora are located. "They've coined terms to capture the polymorphous living arrangements found in these fast growing regions: edgeless city, major diversification center, multicentered net, ruraburbia, boomburg, spread city, technoburb, suburban growth corridor, sprinkler cities." These are places without beginning or end. They're fuzzy fractals of sprawl growing increasingly unsustainable as they deliver continually diminishing returns. DIA could be the foundation of a new kind of city, one that values land, access, and community as precious commodities rather than free goods, and creates urban forms accordingly.

Living next to the airport has a different meaning around DIA. Unlike Stapleton's neighbors, no one lives a few hundred yards away. "You look at the photos and think, 'Oh, that's so close.' But most of Reunion is six or seven miles from the nearest runway," Cal Fulenwider said. "The enormity makes it work." DIA proves we can make our own accommodations with the sound and fury necessary to fly. The question is, How do we make the most of it?

Fulenwider isn't taking any chances. Prospective residents have the possible side effects of the airport's presence spelled out for them, in writing. "Are you living next to an airport? Hell, yes," he snapped. "Is it growing? It's going to double. And before you make your decision you need to know that. If you want to live in close proximity to an airport because you're traveling a lot, then you want to live near one that's *designed* to grow, because you don't want planes flying overhead while you're trying to entertain your family."

Reunion isn't even the closest to the airport anymore; another group bought the mile and a half in between and plans to build townhomes right up to the fence.

The Death and Rebirth of Stapleton

Brian Tellinghuisen moved back to Stapleton in 2002. Not into his old house, although he could practically wave to his mother from his new one, planted in the middle of what used to be the runway he watched from his living room window as a child. He was the first to come home, followed by a few hundred families that year, then a few thousand, and finally—a decade from now—another ten thousand. He never thought he could go home again, "but I wanted to be a part of it," he said. "It was new, it was urban, and it wasn't happening anywhere else."

While he was gone, they'd torn up the runways, pulverizing the tarmac into six million tons of pebbles piled in Commerce City, forming the only mountain lying east of Denver. They would find their way back into the sidewalks, boulevards, and even the foundation of his home. ("Staple stone," they called it.) The terminals had been pulled down and the hangars demolished, until only the parking garage and the old control tower remained. The tower kept a lonely vigil for seven years, while Stapleton reinvented itself as the largest New Urbanist community in America. When it's finished, Stapleton will be home to thirty thousand residents with a downtown half the size of Denver's own.

At the time of its conception, Stapleton was the most ambitious urban experiment in America, New Urbanist or otherwise. But is it ambitious enough to offer a tool kit for fixing our cities? The new Stapleton is the culmination of a decade's planning that began as soon as the final vote to shutter the airport was cast. While it was on its deathbed, the Stapleton Foundation issued the "Green Book," an open call for someone willing to step up and build "compact, mixed-use communities that are walkable and transit-oriented," communities with as many jobs as residents and a thousand acres set aside for parks. The foundation held a bake-off in 1998 to select a master developer, spurning the highest of four bidders in favor of Forest City Enterprises, which pledged a twenty-year marriage to the project and paid its dowry up front to prove it. In turn, it drafted Peter Calthorpe, a founding father of New Urbanism, to help patch the battered and polluted site back into the urban fabric.

Following his movement's scripture, Calthorpe's plan dutifully broke down the site into zones, or "transects," of various densities. Neighborhoods and schools comprised the south side of the airfield, where Brian Tellinghuisen lived, while parks of both the green and office variety would vie for the center. The north third would be split among a "town center" mall, more office space, and warehouses buffering I-70.

It was a good plan, zoned lot by lot with boulevards and bike trails stitching them together, but the whole thing might have unraveled into the New Suburbanism (or worse) if the home builders hadn't seized the opportunity to serve up something besides the last decade's three-car-garage, 3BR model. Stapleton's layout mixes mod condos with neo-Victorians, Nantucket cottages, and stout Federalist row houses—often on the same block. Four centuries and a continent's worth of architectural styles were poured into a blender and set to "pulse," with low-income and senior housing added evenly between bursts to achieve a creamy diversity in people and places. It also explained all the solar panels on the roofs.

The "Green Book" demanded that Stapleton also be a model of sustainable housing, and Forest City's partners have done their best to comply. The first LEED-certified home went up in 2007, boasting natural ventilation, airtight insulation, and a tankless water heater to go with the photovoltaics upstairs. Four builders have so far enrolled in the U.S. Green Building Council's iconic Leadership in Environmental Engineering Design program for homes, the gold standard of green. Stapleton intends to recycle all of its excavated concrete torn from its ground, has ripped the pipes from its wetlands, and intends to plant twenty-one thousand trees—watering them with recycled rainwater. Beneath the pavement, parks.

Stapleton is the textbook definition of a brownfield, a contaminated industrial site begging for cleanup and reuse. Nearly all airports would qualify as one, along with the typically corrosive and polluting neighbors who've historically taken shelter in the noise ghettos around them. Think of the Chevron refinery near LAX and its subterranean oil spill. Or the Ford Explorer plant next to the Worldport in Louisville. Their land is too valuable to let hulks like these fester. We won't live on some of these hot spots (because they're too polluted or too close to the runways), but we might want to in others, and Stapleton teaches us they can be reclaimed.

Anyone needing proof should visit Atlanta's Hartsfield-Jackson, where a local developer named Jim Jacoby bought a decommissioned Ford plant abutting the airport's fence. Ford Fairlanes and Thunderbirds were assembled there for sixty years until the plant closed in 2006. Three thousand workers lost their jobs, while the suburb of Hapeville lost its largest source of taxes. Jacoby is building "Aerotropolis Atlanta" on the 122-acre site, with six million square feet of mixed-use commercial space—as much as downtown Memphis or Nashville. The price tag for creating ten thousand new jobs is $1.5 billion. That doesn't include the year his firm spent disassembling the factory, yielding forty thousand tons of scrap metal and one hundred thousand tons of recyclable concrete.

Auto plants are easy by Jacoby's standards; try cleaning up after a steel mill's mess. That's what he did in midtown Atlanta to create Atlantic Station, a 138-acre constellation of high-rises, condos, townhomes, and big-box stores. Nine thousand loads of contaminated soil were extracted from the foundations of Atlantic Steel, replaced with twenty-eight hundred trees and the first LEED Silver-certified tower in the Southeast. (Ironically, some of the country's greenest buildings stand on its most polluted sites.) To do it, he needed federal, state, and local cooperation and funds. He needed twenty million square feet rezoned and a bridge built across not one, but two expressways to connect the desolate site to civilization. Ten thousand people will call it home by the end of this decade.

"When we started looking at opportunities like these in the early nineties," Jacoby told me, "people were leaving Atlanta. But because of sprawl, people are starting to move back. Why not reclaim these sites? To build something the size of a Ford plant would take two years to get the permits, but we can redevelop it in six months. Atlantic Steel's taxes when we bought it were three hundred thousand dollars a year; when we're done, it will be a hundred million. How many other great canvases are there? Not many, but Stapleton is one."

Stapleton's main entrance is to the west, on the site of the old rental lots. I slipped in through the back door. The airport's renaissance has been slow and methodical, creeping one block at a time. Most of its acreage is still a man-made badlands of mud flats. On Martin Luther King Jr. Boulevard, its old artery, the landscape changed to a sandy expanse gridded by empty streets—like a beach awaiting a slow-motion tidal wave of plywood. Houses ran the gamut of construction on a single block: one was having its foundations scooped; another was nothing but bare two-by-fours; a third was sheathed in blue blankets of insulation, its solar cells already on the roof; and a fourth was only waiting for a fresh carpet of sod.

The control tower stood in the distance, framed against the mountains and a jet bound for DIA making throat-clearing sounds. By now the locals had accepted it as their symbol of Stapleton's hard-earned sense of place. I found Brian's house later while roaming on foot. His was one in a cluster of Spanish Mission revivals, replete with clay tiles, stucco walls, and a *corredor* for a porch. It sat across the street from a grassy postage stamp of a yard, shared equally by a square of cottages and Victorians, their porches offset neatly from the sidewalks with a white picket fence. Down the block, an otherwise boring brick mansion with a wraparound porch boasted a sign proclaiming it one of LEED's pilots.

But the strangest sight lay not far away. Turning a corner, I came face-to-face with a quarter mile of brownstones lining Stapleton's grand boulevard, looking *exactly* like my own back in Brooklyn. They were new, of course—so clean they'd obviously never seen a pigeon—but otherwise packed shoulder to shoulder like the loveliest stretches of my borough, where Jane Jacobs's "sidewalk ballet" of people endlessly dances arabesques below our windows. Stapleton's residents were learning the steps—dog walkers strolled the grassy median, and a few runners loped by—but it wasn't quite Cobble Hill yet.

After the initial shock of meeting its doppelgänger wore off, another one hit me: Who moves to *Denver* to live like they're in *Brooklyn*? And then: How much do they pay for the privilege? The second question was easily answered—a sign in one window listed the building at $900,000, maybe a third of the going rate back home but three times what comparable square footage would cost at Reunion, or almost any neighborhood in town. The asking price has likely risen since then—Stapleton's actually climbed an average of 20 percent during the housing bust. The other question was trickier. I had to knock.

The first to answer was a handsome blonde in her early fifties named Kathy Holmes, who seemed delighted to find anyone on her porch. She had recently moved from Washington, D.C., "and the density feels very natural to me," she said. Her neighbors—or at least the ones she'd met—were fellow transplants from Maryland and Boston. She had moved here for the lifestyle but traveled often for work as an executive coach. It mattered to her that DIA was an eighteen-minute commute on the highway. Stapleton's brownstones seemed to collect the self-motivated. Living on her block were a traveling salesman raised on Long Island, a stay-at-home software engineer, and a graphic designer who proudly informed me she had been a flight attendant on America West for twenty-five years.

If Holmes had one complaint about Stapleton, it wasn't that it sometimes felt like Disneyland, as her neighbors put it. ("A good Disneyland," one of them specified, "not a cheesy one.") "I've been to Celebration," she said, "and that feels fake to me. But anytime you set out to plan, everything ends up perfect, all clean and new, and it doesn't quite feel real, either." She knew from experience, having worked in her previous life on the creation of Reston Town Center, arguably the original New Urbanist pocket near Dulles. In a deliciously ironic twist, the developer was Mobil Oil. The locals did their best to make her feel welcome—smashing her windshield, slashing her tires, and leaving notes along the lines of "Kathy Holmes doesn't deserve to live." So she was inclined to give Stapleton the benefit of the doubt.

Her problem was the lack of diversity—in age, color, class, whatever. Despite the best-laid plans, it was quickly overrun by young families. The demographics were unavoidable—the same wave of pent-up demand cresting at Reunion had also washed over Stapleton. Holmes, two decades older and living alone, didn't fit in.

The New Urbanist Aerotropolis

Tom Gleason joined me outside the Starbucks a few blocks down the following afternoon, iced lattes in hand. The fatal flaw of every instant downtown is the monoculture of chain stores, I grumbled, and the lack of mom-and-pops. He just chuckled. "There are two camps of people here," he said, "those who say, 'By God, you should have a Starbucks!' and those who retort, 'By God, we need something *else!*'"

Stocky and white haired, he spoke in the jovial-but-jaded rapid-fire cadences of a veteran flack. He'd been present at Stapleton's death and subsequent resurrection, first as Mayor Federico Peña's press secretary, then as the front man for both the Stapleton Development Corporation and Forest City's Denver operations. The name on the checks changed, but he hadn't. It was six years ago to the week, he noted absently, as if remembering an old friend's birthday, that construction on Tellinghuisen's house had begun.

We got to talking about what made this place tick and, by extension, how one would go about building it anew someplace else. It was something he'd thought about before briefing visting members of Parliament on how they might go about rehabbing Heathrow. "'New Urbanism' is a funny term, because it's really the old urbanism," he said. "Peter [Calthorpe] would tell you you can have New Urbanism anywhere."

And so would Gleason's boss, Jon Ratner. The youngest member of the Ratner clan is arguably its most radical. Having started work at Stapleton in his twenties, he'd since risen to the post of director of sustainability, in charge of the firm's triple bottom line: "people, planet, and profit." "We're hoping to use the ingenuity of the private sector and the fiscal resources of the public one to build a new vision for what a city can be," he told me. "This approach tends to be controversial," especially when the city in question, like Brooklyn, already has a vision for itself. "But it's also very hopeful, because you're admitting this part of town hasn't achieved what it *should* be."

Stapleton's vision calls for solar cells on every roof and schools a short walk away. This is pretty modest compared to reengineering sick cities. The more pressing question is whether Stapletons can replace the crust of brownfields surrounding our marooned airports. Is it possible to reclaim the noise ghettos along Elvis Presley Boulevard in Memphis, or the abandoned, feral subdivisions of Louisville? And if so, how big can these aerotropoli get? Can Stapleton be a blueprint for the instant ones rising in China?

"It can be as big as you want it to be," he said. "It's an infinitely replicable model, because it's a model of nodes. Each node has the right mix of residential to retail to schools, and once you figure it out, you keep replicating it. I think we'll see New Urbanist communities in places like China and India on a scale that will blow away anything we've seen."

They'll have to top an even bigger bet his family placed in another mountain mega, twenty square miles of desert named Mesa del Sol. Lying on the south side of Albuquerque atop a mammoth plateau, it's the last parcel of its size in America so close to the airport and downtown. Peter Calthorpe drafted a sequel to Stapleton, with a few twists thrown in. For one, it's three times the size of the original, adding a hundred thousand residents to a city of less than a million. Another is on-site employers any mayor (or governor) would kill for, including a film studio and a maker of solar cells that opened a $100 million factory there last year. But taking their cue from Stapleton's tenants, the Ratners expect that nearly everyone here will work from home. As *BusinessWeek* put it, Mesa del Sol "will be the first place of its kind built from scratch and targeted at the creative class."

A big marketing push will be made to coastal knowledge workers looking to cash out of their million-dollar split levels, move inland, and work remotely for their companies. Mansionettes will carry price tags of up to $400,000, about the same as the average Manhattan studio. They'll feature home offices sequestered from family foot traffic and fully wired for transnational connections. Business centers strewn throughout the community—all within a short walk or electric-cart ride—will offer rent-by-the-hour support staff plus state-of-the-art meeting rooms and seamless video-conference hookups to China and India. With the Albuquerque airport only six minutes and one stoplight away, a former regular of the big-city airport crush can leave for meetings in other cities after breakfast and still be home for dinner.

Mesa del Sol is an aerotropolis in the mold of the "no-collar workplace" imagined by Richard Florida: the twilight zone of multitasking knowledge workers drifting between home, cafés, the airport, and clients' conferences and back. Like Florida—who once switched academic posts to be closer to Dulles—the Ratner clan believes the future of work belongs to those of us who do it wherever we want, whenever we want, so long as we do it longer and harder than anyone else. They aim to give us the city we deserve, a hub enabling our dispersal. No one can work from home forever—Kasarda's Law still applies—but we can try. Forty percent of IBM's employees don't have an office, working either from home or at the client. Sixty percent of Agilent Technologies's telecommute at least part of the time. And a third of AT&T's managers are now "postgeographic."

Demographers call this "the distributed workforce." If Melvin Webber were still alive, he might have tried "employees without propinquity"
because we're acting like the companies we work for, looking to live, play,
and pray wherever we see comparable advantage—provided, of course,
we can get from here to there. Joel Garreau calls this the "Santa Fe-ing
of the World"—"places the entire point of which is face-to-face contact"—
although the test bed for his hypothesis is actually sixty miles down the
road.

In searching for an upper limit to the sizes of salvageable aerotropoli,
Mesa del Sol isn't the largest infill project in the West. It's not even the
largest named Mesa. In the next mountain mega over, Mesa, Arizona, is
building an aerotropolis around Phoenix-Mesa Gateway Airport. The
name should be a clue as to what Mesa is all about. Twice the size of
Washington, D.C., and more populous than Cleveland or Miami, it's just
another Phoenix boomburb strung out across the Valley of the Sun.
Since the 1940s, it has grown at nearly a triple-digit pace each decade
until this one. Having built a single-story city reeling from the collapse of
its only growth industry, Mesa has determined to build up instead of out.

Acting on Kasarda's advice, the city council approved plans for an
aerotropolis the size of San Francisco on the edge of the desert. The core
occupies five square miles on the site of GM's former proving grounds,
sold in 2006 to a local developer. After the city agreed to rezone the land,
the firm promised to build the downtown Mesa never had, an exercise in
"twenty-first-century desert urbanism"—New Urbanism with stucco
flourishes. The plan depends on Gateway living up to its name and winning flights from the region's hub, Phoenix–Sky Harbor. Impressed by
their ambitions, *The Economist* dubbed their aerotropolis the "city of the
future" and name-checked John Kasarda as its architect.

We *want* to live near airports, even if we don't care to admit it—even to
ourselves. Stapleton, Reunion, and the Mesas offer compelling evidence.
We flock to them because that's where the jobs are, next door or at the
end of a flight. So how do we build a better aerotropolis than the ones we
have now?

One of the best tools in our kit is something called "transit oriented
development," an idea coined by Peter Calthorpe the same year he helped

found the Congress for the New Urbanism. The name says it all: neighborhoods and cities built along the splines of public transit. Sometimes that can be buses, but typically it means trains. Denver is doing exactly that with its $7 billion investment in FasTracks, which will have fifty-seven stations dotting 119 miles of track when it's finished. That equals fifty-seven new hot spots for development. (Calthorpe whipped up a plan for them too.) At the end of one line is the airport, which happens less often than you'd think.

The failure of most American cities to connect their airports to downtown with trains (or to do so hopelessly after the fact) will go down as yet another of our great infrastructure blunders. Denver, home to the fifth-busiest airport in the United States, is hardly alone in never building one until now. Dallas (fourth) is in the same boat until the line through Las Colinas is finished. Las Vegas (seventh), Houston (eighth), and Phoenix (ninth) have nothing, while the Los Angeles subway has an LAX stop that doesn't stop at LAX (a bus covers the last leg). But the ultimate insult to injury was delivered by New York's master builder, the auto-obsessed Robert Moses. As early as the 1940s, the city's planners were urging him to provide space for mass transit to Idlewild (later JFK) along the Van Wyck Expressway. Moses refused, forcing an overwhelming majority of JFK's fifty million passengers a year to drive. (The teeth-grinding irony is that Moses never drove a day in his life; he had a chauffeur.)

In Europe, the situation's reversed. Nearly every major airport sports a train station underneath. They aren't mere subway stops, either—Paris, Frankfurt, and Amsterdam's all sit astride the Continent's high-speed rail. The train connecting Zurich's to the city's main station is so fast and efficient I once flew there overnight from Brooklyn, explored the old town that morning, and then caught the same day's flight home a few hours later. Hong Kong takes this a step further with an express train covering twenty-two miles in twenty-two minutes, leaping over islands and bridges to collapse the distance between the island and its aerotropolis to almost nothing.

Maybe the most promising transit-oriented aerotropolis in the world is Ørestad, Denmark's own answer to Stapleton. It isn't built on the remains of an airport, but the green brownfield (a hazelfield?) was founded at about the same time. Ørestad's lifeline and raison d'être is the train connecting downtown Copenhagen to its hub. It's a seven-minute ride to one, a five-minute hop to the other. Riding that train and now the new metro every day are twenty thousand students headed to class at either the University of Copenhagen or the brand-new "IT University" that's attracted the likes of Ericsson, Accenture, and GlaxoSmithKline to Ørestad's office towers. Daniel Liebeskind designed its new downtown, and Jean Nouvel its glowing blue cube of a concert hall. When it's finished in twenty years, twenty thousand people will live in Ørestad, and another eighty thousand will make the commute, almost all of them by train.

Ørestad was one of the first things Elizabeth Plater-Zyberk mentioned when I asked about the possibility of a New Urbanist aerotropolis. She and her husband are still the standard-bearers for the movement, and I wanted to know how she would go about creating one, assuming it can be done. "The first thing you have to do," she said, "is get a train to them. Once you do that, you can begin to think about what happens there and how to organize that kind of development. If you were to start from scratch, like Denver, you might plan to put the industrial parts on the far side, so the mixed-use portions can relate to the core, and back to the city. You can start a community that way, so long as you recognize the need for a central transit hub, which allows for more uses." This is starting to happen in Denver and Dulles and Dallas, where DFW is set to become the only rail hub in a region of six million.

I sought a second opinion. "Density alone doesn't solve any problems," said Dehan Glanz, one of Calthorpe's partners. "Density in the right place—near transit, near downtown—and having a system of transportation that links this density into a larger context is what's important. Instead of just putting a factory near the airport, put mixed-use and housing, and create links within the community and to downtown."

Seeking a third, and someone who's done this kind of thing before (building airports *and* cities, that is), I called Moshe Safdie. He's the Israeli architect still most famous for the buildings he dreamed up as a student—a series of modular, prefab, concrete apartment blocks stacked like a tense game of Jenga. Unveiled in Montreal at Expo '67, Habitat was an instant smash, turning a prototype of affordable housing into one of the city's most desirable addresses. Since then, Safdie's designed terminals for Tel Aviv's and Toronto's airports, and his latest assignment is diagramming a new city of 250,000 outside Jerusalem. "People manage to coexist with airports," he said. "They will learn to live with them. The mess is what happens when you fail to plan for it."

He sees the shape of John Kasarda's aerotropolis and raises him, reimagining it "as something that begins the moment you step on the train. If you develop a very efficient transit system and build it close to an airport, every stop is ultimately an opportunity to build out the airport. The airport starts to spread as it develops access to places beyond its borders. The more tightly integrated it is into the city, the more the airport becomes a city. Until it's everywhere."

THE AEROTROPOLIST

Thirty years ago, John Kasarda saw that the future of cities lies around airports. He has spent his career telling everyone who will listen—and now governments are paying attention.

Human Ecology and Hubs

If the aerotropolis is the avatar of globalization, then John Kasarda himself is the latest incarnation in a line of thinkers dating to the turn of the last century. His brainchild is in many ways the culmination of their inquiries into how cities are born, thrive, and occasionally die. "I never wanted to be a pilot," he once said. "I'm interested in competition."

Enrolling at the University of North Carolina in 1968 as a twenty-three-year-old Ph.D. student, he discovered a haven for sociologists who refused to study human behavior under a microscope. They had stayed true to the sweeping structural analysis pioneered by Robert Park and Ernest Burgess in the 1920s at the University of Chicago. The pair took the Second City itself as their subject, probing its Gilded Age formations for the elementary particles of urbanism. Decades later, Kasarda's model of the aerotropolis—with an airport at the center and concentric rings of uses radiating outward—would echo their studies of the Loop and its trains and skyscrapers.

His arrival in Chapel Hill coincided with Amos Hawley's, his future mentor having just left his post at the University of Michigan to join a few of his fellow travelers. There was the statistician Hubert Blalock, who developed the techniques employed by Chicago's Peter Blau and Otis Dudley Duncan. Their monumental study of social mobility, *The*

American Occupational Structure, had appeared the year before; Kasarda lured Blau to North Carolina years later. And there was Gerhard Lenski, whose 1966 tome *Power and Privilege* had advanced a grand unified theory of "macrosociology" explaining the fates of entire civilizations. This was the intellectual ferment it was Kasarda's job to distill.

The group's touchstone was Hawley's own *Human Ecology*, published in 1950, in which he reconceived cities and societies as organisms competing to survive and prosper. He saw life as poetry—POET being his acronym for the interlocking variables of population, organization, environment, and technology. Over time, he theorized, new institutions and technologies evolve to take advantage of their settings; natural resources and geography are put to their best use as civilization becomes more complex, consumption and energy use rise, and populations multiply, diversify, and migrate. He zeroed in on transportation and communication as the fastest-acting catalysts for expansion and change. Hawley was no doomsayer; although he conceded the possibility of planetary overreach, the fact remained that things were getting better all the time.

"I owe him a lot," Kasarda said, "because he gave me a firm foundation for understanding why the world is the way it is and where it's going. He didn't study social problems or behavior, but the structures that shaped and defined them. He studied power. And real power, I learned, resides in systems, not individuals."

Kasarda eventually became chairman of their department before moving across campus to the business school, where he led investigations into competition and trade. Hawley retired to a long and intellectually active life. Receiving me at his home in Chapel Hill not long before he died in 2009 at the age of ninety-eight, he delivered his last lecture on the laws of natural selection that had produced Kasarda's aerotropolis.

Of all the ideas he first proposed in *Human Ecology*, perhaps none is more important than the *friction of space*. Distance isn't fixed, but flexible, a function of the time and energy required to traverse it. One sign of progress is that its coefficient is continually falling toward zero. "The world within which man lives," he wrote, "is defined less by the horizon of his geographical knowledge than by the limits imposed by his means of transportation and communication." Remove these limits via steamboats or railroads or 747s, and our horizons broaden accordingly. Cities are created not in units of distance but in units of time. They are born or explode into suddenly frictionless pockets, and we find ever more clever patterns, forms, and purposes with which to fill them.

Hawley circumscribed the sixty-minute travel radius of daily life several decades before Marchetti coined his constant, and he even preempted Marshall McLuhan, who in *Understanding Media* practically plagiarized him. "The railway did not introduce movement or transportation or wheel or road into human society," McLuhan wrote, "but it accelerated and enlarged the scale of previous human functions, creating totally new kinds of cities and new kinds of work and leisure." And these, in turn, gave way to the air. "The airplane, on the other hand, by accelerating the rate of transportation, tends to dissolve the railway form of city, politics, and association, quite independently of what the airplane is used for."

"Urban development was always contingent upon access," Hawley instructed me. "It's why space, time, and economic organization are inextricably interwoven." He'd discovered a wrinkle in his space-time equations—as the coefficient of friction falls, the time and energy once wasted on conquering distance are reinvested in the exchange of goods and information. "Cities grow fastest at the points where access maximizes the flows of people, products, capital, and knowledge," and the ones with the highest degree of connectivity become hubs.

"Throughout history," he went on, "businesses have concentrated at the intersections of roads and routes, where the access is greatest. They especially favored cities where there was multimodality," the more forms of transport the better.

"Those businesses generate external economies that attract firms which serve or supply them," like Las Colinas or Louisville's satellites. "The growing concentration often triggers further improvements in transportation infrastructure—new highways, rail lines, air service—making them even more attractive. And the process reinforces itself," until these hubs achieve critical mass, as Babylon, Byzantium, Venice, and New Orleans once did.

But hubs are also vulnerable to the vicissitudes of new technology. Each of these cities was supplanted by younger rivals as caravans gave way to caravels, clipper ships, and eventually Pan Am Clippers. The Harvard economist Edward Glaeser has documented how the advent of the automobile (and of long-distance trucking) canceled out the geographic advantages of waterfront cities such as Buffalo, Detroit, and Cleveland.

"The rise and fall of route centers is a familiar phenomenon to students of history," Hawley wrote in *Human Ecology*. "Changes in route patterns, whatever may be their cause, alter the advantages offered by existing locations, leaving some centers to recede into insignificance and sometimes extinction, and enabling others to rise to new heights of dominance."

Natural selection occurs within cities too. Detroit was built in the railroad's image, but its downtown didn't survive the suburban diffusion set in motion by the Model T. It was clear to Hawley as early as the 1930s that the dispersal of our urban cores had been preordained. The apparently frictionless automobile dissolved the radial spokes of trains and trolley lines into the suburban skein of arterial roads and veins.

As cities changed, so did their economies. The size prized by firms during the Industrial Age gave way to speed, as exemplified by Henry Ford's monolithic factories yielding to the nimbler Toyota's. We scattered into the countryside and our employers followed, confident that connectivity would keep us bound together. This is where Hawley's theories leave off and Kasarda's begin. His mentor's survival of the fittest evolved into his own survival of the *fastest*. Whereas others focused on economies of scale and economies of scope, he zeroed in on the overlooked economies of speed.

The state of the art is the Internet and the 787, and their ties now bind us across hemispheres. Air travel, Kasarda deduced twenty years ago, would create a new, likely final network of hubs within a single global ecosystem. Every city, region, and nation, whether they knew it or not, had been plunged into a Darwinian struggle from which a new world order would emerge. Today we call this process globalization.

The Death and Life of American Cities

Kasarda grew up in Wilkes-Barre, Pennsylvania, in the postwar years. Jane Jacobs, who was born in the next town over, Scranton, later noted that the twin cities of the Appalachian coal country "are less populated today than when I was a child in the 1920s, and even then people in search of city jobs were beginning to leave." By the time Kasarda was born in 1945, the Diamond City's veins of shining anthracite were running dry.

Unlike so many of the Rust Belt towns that followed, Wilkes-Barre went bankrupt in two ways, gradually and then suddenly on January 22, 1959, when one of the mines beneath the Susquehanna River collapsed, flooding a warren of tunnels burrowed for miles beneath the hillsides. For three days, a whirlpool one hundred feet across sucked ten billion gallons of water and ice underground. Kasarda and his older brother witnessed rows of boxcars sunk into the pit to plug it, followed by dump trucks laden with dirt, to no avail. Everyone watching knew this was the end, and the miners had known it too. In their greed and desperation, they had dug far beyond the "stop lines" below the river's banks, until they were barely a foot beneath it when it broke through. King Coal drowned with them.

The river again delivered the coup de grâce thirteen years later, when Hurricane Agnes stormed through northeast Pennsylvania. A swollen and still-vengeful Susquehanna flooded downtown with nine feet of water, destroying twenty-five thousand homes and historic blocks that were neither restored nor replaced, except with the lowest bidder's strip malls. The city of his youth—of impeccably dressed men and women strolling past gleaming storefronts piled high with the latest goods—receded with the waters.

These disasters swirled around his family but didn't touch them. His father managed a Ford dealership, driving regularly to New York and later Philadelphia via a new interstate highway system that cut his former commute in half. Kasarda's only brush with the hardscrabble factories that arrived following King Coal's demise was a summer stint assembling grenade launchers bound for Vietnam. He left with an appreciation for the versatility of four-letter words.

Unlike his coworkers, he escaped to college, landing at Cornell on pace to earn both an economics degree and an M.B.A. (with distinction). Somehow he still found time for his hobby, sociology. Organizations fascinated him, but he was flummoxed by his professors. They were fixated on "agency," our innate capacity to shape the world. They seemed to think that we make choices in a vacuum. The circumstances didn't matter, in their final analysis.

This made no sense to him. Recalling his own upbringing, he couldn't help but ask what choice the miners had when the market for their coal collapsed, followed shortly by the mines. How did agency take into account an act of God, or a dying industry? And was his own father's decision to commute an hour and twenty minutes each way to Philadelphia a matter of will, or of the recently completed Pennsylvania Turnpike extension? No one chose to condemn Wilkes-Barre, and there wasn't anything anyone could do to save it, either. Its fate had dictated its inhabitants', not the other way around. They had been crushed by circumstance.

His apostasy led him to Hawley in graduate school. As a young academic, he was consumed with synthesizing his teacher's structural analysis with the latest strategic thinking. Competition and structure are the major forces shaping human life, he concluded, not individual actors. "Competitiveness" became his watchword—not as it applies to companies, but to places. Countries and regions compete as fiercely as any organism or organization, and face a similar pressure to evolve, economically speaking. Each has its own attributes, expressable in site selection checklists: local labor, crime rates, education, transportation infrastructure, climate, a proclivity for red tape, and taxes, to name just a few. Taken together, they are the genetic expression of a place's appeal to anyone thinking of settling there. Kasarda was especially interested in hearing what companies had to say, as they were fast becoming the only organizations that mattered in Hawley's structural framework.

The strategist who pointed this out made a lasting impression on Kasarda. The Harvard economist Raymond Vernon has been hailed as the "discoverer" of globalization, but he was really one of its architects, having lent a hand in the creation of the Marshall Plan, the International Monetary Fund, and the General Agreement on Tariffs and Trade (the precursor to the WTO). While Kasarda was still a student in 1968, he advanced the heretical idea that the size and reach of international trade and multinational firms had already surpassed the ability of any one nation to control them. The balance of power had been reversed; from now on, corporations would dictate the terms. Today, this is so patently true we have Tom Friedman's "Dell Theory of Conflict Prevention," which presupposes that no two countries with pieces of the same global supply chain—such as China, Taiwan, and Dell's—will ever tempt economic suicide by warring.

One of the main drivers behind the rise of multinationals and what Vernon called "globalism" was air travel, which "shrank the Atlantic crossing from four days to seven hours," he wrote. "It turned transatlantic tourism from a rich man's indulgence into a middle-class need. It opened up the possibility for international consultations on a day-to-day basis not only between the officials of governments but also between the engineers, controllers, salesmen and strategists of private firms." These face-to-face encounters were sufficient to begin flattening the world a good three decades before e-mail.

A more detailed explication was folded into his description of the "product life cycle," a modern take on David Ricardo's nineteenth-century theories of comparative advantage and trade. Vernon's model charted the path from cradle to grave of the latest and greatest inventions. Beginning life as expensive innovations, they were created by American firms and sold to American customers. Overseas demand begot overseas factories, ostensibly to serve local markets. But the radical connectivity of air travel had suddenly made it possible for firms to knit together these foreign outposts into a single low-cost network. Foreign copycats inevitably appeared, taking on the work and driving prices lower until production moved entirely abroad. What began as an American export (by air) ended up a foreign import (also by air). Jobs would inevitably vanish overseas, hopefully replenished by the work of building next year's model. Little did he know then he was describing the dynamic between China and America forty years later.

This new breed of company, Vernon wrote, took "the strategic view that business should find the best markets, employ the best technology, finance through the best channels, irrespective of geography." It asked what the value was of each link in their supply chains, and knowing that, where it should go. An elaborate calculus was created to answer these questions, factoring in costs, access, talent, quality of life, and myriad other criteria. Where you ended up depended on what you were worth—a glass tower in Shinjuku or a factory floor in Shenzhen, perhaps. Kasarda grasped the implications, postulating that places would need to capture links in these chains or else they'd sink without a trace, like Wilkes-Barre. He was one of the first to realize it wasn't what a company did that mattered but how it was organized.

This last point was hammered home to him during a visit to Uruguay ten years ago. The ranchers who settled the self-proclaimed "Switzerland of South America" between Argentina and Brazil were among the world's wealthiest citizens at the start of the twentieth century. Much like the oil sheikhs who later built their tenuous economies on the back of a single commodity, Uruguay grew fat on exports of wool, meat, milk, and little else until prices collapsed after World War II. Uruguay's economy soon followed. Several lost decades later, Kasarda arrived preaching his vision of an aerotropolis on the pampas and of the high-tech industries that might appear in its wake.

He recalls a dissenter interrupting his lecture to pour cold water on his previous point. "He said, 'It doesn't really matter whether we're high tech or not; what good is it if we're just screwing phones or laptops together? They could do that in China, and we might as well go back to making shoes.' He was absolutely right," Kasarda says. "Chinese workers do two-thirds of the work in assembling iPods and keep less than a third of the wages. The rest goes to designers and engineers at Apple in California. 'High tech' is meaningless. I learned early on that it's not the industry but the occupation that counts. It's where you are in the product cycle—are you innovating, or are you turning screws? We had that at Winston-Salem at the largest Dell plant in the world, which was slated to close last year. Workers made twelve dollars an hour screwing boxes together. They might as well have gone back to making furniture. Unfortunately, those factories have left too.

"The guy was right, but I was making a broader point," he adds. As Dallas proves, even something as down-and-dirty as the oil business needs a place to park its headquarters, and ExxonMobil's executives in Las Colinas have more in common with their counterparts at Fluor and Kimberly-Clark nearby than they do with the rig pigs in their employ. Uruguay, for example, went high tech after all in becoming the outsourcing hub of South America. Its mix of high skills and low wages make it the place where even Indian firms send programmers to work on American time.

The principle underlying the aerotropolis, Kasarda patiently explains, is "understanding where you are in the product cycle, how much value you add, and how you can harness speed to raise productivity and cut costs." A city or region lusting after highly skilled, highly paid jobs would do better to focus on an organizational niche (design, sales, R & D) for a number of industries, rather than on just one product or company, no matter how high tech it is or, for that matter, how green.

Besides Hawley and Vernon, the other great influence on Kasarda's thinking was the "macrosociologist" Gerhard Lenski, who sought to explain how and why societies evolve from bands of hunter-gatherers to postindustrial superpowers. His answer was that transformation always began at the top. The rich would get richer as resources accrued to innovators, with the rest trickling down to and tugging the rest of society along behind them. The same was true and had always been true for companies, countries, and cities alike.

Kasarda matched Lenski's thesis with Vernon's product cycle and Hawley's history of hubs and began groping toward a new theory of economic geography. So was the rest of the world. Borders increasingly ceased to matter after the Berlin Wall fell and the WTO was established. Supply chains had been redefined as value chains, in which each link is expected to add value to the finished product. And as multinationals grew in size and power, how they chose to distribute their chains—from headquarters on down to the rawest of raw materials—would decide the hierarchy of the world's cities and regions, and redirect the flow of wealth among them. To survive and thrive, regions would be forced to compete for the most valuable links—the innovators and incubators—that were in turn the ones most resistant to outsourcing someplace else.

The quality these firms prized above all, he deduced, was *friction-lessness*—the unencumbered ability to move people, goods, and ideas in and out as quickly as possible. And the first step toward doing that, as Hawley has always maintained, is possessing state-of-the-art connectivity. If that means the Internet and the 747, then cities needed broadband and a hub if they hoped to stay in the mix. No matter where they stood in the competitive landscape—whether their citizens were busy designing iPods or assembling them—the need for speed meant plentiful air service was a must, even for the heaviest industries. Upon isolating what he saw as the common and crucial variable, Kasarda set out to design a competitive weapon—an equalizer for cities like Wilkes-Barre struggling to make themselves more attractive against their peers. What he produced was the aerotropolis.

In essence, the aerotropolis of his imagination isn't necessarily a city but a superconductor, a piece of infrastructure promising zero resistance to anyone wanting to set up shop there. Examine his original sketches for one—with the carefully arranged waves of white boxes and office cubes—and you'll find a city expressly planned on behalf of the companies expected to populate it. An aerotropolis isn't an airport either, and building one isn't a matter of having the longest runways or the largest landmass. Frictionlessness is the product of a whole host of attributes, many of which are invisible: tariff-free trade zones, faster customs clearance, fewer and faster permits, and a right-to-work workforce that knows what it's doing. "It's the way you reduce time, the way you reduce costs, the way you reduce space," Kasarda says. "The aerotropolis is where the elastic mile, the friction of space, community without propinquity, and trade routes all come together."

They combine to cut costs and red tape for corporations, often at the expense of their employees and the taxpayers, in exchange (theoretically) for greater gains for all down the road. Companies wanted governments that would respond to their needs unflinchingly, and so he would give them one that was.

This is why Dubai is so dazzling to Kasarda; China too. It took as long to air the grievances surrounding Heathrow's Terminal 5 as it did to build Beijing's epic new one from raw ground. There was no debate in this instance, nor was there any over a third runway or the second, separate hub planned for the capital—where, no one knows, because the location is a state secret. It almost doesn't matter, because the government will simply do what it did at the site of the current one, which was to flatten fifteen villages and resettle ten thousand residents without compensation. Kasarda was awed by the ministry's rationale: "Democracy sacrifices efficiency."

Many of us spent the 1990s resisting this conclusion, nodding when Ross Perot warned of a "giant sucking sound" from NAFTA, or taking to the streets in 1999 to fight the "Battle of Seattle" against the WTO. Once we resigned ourselves to it, we did our best to ameliorate its effects on our hometowns and cities, rebuilding around services like health care and education, two things we couldn't imagine being outsourced. By the end of the decade, Kasarda had reached the opposite conclusion, designing cities subject to the same ironclad laws of competition, innovation, and obsolescence. Instead of insulating them from globalization, he would accelerate them to the pace of globalization itself.

This is the challenge he faces with the aerotropolis: the threat of runaway growth without planning. "The real question is not whether or not aerotropoli will evolve around airports—they surely will," he stresses. "It's whether they will grow in an intelligent manner, minimizing problems and bringing about the greatest returns to the airport, its users, businesses, the surrounding communities, and the larger region it serves."

High-functioning autocracies such as Dubai's don't faze him. If anything, they're the only ones who move fast enough. "Life is a series of trade-offs," he points out. "You need to make strategic choices as a city, as there will be winners as well as losers. The fact of the matter is anytime there's a change in the economy, some people and places will move up, and others will move down." Speed kills. But maybe it could resurrect too.

Parks and Prototypes

Once Kasarda had thought of it, the idea of the aerotropolis gestated for almost twenty years, beginning with his trips to Bangkok and Hong Kong in the early 1980s and concluding with the publication of his theories in 2000. By then he had missed America's last chance to build a hub from scratch in Denver; everything that came before it, whether O'Hare, Memphis, Louisville, or Dallas, was already locked into its footprint before he had a chance to save it. He would have to look elsewhere for the time being.

For a long time, he thought of it not as a city but as a self-contained factory town with assembly lines literally ending in the bellies of waiting planes. It struck him as laughably simple—these "transparks," as he called them, could be paved anywhere, in the farthest reaches of the jungle, as they'd be connected to each other via the air. He imagined a dozen such airstrips worldwide shuttling spare parts from one to another, assembling whatever it was we needed when we needed it.

In the fall of 1990, he shared his secret plans with the deputies of North Carolina's governor, James G. Martin. By then, he had left UNC's sociology department for his current post in its business school. When he called, they listened. When he suggested that a transpark might create thirty thousand jobs, they wanted in. The governor himself declared it brilliant ("I thought it was radical, but you look at some radical ideas and think: it just might work"). Studies produced even rosier figures:

fifty-five thousand new jobs by 1998 if the transpark was built *right now*, in a state whose traditional industries—tobacco, furniture, and textiles— were beginning to disappear.

The state put its location up for auction, and eleven communities bid for it, including all three urban clusters: Charlotte; Raleigh-Durham; and the Triad of Greensboro, Highpoint, and Winston-Salem. While consultants bickered over which had the best runways, highways, and railways, politics conspired to trump all other criteria. If you could put it anywhere, asked all the governor's men, then why not give it to the one who needed those jobs the most? Which is how it ended up in tobacco fields not terribly far from Kitty Hawk, where the Wright Brothers first flew in 1903. The selection committee chose Kinston, a small town eighty miles southeast of Raleigh. The nearest interstate was nearly an hour's drive away; the nearest city was ninety minutes! Its airport had nothing going for it except a lot of empty acreage and a stubby runway. As any number of economists could have told you, the state had made a classic mistake of economic stimulus, the sunk cost fallacy mentioned earlier: throwing good money after bad at the hardest-hit communities, rather than putting it to work in successful places where it could do the most good.

Kasarda was surprised when they took him at his word that location didn't matter. Maybe raw geography didn't, he thought, but accessibility certainly did. Kinston straddled no highways, no byways, no junctions. It was nowhere. He kept these doubts to himself. Once, following his first and last chance to intercede in a factory's site-selection process, the committee chairman rapped his knuckles. "Don't get involved," he was told, "you're just the guy with the big idea. And let me tell you something else: You have a character flaw, the same one Governor Martin has, and I've cured him of it. And that is, in your overall optimism, every time you turn over a rock, you expect to find a diamond. Most of the time, you'll find a snake."

He'd warned them that the future belonged to the fastest, but the Global TransPark, as it was duly named, didn't get off the ground until a decade had passed. Choosing Kinston took a year, drafting a master plan took three more, and environmental impact studies squandered another five ("which the FAA proclaimed was the bureaucratic speed of light," Kasarda said). Construction wasn't finished until 2001, just in time for

9/11 and a recession; in the meantime, Kasarda had moved on to the aerotropolis.

He'd spent the interim years putting theory into practice. If Kinston couldn't keep up with him, he would find someone who could—a company, not a state or a city. FedEx borrowed his transpark blueprints for its Asian hub in the Philippines. Located seventy miles from Manila over vertiginous mountain roads, on the site of a former U.S. Navy base, the hub opened in 1995 as the fulcrum of the Subic Bay Freeport Zone. Within two years, Taiwanese companies had opened a dozen factories there, loading their wares directly onto FedEx planes bound for all points across Asia. Motherboards, disc drives, and a billion Intel Pentium chips landed in Taipei and mainland China for assembly into PCs. A Korean company would later one-up them all with a single factory there capable of producing three times as many microchips, equal to nearly half of South Korea's total domestic output at the time. It was screwdriver work, but the country was happy to have it. During the first decade of the hub's operation, more than a hundred foreign firms invested $2.5 billion. Their factories were largely self-contained, employing some seventy thousand locals but otherwise relying on the hub's clockwork operations for connectivity. Exports soared from $24 million the first year to $1.3 billion at its peak.

Subic Bay was Kasarda's validation. His ideas really worked, building a billion-dollar economy out of nothing. He tried to replicate its success in Thailand, at a former U.S. Air Force base named U-Tapao, and in China, near the border with Macau. Back in the United States, he was involved with airports in the Inland Empire of California, and in Fort Worth, advising H. Ross Perot, Jr. (the son of the presidential candidate). The pair abroad were never built, scuttled by the Asian financial crisis and the whims of party chairmen. The ones closer to home had better luck, sprouting new appendages from their surrounding cities and nudging Kasarda toward the aerotropolis.

Back in Kinston, signs of trouble had begun to surface. In 1998, FedEx announced it would add a hub somewhere in the state. The Global TransPark's boosters believed they were in line to get it. They were wrong. The TransPark lost to Greensboro's airport, snug in the center of the Triad, and the competition wasn't close. This set the tone for another decade, during which prospective tenants spurned its isolation for someplace with an easier commute. Its near miss with greatness came in 2003, when Boeing seriously considered assembling the Dreamliner there. But the aerospace giant passed after its home state of Washington offered it $3 billion in sweeteners to stay. (The state had previously been burned by Boeing's decision to move its headquarters to Chicago, citing the connectivity of O'Hare. The finalists in that bake-off had been Dallas–Fort Worth and Denver.)

Nearly eighteen years after Kasarda conceived it, the TransPark finally caught a break. After much wooing, a Boeing spinoff named Spirit AeroSystems agreed to build a large factory near Kinston. It would hire a thousand locals in exchange for roughly $200 million in incentives, enough to pay the average salary of its workers for almost four years. The finished product—a long tube of fuselage for the forthcoming Airbus A350—would be trucked to the coast and shipped by boat to France, not flown.

Still, the TransPark's supporters hoped it might yet become the nexus of a thriving aerospace cluster, throwing off thousands of jobs. Their hopes were dashed yet again in 2009 when Boeing settled on North Charleston, South Carolina, as the location of its second 787 assembly line. Their unwavering faith in the transformative power of sheer infrastructure would seem utterly delusional if it hadn't worked once before.

Hidden amid seven thousand acres of pine forest between Raleigh (the state capital), Durham, and Chapel Hill (where Kasarda teaches), the Research Triangle Park is one of the oldest and largest master-planned R & D hubs in the country, home to 150 firms and their thirty-seven thousand employees. Nearly a third work for IBM or its Chinese cousin, Lenovo, whose global headquarters sits outside the park. Astroturf was invented here; so were bar codes, ultrasound, and the HIV/AIDS drug AZT. The median salary in the park is $56,000, nearly one and a half times the regional average.

Begun in 1959, RTP was the Global TransPark of its day—the brainchild of an ambitious governor determined to fight brain drain in one of the poorest and least educated states in the country. But RTP had advantages the TransPark did not: world-class local universities, a million residents, and a governor picked by John F. Kennedy to be commerce secretary, a perch he used to seed RTP with national research institutes. Even then, it took a decade to land its first big tenant, and reproducing its results has proved as elusive as cold fusion. There is a fine line between keeping the faith and throwing good money after bad, and even now the TransPark's true believers point to RTP as a sign they will ultimately be vindicated. "North Carolina has had success with radical ideas when they were able to hold off the critics long enough to get on their feet," affirms former governor Martin. "When I heard Kasarda's idea, I thought it would be the next one."

Airbus and its suppliers have since made a major commitment to Global TransPark. But if one venue in the area has the hallmarks of an aerotropolis, it is Research Triangle Park. What distinguished the two, Kasarda understood belatedly, is that the latter was blessed with both highways and growing cities around it (not to mention flights across the country only ten minutes away). RTP may be an economic engine, but its cogs are able to sleep in their own beds at night.

The Magic Bullet

On a frosty November morning not long ago, Kasarda flew north to deliver his aerotropolis speech before a fresh audience in Philadelphia. This was not an uncommon request. Since the first of his now-annual "Airport Cities" conferences nine years ago, for example, he's given state-of-the-aerotropolis addresses in Dubai, Hong Kong, Frankfurt, and Beijing. In the United States, he's been an adviser and consultant to Detroit, Indianapolis, Milwaukee, and Memphis, all of which see themselves in a race against the others.

The working breakfast in Philadelphia was staged at the request of Rina Cutler, a blunt bubbe who muscled her way through city politics like a glacier, mountainous and unstoppable. Cutler is Philly's deputy mayor for transportation and utilities; the buck for the airport stopped with her. Philadelphia International is one of the busiest in the nation, but it is severely cramped, wedged between a wildlife refuge on one side and the Delaware River on the other.

Kasarda had been disappointed by the session's title: "Envisioning a Truly Great Philadelphia International Airport." It should have read: "Envisioning a Philadelphia Aerotropolis," because an aerotropolis *is not an airport*, he whispered; dwelling on runways and flight delays risked missing the point. The setting was a wood-paneled conference room with a dozen saucer-shaped tables conducive to the brainstorming exercises to follow. The attendees constituted a mix of bureaucrats and policy wonks crossed with architects and urban planners.

It was his show, but he's no showman. Eschewing razzle-dazzle, Kasarda blends in with his crowds to avoid upstaging them. This morning he was wearing one of his customary dark suits and muted ties—the uniform of business class—disguising any signs of tweediness. His hair was swept back from a widow's peak like the wings of a stealth bomber. His eyes flickered in rhythm with his PowerPoint presentation—a symptom of terminal lag. He has spent years aloft by now, and nothing in the glint of silvery wings stirs his blood anymore.

"Let me give you a very, very simple definition," he began from the podium. "An aerotropolis is basically an airport-integrated region, extending as far as sixty miles from the inner clusters of hotels, offices, distribution and logistics facilities." To a layman, what followed for the next hour was scarcely more specific. Kasarda prefers categorical examples to precise ones, befitting a man trained to take a tectonic view of the world. In his words, "All kinds of activities are served by and enhanced by the airport. Whether it's supply chains, whether it's enterprise networks, whether it's biosciences and pharmaceuticals and time-sensitive organic materials, the airport itself is really the nucleus of a range of 'New Economy' functions," with the ultimate aim of bolstering the city's "competitiveness, job creation, and quality of life."

His idiom is a mash-up of consultant-speak and academic jargon, each one wielded to differing but complementary effect. He hammers home his collection of catchphrases like a good thought-leader should. "The Web can't move a box," "business is a contact sport," and "never make strategic decisions on a cyclical basis." And then there's "survival of the fastest," poached from Alvin Toffler.

"My favorite book of his is *Powershift*, published in 1990," Kasarda told the room. "It's a five-hundred-eighty-five-page treatise asking what will define the next hierarchy of countries, of companies, of regions and communities. It can be boiled down to three words: *speed, speed,* and *speed*. It wouldn't be the big eating the small, but the fast eating the slow. By the beginning of this century, one indisputable law would determine competitive advantage: *the survival of the fastest*.

"By the mid-1990s," he continued, "we found ourselves operating in an environment defined by two words: 'turbulence' and 'uncertainty.' How do you adapt to constantly changing and unpredictable environments? The companies that can do that—the communities and regions that can do that—gain competitive advantage." Individual companies no longer compete, he explained; their entire supply chains do. Dell versus Lenovo has been a struggle not between two companies but between hundreds of them, involving hundreds of thousands of people scattered worldwide. Some links in those chains might be cut loose or switch sides; others might hopscotch from city to city or country to country, or even across continents, as the stakes of global rivalry wear down their margins. And more than a few are playing for every team.

As the distance between these far-flung links in the chain increased, so did the need to traverse that distance as fast as possible. Because even as the size of the playing field has grown, the pace has gotten faster, and the increments counted in a just-in-time system have shrunk from seconds to something less. This, he said, led Toffler to declare that "time itself becomes a valuable product."

This combination of the death of distance and the just-in-time world has changed not only how companies compete but how cities compete as well. In the Instant Age, cities and their hinterlands go head-to-head for the most lucrative links in the chains. Civic pride, national heritage, and executive prestige mean little or nothing when pitted against falling trade barriers, cross-border conglomerates, quicksilver liquidity, and the overweening need for speed. The only trump card a city can play is the last one, Kasarda argued. If it's *faster* than its rivals, it can win. With the right infrastructure, a hinterland can become a hub, toppling capitals. The fundamental laws of real estate—location, location, location—have been supplanted by three new ones: *access, access, access.*

Here, Kasarda's framework dovetails with what we already know about globalization. The world is a network. Cities now connect more easily to each other than to the towns and villages that lie just beyond their borders, or to the national capitals that supposedly call their shots. It's how the cities of the Pearl River Delta can become "the world's factory," and why their fate is bound up in the flat-screen TV you dragged home from Best Buy. It's how Las Vegas and Macau—an oasis and an island, separated by seven thousand miles—can duel to become the world's gambling mecca. And it's why the manicured lawns of the Infosys campus in Bangalore still abut urban squalor outside its gates: because the Microsoft of India has nothing in common with the countryside. We think local and act global.

How did this happen? The short answer is the Internet, if you allow it to stand in for the pervasive wiring of the world over the past forty years and all the changes it has wrought. First corporations, then cities rebuilt themselves according to the logic of networks, as hubs and nodes, and soon we will too, assuming we haven't already.

Kasarda is sanguine about this. For all his talk of uncertainty and turbulence, he has no qualms about his prescriptions, and his faith is unruffled by market volatility. His is the best of all possible worlds, one in which growth slopes inexorably upward. Past results *do* guarantee future performance when it comes to urban expansion—we are forever roaming farther and faster.

"As the world has flattened, all kinds of commerce have moved around the globe," he lectured. "They have to remain connected, even more so than before. Aviation is the means; it is the physical Internet, and your airport is the node. What else is going to connect us?" he asked, clasping his hands together, reaching his climax. "We're talking about a new business model; you have to understand this. Airports are no longer a piece of transportation infrastructure, and this is no longer a city airport, but a city itself. *The airport city.*"

Like any city, an aerotropolis must be governed, although in any given instance it's unclear who should be in charge. Philadelphia International is in a particularly tricky situation; while run as a city agency, it actually straddles two cities and counties, and its catchment area spills across three states. At breakfast, there were representatives present from all of the above, not to mention SEPTA (Southeast Pennsylvania Transportation Authority, which runs trains and buses to the terminals), the Greater Philadelphia Chamber of Commerce, and the Delaware Valley Regional Planning Commission—none of which has any sway over the airport but whose cooperation is essential to realigning the region around it.

The problem is that no one has ever thought to build a city around an airport before, especially when there are already a dozen governments blanketing the ground. As the examples of Heathrow, O'Hare, and LAX have proved, simply muddling through is not a viable option. New forms

of governance are necessary. Kasarda endorses at least a regional aerotropolis authority with control of its own destiny and a say in the outlying areas. Even better are public-private partnerships like the one in
effect in Amsterdam, where a series of interlocking, nominally for-profit
companies administer the region on top of local governments, which weigh
in as their shareholders. Toffler once told an interviewer that the common bond linking failing companies and struggling regions in the Instant
Age was a dearth of imagination. He put it this way: "The illiterate of the
21st century will not be those who cannot read and write, but those who
cannot learn, unlearn and relearn."

Except in places like China and the Middle East, where aerotropoli
are invoked by fiat and the authorities brook no dissent, it can take decades to unstitch and resew the civic fabric to everyone's satisfaction,
which explains why Kasarda ended his talk with the following recitation,
borrowed from one of his colleagues:

"There is no 'magic bullet' in economic transformation. True transformation comes about when people across and within all sectors (government, education, business/industry, not-for-profit, arts, and culture) come
together in genuine partnerships for the common good. It comes about
when processes are improved. It comes about when bureaucratic impedi-
ments are swept aside. It comes about when, intertwined with basic improvements, a few bold experiments are launched. And it comes about
when the public and private sectors come together to invest the resources
needed to stimulate transformation."

As he took a seat to polite applause, his host took the floor. "You've
just heard the *Wow*," Rina Cutler said breathlessly. If Kasarda "is the
Ghost of Christmas Past, then I will declare myself the Ghost of Christmas Future. Because from my perspective, for the regional economy—
and in this case the region is three states, and a lot of counties—this is
my vision of the future." It had come to her six months earlier, following
Kasarda's private presentation to the city's assembled CEOs. Cutler converted on the spot, spying a way to overhaul an otherwise intractable bit
of infrastructure. Kasarda's true purpose at breakfast was a laying on of
hands; this indoctrination would be the first of many.

"I'm hearing a lot now about how this will take billions," she told me
later, after polling the room. "'There are too many governments!' 'You'll
never get coordination!' 'Where will the money come from?' And I tell

them, 'Building the next six miles of I-95 is going to cost me two billion dollars.' I don't get nervous about billions; in the scheme of transportation infrastructure, everything is very expensive. If they can afford to fund a war, if they can afford billions to bail out industries, they can afford this. I'm not asking for it tomorrow or next week, but I have a dream. And he articulates that dream pretty well."

6

AEROTROPOLIS OR BUST

A century ago, Detroit consecrated itself to the automobile. Now its hopes for renewal are pinned on an aerotropolis. Can it be the vehicle for new industries?

Eliminating the City

No one can claim to be the Henry Ford of aviation, as the title already belongs to Henry Ford himself. In 1925, he patented the aluminum Ford Tri-Motor, a Tin Goose in the mold of his Tin Lizzies. Ford promptly built an aircraft factory in Dearborn and an airfield alongside it. Ford Airport was the world's first to be equipped with floodlights, paved runways, two-way radios, and a terminal. There was even an airport hotel. Needing someone to buy his planes and somewhere to fly them, he launched Ford Airlines, also a first.

His fleet of Tri-Motors ferried passengers, auto parts, and airmail between Dearborn and Chicago until 1933, when he closed both the airline and the factory. (Always a trailblazer, he'd never turned a profit.) Charles Lindbergh and Amelia Earhart were customers, while TWA started cross-country service using Tri-Motors in 1929. The airport was later paved over for an automobile test track and proving grounds; drivers still swerve around traces of the runways.

But Ford wasn't finished. He never mass-produced the Tin Goose the way he had the Model T. He was given a second chance during World War II, when the army charged him with building an armada of bombers. Before Pearl Harbor, the California factories of his competitors could barely muster one per day. A bomber a day? He would build a bomber an *hour*.

A mammoth plant was built at Willow Run, on farmland twenty-five miles west of Detroit. The main building had two and a half million square feet of open floor space—more than all the prewar factories of Boeing, Douglas, and Consolidated Aircraft put together. On a tour, Lindbergh pronounced it "the Grand Canyon of the mechanized world." By 1944, B-24 Liberators were indeed rolling off the assembly line every hour, where pilots were waiting to take off with them from the new airfield next door. Willow Run's forty thousand workers produced more planes than any factory in existence, earning FDR's salute as the "Arsenal of Democracy."

Following the war, Ford's heirs turned their backs on aviation and returned to the profitable pursuit of making cars. Willow Run was eventually flipped to General Motors, which built Chevys there for decades before downshifting to six-speed transmissions. The plant will close for good this year as part of GM's bankruptcy restructuring; more of its customers (and employees) now live in places like China and Thailand than in America or Michigan, and the transmissions made there were not being shipped to them.

Driving to Detroit from Willow Run, you can trace the city's sad, century-long trajectory from boomtown to arsenal to lemon. Ford's colossus was the pinnacle of mass production and an omen of the city's evolutionary dead end. Detroit became so wedded to making cars—and to remaking itself in their image—that it stagnated within a generation. "Fordism," his philosophy of industrial gigantism, was quickly debunked by nimbler foreign competitors who traded in size for speed. But not before the landscape he created—one of arterial highways and far-flung appendages, the first to Willow Run—bled entire cities dry, starting with Detroit. "We shall solve the City Problem," he wrote, "by eliminating the City." He was half right. When Ford's rivals in Los Angeles expressed their desire to build a Detroit of the air, they couldn't have known the name would become a curse.

"It's Up to Us"

The delegates wobbled into the Sheraton's private dining room one by one, smiling wanly and yawning helplessly. They'd arrived in Amsterdam hours earlier at John Kasarda's behest, not to study old masters but to scrutinize Schiphol International Airport. And they would, tomorrow—the terminal lay just across the street from their hotel. He'd promised them a glimpse inside the gearbox of a fully functioning aerotropolis, and everyone present suspected that together they would build the first one in America to be conceived from scratch.

They were all from greater Detroit: Wayne County and Washtenaw, the outlying cities of Romulus, Belleville, and Taylor, the townships of Huron and Van Buren, and more amorphous entities such as the Southeast Michigan Council of Governments (SEMCOG) and the Detroit Regional Chamber. There were two dozen in all. The only thing missing was the city of Detroit itself. Its mayor at the time, Kwame Kilpatrick, had dismissed this expedition as a conspiracy. But no one cared what he thought after the "hip-hop mayor" quit office to serve time for perjury. Not that he was wrong—each ringleader flew here scheming to raise a new city beyond the ruins of his own.

Can an aerotropolis save Detroit? The city that most desperately needs one is also its worst-case scenario. The self-styled "Renaissance City" has been a laboratory—and cemetery—for urban renewal fads since the 1970s. Perhaps the city's most pathetic symbol of abortive rebirth is the People Mover, an elevated monorail gliding empty past downtown towers deserted for decades.

Kasarda proposes custom-building cities *by* companies *for* companies, guaranteeing their survival by tailoring them to clients' specifications—beginning with the airport. But this is exactly what happened in Detroit: the city was reshaped politically, economically, and geographically to suit the needs of the Big Three—Ford, GM, and Chrysler. Kasarda's cities are nodes in a global network, streamlined and refined for corporate needs; by that standard, Ford's Detroit was the *autotropolis* of its day. Its demise poses questions that go to the heart of the aerotropolis: What happens when the host industry dies? Or leaves?

There is no Henry Ford this time, and no Big Three. Building an aerotropolis on spec is an all-or-nothing bet they can attract something else—what that is, they're not sure. Considering how far Detroit already trails most other cities in almost every quantifiable measure of talent and quality of life you can think of, the odds are stacked against them. But they'll be heroes if they succeed; their communities would become the center of a new city filling forty square miles of farmland and cracked pavement with tree-lined boulevards, bike trails, trains, and research parks stocked with local graduates designing batteries for the 2035 Chevy Volt. Envious cities would rush to duplicate the patented Motor City Miracle—a downtown Detroit resettled by gentrifiers who make the reverse commute to the airport (not unlike the Googlers who live in San Francisco).

The tall one in a safari jacket, his slate-gray face looming above the rest, was Dr. Mulugetta Birru, Wayne County's economic guru. Birru had arrived in Michigan from Pittsburgh a few years earlier with the reputation of a miracle worker; he learned quickly just how easy he'd had it there. The balding one was Doug Rothwell, whom everyone was trying desperately to impress. As the president of Detroit Renaissance, he was a stand-in for the city's CEOs. As their proxy, he had their ears and their wallets; winning him over would make or break this trip.

Kasarda wasn't here yet—he would lead the tour the next morning—and in his absence the master of ceremonies was Robert Ficano, Wayne County's chief executive. A pol's pol who never misses a parade, his generic honorific belied both his rank and the size of the mess he'd inherited. Neither a mayor nor a governor but something in between, he had a mandate that extended far beyond Detroit. Wayne is to the Motor City what Cook is to Chicago or Dade to Miami. It's four times the city's size in area and twice as populous with two million residents, more than Phoenix or Philadelphia. His domain runs from 8 Mile Road in the north—the Iron Curtain dividing city and suburbia—to Grosse Isle in the south, and from Lake St. Claire and Canada on the east to rolling meadows in the west. It contains not one, but two airfields outside city limits: Willow Run, which continues to handle the Big Three's shipments, and Detroit Metropolitan Wayne County Airport.

Miraculously for a city that is literally crumbling, Detroit has one of the best airports in America, endowed with brand-new terminals, a busy Delta hub, and better connections to Asia than any other city in the country—a legacy of Northwest Orient and the expense accounts of Toyota executives. Between the two airports lies an interstate and nearly a hundred square miles of more-or-less empty land. As with everything else in Motown, the Big Three warped the city's maturity, diverting sprawl away from the airport and north toward their factories instead.

The unmolested acreage left behind belongs to Wayne County and to the municipalities whose stand-ins had come to Amsterdam. Ficano, who as a boy attended UAW rallies with his grandfather (who had left Italy to work for Henry Ford), has found himself in partial possession of Detroit's best chance at a postunion, postauto, postindustrial future. He has no illusions as to what will befall them if they waste it.

If there was a canary in the coal mine beneath Bear Stearns and Lehman Brothers, it was Detroit, which shed six hundred thousand jobs during the bubble. Even in an era of no-money-down, no-money-back mortgages, the city's population fled by the tens of thousands. No wonder the jet-lagged delegates were in a raw, truth-telling mood.

At dinner, Ficano sat to my right, while on my left was a high-strung young man named Walter Mears. He was the city manager of Belleville, a hamlet that once doubled as a lakeside retreat for Henry Ford. He was operating on a need-to-know basis—"my involvement began when the plane took off at two a.m. last night," he confessed—but he liked what they were plotting. Alternatives like Governor Jennifer Granholm's "Cool Cities" initiative to resuscitate Lansing and Flint with artists and hip districts had left him cold. "Build a cool city," she had argued, "and they—young knowledge workers and other creative class members—will come." No one shared her optimism. The aerotropolis "is one of the few things that make sense," Mears told me. "It has a beginning, a middle, and an end, unlike some of the other—I don't want to say 'harebrained'— schemes that are just grasping at straws."

He railed against the local politicians "content to watch our downtown die," proclaiming "the sky is falling" while refusing to embrace any plan to save it. "There's always that initial skepticism about any big project, but this is so important for our lifeblood." His father and grandfather worked for Ford, and he remembers "how scared they were when globalization first became real. Now the people sitting around this table are discovering how it can work to our benefit, and what it means for our children."

Across the table, Ficano and Birru were walking Rothwell through a crash course in logistics. Build it, and they might come, the pair argued. The appeal of building an aerotropolis outside Detroit is that it offers a city that no longer *makes* cars but only assembles them a chance to leverage the logistics involved into something more lucrative. As it stands right now, the Detroit Three move some of their most valuable parts by air via Chicago, including the GPS transceivers at the heart of features like OnStar. Upon landing in the United States from China, they're tossed onto a truck for the last three hundred miles.

"If we sell this to the [freight] forwarders," Ficano was saying, "we can lure them from Chicago. We're the largest port of entry in the country," thanks to the trucks crossing from Canada. "You can never do just-in-time from Chicago, but we can do it from here." The shrinking Big Three may be the sick men of the industry, but there's still money to be made from them.

Consider it a down payment on his real vision, one certified by consultants' numbers: a new city stretching seven miles from Metro Airport to Willow Run, with at least one hundred thousand new residents and as many as five hundred thousand, younger and smarter than Detroit has now. They'll commute via planes and trains (but not automobiles) to the local or far-flung outposts of electric auto suppliers, biotech firms, biofuel refineries, and just about any technology-intensive business you can think of. In other words: a city that has less and less to do with making cars. "Our kids will only stay if they have hope," he told me between bites. "If they see that GM, Ford, and Chrysler are laying people off and aren't recruiting, they won't see a future for themselves."

He rose to give a toast as dessert was served. It was his unstated hope that by bringing them here, far from home, he could turn this team of rivals into coconspirators. Ten of the entities present had already signed a "memorandum of understanding" pledging to push forward. Before they could build this city, they must decide how to govern it together.

"This epitomizes what you can do over twenty years," he told a hushed room. "This can really drive the economy if we do it right. This is so important it will determine whether your children or grandchildren will stay in the state with the jobs created here. We're in a crisis right now in Michigan, and this can be the silver lining in turning things around to where we want to go. It's up to us."

The Utopia of the Machine

How did Detroit manage to drive into a ditch? Check all that apply: auto companies failing or pushing out to the suburbs and beyond, leaving behind a skyline full of tombstones; the freeways dredged through city streets, encouraging residents to follow; black and white flight after the '67 riots; hostility to mass transit and any kind of planning; infighting; corruption; Toyota; Honda; Nissan; Hyundai.

Some attribute it to the unalterable ebb and flow of history—Detroit as a cadaver worthy of Spengler or Toynbee—to absolve themselves of any blame. Ficano's nemesis, L. Brooks Patterson, the country-club Republican running suburban Oakland County, unwittingly echoes Amos Hawley: "Detroit's history has gone the way of Rome and Athens and Constantinople. It is what history does. History moves on. And history has moved away from the Babylonian Empire. It moved away from Egypt. It be what it be . . . I think Detroit sees itself in its rearview mirror. But Detroit will never again be where those other cities were, including Detroit."

Unemployment in the Detroit area has topped 27 percent, the highest in the nation by far and *four times* what it was in 2000. Somewhere around 175,000 people have left the city since, and that's counting only the living. The dead are departing too, exhumed by their fleeing families. The foreclosure rate hovers around triple the national average, while Detroit has the highest crime, poverty, murder, and auto-insurance rates of any major city in the country. Only one metropolis has suffered more in the last decade, and New Orleans's disaster was an act of God. Detroit's is man-made.

The consensus is that Detroit is dying because the industry that spawned the city is dying with it. They have it backward: Detroit wasn't born with the Model T and didn't end with the SUV. It died the moment Henry Ford perfected his moving assembly line in 1913. They just didn't know it at the time.

A century before, Detroit (a French word that means "the straits") was a wide expanse in the wilderness ideally situated between two Great Lakes. It started life as a trading hub for Quebecois fur trappers. After the Erie Canal opened in 1825, travel times and freight costs to New York dropped to a tenth of what they'd been. In 1848, a railroad linking Detroit and Chicago cut the travel time between them by two-thirds. By midcentury, Detroit was closer in time to Liverpool than it had been to Cincinnati fifty years prior.

By then, Detroit's economy had moved on from milling grain to building the ships that ferried it across the Great Lakes. These begot shipyards launching the first oceangoing steamships, their construction spawning an entire class of engine makers and machinists. They demanded metal, and by the 1860s, copper smelting was the city's biggest industry. The local ores ran out after only twenty years, but Detroit was so busy making steam engines, tools, paints, pumps, stoves, and carriages that it hardly mattered.

"This was the prosperous and diversifying economy from which the automobile industry emerged two decades later to produce the last of the important Detroit exports, and, as it turned out, to bring the city's economic development to a dead end," read Jane Jacobs's obituary in *The Economy of Cities*, published in 1969. "The Chinese ideogram for 'crisis' is composed of the symbols for 'danger' and 'opportunity'; just so, a very successful growth industry poses a crisis for a city. Everything—all other development work, all other processes of city growth, the fertile and creative inefficiency of the growth industry's suppliers, the opportunities of able workers to break away, the inefficient but creative use of capital— can be sacrificed to the exigencies of the growth industry, which thus turns the city into a company town." Or in this case a three-company town where there had once been three thousand. Reduced to an industrial monoculture, the city was no different in the end from Jacobs's hometown of Scranton (or Kasarda's Wilkes-Barre) after the coal veins ran dry (or drowned).

Detroit's future was mortgaged to pay for America's postwar autopia. Henry Ford and the system he created—mass production, mass markets, and mass consumption by a blue-collar middle class—transformed every city and factory it touched. By the end of the 1950s, however, it wasn't the military-industrial complex we needed to worry about but the *auto*-industrial one. The Big Three and the industries they spawned or converged with—oil, steel, mining, finance, insurance, sales, repairs, highways, and the construction of a vast suburbia navigable only by car—were responsible for as much as a third of GDP. (It's still a tenth today.) The author and developer Christopher Leinberger has suggested that "in 1953, when President of GM Charles E. Wilson sat before the Senate at his confirmation hearing to be Secretary of Defense and said that 'what was good for the country was good for General Motors and vice versa,' *it was true*."

Not anymore. The number of cars and the number of miles Americans drive each year are falling. The Earth Policy Institute's Lester R. Brown, who tracks these figures, believes American car ownership might be in permanent decline, similar to Japan's. The reasons may be more profound than the recession; Brown attributes it to gasoline prices, saturation, and congestion—the annual costs of the latter, measured in time and frustration, have quintupled from $17 billion to $87 billion in the last twenty-five years. If these trends continue, there's no point bailing out the Big Three. They will never again sell as many cars at home and will only face stiffer competition in growth markets overseas.

The knee-jerk rebuttal is that Detroit still makes a lot of cars and probably always will. But should it? A generation ago, people said the same about Pittsburgh. In the 1970s, the United States poured more steel than any other country, under the banners of Bethlehem, Republic, and U.S. Steel. But the failure to modernize factories, the invasion of Japanese imports, and rising labor costs (sound familiar?) sealed the fate of all three firms, leading to consolidation and bankruptcy. The devastation was total: between 1974 and 2005, the United States scrapped 93 percent of its steelworkers, dropping from more than half a million to thirty-seven thousand. Bottoming out was the best thing that could have happened to Pittsburgh, however. In a subsequent moment of clarity, city elders hatched plans to use local universities as high-tech incubators. The city rebuilt around those Rust Belt mainstays, health care and education, while the mills' old suppliers branched out into cleaner industries like glassmaking, nuclear power, robotics, and biotech. Pittsburgh has more jobs today than it possessed in the time of Andrew Carnegie. The lesson for the Motor City is clear: its salvation is at odds with the Big Three's.

But can Detroit learn, unlearn, and relearn? Listen to one visitor in the 1930s, who could look upon Ford Airport and envision an aerotropolis but could not conceive of a future without Ford: Detroit "is the result of three decades of intense progress in the most modern of the great industries. It is what the biggest of big businesses consciously or unconsciously assumes a city ought to be . . . I see elevated to whatever Acropolis Detroit may erect the twin gods of Utility and Comfort. I see arising the beauty of the perfect order, the Utopia of the machine."

Kasarda sounded equally grandiose when he proposed an aerotropolis here ten years ago. He was asked to craft a plan for several thousand acres of fallow farmland beneath the airport's approach paths, bought by the county to appease neighbors upset by the noise. His early drafts became the prototype of the full-blown city Ficano has in mind today.

Within its footprint or lying along its spine is everything Detroit needs to lure the high-paying knowledge work its civic leaders crave. Besides the airports and the dirt, there is I-94, Michigan's east–west artery and the last leg of the "NAFTA corridor" running from Texas to Ontario. It's a logistician's dream. Strung along a thirty-mile stretch of highway are three universities—Michigan, Eastern Michigan, and Wayne State—with one hundred thousand students among them. The first already spends nearly $1 billion a year on basic research and is busy hiring two thousand scientists to fill a new campus furnished and then abandoned by Pfizer. Plans are afoot to connect all three to the airport via commuter trains and light rail, sowing the seeds for transit-oriented developments. In between are rivers, lakes, and hiking trails—not a bad foundation for your own private Portland.

But the question then becomes what to build . . . and where to build it. And by whom, to what ends? The site is a jumble of jurisdictions. The airports are under Ficano's thumb, but everyone else is free to thumb his or her nose at him. The interstates aren't his; the railroad tracks aren't either. Wayne State is in Detroit. Michigan and Eastern Michigan are in Washtenaw County, the next one over. Willow Run somehow manages to straddle the county line; when Henry Ford built bombers there during the war, a giant flywheel spun them around so he wouldn't have to pay taxes in two counties by crossing it. And then there are those seven needy municipalities, all wondering what's in this for them. "People are hungry here," says Robert Guenzel, Bob Ficano's counterpart in Ann Arbor. "We know we need more regionalism, but we don't do that well in Michigan. I've got all these townships and villages, and they've got *turf.*"

Turf is antithetical to the aerotropolis. Turf is why the Daleys have never relaxed their death grip on O'Hare, lest its suburbs stage the same revolt Kwame Kilpatrick feared. And look how much good it did them. "Look down the next time you fly out of O'Hare," Ficano told me. "You'd have to knock it down to squeeze anything else in there." Rest assured, they're trying.

Form follows function, not lines on a map. If Detroit is to build a better aerotropolis than O'Hare—or Dallas, or Denver—then turf battles must take a backseat to what the consultants call "highest and best use," making sure everything is in its right place. Overlaying Kasarda's schematics, this means gritty cargo alleys in Romulus, which encircles the airport, and gleaming R & D centers out in Ypsilanti, hugging the universities. Guess which one Romulus would rather have? So what's stopping it from bidding for them, highest and best uses be damned?

Not the "memorandum of understanding." Seven communities, two counties, and the airport authority signed it in July 2006 after much wooing and wrangling, but it was legally nonbinding. More to the point, there were no promises of help or signals of interest from the private sector, whose embrace (or lack thereof) will decide whether this turns out to be a catalyst or a catastrophe. Before anyone put a shovel in the ground, it was incumbent on Ficano to knit his fractious allies into some sort of confederacy. If they wanted to build a city, they had to think like one, move as fast as one, act as decisively as one, compete as single-mindedly as one. Strike that; they had to be *faster*, able to slash and burn through the red tape holding back their rivals—whoever they turned out to be. But they weren't a city. And as far as Detroit itself goes . . . well, there are better models. The trick is finding one.

Survival of the Fastest

Maurits Schaafsma began the next morning's lesson with a koan. The first slide in his presentation read:

The Airport leaves the city.
The City follows the airport.
The Airport becomes a city.

Reciting these lines aloud, he pointed at the screen and shrugged, as if to say, "See? Easy."

Schaafsma is Holland's analogue to Kasarda: an architect, intellectual, and strategist all in one. He looks the part with his unruly salt-and-pepper hair, head-to-toe black uniform, and thoroughly angular eyewear. But whereas his counterpart is obsessed with efficiency, Schaafsma's urban vision is more urbane. The skyline of Dubai makes him shudder; he prefers to envision Terminal Cities containing the seeds of new Manhattans.

He's also the senior planner at Schiphol Real Estate, in charge of mapping the inner contours of its aerotropolis. Befitting the Dutch's reputation as inveterate planners, Schiphol decided to exploit its growing footprint instead of protecting it. To that end, it spun out a pair of subsidiaries: Schiphol Real Estate owns every square foot "inside the fence," while the Schiphol Area Development Company (SADC) develops every available parcel outside it. Declaring Schiphol not just an airport but an "AirportCity," they were the first to define highest and best uses besides hangars and parking. They made room for cargo outfits near the runways and corporate headquarters in the Trade Center towers, rearranging them when necessary. They have never been afraid to buy, sell, tear down, and rebuild, because they control a scarce resource convertible into the most precious commodity of all: time.

As airports go, the Schiphol Group proved to be a model of sanity compared to Chicago or Los Angeles. A privately run company that's also a public trust, the group does right by its neighbors by doing what's best for the airport and its tenants. Its principal shareholders are Amsterdam, Rotterdam, and the Dutch federal government. Possession of SADC, in turn, is split among the group, neighboring cities, and the province. Their interlocking ownership owes much to the Dutch East India Company formed four centuries ago. Its start-up costs were borne by six cities—Amsterdam and Rotterdam among them—and its immense dividends were apportioned accordingly. Before it was the world's first multinational conglomerate, it was the first public-private partnership.

In Schiphol's case, everyone wanted in. In 1994, they formed another partnership dubbed the Amsterdam Airport Area (AAA) defining a mega-aerotropolis encompassing the airport, port, city of Amsterdam, and the surrounding provinces. The airport had not only become a city, in some ways it was Holland's *biggest* city. AAA recruited companies in a handful of industries especially attuned to the air: electronics, aerospace, flowers, fashion, and Chinese firms seeking a toehold for their EU invasions. More than a thousand companies have settled there since, creating two hundred thousand jobs. Schiphol's daytime population is sixty-two thousand, not counting passengers—roughly on par with downtown Detroit's. Demand in and around the World Trade Center is so great that Schiphol commands the highest office rents in the Netherlands, higher than Amsterdam or even The Hague, which is home to more lawyers per capita than any other city on earth. Asserting itself with an astute blend of control, community, and collaboration, Schiphol has become more than a gateway; it's Holland's financial epicenter.

Its status was cemented with the Zuidas, Amsterdam's answer to Las Colinas, twenty years and $20 billion in the making. It lies along the city's southern ring road, six minutes' drive or train ride from Schiphol. Most of the Netherlands' native multinationals have relocated there—Philips, ING, and AkzoNobel among them. It was supposed to have sat north of the city until the country's biggest bank, ABN AMRO, threatened to leave the country if adjacency to the airport wasn't part of the deal. (Ironically, it later succumbed to a takeover by British, Belgian, and Spanish banks; for months, its headquarters in the Zuidas teemed with foreign consultants shuttling back and forth to London until the financial crisis scuttled the deal.)

Schaafsma's true fairy tale is a quintessentially Dutch one, a story so full of good faith and common sense all around that you have to wonder if anyone else could pull it off. Ficano interrupted his lecture to ask Schaafsma how he brought aggrieved parties to the negotiating table and kept them there until they came around. "We'll keep talking until someone drops dead," he answered coolly, "but usually we reach a solution." The Americans smirked in polite disbelief; their conversations tend to end in litigation.

That night, their last in Amsterdam, they adjourned to one of the old city's brown pubs. The ratio of empty wine bottles to people was approaching two to one by the time I arrived. Sufficiently lubricated, they were fast becoming comrades-in-arms. "I'm tired of seeing this in my campaign literature as a goal," Ficano vented. "I want a road map that says if I do this, this, and this, and we do, then we win." Seeing Schiphol convinced them the road led somewhere, even if their destination was still decades away. They may have been drinking, but they had gelled too. This trip was a turning point; until this moment, they had said all the right things but had scarcely believed them—that they could work together, make plans together, and repair their public sector enough to make it palatable again to private enterprise.

"I asked Rothwell for a hundred million dollars, and he didn't say no," a particularly giddy delegate told Mulu Birru. "He was drinking, but he didn't say no."

"In my experience, if you have a great idea, you will find the fund-ing," he soberly replied. "Money is never the problem."

It wasn't. A few weeks later, Rothwell took the wraps off the "Road to Renaissance," a six-point plan to rejuvenate Detroit, backed by $75 mil-lion in seed money. The aerotropolis was accorded top priority to "trans-form the economy of the region." Rothwell had said yes.

Ficano wasted no time appointing a task force to commission a study bolstering the strategic plan released almost a year later, in April 2008. Everyone marveled at their speed. (When it comes to bureaucracy, it's all relative.) Kasarda calculated their chances: better than fifty-fifty if they hurried. Master planning was farmed out to the real estate firm Jones Lang LaSalle, which got to work sifting the highest and best uses from a hundred square miles of tarmac and dirt.

I dropped in on Ficano not long thereafter, before the flush of his first victory had faded. He received me in the gloom of his wood-paneled office tucked inside a lonely baroque edifice downtown. A map of the aerotropolis was spread across a table; it was blank within its borders. Ficano is stout and square jawed, composed of two blocks, one stacked atop the other. Although able to parrot Kasarda's axioms ("the new econ-omy is speed, speed, and speed"), he prefers practice to theory.

His faith in the transformative power of airports recalls that of an-other Italian-American politician, Fiorello La Guardia. New York City's mayor during the Depression made building an airport within city limits the centerpiece of his massive public works campaign. "Aviation is es-tablished," he said. "Nothing can stop it." He famously held up a flight home to Newark, refusing to deplane there because his ticket said "New York." The crew complied, dumping him at an airstrip in Queens instead. La Guardia's airport, originally called Municipal Field, snatched those flights away from Newark before it even opened, in time for the 1939 World's Fair next door in Flushing. (Incidentally, the hit of the fair was General Motors' *Futurama*, offering a sneak peek of the autopia it was plotting.)

If you do this and you win, I asked, then who loses? Does Chicago have to fall for Detroit to prevail? Is this a win-win or a zero-sum game?

"We're in a fight with the rest of the world, not just Chicago," Ficano countered. "We're in a fight with Beijing, Shanghai, Dubai, Chicago, and New York," ticking them off on his fingers. "We have assets we've never taken advantage of, the airport being one of them. And they have assets too. This"—the aerotropolis—"is a whole new arena where we're on equal footing with Chicago and competitive with New York. Unlike their airports, we're not landlocked. Everything here has always been centered on the auto industry; now it's time to diversify."

His regional rivals feel the same. Cleveland is investigating its own aerotropolis, while Hamilton, Ontario, faces furious opposition to one. Both have significant flaws. Canada's largest steel town is a fading city of industry trying to reinvent itself as a creative one. Its hopes are pinned on the off chance Toronto doesn't build a second airport for the country's financial capital. Cleveland, meanwhile, counts Continental Airlines' smallest hub on its dwindling list of civic assets. But the airline's merger with United may render it redundant with O'Hare—not exactly the commitment you can rebuild a city around.

Ficano has studied the fighting styles of his foreign opponents, making more than a dozen trips abroad to drum up cash from the Persian Gulf and new business from China. Their shared trait is a ruthlessness not seen in the United States since the Gilded Age: Taxation is minimal, labor is disposable, and decision making is instant and irrevocable. They demand highways, railways, and runways, paying in cash. They don't hesitate, don't explain or second-guess themselves, and aren't about to let their citizens stand in the way. They are banking on being the path of least resistance—competitive superconductors so efficient they practically levitate, like the billion-dollar maglev train connecting Shanghai to its airport. Michigan's only hope, he decided, is to be a little more like them.

"One of the things we learned from Dubai and Beijing is that they make quick decisions," he said. "We don't have the luxury of waiting a year or a year and a half to squabble in public meetings anymore. Developers and companies will just go someplace else. It's a global economy now, you know? I want us to be one of the cheapest places to do business."

In fact, the opposite is true: Michigan is one of the slowest and most expensive, finishing forty-ninth out of fifty states on the *Forbes* list of states best for business. Southern states like Tennessee have shown no mercy, handing out kitchen-sink incentives and openly lobbying for the Big Three to fail. The cost of doing business in and around Detroit—as measured in wages, energy, and taxes—is on par with Chicago's. This despite a fleeing population and repossessed mansions listed in the low four figures. It's symptomatic of the panic surrounding the automakers' terminal prognosis. Everyone wants a piece before they succumb as expected: management, the unions, even the governor, who's taken a scorched earth approach when it comes to corporate taxes.

There's nothing Ficano can do about the unions, the number one reason out-of-state employers stay away, according to survey after survey. But he must plug Michigan's brain drain. Here are some gut-wrenching statistics: greater Detroit has more college students than the Bay Area, Tobacco Road, or Boston, and *none of them stay*. Barely a quarter of the region's residents have college degrees—worse than the national average—while Boston is closer to half. "One thing Michigan does better than anyone else is teach," one of the Amsterdam delegates had told me. "Our frustration is that we will bring you here and teach you, and then we will watch you board a plane and leave." Detroit has three times as many industrial engineers as the Tennessee Valley factory towns rooting against it, and spends more on R & D than the Research Triangle or Route 128. And yet none of it seems to matter. Concluding its own grim analysis, Detroit Renaissance (since renamed Business Leaders For Michigan, with an expanded focus) recommended "a meaningful reduction in the cost of doing business . . . with tax reform at its core."

The aerotropolis is a vehicle for this too. More than a gateway or a rallying cry, it's a test bed for new governance—the kind unencumbered by tax codes, turf warfare, and ancient history. The lines drawn between city and suburb never made much sense except to pit them against each other. Internecine strife destroyed Detroit; 8 Mile Road is a DMZ. It sounds inconceivable, but the city whose name is a byword for blight may be our best opportunity to reinvent what it means to be a city in the Instant Age. Detroit has already failed as a traditional one; its suburbs sucked it dry.

To save Detroit, they will need to think bigger. Southeast Michigan may be a jumble of jurisdictions, but it is still a single economic engine, and if there's one thing Ficano learned from his reconnaissance missions, it's that economic geography now trumps all other kinds. President Obama has said as much in decrying the "outdated 'urban' agenda that focuses exclusively on the problems in our cities, and ignores our growing metro areas," pledging "a strategy that's about South Florida as much as Miami; that's about Mesa and Scottsdale as much as Phoenix," and about Wayne and Washtenaw as much as Detroit. His Office of Urban Policy wants to set the agenda, but Ficano—who decided against a run for governor last year to see the aerotropolis through—isn't waiting around.

His efforts to push through legislation recognizing his new city drew fire from neighboring county executives and from Detroit mayor Dave Bing, who complained that the bills gave the aerotropolis an "unbeatable competitive advantage" against his own. Ficano replied he was competing against other states—and nations—not Detroit. (Bing, meanwhile, was drafting plans to tear down ten thousand vacant homes and close fifty-four schools.) Kasarda considers Bing's protests beside the point. "The companies thinking of moving to the aerotropolis would have never looked at downtown Detroit anyway," he says. The "Detroit *Region* Aerotropolis," as Ficano and his allies have taken to calling it, was their best shot at superimposing new lines on the map.

What they've sketched isn't a city after all but an Aerotropolis Development Corp. in Schiphol's mold. Instead of a mayor, it has a CEO, reporting to a board whose members signed its charter. It lacks the trappings of a city too—no police, no schools, no city hall. But it has the de facto power to tax, and to *untax* when it needs to, dangling twenty-year MEGA and TURBO tax credits in front of whomever it sees fit. (The former Speaker of the U.S. House of Representatives Newt Gingrich has gone one better, seriously suggesting all of Detroit should be one big tax-free zone.) The ADC's first task is to plan. It will decide the site's highest and best uses in detail once and for all, bestowing pockets of frictionlessness on those spots in the form of "Aerotropolis Zones." It will also draft ironclad New Urbanist guidelines defining what can be built, how it should look, and who qualifies to set up shop there—no malls, casinos, or stadiums need apply. In return, things will move faster. Ficano vows that applicants can break ground within sixty days, a vast improvement over the usual six months. For many prospects, the interminable wait for permits is a bigger deal breaker than the taxes. Not so in this case, in which the ADC is your one-stop shop for paperwork.

As public-private partnerships go, the ADC is a typically hazy hybrid. Although created with the passage of state law, its powers are mostly borrowed from its constituent communities, and checks and balances ensure it won't outstrip them. A third of its executive committee is composed of private members, while the airport authority has more votes than anyone other than Wayne County. They have to pay to play, however, chipping in for its operating budget until the tax revenue starts rolling in (assuming everyone isn't exempted by then). This way, the public sector gets the private one to pay for vital infrastructure—everything from sewer lines to light rail—while private interests help decide where it should go. The net positive is efficiency. The ADC should cost less and move faster than conventional government. And since no one has renounced their sovereignty in any case, it's what Ficano has to work with.

The software business has a word for this: middleware. Middleware is code sandwiched between incompatible programs—bleeding edge and ancient—translating for the two. It's typically written to coax data from decrepit mainframes, using it to solve up-to-the-second problems. Whether it's software or civics we're talking about, the purpose is the same: to make hidebound institutions reflect the reality on the ground, rather than straining to make reality fit their rules.

The key, to quote Ficano quoting Kasarda, will be speed, speed, and speed. They're racing as much against the Big Three's total collapse as they are against foreign rivals, and Detroit can't waste time reviving an economy that's had a century to atrophy. The city plans to convert vacant lots into farmland for lack of a better idea, while the suburbs are picking the city's carcass clean of white-collar jobs—a strategy labeled "economic cannibalism."

At the Crossroads

What will the aerotropolis look like, and what will it do? It may be that no one really knows, or could give you a straight answer. But taking the easier question first: Aesthetics aren't high on anyone's list. The only approved sketches are leftovers from an old prototype, Pinnacle Aeropark. Picture glass boxes half hidden among poplars while a plane hovers overhead—it might as well be a brochure for Las Colinas circa 1982. A more inspired vision landed in Ficano's lap a few years ago.

In January 2006, the dean of Michigan's architecture school invited fifty students to hole up at the Ypsilanti Marriott, conjuring their own aerotropolis. These brainstorming marathons are known in the trade as charrettes. They operate on the principle that you can solve any conundrum if enough deadline pressure, caffeine, and sleep deprivation are applied. The participants were divided into three teams, each charged with plotting the entire site. One was led by Douglas Kelbaugh, the dean and former partner of Peter Calthorpe, with whom he'd invented transit-oriented development. He brought a battery of faculty, students, architects, and urban planners to assist him, including two of the consultants later tasked with drafting the actual master plan. And then there was Kasarda, who flew in to brief them all on what exactly it was they were building. They left and got to work. Eighty hours later, the groggy teams staggered back into the conference room to show what they had come up with.

The details aren't important, as this was a conceptual exercise—albeit one with more verve and precision than anything Ficano's task force has imagined. Taken together, however, they suggest what the master plan might entail.

Trains, for one thing. Commuter trains trundle between Ann Arbor and Detroit for the first time in decades. Light rail runs to the terminals from downtown Detroit, while buses fill the gaps between tracks. Cars are conspicuously absent.

The airport is only an excuse to build a city around the train stops. The stunted hotel corridor north of the airport has been replaced with a new downtown bigger and denser than Detroit's (or Indianapolis's or Cincinnati's), replete with a horse-racing track, casino, lakeside resorts, and a performing arts center. (It was based in fact. An offshoot of Magna International, one of the Big Three's biggest suppliers, was all set to build the racetrack and casino until its customers collapsed.) Radiating for half a mile around the airport stop is a walkable village of narrow streets and multistory buildings filled with supermarkets, day care centers, shops, offices, and apartments. Farther out of town are bungalows and a retirement community for empty nesters who don't need the hassle of owning a car and could fly on the weekends to visit their grandkids.

It anchors one end of a grand Concourse Boulevard running between the airports, lined with trees, bike trails, and stately buildings better suited to a college campus. It's a city built in Ann Arbor's image—unsurprising, considering that the college town is the refuge of Michigan's creative class. ("That was the best solution," Kelbaugh said with a sigh, "but we just don't have the public sector to pull it off here.")

Bisecting it is a greenbelt connecting the Rouge and Huron rivers with parks, trails, and wetlands. In their sketches, everything is green, even the rooftops. In between solar panels, sod absorbs and recycles rainwater. The entire city is carbon-neutral, selling spare electricity back to the grid. Greenhouses along the boulevard grow produce for local cafeterias, which turn over their leftovers for composting.

That was the dream, anyway. It remains to be seen whether any of these elements will find their way into the ADC's guidelines. But a promising sign is that Michigan has since come around on trains. In late 2008, hoping for a piece of incoming president Obama's stimulus package, the state passed a twenty-five-year, $10.5 billion grand transit strategy for greater Detroit, adding four hundred miles of rail and new bus routes. Track laying was due to commence last year—the first corridor will link downtown to the airport. The Ann Arbor commuter line will begin running again this fall after its own half-billion-dollar overhaul. Twenty-three similar proposals have been shouted down in the last fifty years. What's different this time is the aerotropolis, its new terminus.

Construction has started there too, even in the absence of a master plan. Keen to show progress, Ficano approved a handful of projects on county-owned land. Some made more sense than others. One is the Michigan Institute of Aviation and Technology, an academy for jet engine mechanics. Another is Pinnacle Race Course, a jobs magnet for jockeys, grooms, and blacksmiths. What Thoroughbreds have to do with competitiveness is anyone's guess—"*speed, speed,* and *speed*," Ficano intoned on opening day—but at least they finished it fast, in three months flat, proving his point about slashing red tape. A few additions have been announced since, none of which were ideal: warehouses, a hotel, a cancer radiation lab (since shelved), and an organic produce nursery. That's all well and good for the tax rolls, but if Detroit is going to win this war of all against all that's raging, it again begs the question: *What is the aerotropolis for?*

The answer, given by everyone from Ficano on down, is anything and everything: batteries, biofuels, windmills, and smart grid-building software consultancies. Two years ago, Ficano announced Wayne County would build a Stem Cell Commercialization Center—adding genetic engineering to the list. When we met, practically the first word off his lips was *The Graduate*'s punch line, *plastics*—but in this case a biodegradable kind derived from wheat. Imagine the Big Three supplanted by Big Green. That may sound desperate, but they're being pragmatic. Detroit dead-ended the last time its leaders—Henry Ford, Alfred P. Sloan, and Walter P. Chrysler—knew exactly what it was they needed. Ficano and Co. aren't about to make the same mistake.

They will start with logistics, but for whom? Detroit has as much chance of stealing UPS away from Louisville as Pinnacle does unseating Churchill Downs. They know better than to try. The obvious candidates are the automakers and their suppliers, but they're stodgier than you might think. As much as they try to be just-in-time, all-the-time, the vast bulk of their supply chains travels on the ground. Weight is one issue—engines weigh almost five hundred pounds—and their fragile finances are another. While next year's models may bristle with systems and sensors, margins are so thin and production is so regimented that even circuit boards take the slow boats months ahead of schedule. Logistics beats a racetrack, but a better bet is flying the auto industry's people instead. Maybe the answer they're groping for is already out there, on the shores of a lake in the dead center of the footprint: Visteon Village.

Visteon is one of the larger companies you've never heard of. Bigger than eBay or Eastman Kodak, it has thirty thousand employees. Spun out from Ford a decade ago, Visteon is one of the heavyweights supplying parts for final assembly. At birth, its employees were scattered around Dearborn, working from the closets of former colleagues. Coworkers went years without seeing or speaking to each other. Tired of their nomadic existence, management commissioned a permanent home in 2002. Their criteria were simple: proximity to an international airport and sticking close to their employees. They chose an abandoned quarry between the two interstates, five miles and fifteen minutes from the terminals.

Visteon makes nothing in Michigan, having given its factories back to Ford. Its Corporate Office and Innovation Center, as it's formally known, doubles as headquarters and its hub for R & D. Design studios and "innovation labs" spill across the nine-building campus, home to fifteen hundred white-collar workers—a third of its salaried employees.

"When it comes to product development, everything's here," the company's real estate chief told me. "We've got prototypes flying in and out all the time. R and D's the core of our business, and it's important to have your sales group here, feeding them with what they're hearing from customers: 'We need navigation, we need high-style instrument panels, we need audio systems.' Once we put them together, that seemed to make sense, so we stirred in our manufacturing operations. So now you've got manufacturing, research, and our sales force all under one roof, and naturally we'd like some efficiencies, so we moved our global quality control, global finance, and global HR people in. Essentially the whole company is here, from the ground up and from concept to delivery."

Which is why Visteon Village is meant to feel like one—like a $300 million, LEED-certified mill town, in fact. All of its buildings are open-air lofts, to keep coworkers in sight and collect sunlight inside. None are more than four stories tall, "so you're never more than one flight of stairs away from your colleagues." You might run into them on "Main Street" outside, or perhaps in line at the deli or the bank. The villagers reflect "a new way of working" for Detroit, or a familiar one in Silicon Valley or Manhattan. "We didn't do this for the people who came with us, but for the people we were recruiting. It was about the future. An open floor is an open mind."

While Visteon doesn't make things here, it does invent them. Take the dashboard computer it developed with the help of Intel, the one streaming music off the Internet and synced to traffic cameras via Google Maps for real-time peeks at congestion up ahead. The engineers here had a small assist from abroad. Visteon has eighteen R & D centers worldwide. Only three are in America, another is in Mexico, nine are in Europe, and five are in Asia. The spread reflects its customers' trajectory: Asia is rising, Europe is slipping, and America is crashing.

Like Detroit, Visteon is doing its damnedest to diversify. To start, it's shipping R & D overseas. In 2005, for instance, only 19 percent of its engineering took place in emerging countries; two years later, it was 35 percent. Its engineers are heading where the newly minted drivers are, in China, India, and Brazil. China has not only surpassed America as the largest auto market in the world, but is also the world's largest importer of auto R & D. Chinese automakers are poaching talent faster than Visteon can add them as customers. Former copycats like Geely and Chery have decided to innovate instead.

As with any village founded at a crossroads, Visteon's has become a hub. On any given day, it may receive a hundred visitors arriving on flights from Tokyo, Paris, Munich, Stuttgart, and Seoul. They're passed in the halls by salesmen leaving for Shanghai and Beijing, who carpool with engineers hopping flights to Mexico—or Slovakia, Thailand, and Spain. One in five villagers is likely to be aloft for long stretches this year. Visteon invents less and less here; soon all that will be left is its brain stem guiding vital functions overseas.

On first glance, Visteon Village is what the aerotropolis should be: a home for the Big Three's knowledge workers and a city that's shed the dead weight of manufacturing for a brilliant future in automotive R & D. It's an illusion. The Village is real, but Visteon isn't. The supplier is bankrupt, as unable to escape the Big Three's undertow as is Detroit itself. Given the chance to slip the noose of Michigan's union labor, it sought the lowest-cost allies everywhere and still failed. Visteon has never turned a profit.

"Winter Is Here, but Spring Is Coming Too"

"The U.S. automotive industry has been pushed to the verge of collapse," the chairman of American Axle decreed two years ago. Michigan has shed two-thirds of its autoworkers in barely a decade. If Detroit is to have a future, then its residents must give up their malignant dreams of its past, the dream of Henry Ford's five-dollar-a-day wages and River Rouge, where one hundred thousand men once forged raw coal, sand, and iron into Model Ts. His dream was to build a city on the back of such immense and monotonous efficiency, spurning the "fertile and creative inefficiency" Jane Jacobs recognized as the sign of vitality. For the aerotropolis to succeed in restarting Detroit's evolution, it must turn its back on Ford's legacy.

The city's real strength isn't the auto industry—the whole intractable mess of bad faith and worse contracts—but the engineering talent left in the tank. It's the men and women responsible for a century's worth of stronger, safer, smarter, faster cars. They created steel that doesn't corrode, plastics for outer space, and millions of widgets a little bit cheaper, a little bit lighter, and a little bit nicer than the ones they replaced. There are enough of them at loose ends to stock a Big Fourth. So how do they retool?

In June 2009, General Electric announced it would build an Advanced Manufacturing & Software Technology Center in the aerotropolis footprint—at Visteon Village, no less, moving in as the campus bled out from round after round of layoffs. The center would be one of only five worldwide, joining a network of skunk works in Bangalore, Shanghai, Munich, and Schenectady, New York (where the lightbulb had been perfected). GE promised to hire more than a thousand engineers at six-figure salaries. The lucky ones would tinker with the next generation of wind turbines, smart grids, CAT scanners, and jet engines, applying their know-how in composites, casting, and machining. It was knowledge work in its most tangible form: they wouldn't build jet engines there; they would discover how to build better, cleaner ones.

It was a startling validation of Ficano's vision and a down payment on the jobs and wages he'd promised to create. GE chose Detroit because too much brainpower was being wasted; it chose the aerotropolis because it wanted to sit between the airport and the University of Michigan. Further surprising everyone, its CEO, Jeffrey Immelt, chose the occasion to call for an "American renewal."

"Many bought into the idea that America could go from a technology-based, export-oriented powerhouse to a services-led, consumption-based economy—and somehow still expect to prosper," he scolded the city's business leaders. "That idea was flat wrong."

Just as no city has suffered more than Detroit, manufacturing has borne the brunt of the recession. Although factory output is more or less unchanged from a decade ago, employment has fallen precipitously. In fact, manufacturing never regained the jobs lost in the *last* recession of 2001, shedding six million—a third of the total—since then. When it comes to exports, America ranks last among the fifteen largest developed manufacturing nations. Whether you chalk this up to outsourcing or rising productivity depends on your politics, but the answer is both.

America had spent too little on R & D, Immelt claimed, falling behind in "clean energy and affordable health care." He called for a manufacturing renaissance, doubling its share of American jobs to 20 percent in order "to compete and win with American exports." GE had led the way in outsourcing under Immelt's predecessor, Jack Welch, but now he conceded, "We have outsourced too much."

"I've had people explain to me the Darwinian nature of markets," he added. "They tell me that America has seen a natural evolution from farming to manufacturing to services. After all, they say, this has happened in other mature economies. But there is nothing predestined or inevitable about the industrial decline of the U.S., if we as a people are prepared to reverse it.

"We would do much better to observe the example of China. They've been growing fast because they invest in technology and they make things. They have no intention of letting up in manufacturing in order to evolve into a service economy. They know where the money is and they aim to get there first." They'd already beaten GE to Detroit.

Immelt spoke an inconvenient truth—it may be too late. Detroit may be too far behind, too slow, and too broken for an aerotropolis to make much difference. The worst-case scenario may not be that it doesn't work—if they build it and no one comes—but that it works in reverse, unintentionally vacuuming talent and opportunities elsewhere. GE, for example, plans to siphon off any breakthroughs by its engineers in Detroit to their lower-cost counterparts in Shanghai and Bangalore. As for the remainder, Richard Florida has seriously suggested they will make it only if they're willing to aerially commute to work in distant cities, assuming they don't just leave.

What's different this time from Henry Ford's day is the scope and scale of Detroit's competition, and how far it already trails in this new game. The competitive logic the aerotropolis is designed to exploit—of clusters and creative ecosystems and value chains—has already conspired to move the centers of the auto and clean energy industries elsewhere. While the aerotropolis works in Detroit's favor by connecting them, it by no means guarantees the city can steal them back.

Take the Chevy Volt, for instance. The Volt's raison d'être is its power train, a four-hundred-pound, T-shaped brick of lithium-ion batteries, and it's why GM spent years running a bake-off to choose the best. The winner is made by Compact Power, a subsidiary of LG Chem—itself an arm of Korea's third-largest conglomerate. The American contender, a start-up named A123, didn't stand a chance. Its batteries "are good for power tools," but "LG Chem is just farther along," sniffed GM's voluble vice chairman, Bob Lutz. "The point is LG Chem, thanks to years and years in the prismatic lithium-ion cell business and also thanks to massive financial technological support from Korea Incorporated, has a several-year head start." GM has since built its own factory in Michigan, (as has A123, which has five others in China) but the R & D is staying under lock and key in Seoul.

The Koreans, in turn, have fallen behind the Chinese. The world's first mass-produced electric car is the BYD F3DM, a $21,000 plug-in hybrid. BYD, which stands for Build Your Dreams, didn't start building cars until 2003. Its bread-and-butter business is batteries, and it makes more than anyone else in China. If you have a cell phone, iPod, camera, or some combination of the three, its battery was probably made next door to the F3DM.

Warren Buffett likes the car so much he bought a tenth of BYD for $230 million. But with a little luck, its boyish-looking chairman Wang Chuanfu may go down in history as China's answer to Steve Jobs. He's taking the wheel of the auto industry the same way Apple hijacked music; the F3DM is his iPod. Wang has made it clear he doesn't care about making cars, per se. He's charged only about electricity. Cars are a commodity; a better battery isn't. Which is why Daimler has partnered with BYD to create its own electric models. His goal is to have the biggest automaker in China by 2015, and the biggest in the world by 2025. (The gas-powered version of the F3 was China's best-selling car in 2009.) Thanks to Buffett's backing, a surge in BYD's stock price has already made Wang the richest man in China. "For 100 years, nothing has changed in Detroit," he told *The Atlantic*'s James Fallows. "I think they need to reconsider their product lines."

Maybe the most ironic twist in the city's tortuous saga is that from a global perspective, the auto industry's best days still lie ahead. Car ownership worldwide is poised to boom as part of a broader revolution in mobility. Rising incomes have at last put cars within reach of millions of Chinese, Indians, Turks, Thais, Brazilians, and Iranians. The number of vehicles on the road will easily double from 672 million in 2008 to 1.5 billion by 2018, according to Booz & Company consultants Ronald Haddock and John Jullens. But that won't be much help to Detroit, as the beneficiaries will be automakers overseas. (Even GM now sells more cars in China than in the United States.)

Not that BYD has it all figured out. The F3DM stinks, for one thing. Visitors to its booth at the 2009 Detroit Auto Show held their noses against the fumes emanating from its plastic interiors. It's still on track to make its U.S. debut this year, but its buzz has been superseded by the all-electric, twice-as-expensive e6. No one at the show thought either car was ready for prime time in the United States. BYD may have mastered the batteries, but it could use a lot of help when it comes to making cars people like to drive. That help happens to be taking early retirement in Auburn Hills and Warren right now.

"Some Chinese [manufacturers], like BYD Company, aspire to become global leaders in the industry," Haddock and Jullens wrote. "But many suffer from a talent shortage and inexperience in managing across borders. This may prompt them to acquire all or part of distressed Western automobile companies in the near future or to hire skilled auto executives from established [manufacturers] and suppliers." China aims to get them first, before GE or anyone else.

The face of Detroit's future may be the florid one belonging to Tianbao Zhou, founder of the Tempo Group. Ficano found him six years ago while passing through the city of Bengbu near Nanjing on one of his earliest missions to China. Tempo started out making steering gear, drive shafts, and brakes for local partners of GM, but Tianbao has loftier ambitions. "We want to be like Henry Ford," he told his visitor. Ficano replied that he should come to Michigan. So he did. Tempo opened its engineering center a year later in Canton, a township on the aerotropolis's northern edge. Overnight, it had the largest presence of any Chinese automaker in Michigan. It hired twenty engineers at first, then thirty, and eventually several hundred. Their job was to test brakes and steering gear, posting the results and their suggestions online for their counterparts in Bengbu to fix. All worked for the Big Three. None are Chinese, except Jeff Zhao, the general manager, who flew in from Beijing.

"We're setting up an R and D center to support our factories back in China," he told me. "It's about connecting our people there with engineers in Detroit, combining our resources with their talent and services. Almost everything we need is available here," and by "everything," he meant idled workers and empty buildings. When I asked him about logistics, he cut me off. "All we move back and forth is people, and sometimes we're moving a lot of them."

Tempo has since been joined by China's Big Five automakers kicking the tires on pieces of the Big Three. One struck a deal for GM's Hummer, but the Chinese government blocked the sale. (Even they found it distasteful.) Ford had better luck unloading Volvo on the then-unknown

Geely. Their suppliers hungrily circled Visteon and Delphi. When Ford took seventeen factories back from Visteon in 2005, it immediately announced plans to sell them. It found few takers besides the Chinese. One plant was sold in 2008 to an affiliate of the Wanxiang Group, China's second-largest private enterprise. The factory was promptly packed up and moved out to the aerotropolis, within a mile of Visteon Village. Wanxiang has announced plans to build electric cars too.

Compared to Wanxiang or BYD, Tempo is a speck. It is one link, albeit the first, in the winding supply chains decoupling themselves from the Big Three and reconnecting to China. The auto industry is inexorably headed east, and the aerotropolis will be the air bridge for Chinese firms brave enough to cross, and to pillage. Ficano will be waiting with open arms to welcome them.

Two years ago, on the eve of the Auto Show, Tempo invited guests from the governments of Detroit and the Big Three to a meet and greet at the Henry Ford Museum. The museum stands along I-94 between the city and the airport, next to Ford's proving grounds and test center in Dearborn. The remnants of River Rouge are not far away. The museum's centerpiece is a life-size replica of Philadelphia's Independence Hall. Inside are the homes and workshops belonging to men whose genius Ford felt was modest next to his own. The Wright Brothers' bicycle shop was reassembled here, as was Thomas Edison's Menlo Park laboratory. The latter was the world's first industrial research and development lab for what would later become GE.

As host, Jeff Zhao was joined by the vice mayor of Beijing. They had come to send a message: after sorting through the wreckage of America's financial collapse, China was going on a shopping spree. Zhao punctuated this by musing aloud about which of his guests were on his wish list. Mom-and-pop tool-and-dies? Maybe. Small and insolvent firms? Sure. Visteon? Why not, if the price was right? Tempo could do a better job, he said, and he had Beijing's money at his disposal.

"We are ready to come and invest and buy companies," the vice mayor informed his guests, "or do joint ventures with suppliers. We have money we can bring in. You have equipment, manpower, and technology, and we want to invest." And Tempo did, buying Delphi's brakes and suspension business at a discount and, later, GM's steering unit for $450 million.

Ficano felt it was a fair trade. "The Chinese are going to invest in the

U.S.," he said at the time. "Our whole intent is to bring jobs here." He'd read enough of Thomas Hobbes and Thomas Friedman to know Beijing was winning. But Detroit could win too if the aerotropolis bound them inextricably together. Even if Michigan could not escape its auto heritage, maybe it could slip free of the Big Three. Instead of exporting cars, it could export the raw talent needed to produce them, in exchange for jobs staying put in Michigan—for now, at least. Whereas once its lifelines were the steamships carrying grain and copper and horseless carriages over the Great Lakes, today they are daily flights to Shanghai and Hong Kong, and their connections—aerial, digital, and otherwise— onward across China.

In late 2008, one of those flights carried another Detroit delegation to Beijing, this time for the China International Auto Parts Expo. While the CEOs of the Big Three bowed and scraped before Congress half a world away, Ficano took the podium in the enormous Exhibition Center and invited everyone present to colonize his corner of Michigan. With him onstage, sitting beneath a banner that read, in English, "Chinese auto parts enterprises to enter into the world market against the background of world economic crisis," were Jeff Zhao and the ambassadors of other Chinese companies already around Detroit. One by one, they picked through Motown's rubble, painting the picture of a city ready for repossession: thousands of unemployed engineers, automakers clamoring for the "China price," and a vast stock of abandoned houses. "People have changed," said Zhao. "They have begun to accept Chinese companies now."

The last to speak was one of the organizers, who extended Ficano an invitation to return. "This is the best time for a brave Chinese enterprise to enter the U.S. market," he said, reminding the audience: "After the rain, there is sunshine. Winter is here, but spring is coming too."

7

THE COOL CHAIN

Amsterdam's flower auctions—combined with its airport—transformed a local specialty into a global industry and paved the way for the globalization of food.

Floriopolis

In 1593, a botanist named Carolus Clusius arrived at Holland's Leiden University to plant the school's botanical garden. In his saddlebags was a collection of bulbs, including a wildflower so unusual it was sometimes mistaken for an onion and eaten: the tulip. Tulips had been on the move for centuries, first blooming in the mountain valleys between the steppes and the Yangtze before heading west. The Turks carried them to Constantinople, where Suleiman the Magnificent tried his best to breed them (seeking bloodred flowers, his gardeners poured wine on the beds). Another century passed as tulips wended their way across Europe toward the Netherlands. Clusius's bulbs evaded a knife and fork, but the tulip's fame preceded him—his entire crop was stolen from the ground after one season.

It didn't take long for tulips—the only relief from a gray-on-gray landscape in the cold, wet springs—to become the national status symbol of Europe's youngest and wealthiest republic. For a brief moment, the United Provinces possessed the world's mightiest economy, built entirely on global trade. The Dutch East India Company, chartered in 1602, was the world's first multinational and the first to issue stock, which traded on the planet's original exchange. Detroit's Big Three combined couldn't hold a candle to the firm, which at its zenith commanded a fleet of two hundred ships, its own private army, and fifty thousand employees. Its charter granted wide latitude to wage war, mint money, and establish colonies. It seized a worldwide monopoly of cinnamon at gunpoint, later adding coffee, cloves, and nutmeg to its portfolio. Like the Big Three, however, it grew fat and sluggish on its profits, gradually ceding market share to the nimbler, more aggressive English East India Company—the Toyota of its day.

The Amsterdam exchange made markets in 360 commodities, none of which were tulips. Fueled by the gross margins of the spice trades, bulb auctions devolved into speculative frenzies. At the peak of tulipomania in the 1630s, a single bulb could fetch a row house along Amsterdam's canals. The tulip bubble set the pattern for all that followed—from the South Seas Bubble in 1720 to the railroad bust of 1847 and on through the Roaring Twenties and subsequent Depression. Every bubble, at its core, was a bet on greater global integration—whether by trade or trains or effervescent auto and radio stocks. Most recently, the Internet boom promised us a frictionless, one-click world, while our splattered housing bubble was financed by China's savings and spent on Chinese goods. In the beginning, the tulip auctions were essentially a gamble that the Dutch East India Company would mint profits forever—that its monopolies would last and so would Holland's Golden Age.

The fever broke during an auction in 1637, when a pound of typically exorbitant bulbs found no takers. Word spread through the taverns, and by day's end their worth had evaporated. To unwind the chain of ruinous contracts, the courts ruled they were indeed gambling losses, not debts, and the losers walked away more or less unscathed. As with the railroad and Internet bubbles to come, the orgy of spending in the run-up to its bursting paid for the infrastructure that cemented Holland's dominance in floriculture. Thanks to their monomania, the Dutch had become the undisputed masters in breeding, growing, and trading bulbs, inheriting the industry from the Turks.

The invention of heated greenhouses 250 years later steered ambitious growers toward a wider variety of perennials. Once they could manipulate flowers into blooming year-round, daily production demanded daily deliveries. Roses replaced tulips as the dominant cash crop, and stems replaced bulbs. Flowers were still a predominantly Dutch preoccupation, delivered to Amsterdam by boat or by bicycle, and to Rotterdam or The Hague by train. Transporting such a delicately dying commodity bedeviled buyers for years.

Refrigerated trucks made possible overnight shipments to Paris and Frankfurt, but going farther required flight. KLM invented the perishables business, airlifting seventy-five hundred tons of flowers, fruits, and vegetables to London in 1928. The city's dowagers rejoiced that winter after Dutch planes had at last made possible the year-round enjoyment of strawberries and clotted cream. Door-to-door service from greenhouse to Bloomsbury took five hours; in light of the Heathrow hassle, this record will likely never be broken. It wasn't until after World War II that growers started exporting flowers in earnest. The missing link arrived in 1969, when California's Irvin Industries unveiled the first refrigerated containers you could plug into the wall—or into the belly of a 747. Promising fail-safe temperature and humidity control, its canisters cut packaging costs in half and spoilage rates by 25 percent. Over the next decade, Dutch growers ascended from Europe's leading flower producers to the world's. By 1973, nearly three-quarters of all floral exports originated in Holland. Soon thereafter, the Dutch welcomed the brilliant yellow roses grown and flown in by Israeli breeders, kicking off the outsourcing of rose production. Four centuries after Clusius, flowers began heading east.

The Dutch never abandoned their auctions. Strictly a local affair for most of their existence, they have since consolidated in scope and scale to match the needs of growers. The largest auction by far is the Aalsmeer, where twenty million roses, chrysanthemums, baby's breath, and tulips change hands every morning before its neighbors have had their first cup of *koffie*. The Verenigde Bloemenveiling Aalsmeer, as it's formally known, is the first stop for every freshly cut blossom in Europe and for millions more bound for the United States, Japan, and all points beyond or in between. It's no accident that Schiphol International Airport, one of Europe's busiest, lies just six miles away. The Aalsmeer is the great green hub of the world, and it's only fitting that its concrete hulk rests amid the fields where tulipomania flourished four centuries ago.

Amsterdam and its airport are the model for the aerotropolis John Kasarda has in mind for Detroit. But more than blueprints, the combination of Schiphol and the Aalsmeer offers hope to any city or industry worried about the leveling effects of globalization. Unlike the Big Three, which ultimately crumpled against foreign competition, Dutch growers used Schiphol to elevate their national obsession into a global network of greenhouses, all while keeping a firm hand on the tiller. Just as the Dutch East India Company commissioned ports and canals to accommodate its fleets, they created the "cool chain"—the seamless network of coolers and canisters transporting fresh flora worldwide. In doing so, they once again reasserted their dominance while paving the way for the globalization of food. It's been left to us, however, to decide whether roses grown in Kenya are too far a flight away in the face of climate change, a debate that encompasses more than just mileage.

The Green Hub of the World

The greatest irony of tulipomania is that the most celebrated specimens were secretly diseased. "Broken" tulips bloomed with wild patterns and striations. The virus has since been tamed and the same effect genetically manipulated. I spotted one such variety one spring in Chicago. These tulips were orange, embellished by purple flames licking each petal. Wrapped in cellophane, bunches spilled across the floor of Jayson Home & Garden, a furnishings emporium on the city's north side. An overflow of peonies, lilacs, and miniature calla lillies were arranged in glass vases around them. Ordinarily, they would never be allowed to stand like this at room temperature, but today was the Friday before Mother's Day—D-day for florists. Valentine's Day is bigger, but that crush revolves around roses. Mother's Day is bouquet pandemonium, as husbands, sons, and daughters race to buy them in bunches. A florist thrust a spray at me as her recommendation. An hour later, they were in my mother's hands, four days and four thousand miles after they'd been picked in Holland.

There they were one bunch among billions. The brilliant fields painted by Van Gogh are an industrial by-product, as the vast majority of buds are bred for bulbs meant for replanting in gardens. The Dutch have cornered two-thirds of the world market by blanketing their polders this way. Thousands of extra acres are devoted to cut flowers including hyacinths, daffodils, and especially roses. Mine were likely harvested from a greenhouse equipped with sunlight sensors and computer-calibrated fertilizer drips. They were cut on Tuesday and graded, sorted, packed, and stowed in coolers in time for Wednesday's Aalsmeer auctions.

Flowers begin arriving past midnight and bidding starts before dawn. To ensure their lilies and hyacinths are ready for the auction block, growers move them from cold storage onto carts in the early morning, or else rush them from Schiphol after overnight flights from Quito, Nairobi, and Tel Aviv. It's impossible to see, much less make sense of, the Aalsmeer at eye level, as the floor of its central warehouse is a thicket of carts bearing blooms, all waiting their turn. This is the world's largest commercial building at ten million square feet, more than twice the size of Chicago's Willis Tower or Merchandise Mart. (Not coincidentally, the only larger structures are a pair of airport terminals in Beijing and Dubai.)

From a catwalk running above, you can study the crazy quilt of tulips, sunflowers, azaleas, and hydrangeas bleeding into daubs of orange or pink at the horizon. The quilt continually changes colors and patterns as burly Dutchmen at the wheel of one-man tugs trail daisy chains behind them. The Aalsmeer seems primitive compared to warehouses in Memphis or Louisville. There are no bar codes, conveyor belts, or gantries spiraling upward (although there is a robot-driven freight train). What looks to be a grid for queuing carts, laid out with numbers and letters hung overhead, turns out to be more of a suggestion—tugs zoom right through it.

And yet the pure productivity of this place would awe FedEx's Fred Smith: The Aalsmeer manages to move five billion stems a year in nearly ten million transactions, all before lunch. Almost a quarter of all the cut flowers in the world pass through this hall, with another quarter moving through the smaller half-dozen auctions that fall under its corporate umbrella. They are effectively the hub of a $40 billion global industry, a bigger one than the music business.

The auction rooms are some strange amalgam of college lecture halls, game shows, and offtrack-betting parlors (with all of the unwashed masculinity that implies). The buyers work for wholesalers like the Dutch Flower Group or for themselves. They are men to a man, looking as if they had rolled out of bed at four thirty, smoked a pack of cigarettes on the way over, and drunk three or four cups of coffee to get going—all of which is the case—because they literally cannot afford to be sluggish in bidding.

Each room contains two or more clocks projected on giant screens, allowing simultaneous auctions to take place. The Aalsmeer doesn't waste time waiting for bidders to drive up prices. The auctions use a countdown clock, with prices starting artificially high and dropping to zero in seconds. Buyers race one another and the clock with buzzers to lock in their orders. Buzz too fast and you'll overpay, too slowly and someone will steal the lot from under you. (If no one bids at all, the flowers are shredded into compost.) In this case, the "clock" is more like a stopwatch—a ring of red lights swoops around its face while the buyers clench their buzzers, making last-second, split-second calculations.

Price isn't their only consideration. Also flashed on screen are the number of stems in each lot, their quality rating (A1 is the best and most common here), the pedigree of both plant and grower, and a crisp digital image of what it is, exactly, they're buying. The flowers are here too— slowly cycling through the hall on a track beneath the clocks, entering from stage left or right and leaving through a center set of doors. One of the auctioneers plucks a stem from each lot and holds it high for all to see, but the buyers barely have time to glance at it before returning to the task at hand. Just like that, the flowers are gone, sold before they've even left the room.

The point of Dutch auctions is their speed. The Aalsmeer averages more than a thousand transactions per clock per hour—one every three seconds or so. There are five of these rooms, including one just for potted plants, another for garden varieties, and the Rose Room, which is the largest auction of all. Two billion rosebuds a year are funneled through it, and depending on the prices commanded for each stem, they could end up in an oligarch's manse in Moscow or in the produce aisle of an Essex Tesco.

At first blush, it might seem absurd to sacrifice two or three days of a dying plant's life in exchange for a few seconds beneath the clock. What the Aalsmeer has always promised buyers and sellers is a fair price, paid in full, for a product of guaranteed provenance and quality. This is no small thing in an industry where taking receipt of the bouquets before they wilt isn't taken for granted. The auctions began in 1911 as a hub for information and today are the place where prices worldwide are set, quality is judged, and innovations appear in the form of new breeds and new producers. Logistically speaking, the world's flowers converge daily on Schiphol for the same reason your overnight packages pass through Memphis—because the efficiency gained from bringing so much infrastructure to bear on a hub offsets any lag introduced in moving them here.

My flowers are won by the tulip buyer of Hilverda De Boer, one of Holland's largest exporters. They're for a last-second order by Jayson Home & Garden, whose florist asked for the purple-flamed variety by name. After my Princess Irenes leave the auction hall, they're carried to the Aalsmeer Shuttle, the robotic railway linking buyers' warehouses in a distant wing. The shuttle bridges a highway with ten miles of track and automated carts capable of twenty-six hundred trips per hour, carrying the capacity of 120 semitrucks stuck idling in traffic below. Its tracks run along the ceiling, from which carts hang and sway as they zip overhead. Its design has more in common with a ski lift than a freight train. Orange I beams replace lift chairs, with aluminum racks stacked between them carrying a blur of roses, azaleas, orchids, and even bamboo trees waving in the breeze.

Trains follow one spur or another to their destinations. Mine eventually halts and drops to the doorstep of Hilverda De Boer. Immediately inside are coolers within coolers, and beyond lies the familiar sight of belts, scanners, and flower pickers. Hilverda ships a million stems a day. Trucks bound for Berlin and Bordeaux have already left, and now they're building pallets for Schiphol. Wandering through the racks, you might spy hydrangeas with their passports stamped for Tokyo next to crates of baby's breath, lathyrus, and lilies. In back, bouquet makers shred leaves and stems from bunches of roses, viburnum, and syringa and pack them in boxes lined with ice packs.

Two hundred boxes of tulips, Thai orchids, and Kenyan roses are headed to Chicago. They're the exception; only 5 percent of the flowers sold at auction, or about 250 million stems, make their way to the United States. Blossoms must command a premium to make it worth the trip. They're loaded onto the cream-colored trucks of J. van de Put Fresh Cargo Handling, which are ubiquitous during rush hour. And small wonder— its array of vacuum coolers and rolling refrigerators is more critical to the global flower trade than is the Aalsmeer itself.

While FedEx and UPS worry about supply chains, the Aalsmeer's logisticians are obsessed with the cool chain. It's a supply chain on ice— everything in it is made cold and stays cold until it exits, preferably in a shopping bag. Any break in the chain leads to rot and ruin. Speed matters more than ever, but it's been supplemented by a degree—by a reliable 3° Celsius, to be precise.

The cool chain is the focus of anyone who makes a living shipping flowers or fish or fresh fruit. Before they can "add value," they need to ensure their product doesn't die on them first. Because whether it's rose-buds or bluefin or strawberries, it's been dying since the moment it was cut, caught, or plucked. Even the name for these goods, "perishables," underscores their mortality. It's a given at the Aalsmeer that flowers shed 15 percent of their value each morning, because they have (at most) seven days to live before they're as good as compost. But the cool chain is what makes it possible for roses grown along Kenya's Lake Naivasha to arrive as fresh as ones picked that morning down the street. And it keeps them equally crisp on their next leg to Osaka or Los Angeles. What J. van de Put's customers pay for is the reliably arctic conditions that will buy them time to bring their flowers to market.

Its trucks are waiting when KLM Flight 566 from Nairobi lands at five thirty each morning, ending an eight-hour flight across the savanna and Sahara. Once they're on the ground, they don't have far to go—J. van de Put's hangar-size Frigidaire is wedged between two runways. The roses are rushed into one of eight "blast coolers" that bathe them in an icy gale. If more extreme measures are necessary—if the blossoms awake from hibernation and begin to respire, sending their temperatures skyward—there is always the vacuum cooler. In a chamber the size of a delivery van, the flowers are plunged into outer space. The air is sucked out, leaving them gasping in a void, then replaced at 35° Fahrenheit, all but flash-freezing them. Within minutes, they're back in suspended animation.

At most, they'll stay here overnight, either waiting to catch a flight or for their Aalsmeer debut. There are dozens of pallets, all filled with hun-dreds or thousands of roses neatly packed. Ironically, the weakest link in the cool chain is also the climax of the flowers' costly detour to the auctions—the three-second parade beneath the clocks. Once sold, they're plunged back into the cold by their new owners. Ninety percent of the day's trades depart the same afternoon. Every flight leaving Schiphol has at least one box in the hold.

Mine travel in an American Airlines belly and arrive at O'Hare on Thursday afternoon. USDA inspectors comb through a sampling of stems looking for blight and infestation. Granted their approval, the tu-lips are remanded to Hilverda's importers, who sort and store them in their warehouse on the rim of the airfield. They're waiting on Jayson's doorstep the next morning, and hours later my mother is admiring her bouquet. I tried to explain their origins, but she didn't care; all that mattered was that they were lovely, and that they were from her son.

The Old Masters: How the Dutch Conquered Flowers

"It is impossible to be around the floriculture industry for any length of time without running into the Dutch," wrote Amy Stewart in *Flower Confidential*. "They're everywhere . . . Hang around growers in Latin America, or Miami, or Southern California, and you'll always hear a Dutch accent somewhere in the room. This is, in many ways, their industry, one they have exported to the rest of the world and still keep a hand in, watching over it like the wise, all-knowing company founder who just won't retire."

She might have been describing Henk de Groot. One morning after the auctions had ended, I toured the Aalsmeer with its recently retired director of planning. It was on his watch that the Aalsmeer as we know it was built, after the crosstown rivals of Bloemenlust and CAV merged in 1968, necessitating the construction of a much larger auction. Invented within that hall—the core of the modern complex—was the system of digital clocks, aluminum carts, and automated trains capable of the throughput and speed needed for just-in-time blossoms. During his tenure, the Aalsmeer multiplied *thirteen* times. Imagine Zappos' Louisville hangar bolted to another, and then another, and so on until you've added a dozen. It's so big the easiest way to study it is from space. And it isn't finished—as we drove along its winding exterior, de Groot pointed out the greenhouses destined to be subsumed in its next, and likely final, doubling.

Schiphol's control tower is visible from here, and I wondered whether the Aalsmeer's proximity had been intentional. De Groot, whose sleepy eyes and pointed goatee give him a certain gnomic look, shook his head. "That was a happy accident," he said. "Schiphol opened in 1919," nearly a decade after the auctions, "and the only one nearby was Anthony Fokker building airplanes there."

Amsterdam's airport would still be underwater if it weren't for Dutch ingenuity. A lake named the Haarlemmermeer once covered all of this before the decision to drain it. One corner had proved so treacherous to shipping that it was dubbed *Schip Hol*, the ship's hole. The airfield opened in 1917 on the edge of the muddy polder; Fokker arrived two years later, and KLM flights to London began the year after that. The airstrip was such a quagmire that passengers paid porters to carry them on their backs through the muck. That left them sitting ducks, however, for the farmers pelting them with turnips in retaliation for their intrusion.

Anthony Fokker was Holland's answer to the Wright Brothers. Having spent World War I building fighters in Germany—including the Red Baron's trademark triplane—he headed home when the airport opened. Flying in the face of the Treaty of Versailles, he smuggled an entire train's worth of planes and spare parts across the German border, with which he quickly set up shop at Schiphol. Between the wars, his company was the Airbus of its day, supplying the aircraft that ferried flowers and strawberries to London and composed nearly half of all American airline fleets. After Allied bombing leveled his factories in World War II, the defunct company never recovered. Schiphol's first incarnation was obliterated with them.

"At the time, there was no idea of what would happen in a hundred years," de Groot said. "Later, when we chose the new location here, it was because of the roads." The Aalsmeer sits at the intersection of two highways, one of which connects to Schiphol and to the freeways of Europe. But it hasn't been widened thirteen times to keep pace with the auctions, so by noon the convoy of flowers is at a standstill.

While its location next to Schiphol is an accident, the Aalsmeer's dominance of the flower trade is anything but. The birth of the cool chain and worldwide production placed a nonnegotiable premium on airborne connections and fast transfers on the ground. Flowers grown outside of Holland weren't present when the modern auctions opened; today they compose almost a third of total volume. Likewise, exports beyond Western Europe (typically by air) have also climbed from zero to a sixth of the world market. During that time the other auctions merged or died off, falling from sixteen in 1950 to just four by 2003. Schiphol is the key to the Aalsmeer's supremacy; since its merger with FloraHolland in 2007, it has effectively gained control of 98 percent of Dutch flower exports. (Regulators let it pass with the understanding that the real competition is now the Netherlands versus the world.)

Tacitly acknowledging Schiphol's influence, the capstone on de Groot's career was to have been an eight-mile-long underground railroad connecting the clocks straight to the hangars, with no need for carts, trucks, or even roads. It was deemed too expensive to be practical, but it provided the blueprints for the Aalsmeer Shuttle. As we followed its tracks, de Groot talked about his retirement plans. If anything, his schedule has become more hectic. He finds himself tracing flower-bearing flights back to their sources, ready to offer his services. When we met, he was busy setting up farms and floral auctions in China, Mexico, Ethiopia, and Vietnam. A decade ago he was in India, fixing links in its cool chain and nudging the locals to try something besides roses (because theirs weren't very good).

I was taken aback by this; wasn't it aiding the enemy? Not at all, he shouted as a train blew by. "We don't see it as competition. If we help them develop at home, it won't be necessary to expand here. Rather than bring every flower together in one place, we can develop a network in Dubai and Miami to forge new connections." This assumes Dutch firms would dominate these hubs. "It's the same in China. Instead of bringing roses from China to the Aalsmeer, we'd like to develop a Chinese market. It's better to be working together on a local logistics hub and auction, instead of bringing everything here to Holland. *Think* global. *Act* global," he said.

A Rose Is a Rose Is a Rose

Another old master keeping a hand in the game is Aard de Boer, who looks the part of a patriarch with a shock of white hair cascading over his shoulders and his tattersall work shirt. The namesake of A. de Boer Bloemenexport married his company off to Hilverda Bloemen a decade ago, transforming a pair of midsize firms squeezed by the giants into giants themselves. De Boer sold flowers across America and the Pacific for thirty years, while Hilverda's own roots go back to 1909, when one of its earliest airfreight patrons was the last of the Russian czars. Together, they trail only the export arms of the Dutch Flower Group and Florimex in market share.

The Dutch Flower Group owns twenty-one companies, and Florimex

consists of fifteen in nine countries. Hilverda has three under its umbrella, including Hilverda De Boer. Another breeds gerberas and anthur-
ium, and the third manufactures carnations in vast, industrial quantities.
An additional half-dozen joint ventures fill in the gaps in its portfolio,
including R & D labs in Holland and India, and a massive farm in Kenya
producing millions of stems. The flower trade itself is globalizing and
consolidating as fast as the products; the number of growers present at
the Aalsmeer has fallen by 30 percent since the 1970s, while imports are
expected to double between 2005 and 2015. Thanks in large part to the
conduit and catalyst of Schiphol, Dutch farmers find themselves running, joining, or being crushed by homegrown multinationals.

What had changed the most during his decades in the business, de
Boer said, "is that the buying of flowers, and the production of flowers,
has become more global." Seated at a table in his office overlooking the
warehouse, he began sketching a crude map of the world on a sheet of paper. He drew an arrow pointing north from South America to the United
States, another from Africa to Europe, and a pair of arrows pointing in
each direction between northern and Southeast Asia.

"In the world, there are three flower zones," he explained. Whereas
once America bought its flowers from the Dutch or else grew them at
home, now "the American market includes Colombia, Ecuador, Mexico,
and other South American countries as the main suppliers. Here in Europe, we have Africa as the main production area," with Kenya being the
largest, followed by Zimbabwe, Uganda, Zambia, and an up-and-coming
Ethiopia.

"The third is Japan, Malaysia, New Zealand, and Singapore," he continued, "with half of production and half of consumption going back and
forth, at least for mainstream flowers. Niche markets"—he meant the
hothouse varietals the Dutch keep under lock and key—"always move
from east to west," as they're both grown and sold in developed countries.

"Thirty years ago, you had a lot of flowers produced in the United
States, and while they still do in California, products like roses and carnations have moved to South America. That's going on here as well," he
said, tracing a line from Holland to Kenya. "For all of those bulk items,
production is moving south, as our labor and land are becoming too expensive," and heating a greenhouse in the clammy Dutch climate cannot
possibly compete with someplace warm where the sun is always shining.

While at first the cool chain had made Dutch growers globally supreme, it would also prove to be the root of their senescence. Freed from the contingencies of history, geography, labor, and climate, farm owners could go where they pleased, and they sought places with steady light, a temperate clime, cheap workers, and, of course, an airport. So they found themselves headed to Colombia, Kenya, Thailand, and Malaysia—all hugging the equator, and all underdeveloped. And just like any other industry suddenly faced with the possibility of frictionless, worldwide competition, the blossom business began to make sense.

Having never played a part in their national heritage, America's flowers were the first to go. The colonization of Colombia began in 1969 with the founding of Floramerica, which started flying product to the United States within six months. Thirty years later, having built it into a $50 million business, the American founders sold out to the Dole Food Company, which has since tripled the operation in size. Today it is the single largest producer in the western hemisphere. According to its annual reports, the headquarters of its floral division "is located strategically for easy access to Miami's International Airport," which happens to be the gateway for 88 percent of all flowers landing in the United States.

They arrive via an air bridge from Bogotá and Quito—the capitals of Colombia and Ecuador—which together monopolize the United States' supply of flowers. Unlike Holland, which still produces two-thirds of the Aalsmeer's volume locally, the United States has outsourced virtually its entire industry. Over the last decade, sales of domestically grown roses have plummeted 80 percent, from five hundred million stems to fewer than one hundred million, while imports have risen to 1.3 billion stems annually.

That shift has in turn led to the commercial extinction of varieties too fragile to meet the demands of the cool chain and air transport. As Amy Stewart noted, "It's no coincidence that roses, carnations, and chrysanthemums are among the most popular flowers today; they're also among the most durable. The flower business tries to give us what we want, but it limits our choices, too, offering us mostly what will work within its industrial system." Everything else is gradually phased out of the market—there is one commercial violet farm left in America, for example, and all of its flowers are sold within a hundred-mile radius.

Once flowers clear customs, they're trucked or flown through a succession of distribution centers until they reach one of almost fifty thousand flower shops or supermarkets. Nearly three billion stems are sold through these channels, about 80 percent of what Americans buy. More exotic and expensive varieties—roses with six-foot stems and heads the size of baseballs—are sent to the Aalsmeer instead, where they are auctioned off to the nouveau riche Russians who prize them.

Ecuador's production still lags far behind Colombia's, and its biggest bottleneck is Quito's airport. While roses thrive in the cool climate of the Andes, the thin air and encircling mountains are less conducive to a fully loaded 747. Not helping matters is the airport's tiny sliver of land, which lay on the edge of town when it was built in 1960 and is now encircled by the capital. A new airport opened last year outside the city, in the middle of an empty plateau and free-trade zone. Even counting Schiphol and Miami, it will be the world's first custom-built floricultural aerotropolis.

Miami manages to hold its own against Schiphol and the Aalsmeer, despite the absence of a central auction. It's more of a free-for-all once the flowers are discharged, as they vanish into the warehouses squatting between the airport and the Everglades. The city actually has more office space around Miami International than downtown, where the skyline is full of condos. A sizable fraction is set aside for the importers, a few of whom play a little fast and loose for Dutch tastes.

"We make sure we sell all of our product every day," Aard de Boer said. "We make sure it arrives as fast as possible and goes out as fast as possible. That means we don't speculate by sticking them in coolers," gambling that prices will be higher tomorrow. "That's something you might do in Miami, but to us, it's just dishonest."

His own suppliers are in Africa. The success of American outsourcing inspired Dutch growers to do the same, and by the early nineties, they had erected vast farms on the shores of Lake Naivasha. Sulmac's megafarm once covered forty-five hundred acres with carnations, roses, lilies, and larkspur, producing two hundred million stems a year. It has since been eclipsed by others owned by Homegrown and Oserian, the latter of which gears up for months to produce six million roses in time for Valentine's Day. Even during the chaos following Kenya's disputed 2008 elections—a terrifying spasm of ethnic strife—Oserian's five thousand employees reported for work dutifully each morning, more afraid of losing their monthly salaries of $80 (plus benefits) than they were of any mobs. The London tabloids pleaded with Britons to buy Kenyan roses for Valentine's Day to help the victims.

Like other disruptive innovations, Kenyan roses entered the market at the bottom, with a reputation for being cheap instead of good. Compared to light- and climate-controlled Dutch greenhouses, Kenyan farms (or Colombian, for that matter) are decidedly low-tech, low-cost affairs. Their flowers take shelter under plastic sheets, or are left to grow in the ground and open air. These are the roses and filler flowers that supply the cash-and-carry bouquets at European supermarkets like Tesco. Not that its shoppers can tell; Dutch-owned farms commonly relabel their crop as having been grown in Holland. Floriculture may be Kenya's third-largest industry (ahead of coffee and trailing tourism and tea), but you'd never know it at Heathrow.

They're not worth sending to the auctions. A customer like Tesco lacks the patience for it, especially when it's offering an eight-days-of-freshness-or-your-money-back guarantee across two thousand stores, forcing Hilverda De Boer to snip links from the cool chain in the name of expediency. In these cases, the line between growers and exporters becomes blurry; the former now package prewrapped, prelabeled bunches on the farm, while the latter race to lock up a reliably steady supply. "We have very close contacts with the growers in Ethiopia and Kenya," de Boer told me. "We advise them on what to grow and what they can expect from market prices, and then we make agreements to represent them on the world market. So they stay growers, and we stay importers."

Roses were the first variety to leave for Africa, but they aren't alone. Once a floricultural foothold was in place, consultants like Henk de Groot landed en masse. Having carved out a niche, African flowers are inching their way up in quality. As a result, the bottom has fallen out of Hilverda De Boer's business, forcing the company to climb higher in the value chain. "Bulk products we used to supply to the United States have moved south, and we cannot stop that," de Boer said mournfully. "Products with low value and high expenses—like chrysanthemums—we used to send a lot of to America, but that's over. We used to send a lot to Japan. Fifteen years ago, maybe it was one thousand boxes twice a week. Now it's only a hundred. And that's happening to the entire trade. Meanwhile, our range of niche products," the genetically engineered marvels, "is getting wider and wider. Originally we had a hundred varieties on that list; now we have a thousand."

While Holland is getting squeezed at the top of the market, Ethiopia is doing everything in its power to undercut Kenya at the bottom. Eight years ago, Ethiopian growers earned just $159,000 from flower exports. Four years ago it was $63.5 million, a four hundred–fold increase. And two years after that, the Ministry of Trade shot for $166 million. Roses could overtake coffee as the country's mainstay export very soon, a remarkable development considering the beans were first cultivated there a thousand years ago.

"This crop is a miracle" is the minister's position. Flower farms have created fifty thousand jobs in a country synonymous with famine. The keys to its rapid success have been tax breaks, generous loans, cheap land, and Ethiopian Airlines, boasting Africa's most modern fleet. Combined with the requisite KLM cargo flights, Addis Ababa has all the connectivity it needs to steal Nairobi's business. Loyalty isn't holding any growers back. "We're committed privateers," one told *The Economist*. "We'll just pick up and move somewhere else in Africa."

As I was leaving Hilverda De Boer, I stopped by the firm's trading desk—a glassed-in conference room with a bank of PCs. Bowing to the rise of the Internet, the Aalsmeer opened the floor to digital trading in the late 1990s. A few years later, management uploaded the inventory system, offering buyers a peek of tomorrow's supply today. Fifteen percent of daily turnover is now handled virtually, via online clocks synced to the live auctions.

At first the buyers resisted, just as Wall Streeters once balked at electronic trading. But tradition is crumbling. Hilverda has twenty-five buyers on the clock most mornings, each a specialist in a handful of varieties, including tulips. Where they all once slouched across the street with their coffee and cigarettes, half now spend their mornings here, pointing and clicking. It's only a matter of time before the rest of their colleagues join them.

The combination of virtual auctions with the cool chain has provoked an identity crisis within the Aalsmeer. It was once the hub of a thoroughly centralized industry, and its auctions reflected this with their insistence on *habeas flora*—presenting lots beneath the clock. But the hastening dispersal of the flower business (made possible by air power and inevitable by comparative advantage) casts the model in doubt. Why bother breaking the cool chain for a stem's three-second cameo when it can safely remain in refrigerators throughout? Or, for that matter, why is it necessary to move half the world's flowers through the Aalsmeer at all? What does it say that the auctions' modern architect is spending his retirement setting up outposts in China?

That only begs more questions: While there's no disputing the industry is well served by a hub in Holland, why not add more of them? And why not decouple the cool chain from the auctions, or what the mastermind of the Aalsmeer/Floraholland merger, Jacques Teelen, described as the "disconnecting of the commerce and the logistics"?

The Aalsmeer itself has imagined a future in which the last physical auction takes place in 2017; by then the halls more closely resemble the ghostly trading floor of NASDAQ. The auctions are held three times a day, staggered across time zones, and the integrated "Logistics Advice System" calculates not only prices but also the transportation costs of any specific lot. There are four hubs now: Poland, China, America, and Holland. The complex has doubled in size again, pushing right up to the fence at Schiphol. There's no need to build a tunnel anymore—an extension of the shuttle carries pallets to waiting planes forty-five minutes after they've been sold.

Confronted with such sensible futurism, it's a miracle the Aalsmeer has survived in its current form at all. It's unique in that it represents the last, mightiest attempt to move flowers (atoms) at the speed and pace of purely digital transactions (bits). The Aalsmeer is what Wall Street would be if globalization had taken place without the NASDAQ or electronic exchanges and we still swapped actual stock certificates. But to abandon it as the hub and heart of the flower industry in the name of efficiency must be heartbreaking, and I could hear the flat notes of resignation and sadness in the voices of Aard de Boer and his peers. They are outsourcing their heritage bit by bit and stem by stem to Africa, watching it fly away.

Flying Fish

The cool chain has the power to make or break a species, whether roses or more exotic candidates—bluefin tuna, for instance. Fifty years ago, sushi was a snack of rice balls pickled in soy sauce and vinegar, while the silvery-skinned fish was so worthless Canadian fishermen regularly dumped their catches in a hole and bulldozed them. Sushi's elevation to a paragon of freshness and yuppie emblem—headlined by the fatty *toro* carved from the bluefin's belly—can be traced to a Japanese Airlines executive named Akira Okazaki.

Okazaki worked in the airline's cargo division in the early 1970s, when his job was to fill the empty bellies of JAL's 747s on their return legs to Tokyo. The home islands were already overfished by then, and pollution was taking a toll on the seabed. Okazaki hit upon the idea of adapting the cool chain to tuna, converting a nuisance in Nova Scotia into a delicacy in Osaka.

On the morning of August 14, 1972—commemorated as "the day of the flying fish"—Okazaki brought five Canadian bluefin to Tsukiji, the fish market in the center of Tokyo. The air-freighted fish were four days old, commanding a respectable (and profitable) $4 per pound at auction. The price would rise 10,000 percent over the next twenty years, as the promise of a worldwide supply raised sushi from street food to a national craze. In a 1980s reprise of tulipomania, tuna prices soared in tandem with Japan's real estate bubble, and it's still not uncommon for a four-hundred-pound fish to fetch $175,000 at Tsukiji. From the day of the flying fish onward, sushi has been a global cuisine, prized for its freshness but able to be sourced and eaten anywhere. Today, thirty million Americans regularly eat sushi—an unimaginable number only a generation ago—to be joined momentarily by as many as fifty million middle-class Chinese.

The cool chain has made Tsukiji fishing's answer to the Aalsmeer. "Tokyo's Pantry" covers fifty-seven acres of waterfront, the size of six Tokyo Domes. Its fishmongers move two thousand tons of fresh seafood daily, compared to less than half a ton at New York's Fulton Fish Market—the world's second largest. The morning I dropped by the auctions, there were glistening salmon straight from Norway, sea urchin from Washington State, and tuna flown in from everywhere. When it inevitably moves from its cramped downtown quarters to a new home across Tokyo Bay, Tsukiji will be pointedly closer and more accessible to Narita International Airport.

The loser in all of this is the bluefin itself. While a rose is a rose is a rose, tuna are not so easily replaced. Bluefin stocks in the Mediterranean and Gulf of Mexico have collapsed 80 percent since fishing began in the 1970s, tracing a likely path to extinction. Annual catches are currently four times greater than the sustainable limit, and enforcement appears impossible—as many as half of Mediterranean catches are illegal. An international ban on the fish was torpedoed by Japan last year. Without meaning to, the cool chain created an insatiable appetite for bluefin that probably won't be satisfied until it's gone.

As far as fish go, salmon has fared better, but only in terms of absolute numbers. Wild Atlantic salmon stocks had crashed by the time fish started flying, but unlike tuna they could be reliably farmed in saltwater pens. Farmed Norwegian salmon started landing on American plates in the 1980s, and harvests began doubling within a few years. Sensing an opening, would-be Chilean farmers moved in aggressively despite no legacy of aquaculture, counting on the cool chain and cheap labor to undercut the Scandinavians. They bet they could bring their fish to market faster than even the wild kind caught off Alaska. They succeeded, with prices falling precipitously as harvests increased. By 2005, Walmart could offer Chilean filets for an everyday low price of $4.84 a pound. Only thirteen thousand tons of Atlantic salmon were farmed thirty years ago; in 2008, it was 1.5 million tons.

Farmed salmon are the cattle of the sea, raised in aquatic pens that have much in common with a feedlot, except the ocean floor is their manure lagoon. The salmon are fed a steady diet of antibiotics to keep them free of disease, but it doesn't always work—as Chilean farmers discovered to their horror three years ago when an outbreak of infectious salmon anemia killed 75 percent of their stock. Which is not to say they've quit trying. Chile's farms are expected to finally make a full recovery in 2011, while Norway's have expanded to make up the shortfall. And farming may yet save the bluefin—efforts are under way to breed a sustainable successor off Hawaii. Kona Kampachi are a cousin of yellowtail raised in the open ocean without antibiotics or hormones. There's still the question of whether it can scale to a million tons a year, but the cool chain can deliver it anywhere.

There are so many flying fish aloft these days that the largest "port" in Germany is technically Frankfurt, lying several hundred miles from any sea. Its "docks" are a ninety-seven-thousand-square-foot refrigerator

at the airport, where a veritable Garden of Eden is kept on ice. For carni-
vores, there's New Zealand lamb, Argentine beef, and Nile perch. Roses
hailing from Kenya and Colombia rest alongside Indonesian orchids,
which arrived with rambutans and mangosteens. Three enormous silver
coffins contain a whole swordfish, an entire tuna, and several flanks of
horsemeat from Canada. There are crates of Spanish avocados, Brazilian
mangos, French cabbage, and Thai bok choi. One holds organic fruit
salad mixed in Kenya without any preservatives, with a shelf life of maybe
three or four days. In twenty-four hours, all of this will be gone, replaced
by more of the same.

Fresh fruit or fish is as perishable as any flower, and our obsession
with freshness demands the cool chain expand to cover any produce we
desire. This means refrigerated trucks in the United States, where the
average head of lettuce travels eighteen hundred miles before ending up
an iceberg wedge at a steakhouse in Chicago. Britain discovered just how
much of its produce is grown and flown from overseas during last April's
volcanic ash crisis, when grounded flights led to shortages. Asparagus,
grapes, green onions, and lettuce all went missing at Heathrow. Airlifted
food miles have tripled in Britain since 1992, growing an average of 9 percent annually while total imports barely budged. This, in turn, has
sparked a heated debate on the future of food: Will it be locally grown, or
global? And which is the right thing to do?

Flowers and Food Miles

In January 2007, Sir Terry Leahy, the chief executive of Tesco, Britain's
largest retailer, delivered a speech about climate change. The grocery
chain faced mounting pressure from customers to reduce its carbon
footprint—and, by extension, their own. It was incumbent on him to say
something.

"I am not a scientist," he began. "But I listen when the scientists say
that, if we fail to mitigate climate change, the environmental, social and
economic consequences will be stark and severe . . . I am determined
that Tesco should be a leader in helping to create a low-carbon economy.
In saying this, I do not underestimate the task. It is to take an economy
where human comfort, activity and growth are inextricably linked with

emitting carbon. And to transform it into one which can only thrive without depending on carbon. This is a monumental challenge. It requires a revolution in technology and a revolution in thinking. We are going to have to re-think the way we live and work."

Coming from Al Gore, this call to arms might be expected. Hearing it from Leahy was shocking. Tesco sells nearly a quarter of all groceries in the United Kingdom and has another two thousand stores around the world (including a hundred in the United States). It trails only Walmart and France's Carrefour in reach and revenue. And like Walmart, it exerts enormous pressure on its vendors. Largely at the chain's insistence, Dutch growers had shifted roses to Africa to cut costs. They had no choice; Tesco is their largest customer.

But Tesco had changed its mind. In his speech, Leahy laid out a series of measures aimed at curbing his company's carbon output. Tesco would cut its energy use by half by 2010, he promised, and would do the same to the number of airfreighted goods it carries, labeling the items that remained as such. (Marks & Spencer quickly followed suit; its stickers read "Flown.") He acknowledged he was slapping a scarlet letter on roses and produce from Kenya.

"However, we cannot avoid the fact that transporting a product by air results in far higher carbon emissions than any other form of transport," he said. "We are not willing to avoid the hard fact that there is a conflict between the issue of carbon emissions and the needs of some of the poorest people on earth whose lives are improved by the ability to sell in our markets products which are brought here by air. There is a strong international development case for trading with developing countries. So, the question is: should we shun Fairtrade horticulture from East Africa to save CO_2, or champion it as an important contribution to alleviating poverty?"

It was admirable of Leahy even to ask, but the farmers could guess what the answer would be. "This announcement from Tesco is devastating," said the head of Kenya's Fresh Produce Exporters Association. Flowers, fruits, and vegetables bound for the U.K. make up a third of the nation's exports, and as much as a fifth of its economy. "I think if things continue in this one-sided sensationalist way, purely targeting air freight, labeling our produce with aeroplanes and not looking at other aspects of production, it will cripple Kenya. It will cripple the economy."

Tesco was torn between their fears and ours. Greenhouse-gas emissions are higher than at any point in human history, and rising faster than even the worst-case scenarios of the Intergovernmental Panel on Climate Change. While America dithered and China willfully ignored environmental devastation, Britain led a charge to the barricades. The U.K. was the first nation to adopt a cap-and-trade scheme for emissions and pushed for one encompassing the European Union. Three weeks after Obama was elected promising a similar system, Parliament passed the Climate Change Act, mandating an 80 percent cut in Britain's emissions by 2050, starting from a 1990 baseline. In 1995, the average human was responsible for producing about one ton of carbon per year. Britons now generate around ten tons, while Americans are closer to twenty.

Aviation is exempt from the law, although only until policy makers are able to estimate Britain's culpability. As far as the public is concerned, flying deserves much of the blame. One outlet for their anger is the debate over Heathrow. Another, referenced by Leahy in his speech, is the concept of "food miles"—the distance a product travels from the farm or ocean to your home. Food miles have become a shorthand for measuring food's carbon footprint.

It's logical to assume that food—or flowers—traveling thousands of miles might have a larger footprint than the same items grown or made locally. But we're often highly illogical about both. We are what we eat, and in our identities as consumers we are what we consume—and how visibly we consume it. As a result, food miles and carbon footprints have become wrapped up in a much larger critique of global food chains. Less-than-scientific correlations have been found between how far food has traveled and how it tastes. "Locavores" embrace this idea, spurning movable feasts whenever alternatives exist and eating seasonally when they do not.

Their attitude flies in the face of centuries of exploration and empire, dating to an era when the most valuable commodities were neither gold nor silver but Saharan salt and Indian pepper. Portuguese sailors rounded Africa seeking the latter, while the Dutch East India Company sought to corner it with cannon. The British Empire's finest hour—high tea—was enabled by "tea clippers" racing home from China after exchanging opium. Refrigerated steamships turned bananas into America's favorite fruit (and turned Central America into banana republics). To turn our backs on imported foods would be a rebuke to globalization itself. Which may be their point.

It's no different in America. Researchers at Iowa State University found that your grocery store's produce travels twenty-seven times farther to your fridge than the same lettuce or tomatoes grown locally. Broccoli, carrots, spinach, and strawberries all cover an average of eighteen hundred miles before we eat them. There's no question they have a higher carbon footprint than produce at farmers' markets. Industrial produce consumes anywhere from four to seventeen times more fuel and emits a corresponding amount of carbon. But distance has little to do with it. "Food miles are a good measure of how far food has traveled," said Iowa State's Rich Pirog. "But they're not a very good measure of the food's environmental impact."

The best example of this disconnect is a recent study comparing the carbon footprints of Kenyan and Dutch roses. Adrian Williams, a scientist at England's Cranfield University, sought to measure the effects of each step from field to florist for twelve thousand stems picked in February and shipped to Britain. To account for burning jet fuel at high altitude, he tripled the emissions of the flight from Nairobi. But the results surprised him: the footprint of Dutch roses was *six times* greater than Kenyan ones. Flying didn't matter as much as heated greenhouses and fertilizer drips. The African roses were planted in the earth and left to bloom under the equatorial sun. "Everyone always wants to make ethical choices about the food they eat and the things they buy. And they should," Williams told *The New Yorker*'s Michael Specter. "It's just that what seems obvious often is not. And we need to make sure people understand that before they make decisions on how they ought to live."

What we really want is to be *virtuous*. Accustomed to expressing ourselves through what and why and how we buy, we demand to change the world one purchase at a time—or at the very least, do no harm. We want low- or no-carbon footprints to go with fair trade *and* free trade. We'd like to support local businesses and local farmers—and barring that, poor ones in Africa. We plan to save the bluefin from extinction by declining to eat it. We crave an organic heirloom tomato that has never known the touch of Monsanto and tastes all the better because of it. These are competing, and occasionally contradictory, demands. Which is why we desire, more than anything else, a tomato that claims to embody all of these things, and if someone can deliver one with proof of virtue, we'll take it.

Tesco promised this proof as far as carbon was concerned. The chain would formulate a comprehensive "carbon count" for each of its seventy thousand products, going far beyond food miles. It would be a "universally accepted and commonly understood measure of the carbon footprint of every product we sell—looking at its complete lifecycle from production, through distribution to consumption," Leahy said in his speech. "It will enable us to label all our products so that customers can compare their carbon footprint as easily as they can currently compare their price or their nutritional profile."

This was easier said than done, requiring researchers to analyze every variable in each item, from field to fork, ground to garbage, and cradle to grave. The difficulty, they soon discovered, is that no one can agree on where the life cycle of a lamb or lettuce begins or ends. How far up the food chain should you go to include fertilizers, farm implements, and feed? How far down do you go to account for climate, soil, and waste? How it's grown, where it's grown, and what you're growing all matter as much as, if not more than, how far it's traveled.

How it's grown boils down to energy. Dutch tomatoes have a large footprint for the same reasons their roses do—they're grown in mechanized greenhouses using pesticides and fertilizer. It's better to fly in Spanish ones, which are grown in open fields. Importing produce from Kenya or Uganda—where the farms are small, tractors a rarity, and the fertilizer manure—is better still, even when accounting for the air miles. Economists at Christchurch's Lincoln University found that a British lamb's footprint is four times the size of a New Zealand one slaughtered and shipped eleven thousand miles, due to differences in fertilizer used for pastureland. The Antipodes' well-traveled milk has half the footprint of a British dairy's, thanks to a power grid fed mostly by renewable energy.

Food miles cannot begin to compare in toxicity with flatulent cattle. Anyone who's read *The Omnivore's Dilemma* can recite chapter and verse on the perils of force-feeding corn to livestock in feedlots. Cows produce methane, a greenhouse gas thirty times more potent than carbon, as a by-product of digestion, and they must keep at it to feed a middle class hungry for red meat. A breakdown of the Big Mac revealed that nearly a third of its footprint stems from feed production, another third from storage, and much of the rest from slaughtering, frying, and baking. Food miles contribute 3 percent.

One study of Britain's food chain attributed nearly half its footprint to cattle. The United Nations estimates livestock's share of worldwide greenhouse gases at 18 percent, more than all forms of transport on the planet combined. We could erase the footprint of food miles—and *all* miles—by becoming vegetarians. We could do it if we gave up beef and dairy only once a week.

"Dietary shift can be a more effective means of lowering an average household's food-related climate footprint than 'buying local,'" recommend Christopher Weber and H. Scott Matthews, Carnegie Mellon engineers who analyzed the American food chain. Food miles compose 4 percent of its emissions, the pair found; seen from this perspective, the Big Mac is healthier than a home-cooked meal. But from what perspective does that make sense?

Air Miles and Fair Miles

And thus food miles hit a dead end. "If you care about the environment, there's certainly a case to be made for growing things where they grow best, or at least better than they do now," Adrian Williams told me. Growing food where it grows best and growing food that's good for us matter a lot more than the mileage.

Once again we're debating virtue, pitting local, organic, preferably artisanal foodstuffs against the cool chain and our current globe-spanning system. But we never defined the stakes: growing a local, tasty, organic tomato is a problem facing the developed world; growing enough tomatoes for six, soon to be nine billion people able to afford them is the dilemma facing the developing one.

A century ago, the world faced an impending Malthusian crisis: farmers had run up against the hard limits of soil productivity. The Haber-Bosch process for synthesizing fertilizer averted disaster and was largely responsible for the fourfold increase in food supply known as the Green Revolution. Now the world faces another, with the UN warning us that food production must double in the next forty years to feed, clothe, and fuel nine billion people. More than half of the world's remaining arable land is in Africa and Latin America. Feeding another two billion people will require a second revolution to replace the carbon-spewing fossil fuels behind the fertilizers and pesticides of the first.

Proponents of sustainable, organic agriculture believe this is possible, but not without significant changes in diet and practice. "The average yield of world agriculture today is substantially lower than that of modern sustainable farming," Michael Pollan has pointed out. Researchers at the University of Michigan recently found that bringing international yields up to America's organic levels could increase the food supply by 50 percent. And yield isn't everything, Pollan argued. Growing high-yield corn to be processed into grain-fed beef and high-fructose corn syrup isn't the same as growing food. "We can expect that a food system that produces somewhat less food but of a higher quality will produce healthier populations," with a smaller carbon footprint to boot.

The prescription is more farms, better farms, and a diet more reliant on vegetables. America has all the land it needs to do that, but what about the rest of the world? Perhaps Terry Leahy's choice between the local and the global was a false one; perhaps the African farmers he would have left behind represent a way forward instead. Tesco seems to think so. When the Soil Association, which certifies 70 percent of the U.K.'s organic products, proposed to expand the definition of "organic" to include a partial ban on airfreighted flowers and produce, Tesco successfully lobbied against it. Asked why, Britain's largest retailer explained it was in favor of bringing Africa's farmers into its markets, not shutting them out.

No one has outlined a clearer path to an African breadbasket than Oxford's Paul Collier, author of *The Plundered Planet* and *The Bottom Billion*. At the end of 2008, while the world was transfixed by the financial crisis, he published a plan to avert global famine. Prices had spiked 83 percent in three years, he noted, sparking riots in thirty countries and toppling governments (including Haiti's). The cause was affluence. Asia's growing middle classes were upgrading their diets—buying meat instead of rice—which translated to high prices. The recession temporarily put a damper on consumption, but renewed growth and $85-a-barrel oil would send prices soaring again a year later. While some economists worried about peak oil, Collier fretted about peak food.

"At the end of the food chain comes the real crunch: among the urban poor, those most likely to go hungry are children," he wrote. Assuming they didn't starve, they would suffer stunted growth for a lifetime, physical and mental. "Stunted growth is irreversible . . . some studies find that it is passed down through the generations. And so although high food prices are already yesterday's news in most of the developed world, if they remain high for the next few years, their consequences will be tomorrow's nightmare for the developing world."

If the solution was more food, then the place to start was Africa. According to the World Bank and the United Nations Food and Agriculture Organization, one of the planet's last large reserves of underused land is the billion-acre Guinea Savannah zone, a crescent-shaped swath that runs east across Africa all the way to Ethiopia, and southward through Kenya to Congo and Angola. It is underused because the continent's agricultural productivity has fallen further and further behind that of the rest of the world. Even during the crisis, farmers had begun cutting back because they could no longer afford fertilizer. (Their produce is increasingly organic by default.) At the current trajectory, Africa's food imports are expected to double over the next twenty-five years. Making things worse, it is the first to feel the heat of climate change. The continent will grow hotter and drier, and rainfall will become more erratic, increasing the chances of drought. "Whereas for other regions the challenge of climate change is primarily about mitigating carbon emissions, in Africa it is primarily about agricultural adaptation," Collier wrote.

He called for a "biological revolution" to replace the green one Africa never really had. With new investments, new practices, and new technology, Africa could learn to feed itself, and then help feed the world. Fertilizers were off the table; the sub-Sahara's only hope was to embrace the genetically modified seeds American farmers use but Europe's won't touch. But curtailing subsidies, lifting Europe's ban, starting research, and expanding farms would take years. In the meantime, he advocated commercial farming as the best way to propagate innovations and to gainfully employ millions. Kenya's rose plantations are a model for this— new breeds developed in Holland are rushed to the equator, cultivated, and flown back to Schiphol. More than a million people work in horticulture there, roughly 3 percent of its population. The farms wouldn't exist without air cargo or the Aalsmeer.

"For Africa to develop, it obviously has to go beyond the peasant mode of production," Collier told me. "Nobody ever got to prosperity by staying tiny. Africa needs large-scale commercial organization. And it needs a global market. The two go together because the large-scale farms are particularly good at penetrating global markets. Peasants are particularly bad at it."

He has nothing but contempt for extollers of "peasant agriculture," dismissing small-scale organic farms as "abandoned technologies." The prerequisites for building an African food chain—scale, investment, R & D, and diverse exports to help pay for them—are the same ones locavores would rather dismantle.

"Everyone is fixated on flying this stuff, but it's an illusion," he said. "Suppose it did cost more in carbon—and there's evidence it doesn't. Does the world want to solve its global-warming problem by squeezing poor Africans out of one of the very few opportunities they've got? Africa has to create jobs. And it's very difficult to break into global manufacturing—China already has it under lock and key. And now, of course, we have the global recession, which makes it even harder for them to break in. Horticulture is one of the few ways for it to assert itself in the global market and not face killer competition from cost-competitive producers. It's obscene to shut that opportunity down on the argument that it's bad for the climate."

(John Kasarda made a similar case to the World Bank on behalf of Thai fishermen and farmers. The bank was unsympathetic. "Do we just write them off?" he asked me later. "Exports are their economic ladder out of poverty. What are the wider implications if we knock out that ladder and replace hope with hopelessness? Instability and terrorism?")

One argument against global food chains is that they outsource produce that should be left to local farmers. In reality, horticulture relies on the lowest-cost laborers available—Africans, Latin American immigrants, and typically Poles in Western Europe. (Pollan was shocked to discover migrant workers on California's organic farms.) While leaning on Kenya, Uganda, and Ethiopia for fresh vegetables and roses might be outsourcing, farmers at home are insourcing immigrant labor. The only losers are the immigrants.

A pair of studies by Gareth Edwards-Jones and his colleagues at Bangor University in Wales found that the millions of Africans working on commercial farms are healthier than their communities. Meanwhile, Britain's sixty-five thousand migrant workers are likelier to suffer health problems than the typical Briton. In one study, as the income of Ugandan farmers rose, they were better able to afford mosquito nets, which lessened their chances of contracting malaria. It was a virtuous circle: farmers grew healthier as they grew wealthier, and vice versa. The circle was a vicious one for Britain's workers, whose substandard pay, relatively hazardous task, and homesickness led to a decline.

In the second, the researchers compared the relative health of British, Spanish, Ugandan, and Kenyan farmworkers, with the latter broken down again into domestic and commercial export farmers. The health of European workers declined, while the Africans' improved, led by Kenya's exporters. The lesson, Edwards-Jones told me, is "buy British lettuce, make a Pole sick; buy Kenyan lettuce, and make a Kenyan healthy." The virtue of the transactions was not up for debate. He characterizes the backlash against food miles as "food angst." "The chattering classes have a nice, fuzzy idea of what farming should be," he told me. "They definitely don't like corporate gigantism. Localism is in many ways antiglobalism."

Another effect of the crisis, besides riots, was the decision by major grain producers such as Russia, Argentina, and Vietnam to drastically curb exports in order to bring down domestic prices and quell unrest. The resulting supply crunch sent prices soaring higher, setting off alarms in developing nations already spooked by issues of "food security." While the world was distracted by financial disaster, Asian governments crisscrossed Africa in a literal land grab. South Korea, Kuwait, and Egypt swept into Sudan, buying millions of acres, roughly a fifth of its arable land. The Saudis, who had once resolved to make their desert bloom until they realized they were emptying their only aquifer, intend to spend billions of dollars building plantations in Mali, Senegal, Sudan, and Ethiopia.

South Korea's Daewoo conglomerate went so far as to acquire a third of Madagascar for literally nothing, with the intention of splitting profits with the government. The deal was canceled after a coup ousted the president who signed it. China has officially earmarked $5 billion for African food, while cutting side deals in the Congo and Zambia to build gargantuan biofuel plantations. Gabon signed its own $4.5 billion deal with Indian and Singaporean investors to produce palm oil and timber in exchange for roads and housing. Even Kenya has talked to Qatar about leasing it land in its pristine Tana River Valley.

In total, an area the size of France has been put up for bid since 2006. Outsourcing's third great wave has begun, following on the heels of manufacturing in the 1980s and computing in the 1990s. Most of these deals are for staples or for biofuels, at least for now. But as *The Economist* noted, "The record of large farms in Africa has been poor. Those that have done best are now moving away from staple crops to high-value things such as flowers and fruit." In Ethiopia, commercial farms owned by Arab investors and run by Dutch farmers already produced tomatoes, peppers, broccoli, melons, and other produce, the vast majority of it to be flown to Saudi Arabia and Dubai.

What do African nations get out of these horribly lopsided deals? The investment and expertise Paul Collier stresses they desperately need. All of sub-Saharan Africa spends less than India on agricultural R & D. Their output has grown less than 1 percent a year since 1980, by far the lowest in the world. The Asian states buying into Sudan will immediately boost investment tenfold, from $700 million three years ago to $7.5 billion this year—half of all investment in the country. China has set up eleven research stations across the continent and by one count has made thirty co-op deals covering five million acres. Loans for fertilizer are part of the bargain.

But the price is steeper than it looks. An unpublished World Bank report titled "The Global Land Rush" was leaked to the press in the summer of 2010. The document paints a picture of exploitation, in which private and state investors prey on nations with weak governance and often fail to follow through on investment, "in some cases after inflicting serious damage on the local resource base." The leader of Zambia's opposition has come out stridently against China's plantations, and China has threatened to cut all ties if he's ever elected. A few years before, one of Zambia's largest commercial farms, employing about thirty-five hundred locals, announced it was losing nearly $100,000 a week after British Airways suspended freighter flights, citing the high cost of local jet fuel. By then, flowers were one of the country's fastest-growing exports, along with fresh vegetables, generating $60 million a year with no strings attached.

In *The Bottom Billion*, Collier made the case that the only way out economically for Africa is through trade, and not within a bloc of equally stagnant nations but by exporting to the developed world. The goal is to sell manufactured products, not commodities, but flowers and food are the continent's only toehold besides its vanishing stockpiles of oil and minerals. And for landlocked nations in the Sahel trapped between failed states and the Sahara, "air freight offers a potential lifeline into European markets," he wrote. "The key export products are likely to be high-value horticulture, and so European trade policy does matter."

"Kenya already has forty percent of the European green beans market," he told me, and 70 percent of the U.K.'s. Overall, almost half of Britain's airborne imports arrive from sub-Saharan Africa, and the British consume upward of one million pounds sterling's worth each day of African produce. "The marketing director of Asda, Britain's second-largest supermarket chain, was telling me they plan to switch thirty million pounds' worth of purchases to Francophone Africa. That's a huge start." (At Tesco, Leahy handed off the company in June 2010 to his handpicked successor, the chain's international chief, who spent thirty weeks a year in the air.)

Global food chains require global ethics and have global impacts. Africa's food and flower farms challenge our notions of what a "sustainable" life should look like—a Ugandan family free of malaria, or an unmarried young Kenyan woman with a concrete floor and running water. Oxfam International has suggested replacing food miles with "fair" ones, taking all of these variables into account. Echoing Michael Pollan's dictum, "Eat food. Not too much. Mostly plants," Oxfam adds, "Buy from developing countries. Drive less. Waste less" and "Eat less meat and dairy." If we're virtuous enough to want to save the planet, our own way of life, and Africa (apparently in that order), then perhaps it requires moving farms to the equator just as Holland's flower growers moved their roses.

The agricultural historian and *Just Food* author James E. McWilliams quotes the UN's Food and Agriculture Organization: "'much of the world's human population growth and agricultural expansion is taking place in water-stressed regions.' It's fine and good for naturally lush regions of the developed world to pursue the noble goals of local production and consumption, but the last thing we want to do as stewards of the environment is universalize such an ethic. After all, the imperative of sustainability demands that more than half the world should get its food from elsewhere."

To this end, McWilliams imagines a global food network of verdant hubs "where the climatic and geological conditions justify the midscale production of goods for local and distant markets. The spokes would be the clean, energy-efficient lines of travel and transport. Trade—often long-distance trade—would be assumed, but everything at the hubs would be open to regimes of improved efficiency," in the process creating millions of jobs. There's no reason they have to be outposts of agribusiness, either. Carlo Petrini, the founder of the slow food movement, has knit together a network of "food communities" called Terra Madre that take the idea of the farmers' market to global scale. Eaters in the West support nomadic fishermen in Mauritania by creating a local market for their bottarga, or dried mullet roe. In helping to preserve this way of life, the consumer evolves into what Petrini calls a "coproducer."

Maybe the best way to help African farmers is to be a market for their goods. Our charity clearly isn't enough, and economists including Collier have persuasively argued that foreign aid can be an addiction, hindering good governance and development. Rwandan president Paul Kagame has announced he will wean his country off aid completely. He has struck deals with Starbucks and Costco instead, giving them dibs on his country's coffee. Rwanda flies flowers to the Aalsmeer too.

"Public policy, stripped to its basics, is a choice among value alternatives," Kasarda makes a point of stressing to his M.B.A. students. "What one person will vehemently contend is the correct policy and another will say is wrongheaded will not depend on empirical measurement, but on the person's values, philosophy, and ideology."

Our debate over virtue will never be settled, because we'll never have to settle it. In societies like ours, where beliefs translate to preferences and morals to lifestyles, all virtues are created equal. We'll vote for them, as always, with our wallets. It is not a stretch to imagine a scenario in which we'll be able to pick from pull-down menus: local, organic, sustainable, fair trade, and so on, down to the family history and methods of the farmers. Microlending sites like Kiva.org already offer lenders their choice of borrowers. Who's most worthy: a carpenter in Togo, a rancher in Tajikistan, or a hardware store owner in the Bronx? They all are, but which of their stories resonates with you?

In July 2009, Walmart announced its intention to create its own sustainability index. Unlike Tesco, which took carbon emissions and food miles as its starting points, Walmart calls for a complete life cycle analysis of every product it carries, taking into account not only greenhouse gases but also pesticides, packaging, water use, waste, sustainable sourcing, and sweatshops. The results will appear a few years from now on a scorecard, or color code, or some other way of flagging customers' attention. "We have to change the way we make and sell products," said Walmart's CEO, Lee Scott. "We have to make consumption itself smarter and sustainable"—in other words, more virtuous.

Green advocates hailed its decision as the first step toward sustainable supply chains. No other retailer or company on earth has the reach and heft of Walmart and its $400 billion in revenue. Its suppliers would have no choice but to adopt the index themselves, and in all likelihood, so would other retailers, including Tesco, which is one-fourth its size.

Assuming we're willing to pay for it, we're heading toward a future in which the life cycles of all our worldly possessions are known to us, and after that it will be up to each of us to decide who and how best to reward them for their virtue. It won't be long before we're able to follow the provenance and path of our lettuce and tomatoes more easily than I was able to track my mother's tulips through the Aalsmeer's cool chain. There won't be any need to ask; the information will be right on the label.

8

THE BIG BANGS

Thailand's prime minister brought in Kasarda to create the perfect aerotropolis. It failed, sunk by corruption—but Bangkok is now the world's operating room as the center of airport-based "medical tourism."

Island-Hopping

If cities are shaped by transportation—whether sailing ship or 747—then so are their economies. Colonies belonged to the kings and companies with enough galleons and men-of-war to rule the shipping lanes. The countinghouses lining the docks of London, Lisbon, and Amsterdam tallied the raw materials of empire and industry—bullion, cotton, coffee, tea—and conveyed finished goods to captive markets overseas.

America following the Civil War had different needs—Reconstruction and settling the West. The railroad was the means to both ends, suturing North and South while linking the coasts, binding them all with standard time. One nation led to national markets, centrally served by sweatshops in New York, stockyards in Kansas City, and rail yards in St. Louis and Chicago. By century's end, the Sears, Roebuck catalog regularly ran to more than a thousand pages, promising speedy delivery from its "World Wide Stocks" to every farmstead in the country. Rail carried coal and ore to River Rouge, where Henry Ford made cars by the millions and unmade the railroad cities in the process. The cost of moving goods overland fell 90 percent during the twentieth century, tilting Americans toward sun and sprawl.

The last region of the world to successfully develop had none of these advantages—no empires, no resources, no hinterlands—the Pacific Rim. The original streak of Asian Tigers were islands or effectively so: Japan, protected by kamikaze winds and closed by the shoguns for two hundred years; Korea, the Hermit Kingdom split in two; Hong Kong and Taiwan, cut off by Chinese Communists; and Singapore, the breakaway city-state at the tip of Malaysia.

The jet made island-hopping—and ocean-hopping—effortless. World War II in the Pacific had been an air war, fought by aircraft carriers and won by bombers built in Los Angeles and stationed on unsinkable midocean atolls. From Pearl Harbor to Hiroshima, Japan was the first nation to learn what air power could do.

Following the war, the United States invested billions to keep the Tigers out of Communist hands. Taiwan, for example, received a mini–Marshall Plan of trade agreements, high-tech blueprints, and college tuition for thousands of engineers. Lacking domestic industries and blueprints, they made their biggest ally their customer, and exports to the United States immediately quadrupled. Before long, the island became an electronics powerhouse trailing only America and Japan in exports. The same thing happened on a smaller scale in Singapore and Malaysia, just as Raymond Vernon might have predicted.

Entire industries began island-hopping—Taiwan proved to be a gateway for American firms surreptitiously seeking access to China, arranged via another layer of middlemen in Hong Kong. These interlocking relationships evolved into today's just-in-time supply chains, in which the components of your Acer or Apple laptop are sourced from a dozen locations and assembled in another before heading overseas. This system, which overturned Ford's as the most efficient factory, could exist only via the air.

Over the course of the Jet Age, the Pacific Rim was transformed—aircraft tied the Asian Tigers to China and each other, just as the railroad linked New York to Chicago and Kansas City. The earlier invention integrated America's regional economies, while jumbo jets plugged Asia's into a global one connected directly to Silicon Valley. It's no coincidence Asian nations have spent billions on aircraft and new airports atop manmade islands, or that they've become the most fervent believers in Kasarda's vision. Taiwan is building an aerotropolis, and so are Hong Kong, South Korea, Vietnam, Malaysia, and Thailand. China and India are building a hundred each.

The repeal of geography changed the rules of their competition, as there were no longer any natural barriers to entry. Infrastructure, costs, and expertise decided which pieces of which industries would settle where, and who would accrue the spoils. Thailand's early efforts to make the best of this arrangement would take on a distinctly sinister cast, beginning with its role as a base for B-52s carpet bombing Vietnam.

Quagmire

In Bangkok, the generals decided where to put the airport. The name wasn't terribly auspicious—Nong Ngu Hao, the Cobra Swamp—and the location, a quagmire between the capital and eastern coast, remains inexplicable. Thailand's leader at the time, the visionary if dictatorial field marshal Sarit Thanarat, chose this spot for his country's bridge to the twenty-first century—in the form of a gleaming international terminal. His American advisers, then preparing for war two doors down, were happy to have another airstrip at their disposal, but the choice puzzled even them. The eventual site of Bangkok's current airport makes sense in light of the city's amoebic growth—after quintupling in size to ten million residents, the swamp was the only option. But why was Sarit so dead set on it then?

"We don't know the truth; no one does," I learned from one of the consultants charged with retroactively justifying his decision. "It's all speculation. All of this land—all of the Cobra Swamp—was owned by two dominant families," who presumably had their own sway.

"There was no study of the site's suitability, no consideration of alternatives," wrote Pasuk Phongpaichit, an economics professor at Bangkok's Chulalongkorn University, in her history of the airport. "The choice set off a minor orgy of land speculation."

The airport would be a long time coming. The field marshal's unexpected demise in 1963 stalled the project, until his generals resuscitated it by drafting Northrop—a pillar of Southern California's Warfare State—to design, build, and operate it for twenty years. "Parliament rejected the project three times," Pasuk noted. "The deal was finalized only after the military strongmen abolished parliament and went back to dictatorial rule in 1971." Student agitators seized on the subsequent purchase of eight thousand acres in the Cobra Swamp as proof of the junta's corruption, using it as a pretext for increasingly strident demonstrations. On October 14, 1973, one such march devolved into a riot, and then into slaughter as the army unleashed tanks and helicopters on the unarmed protesters. Horrified, the reigning king Bhumibol exiled the junta that night and appointed a civilian prime minister in the morning. (The monarchy, immortalized in *The King and I*, has nominally ruled an unconquered, uncolonized Thailand for seven centuries.) Not for the last time, the airport had brought down the government.

The once-and-future hub was mothballed for twenty years, until yet another coup in 1991 returned Thailand's generals to power. This time, they had a smiling public face in Prime Minister Anand Panyarachun, and the airport was reconstituted as an independent authority. This just made the infighting fiercer, however, as "there was a battle royale between the air force and the civilian ministers of Anand Panyarachun's government over who would appoint and control the authority's members," according to Pasuk. For the next decade, the project sidewinded its way through successive governments, continually morphing in size and scope to reflect Thailand's ambitions at the time. Under one plan, Pasuk remarked, "The project was reimagined as a hub for the Southeast Asian region." Under another, "The grandiose plans were scaled back because of the economic crisis. Under Thaksin, the project was reconceived as bigger than ever.

"What kept the project moving," she concluded, "was the factor which has marked every significant stage in its long history: a revival of authoritarian rule."

The aerotropolis and authoritarians go hand in hand. The first is a city built from scratch to chase economies of speed; the second are the only ones in a position to sign off on a mammoth construction project before it's too late. It's no accident Kasarda has found early adopters in the Middle East and China, followed close behind by Asian nations with a legacy of military rule—Taiwan, South Korea, and Thailand among them. For a fleeting moment, the latter is where his ideas appeared to have reached their full fruition.

In September 2006, on a still-soggy tract that now lies at the creeping border of Bangkok's suburbs, a gleaming $4 billion mega-airport finally opened. It was envisioned as the heart of a since-stillborn aerotropolis. Thaksin Shinawatra, Thailand's billionaire prime minister and aspiring autocrat, had picked up the field marshal's baton and finished his air bridge, renamed Suvarnabhumi, evoking the Thais' mystical Golden Land. But Thaksin wouldn't be around to see it. He was deposed by the army the week before in the nation's eighteenth coup since 1932.

The generals blamed Thaksin's overthrow on "rampant corruption" and a plot to take power into his own hands. Exhibit A was Suvarnabhumi (pronounced "Soo-wanna-POOM"). In his waning days in office, Thaksin tried to ram through legislation creating a special province for the airport, one reporting directly to him. The proposal immediately drowned in a monsoon of rumors and allegations of bribes and kickbacks. Before construction began, a long roster of government officials, well-connected businessmen, and even one of Thaksin's sisters bought land in anticipation of what was coming: a new "Venice of the East" floating atop a defanged Cobra Swamp, with dry land set aside for golf courses and cargo complexes. Within thirty years, a city of three million residents—ten times the size of the actual Venice—would have emerged from the waters. Imagine having the opportunity to buy long stretches along the Grand Canal when it was still underwater: Wouldn't you be tempted?

Their treasure map was a plan many of them had been privy to during its creation. More than a few sat in meetings and took notes on what to buy and where. Its principal author in fact, if not in name, was Kasarda, and it was titled "Suvarnabhumi Aerotropolis Development Plan." He'd incorporated everything he'd seen in Memphis and Subic Bay, and everything he knew about governance and competitiveness. It was his chance to put theory into practice, and his gift to the Thais, whom he'd come to admire after fifteen years of economic development work at a Bangkok affiliate of his Kenan Institute for Private Enterprise. Kasarda saw the aerotropolis as a hedge against the circling Tigers of Malaysia, Indonesia, and Vietnam.

But it never came to pass. Suvarnabhumi was made to stand in for Thaksin's moral depravity after his ouster. Today, the plan is in limbo and the wetlands are off-limits, while the airport's environs were abandoned to the encroaching sprawl. The tragedy of Suvarnabhumi and the aerotropolis that never was (and will likely never be) is one of a nation's leaders repeatedly acting in bad faith when presented with the best intentions. Kasarda meant well; his mistake was insisting on arming the Thai people for an economic war of all against all they had no capacity for waging.

Kasarda arrived in Thailand twenty years ago on a mission to expand the Kenan Institute's global presence. "It was my strong belief that the twenty-first century would be the Asian century, and that this was where we needed to be," he explains. His goal was to set up a permanent outpost someplace friendly toward Americans where he could make inroads into academic, corporate, and political circles and that was also safe and sufficiently exotic. "Thailand, which was the fastest-growing economy in the world at the time, fit the bill nicely."

The Kenan Institute Asia opened its doors in the early 1990s with a charter to play matchmaker between American and Thai companies, with an eye toward the former investing in the latter. The semiretired Anand Panyarachun signed on as chairman, packing the board with a Thai who's who of CEOs and former ministers. When the lineup was announced, the press dubbed them the "Anand 3," referring to his likely cabinet if he ever ran for a third term. Kasarda's immersion in Thai politics was complete.

He leveraged his new connections to take a second crack at building the Global TransPark—the next node in what he imagined would be a worldwide web of just-in-time airstrips. The Thais already had a plan on the shelf for converting a Vietnam-era American bomber base to civilian use. Given the chance to get it right this time, Kasarda spent the next six years drafting blueprints and wooing Thailand's prime minister at the time, until the whole thing was scuttled in the chaos of the Asian financial crisis.

From 1985 until 1996, Thailand's really was the fastest-growing economy in the world, surging 9 percent annually—faster even than China or India today. Reforms had slashed tariffs and opened the door to foreign investors like Toyota, which moved there for cheap labor, followed by the Big Three. They touched off an industrial boom during which real per capita income doubled, spawning joint ventures and an entrepreneurial class tapping overseas loans. The foreign debt of Thailand's corporations correspondingly ballooned, eventually putting so much pressure on the Thai baht that the government was forced to cut it free from its peg to the dollar in 1997. The baht crashed, the cost of money doubled, and balance sheets totaled. Foreign lenders took their money and ran for the exits—not just from Thailand, but from all of Asia—triggering a cascade of currency crashes in Indonesia, South Korea, and Malaysia. Thailand's growth curve flipped upside down.

But the depreciation of the baht only made Thailand more attractive for exporters, as the costs of labor and materials had been halved as well. Lacking any better options, the country embraced its role as an offshore factory for multinationals, especially automakers and hardware manufacturers. Hard drives—the infinitely elastic brain tissue of every computer—became Thailand's specialty. Major players like Seagate, Hitachi, and Fujitsu flew in pieces from places like Ireland and flew out finished discs to factories in China, where they were slid into laptops winging their way from there to the States. It wasn't long before they were stamping drives by the hundreds of millions, employing hundreds of thousands of Thais in the process. In the decade following the crisis, exports tripled while the ratio of foreign trade to GDP nearly doubled to 150 percent. Exports rescued Thailand but also dragged it unwillingly into Kasarda's global arena of the fastest. There was no going back.

Nakhon Suvarnabhumi

Of course, "going back" was Thaksin Shinawatra's first promise as prime minister. Elected by a landslide in 2001, Thaksin was one of Thailand's richest men, having leveraged his family's modest fortune into a TV and telecom empire. He ran as a self-made populist, ignoring Bangkok's educated elites in favor of winning the hearts and minds of poor farmers in the countryside. He promised them a New Deal of universal health care, public works, microcredit, and outright cash handouts to the villages—in effect buying their votes.

He announced his aim in early speeches to move away from the "East Asian economic model" that was "overly dependent upon exports produced by foreign technology brought in by foreign investors with low value-added content and relying mainly on cheap labor." Pulling the needle would prove impossible, though. After a minor panic ensued among foreign investors, Thaksin recanted and elaborated that he was actually pursuing a "dual-track" strategy: self-reliance on the one hand, and increased exports, foreign investment, and tourism on the other. This could only work so well once China joined the WTO in 2001, starving the Tigers of overseas dollars.

Thaksin realized that his own government needed to lead the charge in domestic spending, which meant big-ticket infrastructure. In 2002, he accelerated the ongoing airport project, making it his top priority. It would open in September 2005, he guaranteed, just in time for the start of his second term. "We are going to free Thais who are slaves of capitalism," he promised in 2003. "We cannot run away from capitalism. But we can increase our competitiveness."

In the years between the crisis and the airport's reanimation, Kasarda had finally synthesized his grand unified theory of the aerotropolis. He was waiting by the phone when Thaksin's chief deputy called for advice about the new airport. Soon, he was deeply enmeshed in the planning of Nakhon Suvarnabhumi, Suvarnabhumi City.

Although the final report, issued in December 2003, does not contain a single mention of him, his fingerprints are all over the executive summary. Under the heading "roles of the airport," all mentions of tourists or passengers or even airlines have been replaced with "fostering business and country competitiveness" and "airports as office, commercial, and professional worker magnets." The result: "a new urban form—the *aerotropolis*." The authors had cut and pasted from the collected works of John Kasarda. Building Nakhon Suvarnabhumi from the ground up, they promised, would boost exports, attract more money, and become the "primary engine of Thailand's rise in global competitiveness. It will also make the Suvarnabhumi Aerotropolis the exemplary model of twenty-first-century urban development."

The plans fit Kasarda's theories to a T. The airport itself occupies a rectangular slab of land longer than it is wide; combined with noise buffers on its north and south sides, it would have neatly divided the aerotropolis in half, following the plans he provided. On one side of the runways were street markets, high-rises, bungalows, and arctically air-conditioned office space. On the other were free-trade zones, factories, and distribution centers radiating outward into the countryside in declining order of their need to hug the hub. Stiching the halves together were boulevards and six-lane "aerolanes," while a half-billion-dollar express train (originally Kasarda's "aerotrain") linked Suvarnabhumi to the city. The planners tried to think of everything: parks, protected wetlands, and even space set aside for Buddhist temples.

As bold as these plans were, they paled next to fantastical renderings depicting floating office parks and subdivisions linked via canals instead of roads. Bangkok itself was the original "Venice of the East" they hoped

to emulate, but their pixellated update on the capital's polluted *khlongs*—
which now run through some of the poorest districts in the city—had
been fumigated of Bangkok's sweet putrescence and sticky vitality. They'd
sketched a lean, mean export machine, a city that had more in common
with the "Asia lite" of Singapore than its own antecedent, just as modern
Singapore (entirely rebuilt in the last forty years) has nothing in common
with its colonial self. Both cities—Suvarnabhumi and Singapore, and all
aerotropoli in general—were laid out in accordance with the whims of
multinationals and foreign capital flows to prove their competitiveness.
And the qualities they prize above all else, qualities at odds with Bangkok's very essence, are order and control. To build the aerotropolis, they
would need to erase the past.

Fortunately for them, this is exactly what Thaksin had in mind. The
most controversial recommendation does not appear anywhere in the executive summary: the legal creation of Nakhon Suvarnabhumi as Thailand's seventy-seventh province, reporting directly to the minister of the
interior—Thaksin's brother-in-law—and essentially to the prime minister himself. It would be carved from pieces of metropolitan Bangkok and
its provincial neighbors, absorbing several existing cities and covering
nearly 150 square miles, or roughly half the size of Singapore. Kasarda
argues it was necessary to avoid the multimunicipal infighting and inertia seen everywhere in the United States. "The point was to put powers
of planning and zoning in one set of hands to guide its development," he
says. "A smooth integration was never going to happen if we left it to six
different government bodies operating independently and often in outright competition. None of them were willing to lose any control over
their jurisdiction, so they took Thaksin's proposal to the mat." Every one
of them had gone solidly against him in the election.

The governors weren't alone in their suspicions that Nakhon Suvarnabhumi was at best a boondoggle and at worst a land grab with electoral
implications. One powerful Thai told Kasarda point-blank: "The aerotropolis is just another way to make Thaksin richer. It will be mired in
corruption the same way the airport was from the start." The planners
were worried too. A pattern had emerged during their briefings. They
would present drafts to assembled ministers, generals, and Thaksin's
own family, only to discover days or weeks later that their audience had
bought the land in question following the meeting. When Interior Minister

Somchai Wongsawat told the press land prices were destined to soar, "perhaps a hundredfold," it might have been a case of self-fulfilling prophecy. Thaksin's younger sister Yarowet Shinawatra (not to be confused with her sister Yaowapa, who is married to Somchai) went so far as to start her own logistics business, despite no previous interest or experience.

That was topped in November 2003, a month before the master plan's completion, when Shin Corp., Thaksin's family-owned conglomerate, struck a deal with Malaysia's Air Asia to launch Thailand's first low-fare carrier. The new airline would go head-to-head at Suvarnabhumi with Thai Airways (owned by Thaksin's government), which was set to sell nearly a quarter of itself to help pay for the airport. The egregious conflicts of interest staggered the planners. "I think it's great Thailand will have a low-cost airline," said one. "But what a shame it had to be owned by Thaksin."

His siblings confined their avarice to flipping real estate and dispensing favors. One miniscandal broke when the airport's parking lot contractor claimed on tape that he'd paid Yarowet $250 million to win the contract. A second tape appeared in which he claimed he hadn't paid her anything, and then he took the whole thing back. (Yarowet has repeatedly denied any wrongdoing.) Well-connected developers, powerful clans, and opportunists began snapping up parcels in preparation for the gold rush.

"But they ignored everything we recommended," one of the planners complained. "Not only did the politicians buy up the land, but they started building houses." I saw a few of these gated communities, which would fit right in to Laguna Niguel, but it was unclear why anyone would want to live on the edge of a swamp, under a flight path. "The authorities who were supposed to investigate this ignored it," he continued, "so now there are twenty thousand people who will need to be relocated. Just think about how much that's going to cost!"

The more pertinent question is whether Thaksin himself understood what the aerotropolis was, or simply saw it as a way to enrich his inner circle. His motives are ultimately unknowable—Kasarda's repeated requests for a postcoup interview were refused—but the educated guess is that he understood completely. And he didn't care.

"Everything Thaksin did was strategic," someone who had briefed him personally told me, "but the failure of the aerotropolis was a lack of communication. He never tried to sell it to the people. And what many foreigners made the mistake of doing was going straight to Thaksin to make things happen. They never got the people to understand what the concept was, or the benefits, or the costs. Even now, they don't understand it."

Thaksin won reelection in a landslide in 2005, but he missed his self-imposed deadline. The airport was nowhere near ready in September, and so a ceremonial opening was held instead. The real opening day was pushed ahead to July, and then to the fall. The master plan had been finished nearly two years before and only awaited passage of the "Suvarnabhumi Act" into law. Then it all unraveled.

In January 2006, Thaksin's family sold their remaining 49.6 percent stake in Shin Corp. to Singapore's Temasek Holdings, on the same day the government relaxed foreign ownership restrictions to 49 percent. Thaksin himself had signed the law allowing him to sell the company. Worse was the buyer. Temasek is Singapore's state investment arm, the owner of its ports, airport, and Singapore Airlines, in addition to dozens of companies across Asia. Cashing out to Thailand's regional archrival went over about as well as President Obama proposing to sell Exxon-Mobil to Hugo Chávez and Venezuela. Rubbing salt in the wound, the family avoided paying taxes on their $2.3 billion windfall (Thailand's Supreme Court later ruled the sale illegal).

It was the opening his opponents had been waiting for. Thaksin had made bitter enemies in the establishment. Some saw him as a usurper, others as a demagogue, and there were fears he might even try somehow to do away with the king himself. Thaksin had done himself no favors with his brutal "war on drugs" and the police's lethal tendency to shoot first and ask questions later. Human Rights Watch estimated that 2,275 people died in the first three months of his administration, many of them in "extra-judicial killings," murder without due process. Half the victims were found to have no links to dealing drugs. To make matters worse, Thaksin's staff had badly botched a counterinsurgency against Muslim separatists in the south, including a bloody raid on a mosque. The Temasek deal was the last straw.

Within weeks, a hundred thousand Thais had taken to the streets, calling for Thaksin to resign. Protests lasted for a month, until Thaksin took the drastic step of dissolving the lower house of parliament, calling for snap elections on April 2. His opponents in the Democrat Party boycotted. A month later, the Supreme Court invalidated the elections. Thaksin, who was now calling himself the "caretaker prime minister," would stand for reelection again in October.

A month later, in June, the Interior Ministry presented the Nakhon Suvarnabhumi plan to Thaksin's cabinet, which approved the plan "in principle," the first step toward parliamentary approval (once a new government had reconvened parliament, of course). Thaksin was pilloried for gerrymandering the provinces opposing him and for rubber-stamping a multibillion-dollar megaproject while a lame duck. "His government went too far," one of the planners told me. "They tried to pass the law—bang, bang, BANG!—in only a few weeks' time, which people were very much against." Why risk it? I asked. Why not wait until the October elections? He shot me a look. "Because of the financial benefits."

The airport was still closed when Thaksin left to visit the United States in September. On the 19th, he was deposed in a coup—bloodless, as most are in Thailand. ("You know they're over when the dancing girls come out and put flowers in the gun barrels. It happens every time," Kasarda said.) The generals appointed a caretaker government, which froze Thaksin's accounts, banned him from politics, and dissolved his party. Thaksin settled into exile in London, plotting his next move.

Suvarnabhumi opened a week later. The terminal—then the largest in the world under one roof—had been designed by the German architect Helmut Jahn, whose previous work included concourses at O'Hare. Jahn's initial sketches were criticized for being insufficiently Thai. A government committee was appointed to ensure that the correct flourishes were included in the final designs, amounting to wooden pagodas sprinkled throughout vast steel-and-glass tubes. The prevailing aesthetic was practically posthuman, resembling a vast spaceship on an interstellar journey to a new home planet. The arrivals area was more traditional—acres of naked concrete.

It was the concrete that would give its new owners headaches. Cracks appeared in the taxiways immediately, caused by water seeping into the lowest strata—a predictable legacy of being built atop the Cobra Swamp. The junta knew a metaphor when it saw one, seizing upon these as signs of Thaksin's corruption and the airport's shoddy construction.

The farce ended when its own engineers reported that most of the damage could be fixed in twenty-four hours. But it set the tone for what was coming—the purging of Thaksin's pet projects from the budget, Nakhon Suvarnabhumi being the biggest among them.

The objections Kasarda and company could just shrug off while Thaksin was around now resurfaced with a vengeance. The aerotropolis would be too close to the runways, too crowded, too loud, too wet, and too expensive. A few weeks after his ouster, large swaths were rezoned as wetlands, sticking a pin in the real estate bubble. A month after that, the new deputy prime minister declared himself dead set against the aerotropolis. "Airports everywhere are built away from residential communities," he blustered. "Now that the airport is up and running, what purpose will crowding up communities around it serve? The noise from the aircraft is loud enough as it is." Bangkok officials chimed in to the effect that building one would cause both cities to flood. Better to let it go back to being a swamp.

That wasn't going to happen. Kasarda had tried to warn them. The areas around airports were so bad because people refused to plan. In Suvarnabhumi's case, it would inevitably lead to an "urbanized swamp." The planners (who had kept their heads down and their eyes open) hadn't missed the steady trickle of people into the Golden Land. "Right now, we're dealing with twenty thousand people, but that could become forty thousand," one complained. "Imagine what you would have to do to convince them all to move. You'd have to pay them a fair market price, at least. But I am sure there would be corruption in the air." Or outright extortion. Thailand's chance to build the Singapore of the skies was slipping away. Nearly a year after the coup, I called the Ministry of the Interior asking for anyone who could tell me what was going on with the remnants of the aerotropolis. An affable voice on the other end apologetically explained nothing was happening, and nothing was likely to happen until after the elections, which were set for December 2007, four months away.

When the elections rolled around, those in power predicted an easy victory (on the assumption the junta wouldn't *let* them lose). To their shock, Thaksin's party rallied around a new flag and new leadership (his old cronies) to carry the day. His base—the impoverished countryside—had spoken again. The opposition denounced the new government as

Thaksin's puppets and tried to rescind the results. Determined to sweep them out of power once and for all, tens of thousand of protesters calling themselves the People's Alliance for Democracy began to riot. PAD's "yellow shirts" stormed the government's offices in August 2008 and occupied them for months. When that didn't work, they decided to shut down the country, starting with its airports. Their comrades occupied terminals in Phuket, Krabi, and Hat Yai, crippling Thailand's beach resorts and stranding thousands. They were ousted after a few days, but PAD had succeeded in finding the economy's choke point. All it had to do now was squeeze.

On the evening of November 25, 2008, a convoy of several hundred yellow shirts armed with knives, steel rods, and clubs blockaded the entrance to Suvarnabhumi and stormed the terminal, startling thousands of passengers. Fighting their way past riot police, a masked group seized the control tower and demanded the flight plan for Prime Minister Somchai Wongsawat's return·leg from a summit in Peru. Somchai's plane touched down safely that night at Bangkok's Don Muang airport instead, before taking off again to Chiang Mai. All other flights were canceled. The yellow shirts dug in for a siege, joined by several thousand reinforcements. PAD's leaders proclaimed "Operation Hiroshima" was the "final battle" in a "fight to the death" against Thaksin's proxies. This was the form revolution took in the Instant Age—disrupt the flow of air traffic. Somchai ordered the Royal Thai Army to intervene; the commander general politely declined and suggested that Somchai resign immediately instead.

Two nights later, a second swarm of yellow shirts captured Don Muang, closing the last international airport within hundreds of miles. The capital of Thailand, home to nearly a quarter of its sixty-five million citizens, had been cut off from the world. In a perverse experiment, PAD would prove how critical the airports are to Thailand's economy by wrecking both.

The tourists noticed first. An estimated three hundred thousand were trapped in Thailand as the crisis unfolded, with no easy way out. Two million others canceled their pending vacations, blowing a hole in Thailand's largest industry. The ones waiting it out in their hotels watched their breakfast fruits vanish, followed by milk (from Australia), cheese (New Zealand), and fresh fish (flown in from Tsukiji). But the lobbies overflowed with orchids, as growers faced the choice of either letting them rot or dumping them on the street for a third of the price they would have commanded abroad.

Then the factories closed. The country's embrace of low-cost electronics manufacturing had blossomed over a decade into a $40 billion industry. Components made in Thailand made their way into everything from the iPod to Google's servers. Suddenly unable to fly components in or finished drives out, the factories around Bangkok stopped. Thirty plants closed shop and two hundred thousand workers were sent home in the first *two days*. All the while, HP, Apple, Dell, Samsung, and Lenovo held their collective breath.

The whole point of just-in-time manufacturing is to keep raw materials away from your factories until the very last moment, which meant the PC and gadget factories in China rarely kept more than a few days' inventory on hand. The longer the grounding of Bangkok lasted, the greater the chance they would run out of the disc drives and semiconductors made in Thailand. Once that happened, the production freeze in Bangkok would begin to spread. Lines across the world would stop, losses would mount, and the entire industry would begin convulsing.

It had happened before. In 1999, an earthquake in Taiwan knocked its semiconductor factories offline for a week, triggering a chain reaction that stretched from Silicon Valley to Wall Street. In 2000, a lightning strike at a Philips Electronics semiconductor plant in New Mexico destroyed the sole supply of a chip critical to Ericsson's latest cell phones. Caught without a Plan B, the handset maker saw its stock price fall 50 percent. Now the biggest names in computing were staring down the barrel of another disaster, a man-made one. You could practically hear them in their Tokyo and Silicon Valley boardrooms resolving never to invest in Thailand again.

Why won't democracy stick in Thailand? In the last five years, there have been a coup, two elections, mass rioting, and three governments toppled. Blame could be assigned to almost anyone, but the real reason is poverty—or in Thailand's case, where huge fortunes were being made, what sociologists call "relative deprivation." Over twenty years, the poverty rate has fallen from 70 to 25 percent, but inequality has mushroomed. Democracy and capitalism may go hand in hand, but only past a certain point.

New York University's Adam Przeworski has found that democracies are "certain to survive, come hell or high water," only if their per capita incomes exceed $6,000 a year. No sufficiently wealthy democracy has ever been deposed above that level. Thailand's is well below it—$3,170 in 2006, the year of Thaksin's overthrow. Poor democracies are more vulnerable to crisis, Przeworski found, and countries stuck at an income level around Thailand's are more likely to die when their economy stagnates, and they are also less likely to boom.

Perhaps the saddest irony of Nakhon Suvarnabhumi is that it was expressly designed to prevent Thailand's stagnation. In Kasarda's appeals to the World Bank for financial support, he stressed that exports of flowers, fish, and semiconductors would help poor farmers, fishermen, and the young women who staff the assembly lines far more than the ruling class. But no one at the bank would listen.

In the midst of the chaos, he began back-channel negotiations with various ministers, drawing upon his old connections to start all over again. The deputy prime minister who once recruited him resurfaced in Somchai's cabinet, only to resign after an angry mob chased him from parliament.

Eight days after the occupation began, Thailand's Supreme Court ended the crisis. It dissolved the ruling coalition as punishment for electoral fraud, disbanding three political parties and banning Somchai Wongsawat from politics—the same fate as his brother-in-law. PAD declared victory and went home, leaving a more sympathetic government to clean up their mess.

Thailand's self-inflicted embargo was an utter catastrophe shocking in its scale. The Thai central bank pegged the damage at $8.3 billion in lost income, a billion dollars a day. Thailand lost 3 percent of GDP in one week, single-handedly plunging it into recession, the first since the baht had collapsed a decade earlier. The number of tourists fell 28 percent, worse than the aftermath of either 2003's SARS epidemic or the 2004 Indian Ocean tsunami. Foreign investment fell by half. Worst of all, airlines began to divert from Suvarnabhumi, rerouting nearly a third of their flights to Hong Kong, Singapore, and Malaysia. "It was only ten days," said the head of the Pacific Asia Travel Association, "but it will probably take ten years to get over that incident."

Thais couldn't wait that long. Six months later, they were at it again, only their roles had reversed. Pro-Thaksin "red shirts" laid siege to Government House as PAD had done before them, forcing the new prime minister to deploy a more pliant army. Calling from Dubai, Thaksin declared, "Now that the military has brought tanks out on the streets, it's time for the people to come out for a revolution." He promised to lead it.

But Thaksin stayed put. (A warrant has since been issued for his arrest on charges of terrorism.) The revolution went on without him last spring as the red shirts barricaded themselves in the center of Bangkok, fighting deadly battles with police and practically igniting a civil war. One confrontation began with protesters lobbing Molotov cocktails at advancing soldiers, only to end with handshakes and an exchange of cellphone numbers. "This situation hurts me here," one officer said, pounding his chest with his fist. "I won't order the troops to shoot. We don't want Thais to fight Thais. How this ends is not up to us; it's up to Thaksin."

The Window Is Closing

One evening I strode into the lobby of my hotel along Sukhumvit Road—the thumping spine of Bangkok's shopping and red-light districts—and nearly tripped over Dr. Suwat Wanisubut. He winced slightly in embarrassment, looking up at me with soft eyes. He looked nothing like the potbellied insiders or patrician consiglieri I'd been braving epic, twelve-lane traffic jams to meet. (Late to one such rendezvous, I almost got out of a cab to walk the rest of the way when a baby elephant passed me on the median.) Dr. Suwat radiated a paternal serenity, dressed simply in a yellow polo with "NESDB" sewn on the breast—his uniform at the National Economic and Social Development Board, the central planning agency of Thailand.

He had been Kasarda's champion and the de facto leader of the Nakhon Suvarnabhumi Aerotropolis steering committee. If anyone knew whether Thaksin had ever acted in good faith toward the airport, or whether the aerotropolis plan might be resuscitated, it was he. Dr. Suwat motioned for me to follow him on to Sukhumvit Road, where we dodged autorickshaws before ascending to the elevated SkyTrain platform forming a concrete canopy over the smoggy street. The SkyTrain was typical of Bangkok's approach to urban planning—the original version had been modeled on Vancouver's, but the contract was canceled and the money spent on expressways instead. Congestion actually increased as the new roads unleashed latent demand. The SkyTrain was eventually built as a privately owned, for-profit system competing with Bangkok's subway.

Alighting a few stops later in Siam Square, we barged through one of the largest malls in Asia to the opposite side, hopped a smelly diesel bus that ambled by, and finally zigzagged through back alleyways before emerging in the atrium of Bangkok's tallest building, the thousand-foot Baiyoke Tower. One story below the top-floor revolving roof deck with panoramic views is a buffet. We headed for the roof deck first: I needed to see Bangkok as it is, he explained, before we discussed what it should be.

Even from a thousand feet, Bangkok resists any attempt by the brain to impose order on it. It is laid out on a grid—but one drawn by a six-year-old who quickly got bored with right angles. The city, as far as I could tell, is a saw-toothed blanket of skyscrapers, parks, and parking lots, bounded by the river on one side and the horizon on all others. There are no cores, no clusters, no visual cues to give away the game. For variety, the rusty skeletons of a dozen "ghost towers" poke through the skyline, untouched since their backers were wiped out during the financial crisis a decade ago. (There have been a few recent additions.) Down below, slums sit cheek by jowl with massage parlors and granite office blocks. "You'll see the most beautiful house surrounded by people living in a box," one resident marveled. "You ask, 'How is this possible?' I would say it's possible because the people living in the boxes are friendly. They don't steal. It's very, very strange, but this is why planning is something of an unknown here."

Dr. Suwat said as much as we took in the view. The city's first land-use plan, drafted on his watch, went into effect only twenty years ago. By then, he said, 70 percent of modern Bangkok had been built. Below us, molten streams of traffic coursed through the streets, coagulating at stoplights. The one sliver of darkness in this tableau belonged to the tracks of the future airport express train, which would someday terminate almost directly below us. "And at the end of that," he said, pointing due east, "is Suvarnabhumi." My eyes followed the highway running alongside, a golden thread connecting the Golden Land.

Dr. Suwat and I had spoken before, in the spring of 2006, under very different circumstances. Thaksin had won his snap elections, and everyone still had every reason to believe the aerotropolis would be approved. "This is the key to Thailand's growth over the next five years," he had said at the time. "No other project is this big. It will bring high-tech companies to this region from Malaysia, Singapore, and even southern China. We are now competing directly with them, and even with Korea and Japan."

There was no trace of such exuberance this night at dinner. Once we'd staked out a private corner, I asked about Thaksin. Had he understood? "I think he understood the land-use planning," Dr. Suwat began hesitantly. "It was similar to places like Singapore, which he liked and thought was very well planned. He looked at the aerotropolis and saw something similar. But I know he didn't understand city planning. When I was assigned to find a site to build a new parliament building, I submitted one to him, and he didn't understand why I had chosen it.

"You know, the king *asked* him to build a new city. And he didn't do it, because he didn't get it. I think Thailand should have a new capital myself, like Brazil and Brasília." My eyes widened at this. Lúcio Costa's plans for a new Brazilian capital in the middle of nowhere had produced a tabula rasa monstrosity in 1960. Conceived as a hub and laid out in the shape of an airplane (with vast, windswept plazas standing in for the wings), its location was so remote the concrete had to be flown in. Fifty years later, Brasília is a failure, inefficient and inhumane. Anyone who can afford a plane ticket flees to Rio or São Paulo on the weekends. ("Don't bother trying to catch a flight out on Thursdays or in on Sundays," warns Kasarda, who knows from experience. "They're booked solid.")

Dr. Suwat tried a different tack. "Or maybe it could be like Kuala Lumpur and its new airport, with the transportation hub and the government together? Bangkok is just much too much." He was referring to the capital of Thailand's southern neighbor, Malaysia, and its late-1990s update of Brasília: the $20 billion "Multimedia Super Corridor." Cooked up by Malaysia's own megalomaniacal autocrat, Mahathir bin Mohamad, the MSC and its offshoots were Malaysia's moon shot—an attempt to build an Asian Silicon Valley. He hailed it as a "global gift to the Information Age," but in reality it was an office park. Matathir planned to lure Microsoft there in hopes that its skills would rub off on Malaysian firms, a process known as technology transfer. If the plan worked, Malaysia's economy would lift off—eluding China, which was beginning to eat away at its low-cost, low-skilled factories—and plant its flag as Asia's next mature Tiger. But if the MSC blew up on the launch pad, it wouldn't be long before Malaysia was squashed between rivals boasting smarter or cheaper talent pools. Thailand is in a similar bind.

The south end of the corridor, an hour's drive from downtown and hacked from rubber plantations, was the new Kuala Lumpur International Airport, making the MSC the world's first intentional aerotropolis—or "aeropolis," as it bills itself. But the crisis struck before it was finished. By the time Malaysia recovered, its intended tenants had chosen India for outsourcing and China's factories for everything else. Does that count as a success? I asked. "In the long term, sure," Dr. Suwat said. "Building a city takes fifty years. Look at Washington, D.C.—it took 150 years create a layout as good as the one today." That isn't saying much.

"But at least you had plans, not just a traffic jam. If you're building for the next ten years, or twenty years, you should have a plan. If we fully support Suvarnabhumi, I think it will move much faster, you know. But I have to run around to talk to many groups. Because my background is in transportation, I think of transportation and city planning as one. I cannot plan transportation without a land-use plan. I can't select where the line for an underground train should go, or an expressway, because I don't know how they will be used."

Dr. Suwat glumly picked at his food. The Thais—from the prime minister on down—seemed constitutionally incapable of planning for their future. I was reminded of something Kasarda had told me before I left: the Thais are terrible planners but excellent copers. Dr. Suwat didn't disagree. But there had been a difference in their motives. He wanted to build a better Bangkok around whatever anchor he could find. Kasarda, on the other hand, had insisted on grafting a competitive weapon onto a host that had rejected the transplant.

Dr. Suwat shook his head when I floated this. "The Thais don't like high tech. The majority of the people here are very, very conservative. I don't think they want to go that way. I like it, I plan for it, but it moves very slowly." He turned philosophical. "It probably doesn't help that we were never colonized. We never had a civil war. People live the easy life. They eat, they drink, they sing all year. I think Vietnam is a better bet to move forward, actually."

He's not alone in his thinking. The next morning, I slid into the backseat of a chauffeured car beside Tom Reese, the former director of USAID in Thailand. He had sponsored Kasarda's proto-aerotropolis plans years before. We were nominally headed to see the city-size industrial park he manages south of the airport. But before we'd even pulled into traffic, he was briefing me on his new franchise in Vietnam. He'd staked out several thousand acres of rubber plantations east of Ho Chi Minh City, beside a future ten-lane highway and equidistant from the city and its new mega-airport, opening next year.

While its neighbor once removed lurched from one political crisis to the next, Vietnam entered the fray with plans for a network of two dozen new-and-improved airports by 2015, at a cost of $7.2 billion. The centerpiece will be Ho Chi Minh City's, with more theoretical capacity than Heathrow or O'Hare. The airports are part of a national strategy to undercut China as the bottom rung of Asia's low-cost manufacturers. Its ready supply of rock-bottom labor doesn't matter without the means to export the finished product.

"Here's the way it works," Reese explained. "If you're going to manufacture in China, and you're an exporter, you're beginning to take a second look at where to go. If you move to inland China, you have huge logistical problems. And coastal China is too expensive," leaving Thailand and Vietnam. Last year, a free-trade agreement between China and the nations of Southeast Asia took effect, making it easier than ever for both sides to woo factories and jobs away from each other. "Once Vietnam stitches this together—good highways, good connectivity—then it's all over," Reese said as the car swung past Suvarnabhumi on the highway. "Thailand's really only got a few years. By 2012, it had better get its act together."

Dr. Suwat was more pessimistic as we picked at our fruit and sorbet. He didn't see Suvarnabhumi becoming the hub Kasarda had envisioned. "The Thai people can't do it by themselves, you know. We don't have the personnel; we're not good enough. So if we want to do that, we have to allow foreigners to do it. Sometimes, we like that. And sometimes, without any reason, we don't like it. We turn on them. Sometimes it's Singapore, sometimes Malaysia, sometimes the Japanese, and sometimes the Americans. Thailand is really close to America, but at some point we saw we shouldn't follow them."

So what is Suvarnabhumi good for, then? "Tourists," he said, popping a bite of melon into his mouth. "And that's about it."

•

The Land of Smiles depends on the kindness of strangers, who have been bitten badly by chaos and crisis. But tourists contributed $17 billion to Thailand's economy in 2007, more than hard drives, fish, flowers, or any one of Kasarda's envisioned uses for the aerotropolis. Bangkok has been a tourist magnet since the 1960s, when American soldiers on R & R from Vietnam began hitting the beaches (and the massage parlors). The number of tourists following in their wake has risen nearly fortyfold in forty years, made possible by the Boeing 747. The economics of its size, speed, and range ushered in the era of international mass tourism via chartered flights and package tours, creating tourism hubs on par in importance with factory towns like Penang in Malaysia (where all of Dell's laptops were once manufactured).

Thailand is representative of the worldwide transformation of tourism in the last half century, when the combination of rising incomes, falling fares, and political freedom produced a bumper crop of globetrotters. Global tourism has grown thirtyfold in fifty years, generating somewhere between 5 and 10 percent of worldwide GDP. The United Nations' World Tourism Organization estimates it will triple again in the next two decades, almost in lockstep with the growth of international air travel. By some accounts, tourism composes 75 percent of all aviation demand today, and we have barely scratched the surface of who might fly—only 7 percent of all the people in the world who can afford to travel abroad have done so. Tripling their numbers might be easier than you'd think. Kasarda's Law predicts that the explosive penetration of mobile phones in the developing world—from near zero to 50 percent in the last twelve years, to four billion subscribers worldwide—will lead to a corresponding rise in air traffic. The emerging middle class has not yet begun to vacation.

Tourism is already a bigger business than either textiles or agriculture in developing nations like Thailand. It's proved so effective at creating jobs—for the otherwise unskilled, for women, for the young, in backwaters where pristine wilderness is the main attraction—that the UN added boosting tourism to its list of Millennium Development Goals. Speaking before the aviation industry in 2005, Secretary-General Kofi Annan described the role of tourism this way: "It can benefit other economic sectors and small businesses, such as traditional agriculture and food production, handicrafts and textiles. Through ecotourism—one of the fastest growing parts of the industry—it can contribute significantly to rural development, while promoting the environmentally sensitive development of basic infrastructure in remote locations." Or, as the head of the UNWTO put it, "Tourism is the best foreign direct investment system ever invented."

Tourism has become more diffuse over the past half century as well. In 1950, fifteen countries absorbed 97 percent of all international arrivals; now these mostly European nations receive barely half. The one thing they all have in common, according to a report published by the World Economic Forum, is "an accessible, high quality air traffic network," with roads, hotels, and banks to match.

The connectivity this represents is so powerful that once built, even if corrupted or squandered, it retains its potential. Nakhon Suvarnabhumi may be dead, but the airport was bursting at the seams the day it opened. Its forty million passengers in a good year (when there isn't rioting) are more than Singapore's, Kuala Lumpur's, or any airport's in India. Thailand's connections and its smiling, educated, below-market-value talent pool make the country a perfect candidate for a person looking to create a new kind of tourist hub. That person was an old friend of Kasarda's, a man named Ruben Toral.

Medical Leave

"This doesn't look like a hospital," Toral said, showing me around. "It feels more like a hotel or an upscale mall."

After studying the gleaming lobby of Bumrungrad International Hospital for a minute or two, I was inclined to agree. Americans in shorts reclined across from Arab couples in flowing white dishdashas and black abayas, the latter accessorized with designer handbags and sunglasses. In August, even the asphalt in Bangkok is overripe and malodorous, but the only scent inside was a faint whiff of espresso from the Starbucks in the corner.

Toral is responsible for luring that cosmopolitan clientele here, thousands of miles from home, for a knee replacement or a triple bypass or even just a checkup. Before he arrived in 2001 as Bumrungrad's marketing director, "We were a Thai hospital serving a Thai community," he said. "Now we're an international hospital that just happens to be in Thailand."

Toral is still amazed, seven years later, that folks who have never set foot on a plane, let alone owned a passport, will log a twenty-four-hour flight—in coach!—to put themselves in the care of a hospital whose name they can't even pronounce. The number of overseas patients more than doubled on his watch, to 430,000, generating the majority of the private hospital's revenue. "It's the high-school-cafeteria person," Toral said. "The independent businessman, the doctor, the lawyer. They tell me, 'We did the math. We can't afford to pay twelve hundred dollars for insurance every month,'" so they go without.

The phrase "medical tourism" was once used to describe early retirees jetting in to Bangkok or Bangalore for a boob job before recuperating on the beach. That image doesn't jibe with the numbers today. As many as a million Americans streamed abroad last year in search of affordable alternatives for hip replacements or prostate surgery. And they went not for the postsurgical tanning but for the savings: up to 90 percent off the going rates in the United States. They went because forty-seven million Americans have no insurance and can't pay for surgery to fix a bad back or clogged arteries. Or they left because they have insurance but can't begin to pay the soaring deductibles a major surgery entails. They're fleeing a system that is by far the most expensive in the world and growing more so by the hour, with diminishing returns in quality of care.

"Your options are paying fifty to sixty thousand dollars in the States or coming here and paying eight thousand," said Toral. "That's the difference between putting it on your credit card or going into bankruptcy."

A journey to Bumrungrad is hardly a descent into some third-world medical hell. It was arguably a world-class hospital even before it became a world-famous one (thanks in large part to a *60 Minutes* segment orchestrated by Toral). Administrators have spent the past fifteen years acquiring state-of-the-art technology, adding beds, and wooing Thai doctors abroad to come home. Bumrungrad replaced its paper records nine years ago with a homegrown all-digital system, an upgrade U.S. hospitals have struggled with for years.

Its outpatient clinic is more stylish than the bar at my five-star hotel in Bangkok. Instead of waitresses, some two dozen nurses tend to a polyglot mix of patients. Arrivals from Asia and the Middle East have separate floors to make them feel at home. The cafeteria is staffed with chefs poached from some of the city's best restaurants. And there's even an in-house travel agency offering visa extensions in case complications arise and patients need to stay. Being located in a tourism hub offers Bumrun-grad advantages its rivals simply can't match, giving it a chance to become the world's first truly global hospital.

But the Arabs sprawled across its lobby aren't oil sheikhs awaiting VIP treatment. They're humble civil servants, shipped in bulk from Riyadh and Dubai because Toral cut a deal with their governments to outsource their surgeries here. Medical tourism, Toral told me, is only the beginning. The next step is globalized medicine, in which millions of fully insured patients in the United States will be flown to hospitals in Bangkok, Singapore, and India for treatment. The patients will belong to Blue Cross Blue Shield, UnitedHealth Group, and maybe your insurer. If Toral has his way, Bumrungrad's next heart- or knee- or brain-surgery patient will be you.

Ruben Toral is an outsider twice over. Not only is he a foreigner in a Thai hospital, but he's neither a doctor, nor an operator, nor an insurer. That may explain his near total lack of empathy for the panic or anger those professions should feel upon hearing his chilling vision of their future.

Born in North Carolina (where he was mentored by John Kasarda), Toral came to medicine only after a stint consulting with Duke University's Center for Living, arriving in Thailand twenty years ago to set up "health and wellness" retirement villages for Westerners. That may explain his idea of health as a lifestyle choice, as opposed to a total war against death and disease. Toral's candor and mellifluous voice recall a weary George Clooney character explaining how the world *really* works. Health care, in his mind, is not necessarily a social compact or a universal right, but a quality product to be packaged and sold at a sensible price: he assumes patients are much savvier consumers than their doctors give them credit for.

Annual health-care spending in the United States has topped $2 trillion—about half from private sources, half from public coffers—to compose a staggering 16 percent of GDP. That's almost double the average of other developed countries and more than half of global spending overall. Despite the best intentions of health-care reform, the figure will keep climbing, perhaps exponentially, as eighty million baby boomers—the so-called silver tsunami—reach old age over the next twenty-five years. Their needs alone could keep every doctor from Boston to Bangalore gainfully employed for half a century, and a shocking percentage is barely able to afford the coverage they have. As Toral put it, with typical bluntness: "God forbid you have a family of four, earning fifty thousand dollars a year. You are fucked."

Some economists have hailed our extreme health-care spending as the central pillar of a postglobalization American economy built on services. In their view, hospitals and their support systems of doctors, administrators, and insurers have been, and will continue to be, the greatest creators of domestic jobs this century—nearly two million so far— especially in the Rust Belt and other areas hit hard by manufacturing's emigration. Health care and education are the only sectors keeping cities like Cleveland afloat after what feels like decades of recession.

The flip side is the staggering costs that have stymied attempts to provide universal coverage, hurt the global competitiveness of American firms, and bankrupted millions of families. "The greatest threat to America's fiscal health is not Social Security," President Obama has said. "It's not the investments that we've made to rescue our economy during this crisis. By a wide margin, the biggest threat to our nation's balance sheet is the skyrocketing cost of health care. It's not even close."

A coronary bypass costs $15,500 at Bumrungrad, including the doctors', nurses' and anesthesiologist's fees ($4,800), surgery itself ($5,000), and a week's hospital stay, meals included ($850). Airfare costs extra. Flights from the United States run as little as $1,000, a pittance compared to a $50,000 or $60,000 bill for the same procedure back home. The real cost in those cases is actually unknown, shielded from the patients by a byzantine series of discounts, kickbacks, and payouts among doctors, hospitals, and insurers.

The $30,000 differential between Bumrungrad and General Hospital is even more convoluted than you might expect. Cheap labor is the least of it—these are American-trained, board-certified surgeons, not country doctors. One reason is that the same stents and other devices that might wholesale for five figures in the United States cost a tenth as much in Asia, where manufacturers like Medtronic sell them at huge discounts and make it up on volume. And then there are economies of scale. India's Devi Shetty is known as the "Henry Ford of heart surgery" for driving the cost down to an inconceivably low $2,000. His flagship clinic in Bangalore has six times as many beds as the average U.S. hospital, and his army of cardiac surgeons perform twice as many surgeries as their American colleagues. The question isn't why is surgery in India or Thailand so cheap; it's why is surgery in America so expensive.

For someone like Toral, the hypertrophied medical-industrial complex is just begging for a dose of disruptive innovation. He calls his vision the "Toyota-ization of health care"—just as Japan's automakers went from being cheaper to better than their American counterparts, so too will Asian surgeons. In his view, medical tourism as we know it is giving way to "globalized health care." Hospital chains at home will buy, partner with, or even sell out to foreign rivals like Bumrungrad, creating worldwide aerial networks of patients who will hopscotch across continents chasing the best care and costs. Insurers will leap at the chance to lower their own bills and offer members more options. And employers, dying to do the same, will induce employees to play ball by kicking back a share of the savings.

We'll learn to love jetting to surgery overseas, Toral insists, just as we came to prefer Toyota Camrys to Chevys. Never mind that globalization gutted Detroit; it gave us cheaper, safer, more fuel-efficient cars and helped lift Japan and South Korea into the ranks of developed nations. Toral believes globalization will do the same for our health care (and quite possibly for India and Thailand). "Medicine has always been so locally driven that it can't think out of the box and ask, 'How does this globalize?'" he complained while we watched translators, collectively fluent in two dozen languages, admit patients into Bumrungrad. "What it's looking at right now is the beginning of the beginning, which is individuals who are franchised, voting with their feet and heading out of the country."

The process will pick up speed as heavyweight for-profit U.S. hospital chains such as HCA ($30 billion in revenue), Tenet Healthcare ($9 billion), or HealthSouth ($1.9 billion) realize that hospitals such as Singapore's Parkway Group or India's Apollo chain aren't competitors so much as links in a global, offshore supply chain that can be bought and brought into the fold just as easily as an auto plant outside Bangkok. Medical hubs will become different stops on the same assembly line: Brazil and South Africa for plastic surgery, Mexico and Hungary for dentistry, Costa

Rica for a little of both, and Southeast Asia for the bodywork of heart surgery, organ transplants, and orthopedics. Patients needing new hips or hearts will be the first sent overseas by their doctors for the same reason medical tourists are headed there now: the procedures are safe, low margin, and high volume—always the first things to go in any globalization scenario.

"There are going to be primary-care networks and emergency care" near your home, "and then there are going to be surgical centers offshore," explained Toral, laying it all out for me over dinner one night in Bangkok. "And the great thing is, we're going to own them!

"In order to ensure continuity of care," he continued, "you'll never leave the system. What could be better than telling an American patient they're going overseas to an American-owned hospital? They're going to discover the same supply-chain advantages Toyota did when it created just-in-time manufacturing. We're going to have the same thing—just-in-time *patients*. Hospitals are not going to spend any more money or any more time in the movement of that patient through the system than is necessary. They're going to get the patient in, get them on that global platform, and get them back. Now, how do they do that in a fast, efficient way where quality is kept, efficiency is gained, and prices don't go up? As Jack taught me, it's classic manufacturing and logistics."

But in this case, the supply chain is made of people, often very sick ones. Our trips through the global health-care assembly line may come to resemble those of Bill Flother, a Colorado peach farmer with a balky back whom I spoke with while he was recuperating in Bangkok. It was his third visit to Bumrungrad, having previously had his heart valves fixed. This time around he'd survived a fourteen-hour spine-crushing flight, arriving on a Sunday, going under the knife on Monday, and checking into his hotel on Tuesday. "It's like a bed-and-breakfast with surgery thrown in," he said. He was confined to bed rest for a few days, "and then maybe I'll go to the beach for a few days, and then I'll fly home."

Flother was no stranger to Thailand, having flown here fifteen times on vacation (there isn't much to do in orchards during Rocky Mountain winters). Outsourcing his surgery halfway around the world was less exotic than it looked; it was really just a change in scale. Once it seemed that every small town had its own hospital staffed with local doctors making house calls, until economics and our desire for cutting-edge care conspired to send us to big-city ones instead. Whereas people once asked why they had to drive for hours to surgery, now they ask why they should have to fly for hours (and hours) to Bangkok instead. The answer is the same as always: because the care is better and it costs less. Toral tells the story of a public school cafeteria worker who flew to Bangkok to fix her back. "She didn't have a passport—hell, she probably hadn't been out of two or three states in her life," he said. "She giggles her way through the thing, her total bill comes to seven thousand dollars, and then she comes back a year later for a hysterectomy. All of sudden, *we are her doctors*, ten thousand miles away. It's crazy."

Even crazier is how, overnight, the United States went from the top medical tourist destination to its single biggest source of refugees. American hospitals were the envy of the world for decades, and open to all comers. Then came 9/11 and the Department of Homeland Security with its draconian visa policies, which made it nearly impossible for certain nationalities to check in. In one year, for example, the United States went from being the single biggest draw for Middle Eastern patients to a nonfactor. The beneficiaries were—you guessed it—India, Singapore, and Thailand. The patient supply chain can change gears in an instant.

It's still unclear who will come out on top in a global wave of health-care consolidation. There are precedents for U.S. companies owning hospitals abroad, and the trend continues with top-tier medical schools such as Harvard and Johns Hopkins cutting deals to open dozens of hospitals and teaching programs overseas. Harvard has partners in Mumbai, Seoul, Istanbul, Xinjiang, and Islamabad, to name a few. "Institutions within the U.S. health-care system will have to think very creatively about how they can participate on a global basis," says Dr. Robert Crone, a consultant and former head of Harvard Medical International. "The magic formula hasn't been developed yet."

Even if the roles of hunter and hunted have yet to be defined, there are clear winners and losers in Toral's scenario, which he sees unfolding over the next few years. The biggest losers by far would be American doctors—especially cardiac and orthopedic surgeons, who face the most damaging blow yet to their pride, public standing, and paychecks. In one fell swoop, they'd devolve from the rock stars of the OR to glorified mechanics, and they'd really have only themselves to blame. Overseas patients routinely return home raving about the personal attention shown by their Thai or Indian surgeons. In a twist on Kasarda's Law of Connectivity, patients regularly trade phone calls and e-mails with doctors before arrival. (Nothing punctures the myth of American medical invincibility quite like the experience of having a doctor who actually speaks to you.)

Foremost among the winners would be the forward-thinking hospitals and their owners—in both hemispheres. They stand to profit enormously from the dismantling of an immense cost base on one side of the Pacific and its subsequent reconstitution as a streamlined profit center on the other. McKinsey estimates that 20 percent of America's forty million hospital patients would be well served by transoceanic care, a potential drain (or savings, depending on where you stand) of $190 billion per year, more than the GDP of Singapore. Also sitting pretty would be expat doctors, who would be free at last to return home from the United States to practice world-class medicine, letting their patients come to them.

Toral's entire road map, of course, is predicated on insurers' willingness to underwrite it. Rest assured, they are. "Once they understand the ramifications of this, you'll see the larger players start crafting policies that allow people to receive treatment overseas," Ori Karev, CEO of UnitedHealth International, the global arm of the UnitedHealth insurance conglomerate, told me. "I think you'll find most of us exploring this. We are a business at the end of the day."

But if insurers will be delighted to cut costs while adding more options, and employers will be equally pleased to see the same trickle down to them, the question remains: What about the *patients*?

Doctors in Thailand and India are arguably outdueling their Western counterparts right now when it comes to better care. That may sound like sacrilege, but the bar is set lower than you think: more than one hundred thousand people die each year in U.S. hospitals from preventable errors alone, more than those who fall to AIDS, breast cancer, and car crashes combined. At Bangkok Hospital's five-year-old heart clinic—really a hospital in its own right, treating some fifteen thousand outpatients a year—stem-cell therapy is part of the standard tool kit for treating battered hearts that might otherwise demand a transplant.

"Most of the patients have been ill for a long time," the clinic's director, Dr. Kit Arom, told me in his art-strewn office. "By the time they come here, they are all but incapacitated. They are waiting for a transplant or waiting to die." After receiving stem-cell injections straight into cardiac muscle tissue—a treatment too controversial to be offered yet in the United States—most patients recovered enough to leave under their own power. On Arom's watch, the clinic has also retired open-heart surgery in favor of a new, decidedly less invasive approach using small incisions. Having also seen the procedure performed in Bangalore, Crone enthusiastically notes its "extremely low morbidity rate, and the patients are literally out of the hospital in a couple of days. It's this kind of innovation— done with well-trained, U.S. board–certified surgeons in a less oppressive environment—that yields the potential for better health care than there is in the United States currently." Arom is more succinct: "It's a question of will."

Will patients embrace that perspective and agree to fly abroad for their care? One thought is to be up-front with patients about the true cost of their treatment and offer to share the savings with them. In light of what it costs for a fresh set of knees in the States—$45,000 and up for the uninsured—and the huge discounts overseas, it's conceivable that patients might come out ahead if they let a Thai doctor install them. Of course, just because insurers won't use a stick doesn't necessarily mean the dangling carrot couldn't be considered coercion in its own right.

The United Steelworkers made that case to Congress, sending every union member a letter declaring, in part, "The right to safe, secure, and dependable health care in one's own country should not be surrendered for any reason, certainly not to fatten the profit margins of corporate investors." A blog on the AFL-CIO website followed up with the headline, "First Employers Sent Your Job Overseas. Guess What? You're Next."

"The problem with exporting people for health care is: Who goes?" asked Stan Johnson, a director for the United Steelworkers, his old-timer's drawl coming across the phone loud and clear. "Is it voluntary now? Is it involuntary at some point? Do you end up sending your eighty-year-old mother to India when she has never been outside of a fifty-mile radius from home? You're going to put her on a plane and ship her to a hospital where they don't understand her language or her culture and where conditions may be suspect?"

I asked Johnson if he thought someone like Toral was being disingenuous, or merely deluded, when he claimed medical tourism could go a long way toward fixing health care. "Either or both," Johnson replied. "There are clearly people who see a significant opportunity from a monetary perspective. There are also people who think that competition is just the thing to fix the system. But I can without a doubt say they are not seeing the bigger picture."

Toral, naturally, sees something else at work in this kind of thinking. "Protectionism and slander," he declared, during a prescient rebuttal of Johnson's points months before. "If you change the health-care equation, they are going to mobilize. *You want a Chinese doctor working on you? You want an Indian doctor working on you? Can you trust these people?* Of course, those doctors studied in your schools and speak your language, and they already mastered their medical system. Now they've mastered yours.

"They say, 'It's outsourcing, you're trying to drive [patients] out,'" Toral said mockingly. "Well, I'm not trying to drive them out; the American system is driving them out! My product is just as good as it was five or ten years ago. The only thing that has changed is *you*. You're now unaffordable, unreachable, and you've got forty-seven million uninsured. So you do the math." At one particularly effusive moment during our dinner in Bangkok, Toral announced that a patient pipeline between the United States and Bangkok or Singapore could fix the most intractable costs facing the industry today: the aggregate expenses of surgery, hospitalization, and administration. "Right there, you've saved maybe forty percent of the total cost," he said, "and all of a sudden the pressure to overhaul the U.S. health-care industry is off you, because you've solved the most vexing problems out there."

But can a free-market solution actually produce meaningful change, measured in terms of more care, better care, and lower costs? Toral is right to insist that the fourteen-hour flights, the Indian doctors, and the hospitals with unpronounceable names are red herrings; the real issue is whether these choices will eventually fix our health-care system or simply extend its dysfunction around the planet. But Johnson also is right: the recent history of health care is marked by elective improvements that soon enough hardened into the status quo. "Before this, there was 'first dollar' coverage," Johnson told me, ticking them off. "Then there was the 'miracle' of HMOs, all of which were voluntary, and all of which quickly morphed into something quite less. It was the same thing with PPOs, and every new gimmick the health-care community can come up with." Will the promise of cash prizes go away, replaced by implied threats? Will our choices simply disappear?

It's hard to imagine how the insurers—operating in the same Hobbesian universe as the rest of us—won't eventually winnow the choices down to having our care paid for in Bangkok or making us cover it if we opt to stay close to home. It's hard not to notice that their argument seems to boil down to "Trust us."

For now patients have a choice, and they are choosing to leave. The crippling cost of staying home may be why they're flying overseas, but it can't explain how they've ended up in Bangkok and India. Prior to its star turn on *60 Minutes*, how would anyone have even heard of hospital groups like Bumrungrad, Apollo, or Parkway, let alone use them as the escape valve for the unbearable pressure of their medical bills?

The one who answered this question was Vishal Bali, the CEO of Fortis Hospitals, one of India's largest chains. He cornered me at a medical tourism conference in Las Vegas (of course) and held forth on the underlying transformations that had taken place. It all boiled down to Kasarda's Law. "The whole phenomenon basically started with *connectivity*, both virtual and physical," he began. "The virtual connectivity was the Web. The patients are online consumers. They're not just part of a global health-care phenomenon, but a phenomenon in consumption itself. When people use eBay or buy iPods, computers, shirts, and shoes online, they're only addressing the physical piece of their desires. They want *services* too. People around the world are buying hotel rooms online, air travel online, and now they're looking for health care on the Web. That's how they find us.

"The other factor—and this has only happened in the last couple of years—is aerial connectivity through air travel. There's been a radical transformation in how countries are connected through the air. The cost of air travel, and of these connections, has actually gone down over the last few years in spite of oil prices. That's being driven by increased competition among the airlines in India and across the world. Distances have shrunk, not because there are more planes or more seats, but because they cost less. That's why more and more people are willing to connect themselves to other countries to receive health care—because the real cost of travel has gone down.

"And that isn't just in India, but globally. Sometimes, supply really does create demand. We went from one airline to ten, and there's been so much competition that not only are we getting better fares domestically, but internationally too. If I were to go back ten years and look at airfares between India and America, and then look at the fares on the same routes today, they will have dropped twenty-five to thirty percent. One of the main reasons medical tourism evolved in India is simply because air travel became less expensive" and more extensive. "It's happening because of the rise of large Indian and Chinese middle classes, and the rapid industrialization of Asia. When I look at it from a global perspective, there are so many people crisscrossing the world. There's been an intermingling of cultures, and distances are truly shrinking."

It all started in India with the outsourcing boom. More than a decade ago, McKinsey predicted outsourcing would be a $50 billion business in India by 2010. It was close; the real number was $47 billion. To top itself, McKinsey predicts that figure will have tripled another decade from now, to $175 billion. As Kasarda's Law would tell us, the tremendous surge in data traffic between India and the United States ultimately led to a parallel rise in air traffic. Business travelers visiting Fortis's hospitals for emergencies provided crucial word of mouth. "So it was virtual connectivity, aerial connectivity—and therefore personal connectivity— between our two countries that led to global health care," Bali concluded.

In 2009, he said, Fortis's hospitals drew nine thousand patients from abroad. More than half were American, and most of them were clustered in two cities, Mumbai and Bangalore. Mumbai because it's big, and Bangalore because it's Bangalore, "probably the best-connected city in the world," in his estimation. The real opportunity, as he sees it, is vacuuming patients from Pakistan, Afghanistan, Bangladesh, Sri Lanka, and Africa, "because for all those regions, coming to India for health care isn't necessarily a choice. In more ways than one, it's a compulsion, because they don't have good health care." Or they have better connections to India's best hospitals than the ones in their own countries. The danger is that someone else will siphon them away with lower costs and better connectivity in the form of nonstop flights; layovers are not an option when you've just come out of traction.

The Vatican of Aviation

Soon after striking out on his own as a free agent, Ruben Toral flew to India for a meeting. While at breakfast in Delhi, he was intercepted by a friend he hadn't seen in years, who had a proposition at the ready: Forget Bangkok, forget Delhi, forget *cities*, even. If you're going to run a hospital for tourists, he said, why not just park it at the airport? Call it . . . *the Healthport*. Even Toral was taken aback. "That's *really* just-in-time medicine," he told me afterward. His friend had an airport in mind—the new Rajiv Gandhi International outside Hyderabad—aka Cyberabad, India's second Silicon city after Bangalore. Designed, in part, by Kasarda under the rubric of the "Hyderabad Aerotropolis," it was India's first greenfield airport in a decade and one of only a dozen in the country with international flights.

This is something we've been looking into for a while, the friend told him, "we" being GMR, one of India's largest industrial conglomerates. But we don't know what to do with it. Are you interested? Sure, Toral replied, but he couldn't see it. His advice was simply to build a better one, "because the biggest complaint about India is that the disaster always begins at the airport."

Some months later, he saw the airport for himself, which by then had been labeled India's inaugural aerotropolis. "It was light-years better than what they had before," Toral noted, but the grounds were a blank slate—several thousand acres of pure potential. GMR had stopped returning his calls, and he wondered if they had any idea what they were getting into. "Their thinking was, 'Here's our airport, we own all this land, and we're thinking about building cities,'" he said. They were building an aerotropolis, all right, but they hadn't yet figured out what to do with it.

GMR's real business is infrastructure—aerotropoli are only its latest offering. It builds power plants—natural gas, coal, hydro—paves roads, and opens airports. It is "getting India ready," according to its tag line. Ready, that is, to steamroll whatever bits of the world its call center operators and office tigers haven't already flattened. India grew at a torrid 9 percent annually for most of the past decade, a pace it can't possibly regain and sustain without much, much more of what GMR is selling—the bones and sinews of modern commerce. The company's namesake and founder is a proud, self-made patriarch who made his first fortune selling burlap, one G. M. Rao. He's the father of India's brand of aerotropoli, and to step inside the prototype outside Hyderabad is to enter a showroom of the modern India he intends to build.

Approaching it from downtown requires navigating the city's hellacious mix of cars, buses, cabs, and ramshackle auto-rickshaws belching black diesel smoke, crawling past moldy shops, bombed-out blocks, and goats, roosters, and homeless families lining the roads. It also means ducking beneath overpasses that are half built and at best unfinished—like just about every other public works project in India—scheduled for completion sometime in our next incarnations.

As you cross the airport boundary, everything changes. Smooth, open asphalt swoops past an immense parking lot with thirty-five hundred spaces, lined by palm trees. The glass terminal and its canopy could fit in comfortably anywhere in the West, which was exactly Rao's intention. If he's leading the tour, he'll take pains to point out that the landscaper's from Hong Kong, the firefighting gear is from Austria, the drinking fountains were made in America, and the staff were trained in Athens and Singapore. He's visibly bursting with pride as he does this because the airport's his baby, GMR's crown jewel. It's not just the satisfaction taken in a job well done, either. He owns this, *all* of it, from the marble-and-teak terminal to the torch-shaped tower, to the thousand-acre aerotropolis going in next door, stocked with schools, malls, hotels, and hospitals—with or without Ruben Toral.

"I want to make Hyderabad the Vatican of aviation," he tells a reporter, meaning every word. And then he wants to build a hundred others just like it, because India needs them. The country's aviation infrastructure mirrors Hyderabad's umpteen lanes of lurching, wailing, hysterical traffic, all seeking passage on overloaded streets laid out in 1948, for a backwater of half a million. The city has multiplied twentyfold since then, while India's airlines grew at an even faster clip until the bust. No one took to the skies with the exuberance of Indians, who sprinted out of what was essentially a standing start.

This is a place where privately owned airlines were out and out outlawed until 1993, when the subcontinent's skies opened a crack in a wave of national economic reforms. Jet Airways launched that year—landing at the wrong airport on its maiden flight—and was the country's largest domestic airline in short order, defrocking the state-owned Indian Airways. But the country didn't have an analogue to Southwest or JetBlue until Air Deccan started service to its hinterlands a decade later. India's answer to Southwest's cigar-chomping Herb Kelleher is Captain G. R. Gopinath—or "Gopi," as he's affectionately known—who was struck during a flight by the sight of television aerials sprouting from mud huts—the first glints of a middle class.

Inspired by Henry Ford's proclamation "I want every American to be able to own an affordable motorcar," the captain wanted an airline on which every Indian might fly at least once in his or her lifetime. He still has a long way to go. Only around 1 percent of India's 1.1 billion citizens fly, leaving plenty of room for growth. Meanwhile, the middle class—defined as 5 percent of the total population, or about fifty million people—is expected to swell elevenfold by 2025, to 583 million. Average household income should triple over that span, and the percentage of income spent on travel has doubled once already, from 5 percent in 1995 to 11 percent ten years later. Indians have more disposable income than ever, and they're spending more and more of it to fly.

The wear and tear of their new migration patterns on the nation's airports is not all that different from the grind of modern Hyderabad's traffic on the city's independence-era streets. Delhi's Indira Gandhi International is poised to become India's premier gateway, with passengers surging from 20 million four years ago (as many as San Diego's) to 63 million by 2020 (more than LAX) to 112 million by 2036, the size of LAX and Beijing combined. What's scary is that it's already a dump. Mumbai's airport is arguably in worse shape, having been overrun by squatters occupying a third of the property. Final approach to Chhatrapati Shivaji International is legendary for its long glide over the slums made famous by *Slumdog Millionaire*.

While Gopinath and the copycats at SpiceJet, Kingfisher, GoAir, and IndiGo waged a dogfight of rock-bottom fares for India's jet-setting families, the aviation system had fallen to its knees. In the midst of this boom-slash-crisis, the Reserve Bank of India reported that "infrastructure bottlenecks are emerging as the single most important constraint on the Indian economy." It wasn't confined to airports—annual spending nationwide as a share of GDP bottomed out in 2003 at just 3.5 percent, or $21 billion. Across the Himalayas, China was in the midst of paving fifty thousand miles of eight-lane highways, building a hundred airports, and tossing up cities the size of Dallas every few months at a cost of

$150 billion a year, or 10.6 percent of GDP (not counting its citizens' blood, sweat, and tears).

India's rambunctious democracy is messier. Prime Minister Manmohan Singh (the architect of the nation's economic turnaround in the 1990s) has made infrastructure a priority, calling for $55 billion to upgrade airports and railroads alone. But between his government's promise to trim the national deficit, cover overdrafts by the individual states, and preserve the people's oil subsidies, it wasn't clear where this money was supposed to come from.

Enter G. M. Rao. He's an outlier among the subcontinent's tycoons—the Tatas, Mittals, and Ambanis—many of whom are English-educated scions busily adding to or battling for their families' already considerable fortunes. Rao has less in common with them than with their fathers and grandfathers, men like J.R.D. Tata, founder of the Tata Group and its sprawling interests in steel, tea, and cars—including India's own Model T, the $2,300 Tata Nano. J.R.D. started India's first airline, named it for himself, and piloted the first flight between Karachi and Bombay in 1932. Later renamed Air India, his entrepreneurial outburst was nationalized in 1953.

Rao is a throwback, a hustler who built one fortune in burlap, then flipped it for another in rice, beer, and banking. He flipped the breweries when he caught wind prohibition was coming and plowed the money into power plants instead, which had just been privatized. Seizing his chance to literally remake the country, he cashed out of his other interests and reinvested everything in infrastructure.

His chance to break into the airport business came in 2001, when he bid to build, operate, and own Hyderabad's new one in a public-private partnership. The state would retain a minority interest, and the winners would keep the rest. GMR and its partners kept their promise, sinking $560 million of their own money into construction, tossing in an elevated expressway, links to the outer ring road and highways, and plans for a downtown train covering the twenty-five miles in twenty-five minutes. More important, they'd beaten Bangalore to the punch, finishing a few months ahead of Hyderabad's archrival in the spring of 2008. By then, Bangalore's answer had become an abject lesson in how not to build an airport, beginning with the fact that it had been stuck on various drawing boards for *seventeen years*. Desperate for someone to kick-start it, the government had privatized it three years ahead of Hyderabad's, but work had repeatedly stalled due to bureaucratic infighting. By the time it finally opened, its troubles had just begun.

The old airport—which even the locals compared to a Greyhound bus station (evidently a universal complaint)—at least had the virtue of being close to downtown, not far from "Electronics City" and the gated communities of India's outsourcing giants. But the new one, Bengaluru International, lay on the far side of town forty miles from their front doors. This wouldn't have been a problem if a new expressway was waiting to cover the distance. But the National Highways Authority refused to pave one. Lawsuits and skirmishes among thirty-two agencies ensued. Widening the existing highway to accommodate the onslaught would take years; it might still be unfinished by the time you read this. Construction of an express train is also finally under way.

Even before the airport opened, the high-tech executives who had long been its biggest cheerleaders had begun begging officials to hold off on closing the old one. Suck it up, they were told; Bengaluru's owners hadn't dropped half a billion dollars to compete with the airport they were hired to replace. Traffic on opening day was as apocalyptic as predicted. Traversing the long stretch of honking, snarling, exhausting traffic—as nasty as Hyderabad's along its entire length—took three hours from Electronics City, "outstripping the charge on most laptop batteries," an alarmed reporter noted. Day trips between back offices in Hyderabad or Chennai, at most a forty-five-minute flight, required five- or six-hour head starts to beat rush hour—about the time it takes to fly halfway to London. Tech executives quailed at the traffic jams and then started finding reasons to stay home.

The fiasco punctuated *The Economist*'s assessment of a city "choking on its own success" while Wipro and Infosys—India's homegrown IBM and Microsoft—were adding a thousand engineers every *month*. "Our body is in India," Infosys chief Nandan Nilekani said, trying to explain away the contradiction, "but our head is in New York or somewhere." Nilekani was the one who informed Thomas Friedman that "the playing field is being leveled"—flattened—by Bangalore's bulging yuppie bracket. But Friedman, lost in a reverie of putting greens and videoconferencing screens, had either missed or willfully overlooked a different set of signs—the private fleets of buses ferrying workers over potholed roads, to cubicles in infocubes powered by diesel generators humming in their basements, ready to kick in when the power (frequently) cut out.

Nilekani, who has since resigned himself to making the best of his city's terrible situation, once went to war with the state government for the funds and the authority to rebuild its crumbling infrastructure. He lost to a provincial minister who'd renounced his predecessor's "urban bias" in favor of the farmers and refused to do his part in keeping the nation's economic miracle going. The new airport was the best concession India's IT billionaires had been able to wrangle, and look where that had gotten them—into the backseat of a helicopter carrying them across town.

Not long after Bengaluru opened, Gopinath (whose airline called it home) began flying helicopters from the old airport to the new, selling seats for $100 each way on the ten-minute hop. Good luck scoring one today. Bangalore has become even more of an abstraction for Nilekani and his colleagues—a metastasizing blob to be studied from several hundred feet in the air, a perverse reversal of the captain's original ephiphany. "Bangalore may be unique in the speed of its decline," *The Economist* posited before the airport even started construction, leaving some wriggle room for later redemption. The departure window may have closed. "Now the local talk is that it's only a matter of time before even obscure Chinese cities—wannabe Bangalores—plan and pull off better airports," one reporter noted. But despondent boosters might want to keep a lookout a little closer to home.

The opening of India's skies didn't begin in earnest until 2004, several years after Hyderabad's and Bangalore's auctions. That spring, the new government of Manmohan Singh named Praful Patel aviation minister. Patel had shadowed the ministry for years, waiting in the wings on various committees. In the meantime, he'd become a tobacco mogul on the side, hawking both cigarettes and India's first nicotine gum—a case of demand creation in action. He was determined to run Indian aviation along similar lines, "doing business the way business does business," as he put it. Within days of taking office, he'd rubber-stamped the motion to sell off airports in Delhi and Mumbai to finance their expansion, then announced plans to raffle off fifteen more. A few months later, he ordered the first new planes for Air India and Indian Airlines in a decade (he would merge the two in 2007) and signed Open Skies agreements with the United States and Britain.

G. M. Rao pounced on his chance to add Delhi's airport to his port-folio, besting Anil Ambani (of the billionaire Ambani brothers) and a pack of multinationals. There was a catch: although (mostly) free of slums, 95 percent of the footprint was off-limits, leaving just 250 acres for devel-opment. To have any hope of recouping his multibillion-dollar grubstake, Rao needed to sell something lucrative, dense, and irresistible to starry-eyed developers. He put out word: "We want the airport to be like a city, an 'aerotropolis.'"

Swooning bureaucrats interpreted this as his intent to re-create Paris. One promised the press it would boast "long avenues of shops, sell-ing everything from cheese to cardigans; internet cafés, a medical cen-tre, a hotel, bookshops, quiet lounges, entertainment centres and baggage check-in counters." The actual plans were more prosaic—a few million square feet of office space, condos, hotels, condo hotels, and a pedestrian-friendly High Street. So was Rao's finding religion. Enterprising number crunchers deduced that the raw dirt of the aerotropolis was already worth more on the open market than what he and his partners had inci-dentally paid for it. With that parcel in hand, they could rebuild the air-port essentially for free.

In short order, a second aerotropolis was unveiled in Hyderabad, this one according to Kasarda's designs, with all the trimmings—infocubes, more hotels, malls (always malls), convention halls, and a free-trade zone open to anyone interested in hauling things through. Rao and GMR had the latitude to build what they liked, going so far as to set aside a thou-sand acres explicitly for Wipro and Infosys, if Nandan Nilekani ever gave in to the urge to give up on Bangalore.

A few months before the word "aerotropolis" was first uttered, Kasarda was summoned to Delhi by Rao himself, who was understandably eager to hear how he should go about building one. Kasarda dutifully gave his stump speech before Patel and the assembled ministers and chiefs of Indian aviation, who received his PowerPoint deck like some long-lost Veda. "Aerotropolis" entered the national lexicon in the spring of 2007, and within months more were planned for Mumbai, Calcutta, and a dozen smaller cities. Let a thousand aerotropoli bloom was Patel's phi-losophy, although the actual number was closer to five hundred. That's how many airports India needs by the end of this decade—five times as many as the country has at the moment. (By contrast, the United States has five thousand of all shapes and sizes.)

Patel envisions adding fifty in the next five years, including a second for Mumbai and new ones in Chennai, Goa, and Pune. Some will be "merchant airports," privately owned and operated, designed from the ground up as aerotropoli. One is slated for Chandigarh, India's original master-planned city—a machine for living laid out by Le Corbusier himself in the 1950s. Others will be "cargo villages," Memphis-style hubs meant to serve a nation the size of Western Europe and half again more populous. The first of these will be built at Nagpur in the dead center of the country, where the Indian post office briefly ran an overnight airmail hub in the 1940s—thirty years before FedEx got off the ground.

As for the nagging question of who would pay for them all, Patel had a simple answer: G. M. Rao. Not him personally, but hundreds or thousands of moguls just like him. India's airport boom, Patel told a roomful of B-school students, would pay for itself with $150 billion from private investors clamoring for the chance to buy in. "It will be one of the sunrise sectors of our country like IT and telecom," he told them. "It will redefine the contours of development in our country." Is it realistic to expect them to rebuild India from the ground up? "I don't think the government is asking too much," Rao said. "The public side has the capabilities—the technical capabilities—but the speed is not there. We are bringing the speed, as well as the best technology, the best financial engineering, and the best talent in the world."

Patel believed him, and so did the bureaucracy, which tripped all over itself in its rush to place an aerotropolis in every backwater. Expectations raged so out of control that Kasarda found himself writing editorials in the Indian press encouraging everyone to calm down—not everybody can be a Hyderabad or a Delhi. "The bottom line is that the Aerotropolis has to be more than a 'build it and they will come' airport dream," he wrote, trying to defuse expectations. "Success rests on market realities and adequate air service." But his *Field of Dreams* reference was lost on the cricket-crazy populace.

At the opening of New Delhi's Terminal 3 last July, Patel and Rao took Manmohan Singh and the Congress Party leader Sonia Gandhi on a personal tour of the vast structure, built in a record-setting three years. The new terminal, Gandhi gushed, proved "we can be not just good enough to pass muster, but right up there with the best." A jubilant Singh was equally impressed, while noting that India's aviation industry had grown from two airlines with one hundred aircraft in the 1990s to ten airlines with four hundred aircraft today. Only Patel was in bad spirits, fretting openly about the need to break ground on a second airport for Mumbai. The day before, he had publicly accused India's environment minister of obstructing the project in order to protect a mangrove forest on the site. "We can't be overly obsessive about environmental issues," he fumed on Indian television. "We can't give priority to fifty to one hundred acres of degradation over a large infrastructure project."

He should be more worried about the state of India's airlines, which compressed forty years of the American experience into just four—one each for boom, bust, a scramble to cut costs, and a return to modest profits. A glut of seats collided with high oil prices and an economic crisis, causing passengers to flee. Indian airlines suffered nearly a quarter of the entire industry's $9 billion in losses in 2009, despite carrying just 2 percent of all passengers. Shotgun weddings between carriers and evasive maneuvers ensued as Patel and Singh prepared to overhaul stodgy Air India. But then the recession ended early and the good times resumed. The World Bank projects India will grow 8 percent this year and for each of the next three, while its airlines are fuller than ever, growing at blistering, double-digit rates. In the meantime, India has had a breather to get started on its aerotropoli.

"This is our time. This is India's time" is how G. M. Rao frames the stakes. "We won't get this opportunity again. If we miss it, we miss it eternally."

9

THE AEROTROPOLIS EMIRATES

Dubai was the world's first aerotropolis nation—an airline and an airport with a city attached to it. Its ambitions never made sense at less than thirty thousand feet. As it struggles to pay for its vision, its rivals in Abu Dhabi, Doha, and beyond are building aerotropoli of their own.

"We Are the Pillars of This Country"

Dubai on the 4th of July is *hot*, 115° in the shade, an even 100° in the evening. All the hype surrounding its malls—the ones with ski slopes and aquariums inside—boils off after a few days. They're absolute necessities in the summer, latter-day oases. I could see one blazing against the night sky nearby—two million square feet of air-conditioning, almost within reach—but I was lost in the blind alleys of Al Badia, wandering cul-de-sac airlifted straight from the O.C. The identical "villas" were packed side by side, their two-car garages facing the street. These were tenements for the emirate's kinetic elite.

I was looking for Assem and Dina Hamzeh, married Lebanese expatriates who left Beirut before the last round of troubles began. When I finally found their door, Dina greeted me with her mouth agape. "You walked here?" she blurted. "Nobody walks in Dubai!" For good reason—I'd instantly sweated through my shirt. While I freshened up, her husband poured me a beer. After a week in the desert without one (Dubai is technically dry), it was the best I'd ever tasted.

Assem is a chocolatier. He struck out on his own six years ago, choosing Dubai as his base of operations. He filled a small factory with machinery flown from Belgium, along with now daily air shipments of cocoa, caramel, and cream fillings—the raw materials for his confections.

Before long, he and his chefs were moving tons of milk chocolate through the emirate, bound for customers in Saudi Arabia and Kuwait. His goal is to build the Godiva of the Persian Gulf.

He was still in awe of how happy Dubai was to help. Its civil servants processed his paperwork in three days flat, no bribes required or questions asked. His factory was airborne a week later. "They treated me like an investor" instead of a refugee, Assem told me in his living room. "They *want* me to stay. Although it's getting more expensive, the volume, the turnover, the scale of this place is so big you can work hard and get what you want." Sales have tripled in the last four years.

"Originally, I said I wanted to set it up in Lebanon," Dina interrupted. "We know so many people there, I thought it would have been easier for us. But Assem said, 'No, Dubai,' and that was the right move." Their friends at home reached the same conclusion, convinced by Hezbollah rockets and yet another Israeli invasion. The Lebanese outnumber the natives here, composing a tenth of the emirate's one and a half million inhabitants.

"We are the pillars of this country," Marwan Bibi announced at breakfast the next morning. One of the Hamzehs' neighbors, he's lived in Dubai off and on for more than thirty years. "Because of the war in Lebanon, we had to leave," he explained. "The first time I came here, in 1975, I had to walk through the sand to reach my home. But the good thing about Dubai is that it sits between continents and has always been a center of trade and a home to those of us who travel. This was the intersection of India, Africa, Iran—you name it. Its strengths—simplicity, accessibility, and mobility—were so strong that it was easy to make money here. And there are no taxes, either."

Bibi started as Pepsi's point man in the region. Now a free agent, he's a trader at heart, flying medicines and cheese from Australia and passing them around the Gulf. "Dubai was always unique in the Arab world because it had an educated elite" borrowed from its neighbors and seeking a haven at its crossroads, he said. "They offered an expertise multinationals could build on" and could build new lives upon in turn. Bibi's parents were refugees—his Palestinian father was born and died in exile—while his daughter went to Harvard and works for Google. "I could live anywhere," he boasted, and after several decades milking the trade routes, he owned the homes to back it up. But Dubai offered something more, he claimed—the means to go anywhere instead, a hub for his sales calls in Arabia, vacations in Australia, and visits to his grandchildren in California.

The Hamzehs aren't leaving anytime soon. "We have our own business here, and the kids are settled," Dina said as I was leaving, casting a glance at their two young sons watching television. (She was pregnant with their third.) "I love Dubai," Assem cut in. "To be honest, for me, it's 'Wow.' And I'm not talking about the towers or the Palms," the man-made islands that put the emirate on the map.

It struck me on the steamy walk home that maybe I'd seen the true face of Dubai in the Hamzehs—that of its displaced melting pot of a middle class. They occupied a band on the emirate's socioeconomic spectrum that had been washed out by its surreal extremes, with the visiting Saudi royals, Russian oligarchs, and hard-partying Brits at one end, and the Indian "guest workers" slaving to build the city at the other. But there were gradations to this "evil paradise" that its critics had missed. Not everyone with white skin was a mercenary, nor was this some frontier town of oil arbitrageurs and human traffickers in lieu of card sharks and cattle rustlers. Dubai was building something unprecedented before the crash, and it wasn't only the archipelago arranged in a map of the world.

The year before, all of this was sand. I'd stood where the Hamzehs' villa now stands and watched an army of workers march onto buses at dusk for their trek back to a labor camp in the desert. They had just finished sculpting dunes into "cliffs" using bulldozers, and by my next trip those had been accessorized with imported boulders. Al Badia Hillside Village was the neighborhood's latest installment, a half-dozen apartment towers camouflaged by the cliff face and given a *One Thousand and One Nights* motif. They weren't finished yet, but the leasing office was open. I spent a weekend afternoon watching hopefuls file through. Most were Asian families interested in the neighboring international school, which had just doubled in size to six hundred students and tripled in nationalities present, from twenty to sixty-five. "The emirate is broadening its recruiting base, so they're bringing in Brazilians, Mexicans, and Pacific Islanders now," the school's principal (a New Zealander himself) told me.

The rest were global nomads seeking a temporary oasis. One was an American oil engineer who refused to divulge either his name or his employer's. Another was the Indian salesgirl who moved here from Mumbai a decade ago, "when the salaries weren't that hot." They brought to mind still another resident, a thirtysomething German named Iris Kraska. She'd been globe-trotting for so long in the service of Volkswagen that she'd forgotten home, and Dubai was just her current stop. "For me, it's not a city, it's a case study," she said one night while packing for a business trip. "The sheikh is living out his vision here, and we're all part of his business case. That's what I like about this place—where else on this planet can you be a part of that? It's not about how beautiful it is here, or historic monuments, because there aren't any. I was spoiled when I lived in China, with a five-thousand-year-old wall."

I scampered up the hillside later, this time at dusk, sneaking past security and making my way to the roof. From there, I had a panoramic view not of Dubai per se, but of Dubai Festival City, a city within a city covering several square miles of a desert within the desert of greater Dubai. To the west was the megamall hugging the Creek, the city's natural harbor; to the south was a Four Seasons golf course. Al Badia and its spin-offs would theoretically multiply until they encircled the links; beyond them, where there is now only more sand, would be taller apartment blocks. If and when Festival City is finished, it will be home to one hundred thousand or so Hamzehs, Bibis, and Kraskas, complete with their own schools, malls, marinas, and office towers along the Creek.

To the north, only a mile away, was the scarab-shaped control tower of Dubai International Airport, flanked on either side by cylindrical terminals tapering to points at each end. From this distance, they resembled giant sandworms burrowing into the desert. Festival City was in fact an aerotropolis within an aerotropolis, a microcosm of the emirate itself. Everyone and everything in it—its luxuries, laborers, architects, accents, even its aspirations—was flown in from someplace else.

Playing SimCity for Real

Festival City is barely a speck on the city's maps. The snub has more to do with politics than size, as it's one of the few megaprojects, real or imagined, that weren't controlled through one holding company or another by Sheikh Mohammed bin Rashid Al Maktoum, the ruler and

"CEO" of Dubai Inc. "Sheikh Mo," as he's affectionately known, runs the emirate as a state-owned conglomerate. Imagine if the Department of Defense had been chartered at birth as Halliburton (which moved its headquarters here in 2007).

The other reason for Festival City's relative obscurity is its modesty. It never claimed to own the world's biggest or most "iconic" anything, unlike nearly all of its contemporaries. Its backers, a family of local billionaires, decided against a statement piece because what was the point? "In Dubai, there is no 'biggest,'" one of their factotums said. "Someone will always be bigger."

No one will top the Burj Khalifa anytime soon. The world's tallest building is a slender silver spire twice the height of the Empire State Building. Inside are an Armani hotel and a hundred floors of apartments, all of which sold out in two nights, by invitation only. At its base is the Dubai Mall, the world's largest if you include the aforementioned fishbowl. "The Earth Has a New Centre," its billboards boast. The competing developer, Nakheel, waited until the last piece of steel went up before unveiling a taller tower. Al Burj ("the Tower") would soar a solid kilometer (3,280 feet). It's been postponed indefinitely. Nakheel is more famous for sandcastling the islands of the Palm and the World into existence, and for doing it with other people's money. "There is nothing after the World," its executives claimed, and it looked as if they might be right.

Before the financial crisis, the old saw about Dubai commandeering a quarter of the world's construction cranes sounded plausible. By one count, there were seven thousand projects under way in the United Arab Emirates, worth $1.3 trillion on paper. Then prices in Dubai fell 50 percent, and $330 billion in new developments were put on hold or canceled. The cranes moved down the coast to oil-and-gas-rich Doha and Abu Dhabi, which could afford to keep writing blank checks. Not so in Dubai's case, having borrowed $80 billion (or more) to pay for islands literally and financially underwater.

The emirate threatened to unravel during 2009, as the credit crunch caused a vicious cycle of insolvency, distress selling, layoffs, and a mini-exodus of expatriates forced to leave upon losing their jobs. The simmering crisis came a boil that November with the bombshell that Dubai Inc. was asking creditors for a standstill on its debts, admitting it was unwilling or unable to pay. For a moment, it appeared the entire emirate might default. Abu Dhabi eventually arrived with an eleventh-hour rescue, and the bankers agreed to take a haircut on their loans, but the damage to its reputation had been done. No one will lend Dubai no-questions-asked money ever again. It will have to pay its own way.

Dubai Inc. has endured heavy restructuring since. Many of Sheikh Mo's top lieutenants have been merged or purged; high-profile developers have been jailed for fraud. Financial markets wait for the other shoe to drop, while emirates Kremlinologists wonder what price Abu Dhabi will ultimately charge for its help. (Naming the onetime Burj Dubai after its ruler Sheikh Khalifa bin Zayed Al Nahyan is suspected to be a down payment.)

In hindsight, Dubai was almost fatally overleveraged in hype as well as debt. Unwinding its untenable positions entailed the world's awe curdling into schadenfreude. Planeloads of journalists who once breathlessly touted every pleasure dome in Xanadu returned to pass judgment, switching their metaphors to *Ozymandias*: "The towers of Dubai will become casualties not of human greed but of architectural folly," predicted one screed in *The Guardian*. "Their lifts and services, expensive to maintain, will collapse. Their colossal façades will shed glass. Sand will drift round their trunkless legs." The roots of the "Dubacle" are less melodramatic.

During the boom, the sheikh's chosen instruments played SimCity for real, without bothering to read the manual. They had two building blocks: cities within a city and corporate "free zones" interspersed between them. The former are cocoons for expatriates, the latter the reason they set up shop here in the first place. Anything goes in the zones, where the last vestiges of sharia law are checked at the door. There are no tariffs, no corporate or personal income taxes, no censorship, and no prying eyes inside. Local laws are suspended at the host's discretion.

The largest is the Jebel Ali Free Zone Authority, which blankets fifty-two square miles with warehouses wedged between the Gulf's busiest port on one side and what Dubai hopes will be the world's busiest airport on the other. Five thousand foreign companies do business inside, making it one of the busiest commercial hubs on the planet. There are dozens of smaller ones just like it, one for every industry. "The beauty of these oases," I was told by an American setting up one himself, "is that they're really countries within a country. You can do anything you want

there, even issue your own visas. They're about doing business with absolute simplicity," by which he meant no interference, "and what's at stake
for Dubai is competitiveness."

The urban fabric has the pixellated sheen of SimCity too. Most projects achieved their platonic form not at completion but as animated,
swooping "fly throughs" of renderings that may or may not have a passing
resemblance to the real thing. Their names echoed the game's generic
'burbs. You might live in the Lakes, the Springs, the Meadows, the Views,
the Lagoons, or the Gardens and work at Internet City, Media City,
Health Care City, Studio City, Motor City, Industrial City, or, more omi-
nously, the Outsource Zone. Or you might attend school at Knowledge
Village or Academic City. These enclaves render Dubai dense sprawl—
high-rise monocultures that are classical urbanism at its worst.

The Western architects who stumbled onto this scene soon found
themselves punching buttons as mindlessly as their clients, ordering up
yet another "iconic" edifice destined to be trumped a second later (or
dumped during the downturn). The emirate was poised to more than
triple its theoretical population by 2020—the equivalent of dropping a
Berlin on top of what was already there.

The architect Rem Koolhaas barely came to grips with this while
designing Waterfront City, Nakheel's abandoned city within a city within
a city (and the collateral on Dubai World's debt). "There is a weird alter-
nation between density and emptiness," he confessed. "You rarely feel
you are designing for people who are actually there but for communities
that have yet to be assembled." He learned that its "density is virtual.
Almost everybody who lives in Dubai also lives somewhere else . . . The
actual inhabitation of the city is a fraction of its maximum capacity."

This is becoming the norm. Kasarda argues that virtual density isn't
limited to Dubai, but is already a fact in London, Las Vegas, and Miami—
all places where the global overclass owns homes, yet has no intention of
living full-time. "Go to the Strip, to South Beach, to Belgravia and look
up at the darkened windows," he says. "They are residential neighborhoods without residents." His point was hammered home when I visited
Nakheel's showroom before the crash. The custodians who let me in late
one afternoon were busy hanging signs and tweaking models ahead of
the next morning's instant sellout. After lingering over a tableau of the
Palm for a bit, I found a wrung-out young Brit who sipped mango juice

while I peppered him with questions. How would its trunk handle the crush of seventy thousand commuters through six lanes of traffic? He sipped thoughtfully for a moment. "There will never be a traffic jam on the Palm," he said quietly, because no one would ever be home. A survey of the buyers' demographics bore this out: a third were UAE natives or else lived in the Gulf; another third were British (including David Beckham); while the rest were German, Russian, Indian, and the emirate's typical panoply of nationalities, for whom these were almost certainly fourth or fifth or phantom homes bought only to be flipped.

The Navel of the Middle of the World

The Burj Khalifa mirrors Dubai's conundrum: sold out but two-thirds empty. Was this deliberate or delirious? The emirate feverishly assembled itself from modern analogues of the Bedouins who first settled here: unmoored Lebanese entrepreneurs, footloose multinationals; British bankers and their Saudi investors, and Russians buying condos with suitcases of cash. Waiting in line behind them were Indians, Iranians, Kenyans, and Nigerians, all eager to buy into the last best place in the region. ("Dubai," the line goes, "is the nicest city in India." The same goes double for the others.) Bricolage on an imperial scale was Dubai's only shot at building a world-class city out of sand. Sheikh Mo doesn't have enough subjects of his own, and he was already out of oil. He solved the lack of shoreline by creating his own.

The United Arab Emirates possesses a full twelfth of the world's proven oil reserves, enough to keep pumping for a century. But almost all of that lies under Abu Dhabi; Dubai is running dry. This was hardly unexpected—Sheikh Mohammed's father, Sheikh Rashid, knew it not long after oil was discovered in the 1960s. The knowledge defined Dubai, forcing its rulers to diversify and imagineer. While Abu Dhabi threw up topaz and tourmaline towers *Dallas*-style in the 1970s, Sheikh Rashid plowed his oil-shock profits into infrastructure. It was during his reign that Dubai built its ports, airport, drydocks, World Trade Center, and the first banks and hotels to cater to traders like Marwan Bibi. His greatest legacy was Jebel Ali, the largest man-made harbor ever created, carved from a stretch of empty beach. "I'm building this port now," Sheikh

Rashid told his son, "because there will come a time when you won't be able to afford it."

Dubai discovered after 9/11 that its greatest asset wasn't oil but *geography*, defined not by the contours of any map but by the flying times of modern airliners. Living within four thousand miles of the emirate, less than an eight-hour flight away, are 3.5 billion people, more than half the world's population. And they're the ones learning the world is flat— billions of the most deprived, the most striving, and the most nouveau of the world's riche, all dressed up with no place to go. They're the beneficiaries of a quintupling in oil prices and a tripling in outsourcing. The crossroads of the Gulf sits squarely in the wide strip of longitude between the developed nations of Europe on one side and the Pacific's on the other, in what was once a time-zone dead zone between Frankfurt's bourse and Tokyo's stock exchange. The world's onetime backwater now includes China, India, most of OPEC, and half of Africa. With no hinterland of its own, this desert enclave scrambled to offer the only hub they'll ever need—their London, Miami, Las Vegas, and Singapore all wrapped up in one—the navel of the middle of the world.

In effect, Dubai was a gigantic arbitrage play, a pure experiment in funneling and funding globalization. A tiny city-state with literally nothing—no oil, few people, and little education—sought to become a global capital in a single generation, in the process becoming the most obscenely wasteful city on the planet. (How else are you supposed to build a civilization overnight in the desert?) Sheikh Mo's grand plan was to harness the greed of the world's talented, the desperation of its poorest, and the flows of money, goods, and energy running through the region. That's why everything was so oversize, including Dubai's ambitions.

The emirate set out to transform itself into an aerotropolis nation, built from the ground up to take advantage of the sky. It's building a second airport on the far side of town, initially as a cargo hub, but one with more theoretical capacity than Heathrow, O'Hare, and Memphis combined. They'll need it someday, as the Gulf's residents haven't quit flying; Dubai's air traffic tripled over the last decade and has kept climbing steadily through the bust. This is why Dubai International is the busiest airport in the Middle East, and why its hometown carrier Emirates has enough planes on order to overtake all rivals as the largest long-haul airline. Dubai made sense only if you saw it through Kasarda's prism. It is the aerotropolis writ large, a city of hubs designed to lure the world's wealth to its door.

Take Internet City. The free zone opened in 2000 as the Gulf headquarters for Microsoft, Oracle, HP, and IBM—the usual suspects found everywhere from Las Colinas to Schiphol. But it quickly became a haven for more than a thousand start-ups and transplants looking for a base from which to crack three continents. A quick scan of its phone book yielded more Arabic and Indian names than *Fortune* 500 tenants, all of which came for the same reasons—simplicity, accessibility, and mobility. From Dubai, they can be in front of any customer within hours. They moved *here* to get to *there*, wherever there may be.

Dubai would be a new kind of city because of it, as virtual as advertised, scattered across a million square miles and drawing on a billion residents who will live only a sliver of their lives within its city limits. They'd fly in to see the sights, visit their villa on the Palm, or serve a two-year tour of duty in one of the zones. Half its population would be flown home to Kerala or Karachi when these sand castles were finished, making room for millions spending the prime of their lives here, having left Baghdad and Beirut permanently behind. Dubai repudiated our idea of a city as a place with only one population, one niche, and one identity. It has stretched the elastic mile until it threatens to snap; its enclaves are psychologically closer to London, Sydney, Chennai, Mumbai, and Moscow by air than to each other along the emirate's hopelessly clogged roads.

Dubai didn't need oil when its GDP was climbing at a 13 percent clip, as it did for more than a decade, outpacing even China's. It didn't need the dull grind of Asian Tiger–style industrialization, either, not when it could skip ahead to a new economy built on the most supple sectors of all: trade, transport, tourism, and "services." The emirate would borrow Singapore's blueprints for building an entrepôt from scratch, an aerotropolis tailor-made for the Instant Age. But seduced by the paper gains of real estate during the bubble, Sheikh Mo and his lieutenants lost their way.

They convinced themselves their follies were a necessary smokescreen. "If there was no Burj Dubai, no Palm, no World, would anyone be speaking of Dubai today?" one of the city's banking chiefs mused. "You shouldn't look at projects as crazy stand-alones. It's part of building the brand." On the morning I took off for Dubai, for instance, one of its subsidiaries bought a suitably iconic ocean liner, the *Queen Elizabeth 2*, and planned to park it off the Palm.

But the story was pushed off the front page by more urgent news from Paris. His Highness's debonair uncle and right-hand man, Sheikh Ahmed bin Saeed Al Maktoum, had announced at the Paris Air Show that Dubai would spend $82 billion on aviation in the coming years—on its airline, its airports, and ingenious combinations exploiting the two. They were key to the emirate's plans to double the annual number of tourists to fifteen million by 2015. The sum represented a third of the emirate's budget for infrastructure. Sheikh Ahmed had given notice that he and his ruling nephew would stop at nothing to ensure that the world connects through Dubai. And as chairman of Emirates Airlines, the airports, and the Supreme Fiscal Committee, no one doubted he could back it up. To punctuate his challenge, he signed a multibillion-dollar order for an additional eight A380s, bringing Emirates' total to fifty-eight. He would trump it a few years later with an order for thirty-two more, the largest in history. Airbus estimates 95 percent of the world's population is within the plane's reach. Emirates owns a third of the superjumbo's entire production run. None have been canceled.

"What we are witnessing today is the rewriting of the world's aviation history and the beginning of a new era of global aviation," he said that morning. A year later, just to remind the world what those jets were for, he began his presentation of Emirates' annual results with a slide reading: "Dubai's future = Emirates' future," and Dubai hopes that is still true.

Dubai is chasing a dream that has haunted men since the first camels strode the Silk Road, the dream that led Marco Polo east to Kublai Khan's court and Christopher Columbus west across the ocean: the dream of linking East and West, of seamlessly exchanging the coin of one realm for the goods and mysteries of the other. And Dubai might yet succeed where its fellow Arabs failed.

Dubai aspires to be what Baghdad was a thousand years ago—the western terminus of the Silk Road. "This island, between the Tigris in the east and the Euphrates in the west, is a marketplace for the world," wrote Al Mansur, the eighth-century founder of the city. "It will surely be the most flourishing city in the world." And for five hundred years, it was. Baghdad was the seat of the Abbasid caliphs, and as the Muslim empire's commercial and administrative capital, it drew as many as a million emigrants—including Persians, Aramaeans, and Greeks—to its splendors. With them came science, mathematics, medicine, and astronomy, discoveries that would later help Europe escape the Dark Ages. Baghdad fell when the Mongols appeared at its door in 1258, destroying most of the city and massacring its inhabitants.

Historians often trace the beginning of the Muslim world's decline to that moment, which accelerated after the European voyages of discovery a few centuries later. New trade routes to Asia via the sea instead of the Silk Road left out the Muslim middleman. Without trade and contact with neighboring cultures, the Middle East suffered a depression too deep for oil to be of any help. Dubai can be seen as a heroic attempt to reverse history by reopening the Silk Road after four hundred years— only this time via the air. It aspires to be the twenty-first century's Baghdad, rekindling the tolerance, openness, and diversity of Islam's golden age to become the undisputed hub of the Near East. It's profited from the misfortunes of its neighbors, collecting the best and the brightest fleeing Lebanon, Iraq, and Iran. "How do you build a society based on expatriates, Islam, and capitalism?" one Western diplomat asked me rhetorically. "That is the great societal challenge."

If Dubai seems irredeemably exotic, despotic, and unsustainable to American eyes, it's because all we have in common is the questionable materialism of the American dream—the glass towers, McMansions, and SUVs (subsidized by dollar-a-gallon gasoline). But Dubai has nothing to do with America, even though our gas money and our fear of the Arab world after 9/11 helped create it. The machinery of its aerotropolis is designed to drive a very different dream.

Not long after my first trip to Dubai, I spoke to the urban anthropologist Paco Underhill. He was the first person to systematically study how and why we buy, and I wanted to know why Dubai was building shopping malls on a scale Americans had never imagined. He spent a lot of time there in those days, and he urged me to see the city through their eyes.

"Dubai is full of 'tourists,'" he said, "but they aren't the tourists we know. These are economic tourists, and they're coming from the Middle East and eastern Africa for the express purpose of shopping, because there is nothing to buy where they are. We don't get it in the West because while we live in a world that is overstocked, they live in a world that is understocked. The tourists Dubai is reaching out to are a giant audience whose appetites just aren't as jaded as ours."

He then asked me to imagine Dubai sitting at the bottom of a vast drainage basin of new wealth, as wide as the reach of Emirates' long-range 777s. Within that basin, he said, there is no Paris, no Tokyo, and no Shanghai, so Dubai was building *all* of these cities at once. If it didn't, its neighbors would; Doha, Abu Dhabi, Saudi Arabia, and even Iran have aped the "Dubai model," and all are still as solvent as ever.

Seen this way, the calculated vacancy of the Palm and the World almost began to make sense. No one in the West would have ever thought to build barrier reefs with enough pieds-à-terre to house all of San Francisco, but America's second-home market wasn't twice the size of China. Ditto for the sail-shaped Burj Al Arab. Dubai needed all of its hotels if it hoped to play Vegas for a third of Earth's surface.

It hasn't worked out that way. Yet. To many, Dubai is still a success. It's an oasis of peace and (relative) tolerance in a volatile region, and a haven for the dispossessed. It found a life after oil (which Abu Dhabi and Saudi Arabia are still searching for). To Iranians, Dubai represents freedom and a lifeline; to Indians and Africans, opportunity; to its neighbors, vice. And to Arabs, it points the way toward modernity.

As Americans, we want Dubai to fail, as we're blinded by the reflection of our own inequality, unsustainability, stupidity, and greed. But what if it doesn't? What if the hub of the trillion-dollar economy we paid for manages to succeed?

The Emirates Empire

Dubai's reinvention as the mother of all hubs was born of necessity. For the first twenty-five years of the airport's existence, the emirate didn't have an airline. When Sheikh Rashid cut the golden cord at Dubai International in 1960 (six years before the discovery of oil, or construction of the city's first hospital), he ushered in the era of Open Skies. Unlike the treaty of the same name signed by the United States and the European Union nearly fifty years later, Dubai's Open Skies was unconditional—any airline was welcome to land at any time. The decision to offer such access followed Sheikh Rashid's motto, "What's good for the merchants is good for Dubai." (Another aphorism expressed his unease about oil: "My grandfather rode a camel, my father rode a camel, I drive a Mercedes, my son drives a Land Rover, his son will drive a Land Rover, but his son will ride a camel.")

Dubai had been a free port since 1901, when the reigning sheikh abolished all tariffs in response to its Iranian rival across the Gulf abruptly hiking its own. The Persian traders emigrated en masse, comprising the city's first expatriates. Open Skies had a similar effect—for twenty-five years, the emirate's population rose exponentially in lockstep with the airport's as the latter became one of the busiest in the Gulf. The policy eventually drew Dubai into conflict with Gulf Air, formed in 1973 as the flag carrier of Bahrain, Qatar, Oman, and the UAE. It demanded the same protections it enjoyed at its other hubs, which is standard practice in the industry. When Dubai demurred, the airline retaliated by drastically cutting service. Rather than knuckle under to its demands, Sheikh Rashid and Sheikh Mo countered by launching their own airline instead.

As with most white-collar work in Dubai, the actual toil of starting an airline from scratch fell to a team of British expats led by Maurice Flanagan, a former British Airways executive then running the airport. His star hire was Tim Clark as president. Clark's task was figuring out where the new airline should fly. When Emirates launched in 1985 with a pair of used planes and a check for $10 million, Clark zeroed in on routes its rivals had overlooked. Pakistan, for instance, had eighty-five million people but only one international airline. India, nearly ten times as large, had the same. Emirates began life with daily service to Karachi, followed by Delhi and Mumbai.

Before long, however, Emirates would run out of cities that needed it more than it needed them. So Clark, Flanagan, and their new boss—twenty-six-year-old Sheikh Ahmed—hit the road to broker deals for new destinations. Its tiny fleet, route map, and name recognition proved ideal for negotiations, as otherwise paranoid governments like Singapore happily forked over landing rights. In that particular case, "We signed the deal and were off to lunch before the meeting even started," Clark recalled. Today, Emirates flies ten times a day in the teeth of Singapore Airlines and its fortress hub, to its rival's regret. By 1991, the airline had signed similar deals with unsuspecting parties in Germany, Thailand, the U.K., and Hong Kong, battering its way into any place possessing the raw materials of the Instant Age—talent, ideas, trade, tourists, cargo— and carrying it back to Dubai. Service to London, Frankfurt, Hong Kong, and Singapore tied the emirate into the world's financial centers, while its routes to the subcontinent became a conveyor belt of inexhaustible labor.

It wasn't until the 1990s—after the death of Sheikh Rashid and transfer of power to Sheikh Mo—that the master plans of Dubai Inc. and the emirate aerotropolis were hatched. While His Highness spent $500 million on a new concourse at Dubai International and $650 million more on the spinnaker-shaped, skyline-defining Burj Al Arab, Clark and Flanagan acquired a handful of new 777s, twin-engine long-haul jumbo jets that fly farther on less fuel than 747s. Armed with these state-of-the-art aircraft, Emirates made it its mission to rewire the world's paths from Point A to Point B.

After it broke into Australia, for example, it pounced on the lucrative "kangaroo routes" linking the Antipodes to London. The cities are far enough apart that no aircraft can make it on a regular tank. There's no reason why they shouldn't lay over in Dubai, especially if Emirates could use its hub to lower costs and offer lower fares. This insight had enormous ramifications for strategy; any flight between two cities in the East and West that didn't warrant its own nonstop—Milan-to-Tokyo, or Frankfurt-to-Bangkok—could connect via Dubai as easily as anywhere else, and should. And by virtue of being a hub, it would link cities that had never been connected before. When Emirates started service to Shanghai, for instance, the flights were quickly full of Egyptian traders traveling in packs to the Yangtze's factory towns—a postmodern spin on their ancestors' Saharan caravans. As Emirates wove a tight web of destinations, Dubai became the O'Hare of the Orient, a switching station that made the airline frighteningly efficient and the tax-free emirate a steadily sweeter place to do business.

Once Emirates achieved sufficient size and economies of scale, profits and passengers shot skyward, doubling and tripling in size every three or four years. The airline has turned a profit twenty-three years in a row according to its independent accountants, including a $964-million-dollar profit last year—more than all American carriers combined. It carries more international passengers than any U.S. airline.

As of this writing, Emirates has 141 planes in the air and more than 200 on order or optioned, with a book value of $70 billion. Despite Dubai's debt woes, financing hasn't been a problem. The list includes the A380s and more than a hundred A350 XWBs, Airbus's still largely conceptual knockoff of Boeing's 787. Emirates won't take receipt of those until sometime in the second half of the decade, underscoring that it's in this for the long haul. American carriers, meanwhile, find themselves caught in a vicious circle—ruinously expensive fuel crossed with the recession has left them too cash-strapped to buy more fuel-efficient planes, leaving them stuck with aging gas-guzzlers bleeding them white.

"Anybody that can control the airline, government policy, and the airport should make a lot of money," the CEO of Qantas groused, and Dubai has with Sheikh Ahmed handling all three. What would be considered socialism in America is regarded as best practices in Dubai. His Highness's first act was to run the airport 24/7, regardless of neighbors, noise, and circadian rhythms. Emirates' hub operates round the clock, with waves of planes coming and going through the early morning. The airline makes millions while its competitors sleep, with its planes in the air as theirs sit at gates depreciating. It doesn't pay taxes, either, although its biggest advantage is labor. Emirates spends nearly half of what Southwest or Lufthansa does on its people, recruiting Africans and South Asians for ground staff and cabin crews. It houses its catering staff in a labor camp in Dubai's poorest neighborhood.

Like Dubai itself, Emirates has built its empire on the backs of workers earning as little as $175 a month, wages comparable to what a Chinese factory worker makes. But where the grind of assembling iPads has been outsourced to Shenzhen and passed back to the United States via an aerial umbilical cord, in this case the worker himself has been outsourced to Dubai; he's been insourced. What makes Dubai so hallucinatory is the simultaneous coexistence of the developing world within the developed one—a brown worker toils on the other side of the glass from the white one, both enticed to move here for the fruits of their labors, the pair separated only by the surface tension of extreme inequality and the threat of deportation.

Sheikh Mo's management style might charitably be described as enlightened despotism. The emirate walks a tightrope between the conservative Wahhabi Islam of its neighbors and Western hedonism. The same is true of its geopolitics: Jebel Ali is the port of call for U.S. aircraft carriers patrolling the Gulf, while a huge body of investigative work points to Dubai as the money-laundering hub for Al Qaeda and the Taliban. Journalists probing the "dark side of Dubai" after the crash missed the point: Dubai is all dark side. This is a place that made its first fortune smuggling gold into India, at one point cornering a fifth of the worldwide market. Today, as the hub of hubs—where one does business with "absolute simplicity"—it is effectively amoral.

Its free zones are hubs for smuggling embargoed American goods into Iran, and for smuggling Chinese counterfeit drugs into America. Dubai also traffics in sex and death. An estimated ten thousand kidnapped girls move through here, while the weapons dealer Viktor Bout reputedly armed both Hezbollah and the Iraqi insurgency from the emirates. His fleet of fifty aircraft is the black market FedEx, exchanging assault rifles and ammunition for oil money and blood diamonds. Defying all sanctions, his planes supplied more or less every warlord in Africa, including both sides of Angola's civil war. Al Qaeda and the U.S. military were also his customers, as was the United Nations, which unwittingly relied on him to deliver aid to Darfur. (Bout was extradited to the United States in the fall of 2010.)

What people find most repugnant about Dubai is the inhuman way of life forced on the "guest workers" who compose a third of its population. Slavery was abolished here in 1963, although the practice lives on whenever a laborer from Dhaka, Karachi, or Sri Lanka has his passport confiscated upon arrival. Investigations by Human Rights Watch have uncovered horrific working conditions and the withholding of wages, and even the UAE's minister of labor was reportedly shocked by the utter squalor of labor camps in the desert. But the unbelievable truth is that Dubai still offers these workers better opportunities than anything they had at home. For an unskilled laborer from the Indian province of Kerala, for example, hard labor in the desert is a ticket to the middle class. India is the largest recipient of remittances from the Gulf, receiving $27 billion in 2007.

Emirates made this Marxist dystopia possible. The airline is a reflection and an extension of Dubai, run like a strategic arm of the state. "It's a massive virtuous circle," Flanagan has said. "Neither can succeed without the other." The Emirates Group constitutes a full quarter of Dubai's

GDP and is its largest company, with fifty thousand employees. There isn't another city or country so invested in transportation, in which the flagship company is an airline. And the way the economies of scale shake out, Emirates is still getting better as it gets bigger.

"From July, we will be taking on two big aircraft a month, and that will go on for fifty-eight months. And it won't stop there," Flanagan said in 2008. It hasn't. By 2020, he and Clark intend to have four hundred aircraft, making theirs by far the largest international airline in the world. And it's not enough. Flanagan would like to have six hundred, but he'll settle for fewer because Dubai International can't handle them all. Presumably, that's where the emirate's second airport comes in.

Abu Dhabi's Ivory Towers

The only threats to Emirates' dominance are taking shape just down the coast, an hour's flight away in Doha, the capital of Qatar, and an hour's drive in Abu Dhabi. Both are building aerotropoli, and both have airlines with orders for hundreds of new planes. They've studied their neighbor's suffering with a measure of schadenfreude, awaiting their opportunity to supplant it as the epicenter of the Gulf.

Abu Dhabi has all the leverage as the wealthiest of the emirates and Dubai's lender of last resort. The price of its $20 billion bailout is widely expected to be more than just interest—it may end up costing Dubai its independence within the UAE. Others predict it will be forced to ransom Emirates, estimated to be worth $30 billion.

But Abu Dhabi has an airline, owned by the other Sheikh Mo— Crown Prince Mohammed bin Zayed Al Nahyan. He decreed the launch of Etihad Airways in 2003, spending $8 billion at the outset on aircraft— a record for a launch by a factor of fifty—supplemented by another $20 billion a few years later. Drafting in Emirates' slipstream ever since, Etihad is now climbing an even steeper growth curve, adding new destinations every month—Baghdad, Nagoya, and N'Djamena are recent additions—and doubling in size every other year. Compounding its hypergrowth with Emirates' begs the question of whether these cities eighty miles apart need their own world-beating airlines. Why can't they just share? A merger would make sense. Sheikh Ahmed insists they haven't talked about it; why they won't underscores how aviation has redrawn the map. In their minds, the emirates might as well be oceans apart. But both believe aerotropoli will be the only cities that matter going forward.

"The Middle East is the new center of air travel thanks to advances in aircraft technology," Geert Boven explained in Abu Dhabi. "Because we can fly nineteen hours nonstop now, we're able to reach any city in the world from here. And because of that, traffic streams are being rerouted worldwide." The avuncular Dutchman spent eighteen years at KLM before joining Etihad. He's been charged with stealing those streams from Schiphol and keeping them away from Dubai.

"If you look at the old European airlines, they were always hopping," he continued. "Amsterdam-to-Australia was really Amsterdam-to-Athens-to-Abu Dhabi-to-Bangkok-to-Australia, because they didn't have the technology. Now the world is divided into two brackets," East and West, "and we sit between them, in the center of the world. We can tap into those streams and then control them."

Abu Dhabi's airport is in the midst of a $7 billion expansion that will double the airfield's physical size and raise its capacity exponentially. Before Etihad, it was as sleepy as Oklahoma City's; when they're finished, it'll be on par with Bangkok's. Boven spelled it out for me, and in doing so revealed his owners' insecurities. "Etihad is the vehicle to put Abu Dhabi on the map—financially, culturally, and as a tourist destination. We're a part of 'Abu Dhabi, Inc.' We're inextricably linked."

Abu Dhabi is already on the map, with a star next to its name as the capital of the UAE. It's the richest city in the world, with almost a trillion dollars invested abroad and a century's worth of oil still in the ground. Its mature skyline is molten gold at dawn, framed by a resplendently green corniche. You'd think this Sheikh Mo would have nothing to prove, but that was before his namesake diverted the world's attention next door. He wanted it back. "Abu Dhabi has a desire to be taken seriously on the world stage, and an almost unique assembly of resources with which to buy it," said an American architect who's worked closely with the sheikhs. "They have the means to bring the world to them, but they're thinking very, very carefully about that. Do they become so international they lose their character?" How do they steal Dubai's thunder without sinking to its level? "Dubai is Las Vegas; we want to be Palm Springs" is how one tourism official put it.

Abu Dhabi needed a strategy; Etihad was the first piece. Master plans for the airport's expansion followed in 2005, and the unveiling of Abu Dhabi's pièce de résistance two years after that. Saadiyat Island—a real one, lying just off the coast—will follow the Dubai model of condo hotels, marinas, golf, and glass boxes headlined by a "cultural district" of museums and edifices undersigned by some of the world's top architects. The Guggenheim will be here with a supersize riff on Frank Gehry's titanium whorls, while Jean Nouvel is supervising the first branch of the Louvre outside France, procured for a billion-dollar franchising fee.

Perusing the plans at the Emirates Palace (the world's most expensive hotel), I was surprised that no Arab architects had made the cut. But it struck me that these monuments weren't meant for Arabs anyway—they were being pitched to a moneyed, global tourist class expecting Guggenheims and Gehry wherever they went, whether New York, Bilbao, or Abu Dhabi. Reading the fine print, I found a cost-benefit analysis ("value generation = direct return, real estate value . . .") with Thomas Krens's name attached. The former Guggenheim director was the godfather of the "Bilbao effect," coined to explain how a Spanish rust belt city rebranded itself as a creative center around a single piece of "starchitecture." Bilbao has been a template for aspiring cities ever since. Krens was eventually pushed out of his post by a board tired of hearing about the Guggenheim "brand" and exhausted by his empire building. But he has stuck around to babysit his final brainchild, conceived when Abu Dhabi's Sheikh Mohammed came to him with vague notions of becoming a "cultural destination."

As Krens recalled, "The question was: 'How do you achieve an effective critical mass . . . that could make Abu Dhabi an international cultural destination?' A single building—a Bilbao-type structure—would be irrelevant in this context." What they needed, and what they got, was a smorgasbord of Bilbaos. If Dubai wanted to corner the market on theme parks and fake archipelagos, then fine, let them. Abu Dhabi would spend its billions to monopolize museums and art *biennales*, drawing a cosmopolitan flock of artists, collectors, and hangers-on who already flit from Miami to London to Venice to Basel. They could confer, with a laying-on of their moneyed hands, the one thing Dubai doesn't have: class.

The telling detail in Saadiyat's blueprints is the new span of highway between the airport and island, bypassing the city completely. It's possible millions of visitors will leave without ever having set foot in Abu Dhabi proper, which is all part of the sheikh's plan. He envisions the city tripling in size by 2030, with its center shifting inland toward the airport. Just south of the runways will be the new CBD and Capital District, a forest of towers ringing the capitol of the UAE. To the west, on the way to the Guggenheim, is Yas Island, home to a Formula One track and the site of Ferrari World. Abu Dhabi has blown some of its oil wealth on a few trophies of its own—stakes in Virgin Galactic and the Ultimate Fighting Championship, the Chrysler Building, and Masdar, a "zero-carbon" solar-powered city in a country with the highest per capita carbon footprint on earth.

Envisioned as a test bed for every type of renewable energy under the sun—picture solar cells powering personal monorails instead of cars—Masdar is a retort to the unsustainable sprawl of Dubai. "One day, all cities will be built like this," its backers promised, hinting at a multi*trillion*-dollar industry to follow. MIT faculty consulted on the Masdar Institute of Science and Technology, while the emirate is trying to coax clean-tech companies to move here with the carrot of $250 million in seed money and the usual lures—no taxes, no oversight, and the great basin of two billion customers within a few hours' flight. So far, there have been few takers; the opening has been pushed ahead until 2020 and plans for the city are under review.

Abu Dhabi's niche may turn out to be neither culture nor carbon, but college. Its stable of blue-chip brands includes branches of both the Sorbonne and London's Imperial College to go along with a complete New York University campus on Saadiyat Island—the first time a major U.S. research institution has cloned its entire curriculum offshore. NYU Abu Dhabi's students are admitted under the same standards and handed the same diplomas as their American peers. NYU's wish is to open "the world's first global university in the world's first truly global city," according to its president. And while you might think NYU already fits that description in Manhattan, it's not true. Not anymore.

Before 9/11, more than half a million students from developing nations applied for visas every year to study in the United States. They composed the bulk of science graduate programs at elite schools like Johns Hopkins. Then the twin towers fell, America's borders went up, and the number of students—which had been rising by twenty thousand or so annually—fell 10 percent, the first sustained decline in thirty years. (The drop is even steeper for students from the Gulf.) Not that they have many options back home—the United States has a third of the world's colleges and universities and nearly all of its best teachers.

Like the medical tourists heading to Bangkok and Bumrungrad instead of the Mayo or Cleveland clinics, they're flocking to the few top-notch institutions at hand. And as hospitals in India and the United States are starting to figure out, it's faster and easier to buy or clone new ones than build them. Qatar thought of it first, creating an "Education City" in Doha with branches of Carnegie Mellon, Texas A&M, Georgetown, and Cornell's Medical School. Abu Dhabi went them one better by buying a first-class university outright and pieces of two others for $50 million down and a pledge to cover operating expenses (no doubt a rounding error on Saadiyat Island's budget).

Whereas the Middle East's and India's best and brightest once trekked to New York, Paris, and London for their degrees, now they need only hop an Etihad or Emirates flight to the Gulf instead. The inaugural class attracted more than five hundred early-decision applicants, accepting students from China, Ethiopia, Hungary, India, Indonesia, Jordan, Morocco, Russia, and Taiwan. "Everyone introduced themselves, in English and whatever language they wanted," recalled the NYU vice provost in charge of admissions. "From French to Russian to Arabic to Hungarian, they'd say things like 'I traveled 30 hours to get here,' or 'I've never been on a plane before.' It was kind of a goose-bump moment."

What NYU gains from this arrangement besides money is harder to put a finger on. University president John Sexton is frank about his desire to see a host of "glocal" offshoots worldwide, framing expansion and confrontation in the context of 9/11. "After that day, we were forced to confront the critical choice of the 21st century," he said. "What is our attitude toward 'the other' going to be? Is it going to be a clash of civilizations? Or is it going to be an ecumenical gift?"

The others in question couldn't care less. The sheikhs' strategy is craftier than anyone in the United States gives them credit for. Transplanting NYU to the Gulf, where the children of the East can study in the "West" without exposure to the corrupting influence of its freedoms, isn't a case of cloning another trophy property. It's turning the source of America's last great competitive advantage—its unmatched universities—against itself, counting on Harvard and Yale to think like brand managers and multinationals rather than national trusts. They seem to have forgotten in their haste to go global that America thrived by drawing the planet's talent to its shores and then convincing it to stay awhile.

NYU Abu Dhabi erases the old equation. It isn't NYU and Abu Dhabi University competing anymore, but Manhattan and Abu Dhabi, and while one is several oceans away with a suspicious Department of Homeland Security, the other is flush with petrodollars and sprinkled with university zones offering as few or as many freedoms as they'd like. For an aspiring software engineer from Chennai, it's not even close. And just like that, the emirates have hijacked another stream of people who were once the exclusive property of the West.

Saudi Arabia has also chartered new universities as part of its plans to build six instant cities around the country, at a total cost of $70 billion. The aim is to establish a Saudi Silicon Valley, one designed to create a million jobs and increase nonoil GDP by almost 50 percent in barely a decade. These "economic cities" are explicitly intended to house and employ nearly half of the ten million Saudis under the age of seventeen—a largely uneducated workforce described as a "human time bomb." It's the cities' job to defuse it. Scattered across thousands of miles of desert, each will be an aerotropolis. The kingdom is spending billions of dollars to upgrade all of its twenty-seven airports and build an aerotropolis at Jeddah, the gateway to Mecca.

Tallying all of these aerial ambitions, the Gulf expects to receive 280 million passengers a year by 2015, at least in the best of all possible worlds. It works out to 770,000 passengers daily, enough to fill fifteen hundred A380s. This assumes every airline hits its growth targets—imaginary numbers, in other words. Just as Dubai Inc.'s subsidiaries dared one another to outdo themselves, betting their Burj or Palm would not be the one to fail, so are the Gulf carriers. Kasarda calls it "aeronautical fratricide."

Whoever wins (and Emirates remains the front-runner), their vast order books guarantee they will run out of room on the ground. To that end, Abu Dhabi is busy overhauling its airfield while Doha builds a new airport a mile from its old one. Dubai International, meanwhile, makes Heathrow and LAX feel spacious. Although the all-Emirates Terminal 3 has more capacity inside than all of JFK, the approach roads are a round-the-clock traffic jam. Kasarda was once forced to jump from his car and jog the final quarter mile to catch his flight.

There was never any question whether Dubai needed a second air-port; it was only a matter of when. One was set for 2020 until Sheikh Mo sagely determined this was fifteen years too late. Announced in 2005, Al Maktoum International would occupy a raw piece of desert near the border with Abu Dhabi, leaving plenty of room for five runways. When finished, it would handle 120 million passengers per year, and twelve million tons of cargo—more than all three of New York City's airports now. Surrounding it would be an aerotropolis within an aerotropolis named Dubai World Central. The up-front costs for infrastructure would start at $33 billion, more than the United States originally earmarked for the reconstruction of Iraq.

It isn't difficult to imagine the sands reclaiming the runways of an airport Ozymandias once all the oil beneath them has been drained. It was with this picture in mind that I went to see the dunes of Dubai World Central shortly after work began, envisioning an army of pharaonic slaves toiling under the sun. I wouldn't be disappointed.

The City of the Pillars

There were four of us in the Jeep when our driver veered off the highway into the desert, past a cantilevered gate like you might find at a railroad crossing, only there were no rails, no roads, nothing on either side besides rock and sand for miles. The gate was open anyway, and we blew past it aiming for distant cranes. Our guide was at the wheel, while Mohamed and I hung on in back and the Nephew lurched in front.

The Nephew had picked me up that morning in a company Mer-cedes, wearing a white dishdasha and a glazed, placid expression rippled by giggles when I hopped in the car. We'd barely left the parking lot be-fore he'd flipped to one of Dubai's hip-hop stations, singing along to Jay-Z in a fluent gangsta cadence. *If you havin' girl problems I feel bad for you, son. I got 99 problems, but a bitch ain't one.* He waited until we were stuck in traffic to ask if he could light up, punctuating his request with a flour-ish of his lighter and mimed puff of his lips. After I nodded my assent, he produced a one-hitter from the depths of his sleeves and proceeded to take a deep and herbaceous breath, exhaling with a more maniacal giggle this time.

The Nephew was probably just that, some sheikh's nephew needing the cover of gainful employment as a VIP driver. He's Sheikh Mo's nightmare, the spoiled product of a nanny state that's insourced foreign talent for every opening from airline president on down. The government has since launched a campaign of "Emiratisation" to create work for the natives, but day-to-day operations still depend on expatriates.

Mohamed Al Mustafa was waiting patiently for us in front of DWC's headquarters along Sheikh Zayed Road. Tall, obsidian skinned, and nattily dressed in a three-piece suit, how he managed to cross the parking lot without combusting, I'll never know. Sudanese by birth and a surveyor by trade, he once spent summers assembling schools in Darfur before it was *Darfur*, a decade before the Janjaweed appeared and the killing began. "You had to worry about bandits then, but not millions of refugees," he said mournfully as we sped toward the site. The work stopped in the mid-nineties due to budget cuts, and he flew to Dubai. "I would have preferred to stay," he insisted, while acknowledging that all of his work has gone up in flames. His new assignment "is a once-in-a lifetime project," or maybe once in several lifetimes. "Maybe our kids will work on this after we are gone." He laughed.

Our guide was ready with the Jeep at base camp. Mohamed stuck a GPS transceiver on its dash, and once we'd vaulted off the highway, his laptop tracked our position as we rolled across the landscape. His map was overlaid with schematics of thousand-foot glass towers, golf courses, hangars—a mirage completely at odds with dune after dune. We cut a swath through the phantom grid of "Commercial City," which was marked only by fluttering stakes in the sand.

You can see the site for yourself on Google Maps. Type in "Dubai" and scroll south-by-southwest until you're between the two Palms (the sequel is all but abandoned), staring at an upside-down F carved from the coast. This is the port of Jebel Ali, surrounded by its eponymous free zone, bounded on the southeast by Emirates Road. On the far side lies the nascent aerotropolis, and beyond that is nothing but boundless desert. The forbidding *Rub' al-Khali*, the Empty Quarter, begins not far from here.

Dubai World Central would be "the final gateway," in the words of its chairman—proof that there could be the biggest of something in Dubai. Built to last through 2050—which might as well be the twenty-seventh century here—the master plan envisions a "Commercial City" slotted on one side of the runways with eight hundred towers and a half-million residents, next to a "Golf City" (picture a prefab Palm Springs) and the hangars of "Aviation City."

Opposite the airfield are "Exhibition City" (convention centers and hotels) and "Residential City," on-site housing for working-class expatriates. In light of Dubai's real estate crash and vacancy rate, these "cities" will likely never be built, or at least not anytime soon.

The airport itself opened last June, albeit for only a handful of cargo flights on one runway. Passenger flights are scheduled to start this spring. Its intended tenant, Emirates, has pushed ahead its moving day as far as 2030. By then, Abu Dhabi and Dubai may have sprawled together into a single urban landscape, in which case Dubai World Central would actually be at the center. One could easily imagine a merged Etihad (Arabic for "United") Emirates locating their main hub here, equidistant from both cities. After all, a similar thing happened with Dallas–Ft. Worth and DFW.

But all of that is still years away, if ever. (If Dubai International reaches its maximum capacity, it will still rival Atlanta's as the busiest in the world.) At the time there was nothing to see here except the airport's guts being sunk into the desert. Maybe it was the desolation of the terrain, but the airfield had the feel of an archaeological dig, as if they were excavating the future instead of building it.

The stump of the control tower, still visible for miles, was hidden beneath a black shroud, bristling with rebar. "It will be the tallest in the Middle East," Mohamed said casually. Then his eyes lit up. "Of course it will. It's Dubai." The rust-colored beams of the cargo terminal were being hoisted into place one by one like the painstakingly reassembled ribs of some dinosaur. Everywhere I looked, there were relics piled beside the paths, wrapped in plastic against the grit. They are all built now, along with some office buildings, which sit vacant. Work went on around the clock by sixteen thousand men, clad head to toe in jumpsuits, hard hats, and goggles against the sandstorms kicked up by bulldozers. Watching one group be engulfed, we fell silent, suddenly self-conscious of the fact we were on a glass-bottomed boat tour through the inferno.

Crawling along in the Jeep, we came to a petrified forest of steel columns stuck fast in cement. These were the foundations of the temporary terminal. Considering one can burrow through a hundred feet of gravel and never touch bedrock, there was no choice but to build it from the ground up. Seeing these stunted pillars dusted by the sands reminded me of Iram of the Pillars, the lost city swallowed centuries ago by the Empty Quarter, what Lawrence of Arabia called the "Atlantis of the Sands." The ancient capital of the frankincense trade, Iram was a trading hub for three millennia until, according to the Koran, its king ignored a prophet's warnings. In his anger, God smote the city and its people, "possessors of lofty buildings," for their insolence, driving them into the desert, never to be seen again.

At last we came to the runway, shimmering in the heat like a shallow lake of oil. A fleet of steamrollers floated on its surface. Driving in lazy circles, we spotted a trio of saddleless, rudderless camels milling about on the blacktop. A foreman was reading them the riot act. We passed the three again jogging along the highway. The leader shook his head haughtily at us, and Mohamed spun about, searching for something in the dunes. "Their owners are here somewhere," he muttered. There are still Bedouins camping on this fast-receding edge of the desert, until this all vanishes forever beneath tarmac.

The Final Gateway

They planned it without asking John Kasarda. He was summoned once before construction began to a headquarters that could have doubled for a Bond villain's lair. Models of their aerotropolis occupied the center of the room, with Lucite dominos standing in for office towers. Emiratis milled around it wearing dishdashas—no suits. This was a significant detail; in a city run by expatriates, their exclusion sent the message this was too important to be left in foreigners' hands.

Seated before the assembled heads of Commercial, Golf, Aviation, Exhibition, and Residential cities, Kasarda quickly realized how much the project was a microcosm of the emirate. Like Sheikh Mo's lieutenants running the various arms of Dubai Inc., each man around the table saw his "city" as his private domain, and each was locked in open competition with the others. They made it clear they saw Kasarda as an interloper. ("I think he fell a little bit in love with it," one of them told me later, rolling his eyes.) He never heard from them again.

After the crash (and after they'd left), the new regime called him in to find a new purpose for the airport. One piece of its stunted aerotropolis had made sense from the beginning. "Logistics City" is a giant cargo complex with enough room to grow to four times the size of the FedEx hub in Memphis. It was a remake of his 1990s model; at first, it was called TransPark Dubai. Picture gleaming cargo terminals, conveyor belts, factories, and distribution centers, each inserted in the precise order goods flow through them. Every square foot has been allocated, and every process sanded down, automated, and lubricated. You can't just buy a plot and set up shop here—you need a business plan proving you require proximity to the hub. Fail to pass muster and you're added to a waiting list with several hundred names ahead of you. Once admitted, you can choose to construct the warehouse of your dreams or else just flip on the lights in one that's already built. Either way, in thirty years or whenever something bigger and better comes along, a demolition crew will rip and replace the depot you're standing in to ensure a steadier supply of whatever the Gulf needs right that second. Kasarda calls it "functional renewal." An overpass across Emirates Road connects the airport and Logistics City to the port and free zone at Jebel Ali, so anyone hauling containers from a boat just arrived from China to a plane bound for Africa has a straight shot. And it's all duty-free. Everything between the water and the runways—what's being called the Dubai Logistics Corridor—has been engineered with an eye toward being faster and easier than any other hub in the Gulf. If it can do that, economics should take care of the rest.

In light of this, Kasarda's advice for the airport and the emirate was to forget about real estate and go back to being the region's tourism, trading, and logistics hub. Even now, Dubai attracts more international tourists than India and still finishes ahead of everyone between Frankfurt and Shanghai in rankings of the world's top business centers. "Don't count Dubai out," says Kasarda, who is naturally bullish on its prospects. "There's more leadership, ingenuity, and resilience in its superb connectivity than most people recognize. It still holds two trump cards in the form of Emirates Airlines and the Jebel Ali port and free zone." (In a sign of the times, the latter has been put up for sale.)

Sheikh Ahmed agrees, telling reporters that's been the plan for recovery all along. "This is what made Dubai move forward," he said, "not what happened in the past seven years in opening the real-estate market." It's finally moving forward again—trade rose 18 percent in the first six months of 2010. Instead of bringing the world to Dubai to shop for fifth or sixth homes, Kasarda suggests Dubai bring the world to them—an empty vessel for the region's excess cash should be the vessel for its goods. And if this sounds like an ignominious fate for the "kingdom of bling," then Sheikh Mo will sleep better knowing this is how Singapore and Hong Kong became the other great entrepôts of the East.

Dubai has serious soul-searching to do. It's still an open question whether the Gulf's playground must clean up its act to appease the conservative older brother who's picking up the check. It's just as likely that Dubai's dark side suits Abu Dhabi's purposes. But during the rush to soak up the world's excess liquidity with the sponge of off-plan condos, the emirate lost sight of the qualities that made it so attractive to someone like Marwan Bibi or Assem and Dina Hamzeh. The absolute simplicity they prized has been replaced by bloated bureaucracy. Thousands of talented expats have left, not because they're fleeing creditors but because they either can't obtain visas without employment or because Dubai's famously tolerant rulers have become schizoid of late trying to balance conservative Islam with permissiveness. Expats and emiratis alike have called for some form of long-term residency, and for a breakup of Dubai Inc., which often places the government in competition with the entrepreneurs it should be helping.

Once those issues are resolved (assuming they can be), there is still plenty of money sloshing around the Gulf. Higher oil prices were expected to double the surplus of Dubai's neighbors to $140 billion last year, meaning they'll be able to pay for Ferrari theme parks and their own artificial islands into the foreseeable future. As the regional hub, Dubai is poised to be their enabler. (Or their sanctuary if unrest—or Israeli air strikes—shake Iran.)

Kasarda also believes Dubai will be the Gulf's portal to Africa and India in the same way Miami has been the gateway to Latin America. India trails only China as the UAE's largest source of imports and is its top destination for exports, not including oil. The emirate has become a destination for African strivers who have no chance of obtaining visas to the West. To them, Dubai is nicer than any city in Egypt, Ethiopia, Kenya, the Congo, and Nigeria—the capital of a region with four hundred million people.

If it succeeds at doing all of these things, the emirate may yet fulfill its destiny of reopening the Silk Road to China. Arab medical tourists weren't the only ones locked out of America following 9/11—traders were too. The visa restrictions put in place after the attacks, coupled with rumors of detentions and disappearances when names mistakenly matched watch lists, caused the number of Arab visitors to the United States to plummet by a third. That same year, China joined the World Trade Organization, using free trade as an excuse to relax its own travel requirements.

The American-led invasion of Iraq two years later triggered the rise in oil prices that has funneled trillions of dollars to the Persian Gulf. China needed oil to keep its factories running—as of last year, Saudi Arabia supplied more to China than to the United States—and wanted to pay for it with its goods. So while America threw up walls in Baghdad's Green Zone, China lowered a few of its own. It wasn't long before planeloads of traders from Cairo, Damascus, and Amman were en route to Shanghai via Dubai.

The original Silk Road was not one road but a web of trade routes crisscrossing Asia by camels, dhows, and junks. They lasted fifteen hundred years, from Roman times through the Mongols. The New Silk Road is less than a decade old and travels through the air. Ben Simpfendorfer may be its Marco Polo. The chief China economist for the Royal Bank of Scotland once found himself on a flight from Guangzhou "seated next to a group of elderly Romanian women dressed in black, their teeth capped gold . . . On a later flight, I was seated next to an Egyptian shoe manufacturer, a Christian Copt who was wearing a necklace with a heavy gold cross. He owned a factory outside of Cairo, but it was empty, and he now imports all his shoes from Yiwu. 'What can I do?' he said with palms raised upwards. 'I have to make a living and it's cheaper to import from China than to manufacture locally.'"

These caravans flying coach are one reason why China's exports to the Arab world soared from $6 billion at the start of the last decade to $60 billion by 2009, pulling ahead of the United States. And as Simpfendorfer points out, a large share of America's exports to the Middle East are Boeing planes and GE engines bought by the likes of Emirates, Etihad, and Qatar Airways—the airlines plying the Silk Road, which now runs all the way to Africa.

China's trade with the Continent has risen from $2 billion to $100 billion in just the last ten years, "and thirty-five percent of China's trade with Africa goes to North Africa," Simpfendorfer told me. "It makes more sense to hub that out of Dubai than Johannesburg. If you're going to build a regional hub somewhere, it's Dubai. There's a lot of interest from Chinese companies and private equity to pick up assets cheaply there." China's state-owned banks were reportedly ready to aid in Dubai's bailout until Abu Dhabi stepped in.

Is the aerotropolis the next phase of globalization? Is it the way we'll live next? If Kasarda is correct—if the aerotropolis is a breakthrough in the size and scope and skeletal structures of cities—then the scale of what Dubai has built should be transformative instead of additive. Its fusion of airports, port, and logistics should yield something more than just steady upticks in tourists and cargo. Sheikh Mohammed wants to reopen the Silk Road, but what does that mean for the Hamzehs, Bibis, and other strivers in his shadow?

Survival of the Swiftest

One of the companies blazing the trail into Africa is an outfit named Swift Freight, which started hauling Ethiopia's bumper crop of roses through here on its way to all points in Europe, Asia, and America. Swift's cornering of the flower market was an accident—all it had wanted was to quit losing money on every chartered flight returning empty from Addis Ababa. But Swift had stumbled onto something bigger: a back door into Africa, and a deceptively modest plan to airlift goods into some of the most desperate corners of the world.

The mastermind of this plan wasn't Sheikh Mo or some NGO but an Ugandan émigré named Issa Baluch. We met at his warehouse in JAFZA after my flora tour. Baluch is a bear of a man sporting facial hair last seen on nineteenth-century presidents. "I got into the industry by accident," he said, escaping Idi Amin's reign of terror by moving to Dubai at age nineteen. After a short stint with the police ("Boots and khakis are not for you" was one piece of advice), he joined the American oil drilling firm McDermott as a field manager. He "lasted one day," before working outdoors in Dubai's climate struck him as patently nuts. He ended up at a shipping firm, rising through the ranks to general manager before leaving to launch Swift in 1989.

By then he'd made his reputation with a novel shipping technique, one made possible by Dubai's unique confluence of infrastructure and geography. Baluch had managed to combine two modes of transport that almost never go together, because one is cheap (and slow), and the other fast (but expensive): the container ship and the jet. He called it the Sea Air Model, or SAM. The idea had come to him in the 1970s, when the volume of air traffic between Europe and Asia was a fraction of what it is now. In those days, an air shipment might sit in a hangar in Hong Kong or Bangkok for weeks until space opened up or the client paid extra. Faced with such delays, Baluch thought it would be both faster and less expensive to ship it by boat to Dubai and then load it onto a plane for Paris. The only thing leaving the emirate in those days was oil. Dubai handled 170 tons of goods via SAM at the end of the 1970s; it was 20,000 tons a decade later, and 45,000 tons a decade after that.

But it wasn't until SAM was introduced to Africa in 2006 that Swift discovered its niche as FedEx for the bottom billion. Many of Africa's capitals—Kinshasa, Lusaka, Kigali, Harare, and Khartoum among them—are impoverished *and* landlocked, rendering conventional sea or air shipments either too costly or unworkable. Flights south of the Sahara—typically via their former colonizers' flag carriers—are stratospherically expensive and often run just once a week. "Africa-bound traffic can afford to be beaten up and tossed around, because the choices are limited," Baluch said. His solution was a deal with Ethiopian Airlines, which possesses a fleet of modern Boeings (including, improbably, the 787 starting later this year) and a network crisscrossing the continent.

Four years ago, Swift started service to Kenya, Rwanda, and "failed states" such the Congo, Zimbabwe, Nigeria, and Uganda. Up next are the nations along the southwestern edge of the Sahara, including Niger, Chad, and Mali. Swift operates virtually unopposed from Dubai, controlling 80 percent of the market. "The key to Dubai is Africa," an American opportunist told me. "All the infrastructure, roads, telecommunications, food, water—everything—has to be imported, which means the opportunity here is to do just that."

"We're focusing on these corridors," Baluch explained. "I don't want to grow in the Middle East; everyone is doing that. We want to put more thrust into Africa. We have a lot of finished goods going there and very little coming back. Everyone only pays to go one way, so we need to create balanced trade. We're looking at flowers first, and then perishables. We're busy delivering a lot of flowers to the Far East, northern Europe, and North America," another growth market. "When it's snowy in Denver, we're flying a lot of flowers there."

Everything consigned to Africa is made in China. Baluch is running the last leg of the New Silk Road. His clients are African traders and merchants like himself, who've made their ways to Dubai's souks and China's bazaars to hunt for bargains in Guangzhou. They're bringing globalization back to Africa, piece by piece: computers, cell phones, even Toyota Corollas. He calls them the mamas.

I met my first mama later that same afternoon at Swift's airport outpost. She was pacing the loading dock amid pallets groaning under gasoline generators, flat-screen Korean TVs, HP LaserJet printers, refrigerators, and more obscure bundles. She was barefoot, dust covering her feet and her face except for the two circles around her eyes where her sunglasses had shaded them. Every now and then she stopped to bark orders at her assistants, a pair of shirtless young men packing boxes with what looked like black, bedazzled Chanel purses. "My business is ladies' handbags," she said wearily via hasty translation. These were earmarked for her regulars in Kinshasa, the shreds of the Congo capital's "middle class," although a few cartons would wing their way aboard decrepit propeller planes to cities deeper in the jungle—islands of civilization where the only goods of any kind arrive by air. Come tomorrow she would be back in the souks, hunting for counterfeit and factory reject merchandise at discount prices. Around a thousand mamas call on Swift each month, the overwhelming majority in the firm's China and Thailand offices.

A month later, I sat in the conference room of its Guangzhou branch (run by Issa's younger brother Behram) interrogating the mamas packing the waiting room. Many were proud, poker-faced women, but there were some men bearing a manic edge and a hustler's mien. One interrupted our conversation midsyllable to take a call. He was Mwanje Ali, a trader from Uganda who'd been living in China for two years, making a go of locating materials for Khartoum's construction boom: "tiles, ceramics, plumbing, lamps, lighting—everything apart from the stone and cement," he said. "Because the problem in Africa isn't that the raw materials aren't there, but that the finished products aren't as good. Here, you find high-quality product because the factories are actually competitive." His MO is to search Alibaba.com and track down resellers hawking excess inventory. Most of his customers are in Uganda, Zambia, and Tanzania, "but Sudan is very promising because they need basically everything. Everything!"

There are now an estimated twenty thousand Africans living in Guangzhou—enough that Kenyan Airlines made it the destination of the first nonstop flight between Africa and mainland China. They've colonized their own quarter of the city with mosques and cafés, where mamas haggle with customers in Lagos and Lusaka deep into the night, in tune to Africa time. They landed en masse once China joined the WTO, cutting out the middlemen in Hong Kong by tracing their supplies to the source. They're beating the Chinese at their own game.

"It's now likely that the bulk of Chinese goods sold in Africa are brought there by Africans, rather than by the Chinese, contrary to the impression created by Western media," said Barry Sautman, a politics professor at Hong Kong University of Science and Technology. "In fact, Chinese merchants in Africa complain about the competition from African merchants bringing in Chinese goods. Africans do, after all, have a competitive advantage in knowing their local markets."

With SAM, Issa Baluch discovered a way for Africa to make a meal of, if not exactly feast on, the scraps of globalization. Even in the Congo, the story is still the same: They need it, and they need it now, not in a month when their ship comes in or Air France finds an empty crevice in the hold. The mamas' customers can't wait, so neither can they. Swift has found a third passage for them, bypassing the world's more congested trade lanes in favor of Dubai's immense idle capacity. They're hanging on to the global economy by this, the barest of threads.

I'd arrived in Dubai in time for SAM's moment of truth. Before Swift could blaze a trail above the sub-Saharan jungles, Baluch wanted his own man on the ground in Addis Ababa. He and his partners at Ethiopian Airlines needed each other, but he didn't quite trust them. They were falling all over themselves in their headlong rush to add freighters to pack full of roses. Swift was opening an office there, and I was invited to tag along with the new station chief, Shaju Unnithan, to see SAM in action.

Check-in for our early morning flight was blocked by a trio of mountainous mamas and their Kilimanjaro-size pile of shrink-wrapped stereos, baby carriages, and miscellaneous luggage. "Carry-on cargo," Unnithan joked. Before we could shuffle to a shorter line, he was intercepted by a wiry trader. "How's business in Nigeria?" he asked obligingly. The man looked crushed. In a snit of protectionism, the Nigerian government had outlawed the import of furniture—no tables, no chairs, nothing. The hope was to stimulate local industry, but until the country's elites found a way to wean themselves off oil and its poisoning of the economy, Nigeria's 130 million citizens still needed places to sit and sleep. Swift and the mamas would swoop in once they changed their minds.

Unnithan moved to Dubai from Delhi fourteen years ago, while still in his twenties, after an uncle pulled a few strings with Issa Baluch. His face was a series of circles—for his balding head, for his glasses, for his chin. It wasn't a face made for expressing anger, although he was about to spend his days here furiously marrying the rhythms of just-in-time with the inalterably languid "Africa time." He lived in Sharjah, the next emirate over, with his parents, grandparents, wife, and two young children. They would all follow him to Addis.

Just-in-Time and Africa Time

Addis Ababa is melting. Not from the heat—it practically floats above Africa in the crisp mountain air—but from ruin and neglect. Despite a few halfhearted pockets of new tenements, the city's skyline is steadily being rendered, like fat from a carcass, into the tin shacks cramming its slums. An astounding 99.4 percent of Ethiopia's city dwellers live in slum-like conditions, according to the United Nations, and while that percentage is Africa's highest, Addis's three million residents would fill less than half of Lagos's or Kinshasa's vast shantytowns.

The aerotropolis effect reaches even here. Bole, the neighborhood nearest the airport along the southern edge of the city, is the one-half of 1 percent that isn't a slum, where a few new high-rises, malls, and nightclubs stand out from fading villas. The airport itself has been hailed as one of the most modern in Africa. Only three years old, the cargo terminal was as brawny as anything you'd find in Louisville. It was surprising precisely because it was so unexceptional. The same was true for its contents. Piled on racks rising sixty feet high were crates of spare parts for ministers' Mercedes-Benzes, refrigerators, plasma screens, and industrial-strength PCs reserved for one of the city's Internet companies—a litany of goods most Americans would never expect to find traversing the sub-Sahara, where three hundred million people scrape by on less than a dollar a day. There were roses too. A cooler the size of a railway car was stuffed to the ceiling with pallets ticketed for the Aalsmeer.

What we didn't find was our cargo. "They're gone," barked Berhanu Kassa upon spotting us nosing around the heaps. Puffing his chest and grinning as he strode toward us, the airline's cargo chief radiated competence. By way of a greeting, he briskly informed us that everything had left on earlier flights and there was nothing to see here. It was about then that Unnithan—whose eyes had never quit roaming the floor—began moaning.

They were still here. Or the previous shipments were, anyway, and the ones before that. Half hidden beneath assorted parcels lay a pair of tightly bound gray bundles bearing Swift's logo and a hand-scrawled address. "Brenda Ghondo, Lusaka-Zambia," read one, while the other was postmarked to Kampala, Uganda's capital. They should have left days ago, and according to the airline's records, they had. (In lieu of scanners and tracking numbers, both sides relied on e-mail and Scout's honor.) Kassa deflated. Deputies were summoned, angry inquiries made, blame and responsibility assigned. Finally, it was decided the bundles were too bulky for their own good; they kept getting bumped to make room.

Unnithan's face froze into a rictus grin. "It's priority cargo! You have to give it priority!" he spat. An Easter-egg hunt ensued, the two of us bounding through the room comparing serial numbers, turning up additional parcels bound for Harare and Luanda, days after they'd supposedly been delivered. "Oh, my God," he muttered under his breath, picturing a horde of angry mamas on his doorstep back in Sharjah, demanding to know where in the Congo their merchandise went. He cornered Kassa. "They're saying, 'It all arrived yesterday, boss,'" his deputies having closed ranks to blame Dubai's customs for the holdup. It was a good excuse—one package had been torn open and resealed, barely, with official-looking tape.

At length, after many protestations, promises, veiled threats, and assurances that every last package would leave tomorrow, we adjourned for the afternoon. I made my excuses and slipped away via taxi—one of the city's fleet of vintage diesel Mercedeses circling aimlessly—to the Merkato, billed by the guidebooks as "the largest street market in Africa." But it's no street fair—more like a hundred city blocks razed and replaced by a bazaar of bewildering proportions, with no one bothering to clear away the rubble. Seven thousand stalls throng the muddy streets and cracked shells. The most famous sell coffee, first grown on these hillsides a thousand years ago.

There are markets for everything, from sheet metal to mattresses to "local handicrafts" made in China. Ephram Endalamaw told me as much when I popped in his closet-size shop along Stationary Row. He's Addis's one-man answer to OfficeMax, the fixer the embassies call when they run low on toner. His own supply is courtesy of a gang of mamas who fly it here by the crate, nonstop from Guangzhou.

Also for sale is Ethiopia's most perishable good, a leaf with a bigger kick than coffee. Khat (rhymes with "pot") is the drug of choice in neighboring Djibouti, whose capital grinds to a halt upon receiving its daily fix. Similar to cocaine, but with an unusually lucid high, khat leaves lose their potency within forty-eight hours of being picked, with prices falling in tandem. And so every afternoon, an Ethiopian Airlines khat shuttle departs for Djibouti City, where dealers are in a frenzy by the time it touches down. A demolition derby follows as they tear through the streets, lobbing standing orders to customers who proceed to lock their doors, clear their heads, and stuff their cheeks for the day's duration. Not since the Opium Wars has one country, through a combination of maliciousness and logistics, pushed another into drug addiction.

Last Call

Unnithan was triumphant at breakfast the next morning. "They're lying to us," he said, laughing, relieved to have caught them. As if it were ever in doubt. The home office confirmed our cargo had been lingering here for days. When we entered the terminal an hour later, rolling our shoulders and ready for round two, Kassa had had the good sense to disappear. On the undercard were a series of deputies who did what came naturally to them: stonewalled us. The first, sizing us up from behind his desk, opened by strangely insisting the shipments weren't here at all.

"They left on the twenty-ninth," he said, officiously consulting his database. Unnithan's cheeks sank deeper and deeper into a nest of dimples; the angrier he got, the cuddlier. But he was more puzzled than anything else, trying to wrap his head around the institutional languorousness. "Why isn't it gone? Why didn't you tell us?" *Have you no respect for commerce?*

Having exhausted his capacity to catch flak this morning, the deputy handed us off to another manager, this one gaunt with watery eyes, looking as if he was about to cry. Unnithan did his best to oblige. "They're going out today," he said. "We want to see it. Today, our shipment will move."

Kassa reappeared to hear our list of demands. He would personally escort us onto the tarmac, he said, but until then there were hours to kill and security passes to arrange. In the meantime, we were granted an audience with the airline's chief operating officer, Tewolde Gebremariam, who received us behind a burnished desk in an office doubling as a midcentury time capsule. He waxed rhapsodic about his forthcoming 787s, unintentionally echoing the sheikhs three hours away. "We know the 787 can fly ten hours nonstop," he said. "Within that ten-hour radius are five billion people. This is tremendous! Although we've always developed Addis as the best hub in Africa, we have an opportunity to make it even bigger by moving these five billion through it. Being a landlocked nation, air freight plays a major role, but connecting Africa to the forces of globalization is ultimately about connecting people. The 787 is globalization in action."

The last flight was boarding now. A bus dropped us at a 737 where a dozen ramp workers were busily loading luggage. "First the luggage, then the SAM. Hopefully," Unnithan muttered. His bundles were half hidden beneath a tarp; the sky was gray and ominous, the forecast calling for rain. It was a full flight, so the hold was jammed with carry-on cargo. It was time for triage—what needs to go? To Unnithan's satisfaction, one of his bundles was added to the conveyor belt propped against the hold. One down, a dozen to go.

It began to rain, softly at first. The three of us—Unnithan, Kassa, and I—took shelter beneath a wing. More luggage arrived, and space dwindled. The summer squall arrived in force, the tarmac appearing to undulate as raindrops smacked it. We crowded closer under the wing, watching water pool on the tarps and dribble onto cardboard. Bound for the Congo, according to the manifest, were shirts, jeans, belts, shoes, dolls, handbags, a TV and stand, a computer, a "medical machine," two tons of diapers, and eight hundred pounds of "rubberized alphabet letters." All this heading to a country where 80 percent of its sixty-five million citizens live on fifty cents a day.

Headed to Luanda, capital of Angola, where twenty-three children die out of every thousand born: shoes; clothes, and DVD players. To Lusaka, capital of Zambia, where two-thirds of the inhabitants live in slums: T-shirts, TVs, and a "home theater system." To Lagos, the world's fastest-growing megacity, where more than half its residents live on less than a dollar a day: five thousand pounds of clothes, hot plates, cell phone chargers, speakers, DVD players, handbags, and "ladies' shoes."

And to Harare . . . I never learned what was headed to Zimbabwe, but I took it as a miracle anything made it there at all. Inflation was running between 1,000,000 and 9,000,000 percent at the time, when your morning coffee cost twenty-five billion Zimbabwean bucks—a billion more than an hour ago. I stood slack-jawed before those bundles whenever I saw them in Addis, Guangzhou, and Dubai, amazed that anyone had bothered keeping the trade routes open when prices were likely to double between the order and delivery. Harare's supermarket shelves were empty; there was no meat, no milk, no bread, no fuel. They had *nothing*, and yet the airlift continued—the filaments of human desire, vanity, and necessity spinning the thinnest of lifelines from the sky.

10

THE SUSTAINABLE AEROTROPOLIS?

Are airports the ghost towns of tomorrow? Skeptics say that high oil prices and concern for global warming will stem the trend of air travel. Kasarda says it will never happen. We will keep flying—and the world's poorest will suffer if we don't.

Judgment Day Postponed: Peak Whale and Peak Coal

One hundred and fifty years ago, the world faced an energy crisis. Call it "peak whale." Whaling was one of the first truly global concerns. Tea clippers rounding Cape Horn passed fleets of whalers bound for both the Arctic and South Pacific. By the mid-nineteenth century, it was one of America's largest industries, immortalized in *Moby-Dick*. For more than a hundred years, oil extracted from whale blubber lit the lamps of drawing rooms and hovels alike, and made its way into candles, perfume, and lubricants. Without it, the West would have fallen quite literally into darkness.

The peak came hard and fast. After doubling and redoubling again in the 1820s and '30s, the size of the Yankee whaling fleet peaked first in 1846, consisting of 735 ships out of some 900 worldwide. "Production" peaked shortly thereafter, following several seasons of mass slaughter in the Bering Strait; eight thousand humpbacks died in 1853 alone. Prices climbed above $2.50 per gallon—$57 adjusted for inflation!—enriching whalers but leaving consumers in the dark. Six years later, petroleum was discovered in a strike at Titusville, Pennsylvania. Crisis averted. The first fuel refined from black gold was kerosene for a grateful nation's lamps, exactly a century before the first 707 guzzled kerosene-based jet fuel.

The discovery destroyed New England's whaling industry but saved the whales. "Had it not been for the discovery of Coal Oil, the race of whales would soon have become extinct," a California publication noted at the time. "It is estimated that ten years would have used up the whole family."

But the world wasn't out of the woods. Six years later, the British economist William Stanley Jevons declared another long emergency. *The Coal Question*, published in 1865, was *An Inconvenient Truth* for Victorian England—a clear-eyed description of Britain's looming peak coal reckoning, complete with a sobering analysis of the country's coal reserves cross-referenced with its ravenous consumption. The country would run out of coal in less than a hundred years, he estimated, and the result would be cataclysmic. "It is the material energy of the country—the universal aid—the factor in everything we do," he wrote with spooky prescience. "With coal almost any feat is possible or easy; without it we are thrown back into the laborious poverty of early times."

Once Britain had run out, its ability to sustain 10 percent population growth each decade (as it had done for the previous seven) would collapse under its inability to grow or transport enough food. Worse, there appeared to be no alternatives—no fuels to replace it, in Jevons's estimation—and any increases in the steam engine's efficiency would only make it cheaper and easier to use, thus stoking greater demand and faster depletion.

These were not the ravings of a fringe theorist. Jevons was as sober and as mainstream an economist as any Nobel-winning member of the Chicago School today. His suggestion made its way onto the floor of the House of Commons, where no less than future prime minister William Gladstone—then chancellor of the exchequer—referred to the looming peak coal crisis in his budget speech of 1866. A "coal panic" ensued, leading to the appointment of a blue-ribbon royal commission. Five years later, it published the first detailed estimate of Britain's coal reserves but managed to sidestep Jevons's conclusions altogether. The public went back to sleep. Britain's coal did not run out, and the isles didn't become fully reliant on oil until after World War I.

The "Jevons Paradox" still troubles us: *The more efficiently you use a resource, the more of it you will use.* Put another way: The better the machine, the broader its adoption. And there has never been a better machine for transportation than the jet engine. A pair of General Electric

GE90-115B turbofans mounted on a 777 are capable of generating 230,000 pounds of thrust between them—enough to propel four hundred passengers between New York and London in six and a half hours, with gas mileage equivalent to fifty-five miles per gallon per passenger. But the aggregate cost is still staggering: twenty-five thousand gallons of fuel ignited in the upper atmosphere. Fifty years of refinements have yielded engines cleaner by an order of magnitude, but any gains in efficiency have been far outpaced by exponential growth in the number of passengers—the inevitable result of falling costs and ticket prices.

The Jevons Paradox illustrates why infinitely renewable, zero-carbon fuels are a necessity—because merely efficient solutions only postpone the day of reckoning. Peak whale teaches us how an entire way of life underpinned by a single source of energy can be transformed or vanish overnight thanks to timely substitution. If you had told Herman Melville in 1851 that whaling would be a historical footnote within a decade—replaced by viscous tar oozing out of the ground—he would have been dumbfounded. "One day the planks stream with freshets of blood and oil," he wrote in *Moby-Dick*, and the next day, they were gone. How could he have imagined the sweet crude yielding light, flight, locomotion, and the Green Revolution?

Peak whale ended when whalers "ran out of customers before they ran out of whales," quipped the environmentalist Amory Lovins, who was charting paths to a renewable future before Jimmy Carter wore cardigans in the White House. So how will peak oil end?

The Reckoning: Peak Oil

You couldn't ask for a more ominous example of the Jevons Paradox circa 2020 than the prospect of a hundred million tourists and traders transiting the Gulf on the New Silk Road. Anyone paying close attention to oil prices and carbon footprints might reasonably conclude that a Middle East remade in Dubai's image is a looming catastrophe. There is a growing consensus among activists, energy analysts, and fliers alike that aviation is unsustainable at its current pace, ethically and economically.

Their reasons for feeling this way can be narrowed to a pair of culprits—peak oil and climate change—entwined in a single, suicidal braid. We are running out of cheap, plentiful oil, this argument goes, because we are burning more of it every day, releasing greenhouse gases in the process. As we do, both oil prices and temperatures rise until one of two disasters befalls us: the glaciers melt, oceans flood, crops fail, and the world sinks into famine; or the wells run dry and civilization as we know it ends. Right now, we're in a race to see which happens first. Worse, the two form a sort of Chinese finger trap—the harder we struggle to find more oil, the higher we turn up Earth's thermostat. We can't just drill, baby, drill without making things worse—the oil spill in the gulf taught us that.

Air travel's complicity in peak oil and climate change evokes the food miles argument writ large: moving people and goods halfway around the world when they could be made or grown or live closer to home is ethically indefensible. And it depends on a fuel we happen to be running out of, with no substitutes ready to take its place. One way or another, proponents believe, tomorrow's flights should and will be canceled.

We may choose to fly—or not to—but from a carbon perspective, the obvious choice is not necessarily the most meaningful one, or the most destructive. Remember the sun-drenched Kenyan roses and their hothouse-bred Dutch cousins—computing carbon's bottom line requires calculus, not simple addition.

Calculating peak oil requires different equations. When we talk about peak oil, we're really talking about two things. One is Hubbert's Peak, the moment when global oil supply reaches a maximum production rate—eighty-six million barrels a day and climbing (for now)—and then plunges into irreversible decline. It's named for M. King Hubbert, the Shell-employed geophysicist who formulated the theory in 1956. He saw oil production following a bell curve, rising quickly in the beginning as easy gushers are tapped, then leveling off as the obvious fields are discovered and drilled, and finally falling when all that's left are the pockets that are more difficult to recover. In the fifties, he predicted that America's own oil production would peak by 1970, and nailed it. For an encore, he predicted a global peak by 2000. That day of reckoning has been postponed by new discoveries, higher efficiency, alternative energy, and unconventional sources (such as the Canadian tar sands), but in any case where the resource in question is finite and nonrenewable, a peak is inevitable. Especially when global demand is projected to reach 125 million barrels a day by 2030.

And then there is peak oil, the reckoning. Once we tip, rising demand will forever outstrip supply, and the widening gap between the two will place unparalleled stress on the global economy. In 1998, a barrel of crude fetched $8.50 on the futures market; a year into the Iraq War, it was $30 a barrel. Four years later it hit its peak of $147.27, and that was with the Saudis insisting they could still pump faster. Once the peak is apparent, prices will never fall again. The best-case scenario is global recession and maybe depression, as the cost to manufacture, transport, and consume anything becomes prohibitively expensive. In the worst-case scenario, we're tagging along with Mad Max in *The Road Warrior*, battling neobarbarians for the last drops of the "precious juice."

The world doesn't need to slip into a second Dark Ages before aviation ceases to be feasible. By last spring, oil prices were creeping toward $100 again, and there are plenty of economists who believe renewed demand will drive the price to $200 or higher. There's no aircraft flying now or in the next twenty years that could turn a profit carrying those costs. "Many airline business models cease to work at $135-a-barrel oil prices" was one analyst's widely noted estimate.

The stagflationary combo of 2008's unprecedented spike and a weak dollar forced American carriers to jettison free baggage, free tickets, food, flight attendants, planes, destinations, and even themselves (via merger) in increasingly desperate attempts to offset an 80 percent rise in the cost of jet fuel. Twenty-five airlines worldwide filed for bankruptcy in its wake. Passengers, meanwhile, are more miserable than ever, as there are more of us crowding into fewer planes as the industry tries to shrink itself back to profitability.

Not to downplay the devastating effect this has had on central Florida's time-share market, but the much scarier question is what effect such prices would have on the world's airborne supply chains. In 2005, Jeff Rubin, then the chief economist of the Canadian investment bank CIBC World Markets, set out to answer just that. "Soaring Oil Prices Will Make the World Rounder" was the title of his first report, in which he persuasively argued that higher oil prices, translated into higher transportation costs, would shortly undo forty-five years' worth of free trade. The real flattener of the era, he claimed, had been cheap shipping. Beginning in 1960, exports as a share of global GDP boomed by more than

50 percent—until the OPEC oil embargo in 1973. Export growth flat-lined for the next dozen years, through a second oil shock and relatively high prices, until the glut of the 1980s caused exports to soar again.

Falling trade barriers and steady growth didn't make a dent in the 1970s. The X factor had been oil, and the free ride was over. "In a world of $100 per barrel crude prices," he wrote, "distance costs money," and substantially more of it to move a forty-foot shipping container from Hong Kong to New York than from Mexico. The world's factory would come undone as soaring transportation costs took precedence over cheap labor.

Rubin revisited the topic when oil prices approached their all-time high of $147 in a research note beginning "Globalization is reversible." There were signs of entire industries leaving their low-cost outposts and heading home. Steel, the symbol of America's vanished industrial might, was now cheaper to roll in the United States than in China, once you factored in the seaborne shipping costs. The next to go, in his estimation (and to Mexico, probably): "furniture, apparel, footwear, metal manufacturing, and industrial machinery," all of which travel by boat, at triple what it cost in 2000. Rubin left the bank shortly thereafter to write a book, ominously titled *Why Your World Is About to Get a Whole Lot Smaller.*

Airborne misery, grounded planes, shrinking supply chains, and a hot, round, and thirsty planet. *This* is the age of the aerotropolis? When you put it that way, it does sound implausible. As one letter to *Fast Company* put it: "As I see it, an aerotropolis is a multibillion-dollar infrastructure balancing precariously on a petro-dependent air-freight industry, to accelerate the creation of a planetwide sweatshop producing gewgaws for Walmart. And it is doomed. Oil-fueled, growth-dependent megacorporations, militaries, and governments are dinosaurs, frantically mating in their desperate attempts to survive, and producing monstrous offspring such as aerotropoli. Wasting our precious time, money, and energy on nightmare projects like the aerotropolis is criminally insane."

Supposing the end of aviation is indeed at hand, with the aerotropolis reduced to rubble. What are the alternatives? The prevailing assumption is there aren't any, even in a future of otherwise clean, renewable energy. At least one treatise on the subject dismisses air travel in a few sentences, as if flying—once restricted to all but the wealthiest passengers—could quietly return to the rarified air of Pan Am Clippers and the jet set without leaving any turbulence in its wake. With few exceptions, aviation's staunchest critics have more or less demurred on imagining what a grounded world might look like, probably because they can't begin to fully wrap their heads around it.

One detailed postpeak oil scenario in which flying is still with us was advanced by Anthony Perl and Richard Gilbert, a pair of Canadian transportation experts. They imagined a world in which continually rising oil prices have cut domestic flying by 40 percent by 2025, in which the number of primary airports has fallen from around four hundred to fifty, and instead of multiple flights on the hour between New York and San Francisco, only a handful of super-duper-jumbo jets carrying eight hundred passengers ply the route daily. The rest of America's transportation network has switched over to trains, trolleys, and assorted vehicles capable of plugging into the solar- and wind-powered grid. Life goes on over e-mail, although Kasarda's Law has presumably been repealed.

But don't dismiss the aerotropolis just yet. In its ability to redraw the map, aviation possesses the power to sketch a more prosperous world. Even if there were no clean, renewable substitutes for jet fuel on the horizon, it would still be necessary to rearrange the rest of our overheating civilization to save it.

Flying's Inconvenient Truths

In 2007, the Travel Foundation, a British nonprofit promoting sustainable tourism, asked a thousand Britons, "From what you have read and heard, roughly what percentage of carbon dioxide emissions do you believe are due to aircraft?" The percentage in question was the global total, a figure including everything from China's coal-fired power plants (where a new one is opening every week) to Mumbai's surging traffic jams, to the hungover sprawl of our housing bubble. Put another way, how did binge flying's sins stack up against the rest?

The foundation suspected the answers might skew high, as the link between cheap fares and climate change had been hotly debated in Britain for years. The opening of Europe's skies with 1992's Single European Market agreement opened the door for Ryanair, easyJet, and a host of continental copycats. In short order, they convinced blue-collar Britain that a weekend jaunt to Spain could cost less than cab fare to Heathrow. Of course, they didn't fly from Heathrow, and their customers could rarely afford the Costa del Sol. Their destinations were second- and third-string ones like Murcia, a hardscrabble Spanish city quickly overrun by beach resorts, golf courses, condos, and Cockney accents (and which later became ground zero of the Spanish housing bust). Even when oil was still hovering around $130 a barrel, the average fare aboard Ryanair was only $63 each way.

As you'd expect, the dangling carrot of rock-bottom prices between any two points in Europe galvanized travelers. The number of packed flights from Blackpool to Nice and Budapest to Barcelona doubled, redoubled, and somehow doubled again. During the two-year run-up to the recent peak, the passengers aboard Europe's no-frills fleet doubled from 60 million to 120 million. Two years after that, Ryanair, easyJet, and Air Berlin alone carried 140 million among them. The number alighting in Murcia, meanwhile, rose twentyfold in just over a decade, from 88,000 in 1995 to 1.9 million in 2007. To calculate the cost of its boom in carbon terms, those flights generate 1.1 million tons of CO_2 each year. If a couple flying from Leeds chose to forgo the Med for a drive to England's Lake District instead, they would emit about one-seventieth of the amount needed for Murcia. But the odds are good they chose the sea.

Britons are now the world's highest per capita owners of foreign second homes. An upscale answer to Murcia is Carcassonne in southern France, where more than three thousand jobs have been created since Ryanair started flying there in 1998. The additional economic activity brought to the region is estimated at 374 million euros. The full scope of Europe's decade-long tourism boom (aka the "Ryanair effect") is said to have created 1.4 million jobs and $85 billion for all involved. Some effects have been harder to quantify, like the Polish doctors who work the weekend shifts in Britain and fly home Monday morning.

But at what cost to global warming? The European Environment Agency released a report in 2008 stating that aviation's emissions had "far exceeded growth by any other mode," rising 73 percent between 1990 and 2005. No one really knew how much the no-frills carriers were to blame. Into this information gap charged protest groups like Plane Stupid, which earned its militant reputation by unfurling banners atop Westminster Palace with slogans like "WE FLY, WE DIE."

The group contends on its website that "despite myths propagated by the airline industry, aviation already accounts for 13% of the UK's contribution to climate change . . . We could close every factory, lock away every car and turn off every light in the country, but it won't halt global warming if we carry on taking planes as often as we do." The group also asserts that most aviation is unnecessary (because the flights are so short), noisy, poisonous, and fundamentally corrupt, placing a huge tax burden on Britain and receiving only CO_2 tonnage in return.

Last but not least, they charge that "'cheap' flights are for the privileged," the weekenders heading to Carcassonne, not the nation's have-wrench-will-travel plumbers. This claim is meant to deflect counterattacks from aviation's dwindling British supporters that climate change is really a cover for class discrimination. As Ryanair's salty chief executive, Michael O'Leary, put it, "Their solution is, stop ordinary people or poor people from flying. Let's have flying back with just the rich people, and then all will be well again. Yeh know, bollocks." Climate change, in his opinion, is "horseshit."

Attempts to reframe the argument as class struggle haven't gained much traction. If anything, a social stigma against flying has begun to settle across Europe, akin to Americans' nausea over SUVs. The EU has voted to incorporate aviation into its cap-and-trade scheme, requiring airlines to pay for 15 percent of their pollution beginning in 2012—a lot to ask from an industry barely breaking even. Three U.S. airlines are suing for an exemption, and the governments of the United States, Canada, and Mexico have lobbied the United Nations for the same. "When you look at some of the taxes and fees being discussed in Europe," said an MIT researcher, "we might as well bankrupt our industry today."

It was against this grand tableau of grandstanding, stat-slinging, politicking, and weekend homes in Languedoc that a thousand Britons—all of whom, incidentally, had taken trips abroad in the past year—were asked: Just how bad *is* flying, anyway, as a percentage of all the carbon emissions in the world?

Nearly a third were honest, confessing they had no idea. A fifth guessed 40 percent or more. Half thought it was at least 15 percent. The remainder penciled in 5 percent or less.

The answer: 2 *percent.*

How did they overshoot the real figure so badly? Because we tend to think of our carbon footprints as the outcome of personal choices and personal virtue—"What can *I* do to shrink mine?" we ask. The answers, inevitably, are drive a hybrid, eat organic, and recycle. (When it comes to flying, the Japanese airline ANA discreetly asks passengers to use the terminal bathroom before boarding, in order to lighten the load and save fuel.) Seen from this perspective, boarding a transoceanic flight is maybe the single most destructive thing you could possibly choose. But underlying our individual choices are nearly invisible networks and systems of which aviation is just one, generating 2 percent of emissions. The others that make up everyday life are much worse:

Housing. The true cost of America's housing bubble is a landscape generating half of all greenhouse-gas emissions, according to estimates based on data from the U.S. Energy Information Administration. Residential buildings alone account for 21 percent of national energy consumption—a number driven by the expanding size of the average U.S. home, which today measures twenty-four hundred square feet, a 140 percent increase since 1950.

Food. As mentioned earlier, the United Nations estimates livestock's share of worldwide greenhouse gases at 18 percent, a combination of methane produced by the animals and the fossil fuels used to raise and eat them. Even a contrarian like the agricultural historian James E. McWilliams—no fan of organic labels or Michael Pollan—readily concedes meat carries too high a price for us to keep eating it.

Driving. Every form of transport known, save those powered by foot or by wind, combines to emit 13 percent of all emissions. Aviation is a fraction of that fraction—a sixth of the exhaust from cars, trucks, and anything else powered by an internal combustion engine. And that's before everyone in the developing world receives a driver's license.

But aviation is growing faster than any of these, a statistic its critics have zeroed in on. In echoes of the Jevons Paradox, it's growing fast enough to outstrip all of the industry's earnest efforts to increase fuel efficiency, whether that means younger, lighter, and fuller planes, cleaner engines, or smoother descents—although the airlines are striving to keep up. In the United States at least, their emissions actually *fell* for most of the last decade due to belt-tightening—by 2.6 percent between 2000 and 2007, despite carrying 20 percent more passengers and cargo over that span. For similar reasons, the price of jet fuel actually peaked ten years ago, just before 9/11. But Europe's easyJet addiction will prove harder to quit, and coupled with renewed growth in the Middle East and Asia, flying's total carbon contribution will likely rise to 5 percent by 2050.

Another caveat is that commercial aircraft release their carbon in the lower reaches of the stratosphere, where greenhouse gases collect. To account for this, the Intergovernmental Panel on Climate Change has raised aviation's effective contribution to 3 percent—a figure equal to a quarter of the traffic on the world's highways, or half the respiration of our homes. Even at its highest estimates, it isn't likely aviation will overtake driving as one of the most ergregious global warmers, let alone factories and electric turbines. So why don't we focus our energies on fixing them instead?

The biggest smokestack in the world is China, and this has nothing to do with its airports. Its power plants and factories consume a third of the world's coal—2.4 billion tons annually and growing, already double what it was burning a decade ago. China expects to have 130 million cars on its roads by 2020, and more than the United States by 2050 (or maybe 2040). It has overtaken the United States as the world's worst polluter, partly because of its size, but mostly because of its waste. China posted the highest six-month rise in carbon emissions of any nation in history through the winter and spring of 2010. The World Bank estimates as much as half of China's miraculous growth would vanish if the costs of rampant pollution and environmental degradation were factored in. If China's emissions continue climbing at the same rate as they have for the past thirty years, the country will emit more greenhouse gases in the next thirty than the United States has in its entire existence. For these reasons, China is going green by building the world's largest domestic market for batteries, wind, and solar energy, and then cornering our market via air.

As for peak oil's collision with the world's factory, it's worth restating a few fundamental statistics quickly: a third of the value of all the goods made in the world, three trillion dollars' worth, travels by air, while composing barely 1 percent of their weight. Air cargo's growth outpaced world trade's by a factor of four-to-one over the last thirty-five years, and blew past global GDP growth by nine-to-one, meaning more and more of what's worth making and moving (including half of American exports) is aloft. In the Instant Age, Kasarda says, "The price of oil matters less than the price of speed."

Contrary to Jeff Rubin's assertion, the real costs of air transport have not fallen or risen much since the early 1980s. We don't send an increasing array of goods by air because it's cheap; we do it because those goods have grown lighter and more valuable over thirty years. As Chinese manufacturers have learned, waiting for your ship to come in carries its own costs in the form of lost sales and obsolescence. As high as oil prices have climbed, they must still climb much further before they outweigh the premiums we place on labor, economies of scale, and time.

The same is true for moving people. Increasing productivity in a global economy of ideas is predicated on reach, connectivity, and speed. So is tourism, which makes up about 10 percent of worldwide GDP and as much as 30 percent in developing countries. When you boil down the multiplier effects of such concentrated speed and efficiency, aviation's contributions to our well-being are larger and growing more rapidly than its carbon emissions. This is all a complicated way of saying aviation does less harm than good. So why are we trying to strangle it?

The Doomslayers

"If aviation were to stop, we would be inconvenienced. But for those at the bottom rungs of the economic ladder, it would mean their livelihoods disappear," John Kasarda said. Whether Kenyan flower farmers or Chinese factory workers, the end of aviation would mean the end of their incomes. "Those are millions of jobs and billions of dollars. How we will address climate change is through new technology, and not at the expense of growth and connectivity. When Park and Burgess created their model of how cities develop—in which the poor move up and move outward—what was unspoken is that it depends on growth. There's no empirical evidence growth has damaged people; in fact, all the evidence is to the contrary."

And if I needed proof, all I had to do was look outside at a dozen lanes of traffic lurching along Beijing's Third Ring Road. Rush hour was a little more sluggish than the day before, after absorbing another thousand new cars in the night. A few months later, the city would experience a two-week, sixty-mile-long traffic jam smoking all the way to Inner

Mongolia. Several floors below me, hundreds of Chinese and American officials attending Kasarda's "Airport Cities" conference were learning how to build an aerotropolis back home. "There are those who would say I'm like the person who's jumped off the Empire State Building and says, 'So far, so good,' as I pass the fortieth floor," he said. "But in the long term, all the indicators are up.

"There's so little objectivity in this debate," he said, then sighed. "Without it, the politics override the empirical data. You see serious people overreacting so they can claim they're 'doing something,' and they're doing something before they assess the real costs of whatever it is they're doing, not to mention the benefits of what we already have. We could go back to the Stone Age if we really wanted to reduce our carbon footprints to zero, but the cure would be worse than the disease.

"People seem to be very Malthusian right now," he added. "Thomas Malthus argued food supply would increase, and so would population— only faster—until the latter outraced the former and then you would have famine and catastrophe. Instead, for the last two hundred years, population grew, standards of living went up, and life expectancy soared. Connectivity was the key—connectivity and trade. Every study has shown that more connectivity equals more opportunities for social mobility. What the critics miss is that if you take away aviation, you're pulling rungs out of the ladder. They simply don't realize how interconnected these things are."

As a thought experiment, I asked what would happen if we preemptively grounded every plane but otherwise left the world unchanged— imagine a volcanic ash crisis that lasts forever. "Many foods would disappear. Fresh fish? Fresh fruit? Gone. Global supply chains would be crippled. Over the long run, the efficiencies of manufacturing in China would vanish, and so would the low prices we're used to. We'd suffer dramatic inflation, along with a corresponding rise in interest rates that would hurt the entire economy. The poorest will be hit first and hit hardest, because the cost of everyday life would go up dramatically."

When it comes to peak oil taking the choice out of our hands, he's heard this story before: in 1968, when Paul Ehrlich wrote *The Population Bomb*, and in 1972, when the Club of Rome published *Limits to Growth*. Both soberly concluded billions would perish in famines and plagues by the 1980s or, at the very latest, 2000. They were wrong then, of course—or maybe just early? The economist Julian Simon (a colleague of and an inspiration to Kasarda in his younger days) took on these gloomy Malthusians, earning the sobriquet "the Doomslayer" for demolishing their critiques. Drawing on raw statistics, he proved the opposite was true—we are actually living in a world of increasing abundance, made possible by a cornucopia of innovations. Commodity prices have fallen across the board for two hundred years—oil, copper, steel, lead, rice, cotton, you name it—thanks to new technologies, more efficient production, and timely substitutions. Simon believed the population bomb was really a boom. "Resources come out of people's minds more than out of the ground or air," he argued. "Minds matter economically as much as or more than hands or mouths. Human beings create more than they use, on average. It had to be so, or we would be an extinct species."

Simon was right, up to a point. He blithely asserted growth could continue unchecked for the next *seven billion years*, never minding that earth would be a bit crowded by then. But he also placed his bets on human ingenuity before he had the benefit of the Internet. One way of reading Kasarda's Law is to substitute the speed and frequency of human connections for the sheer numbers in Simon's predictions. Just as consciousness is a function of firing synapses rather than raw gray matter, Kasarda believes the key to cracking peak oil and climate change is collaboration, unfettered by space or time. This is counterintuitive, to say the least, but the same effect is already seen in cities. Researchers at the Santa Fe Institute have found that cities grow smarter and faster as they get bigger. "By almost any measure," they wrote, "the larger the city's population, the greater the innovation and wealth creation per person." Their growth becomes "superlinear" as the number of connections between people increases exponentially. Who's to say the same isn't true at a global scale, and hasn't been for fifty years?

"People keep saying things are different this time," Kasarda said, "but the data refutes this. If you correlate revenue seat miles"—a measure of how many passengers are flying, and how far they fly—"with GDP, it's basically a one-to-one correlation. As people grow wealthier, they fly more," because of the rising premiums we place on our time. "If you compare seat miles with oil prices, however, there is no correlation. It just keeps growing.

"One of two things will happen," he added. "Either oil prices will stay down, or the airlines will adapt. They always do. We talk endlessly about their individual losses, but the industry has only grown. So what if oil goes back above a hundred dollars a barrel? They'll adapt, they'll restructure, some will fold. What does that mean for the aerotropolis? It means businesses are going to aggregate even more closely around the major hubs, because that's where connectivity will be the most abundant. Telecommuting won't make a dent. From the invention of the telephone to Facebook, every advance in communication only increases our desire to travel. The trillions of connections occurring now will create a need for mobility that never previously existed. What would we turn to without planes? Trains? Cars? Think of the carbon that goes into paving a fifty-mile stretch of highway. Think of the noise high-speed trains would create along their entire length—and where will you put them?

"Where aviation's critics get it wrong is in their assumption that the technology never changes, or changes very little. That's crazy! The first flight was at Kitty Hawk in 1903. Between then and 1969, when the Concorde took off, we went from the Wright Brothers flying a few hundred feet to traveling at Mach two across the Atlantic. No form of transportation has ever changed so quickly. Look at biofuels, new engines, and composite planes—aviation evolves faster than anyone thinks."

Its role in halting climate change boils down to a classic debate of *equity* versus *efficiency*. Plane Stupid demands equity—if the airlines are responsible for 2, 3, or 5 percent of greenhouse gases, then they should be required to contribute 2, 3, or 5 percent of the solution. Doing their fair share could mean burning biofuels; flying lighter, fuller, fewer planes; or grounding them completely. Efficiency advocates prefer plucking the lowest-hanging fruit, pursuing the fastest, cheapest, most effective solution to the problem at hand, regardless of who is to blame or who will shoulder the burden. (This is why efficiency is often politically untenable—because it isn't fair.) The problem in this case is sharply curtailing CO_2 emissions globally, which means the answer might not necessarily be found at Heathrow. The aftermath of previous oil shocks suggests efficiency is winning the argument.

In the 1970s, when oil prices were the pressing issue instead of climate change, petroleum was hastily replaced wherever alternatives existed. Coal, natural gas, and nuclear power were pressed into service for heating homes, powering factories, and generating electricity. What we couldn't phase out was gasoline—which continues to fuel 95 percent of all vehicles—although consumers rushed to embrace fuel-efficient Japanese imports, just as they do now. As a consequence, transportation's oil consumption grew by about 1.3 percent per year between the first oil shock of 1973 and the 2008 peak. But residential uses fell 2.1 percent, commercial uses 2.4 percent, and power generation 4.8 percent. Americans use *half* as much energy per capita as they did in 1973. While the decade's oil shocks weren't enough to wean us off fossil fuels—"the moral equivalent of war" in President Carter's famous formulation—they did spur us to greater efficiency.

Before the crisis in 1973, global oil consumption grew 8 percent a year. It fell to 4 percent afterward thanks to substitutions, but this was still fast enough to terrify Carter, who estimated in his 1977 fireside chat, "This means that just to stay even we need the production of a new Texas every year, an Alaskan North Slope every nine months, or a new Saudi Arabia every three years. Obviously, this cannot continue." And it didn't. Following the second shock of the Iranian Revolution, growth fell to 2 percent during another successful hunt for efficiencies. Demand kept falling through the 1980s and 1990s, until the past decade's bubble began to inflate it again.

Just as the 1970s shocks were enough to convince heavy industry and utilities to shy away from oil, the combination of the recent peak and climate change appears to have had a similar effect on driving. Americans at last seem ready to swap gasoline for electricity, while Chinese automakers like BYD plan to skip over internal combustion engines completely. ExxonMobil is convinced we are already past our peak use of gasoline in this country, as the combination of fuel efficiency and renewable sources permanently destroy demand, driving gas consumption downward. The International Energy Agency believes the same is true for oil throughout the developed world. As Amory Lovins predicted, the world's supermajors may run out of customers before they run out of oil.

The last holdouts are likely to be the airlines, which require a dense and ferocious amount of energy to defy the laws of physics. From an efficiency standpoint, the best solution for halving transportation's share of carbon emissions is to electrify cars from renewable sources, leaving whatever oil is left for aviation. Its share of emissions would look progressively worse while the total shrinks, but we'd get over the cognitive dissonance.

"We are driven as humans to adapt to new technologies, and we're blessed with the ability to transfer them quickly across societies," Kasarda told me in Beijing. "But people don't change their ideas and beliefs nearly as fast. In anthropology, it's known as 'cultural lag.' And the lag in this case means we're able to envision disaster but not the future. Will we find alternatives? Absolutely. When pressed, we have always found substitutions."

Don't take Kasarda's word for it. Ask James Hansen, NASA's chief climatologist—and climate change's chief catastrophist. He tutored Al Gore and survived multiple attempts by the Bush administration to silence him. He is utterly convinced the world stands on the precipice of disaster. But Hansen is also an ardent believer in efficiency over equity. In his view, the culprit is coal, pure and simple. "Coal is eighty percent of the planet's problem," he has said. "You have to keep your eye on the ball and not waste your efforts. The number one enemy is coal and we should never forget that." He has called for the shutdown of all coal-fired power plants within twenty years.

He has also likened coal trains to "death trains" carrying endangered species to the ovens. He once testified on behalf of protesters charged with criminal damage after occupying a coal-fired power plant in Britain. Their actions were justifiable, he told the court, because rising CO_2 emissions could lead to the extinction of four hundred species. They were acquitted.

Hoping to land him as a character witness, the protesters battling Heathrow's third runway asked for his benediction. Hansen declined. "I don't think it is helpful to be trying to prevent air flight," he told the London *Observer*. Hindering the third runway will hurt more than help, he said. "The number of runways you need for your airports depends on their traffic. You don't want to be so restrictive that you end up burning more fuel because planes are having to circle and wait to land because of lack of runway space." Aviation wasn't the problem in any case, he stressed.

After angry environmentalists stuffed his in-box, Hansen clarified his comments but didn't retract them. "All I intended to say was that aviation fuel is not a killer for the climate problem," he wrote in a mass e-mail. "At worst case we can use carbon-neutral biofuels . . . There are ways to do biofuels right, for the fuel volume needed for global air traffic."

Which brings us back to the seemingly intractable problem of peak oil—no matter how efficient we are, sooner or later the Jevons Paradox will catch up to us. Switching the world's automotive fleet to electricity will take decades at least, leaving airlines and passengers vulnerable to the whipsawing price of oil. The failure of major exporters to invest in spare capacity during the downturn has only made a second spike more likely. Efficiency gains, renewable sources, and fuel-efficient vehicles may have bought us time, but the peak still looms in the distance.

In fact, we may already be standing on the summit: the IEA, no doomsayer, predicts conventional oil will peak by 2020 if current trends continue. Not to be outdone, the U.K.'s former chief scientist, Sir David King, has circled 2015. (OPEC, he claims, has inflated its reserves for years.) Kuwaiti researchers agree, placing their bet on 2014. And depending on how quickly the world's economies recover, McKinsey estimates the crunch could arrive as early as this year. We don't need Mad Max conditions before airlines can't afford the precious juice.

A magic bullet is necessary—a sustainable, replenishable synthetic fuel identical to kerosene-based Jet A. It needs to burn just as hot but ten times as clean, to appease the quotas of present and future carbon-trading schemes. The obvious building blocks, ethanol and biodiesel, are hopelessly inefficient and have a nasty tendency to freeze at thirty-five thousand feet. Once an alternative is found, enough "refineries" must be built to pump fifty-five billion gallons a year for less than the industry's $61 billion fuel bill. Which is where Sir Richard Branson and a brewery filled with pond scum come in.

Branson, Biofuels, and Balance

Branson is the silver-maned billionaire who is that rarest of creatures: an ardent environmentalist who happens to own an airline—several, in fact, including the spaceships of Virgin Galactic. The Virgin Group chairman reconciles his split personality with earnest displays of penitence: "If you run a dirty business," he has said, taking pains to lump himself in with the sinners, "you should pay for the privilege because you are doing damage."

Not long ago he was an apostate, clinging fast to his disbelief until Al

Gore paid him a visit. After sitting through a live performance of *An Inconvenient Truth*, Branson promptly converted, displaying a neophyte's zeal. Shortly thereafter in 2006, he announced at Bill Clinton's annual summit he would divert all profits from his transportation businesses— mostly planes and a few trains—to develop sustainable, renewable fuels. "We have to wean ourselves off our dependence on fossil fuels," he said between bursts of shocked applause. "Our generation has the knowledge, has the financial resources, and, as importantly, has the willpower to do so." The pledge totaled $3 billion, the most by far any corporation has made to battle global warming.

Branson brilliantly sublimated his savvy airline chief persona into his newfound idealism. Virgin's profits are earmarked not for charity but for R & D. Four years later, the Virgin Green Fund has invested $400 million and counting in various efforts to refine a green alternative to jet fuel and will eventually bring a winner to market as its own proprietary "Virgin Fuel." If he succeeds, his pledge will earn him more than his airlines ever will.

A week after the announcement, Branson held a second press conference in New York, this time under the banner of his airline, Virgin Atlantic. Clearly still feeling his way as the industry's Saint Paul, he tersely explained a series of measures the airline was taking to save fuel and cut emissions in the air and on the ground. These included slower, more gradual descents; using tugs to move planes to and from the runways at JFK and Heathrow; and removing excess weight from every plane by replacing some components with carbon-fiber composites. Taking care to frame the savings in CO_2 tonnage instead of dollars, he noted the tugs would reduce Virgin's carbon footprint at each airport by 90 percent and save two tons of fuel on each of its dozen daily flights between the two cities. If the entire industry were to follow suit, he added, the savings could amount to anywhere between 150 and 180 million tons of CO_2 per year, or about a quarter of aviation's annual emissions. To that end, he had already sent letters to dozens of airlines, airports, and regulators asking for their help in reforming the industry. None of his competitors rallied to help him.

It isn't as if Virgin's tactics have proved to be unsound. Indeed, they were endorsed—in fact if not by name—by the United Nations' environment, weather, and tourism bodies, which jointly published a report two years later recommending essentially everything Virgin had done unilaterally. Their checklist included flying younger, more fuel-efficient planes with more passengers and less dead weight aboard each one. Airlines everywhere have taken steps to trim their fleets of their oldest gas-guzzlers and speed up the delivery of their replacements. Boeing's 787 will be the first in a new generation of aircraft made entirely from lightweight composites, cutting fuel burn (and CO_2) by 20 percent or more. Engine makers Rolls-Royce, GE, and Pratt & Whitney are tinkering with "open rotors" and "geared turbofans," which promise to cut fuel use by a quarter and noise by half.

"None of these ideas are a net cost to the industry," Branson told me after the press conference. "The way to tackle global warming is to come up with ones that are net gains for all involved." The double-fisted appeal to the heart and the head is classic Branson, and animates his entire approach to stopping climate change. Rather than frighten people or plead with them, he has presented the gravest challenge facing the world as an opportunity for both profits and nobility. He acknowledged as much during our conversation. "If you want to achieve something," he said, "it's good to appeal to all aspects of their character. And it's certainly worth pointing out that their children and grandchildren will not forgive them if they don't do something about it. But if you can appeal to their bottom line, that helps enormously."

Branson's sincerity is atypical of the industry's lip service to climate change, which has understandably earned the ire of environmentalists. Airlines were excused from 1997's Kyoto Protocol (never ratified by the United States anyway) and escaped without sanction from the standoff of the Copenhagen Conference. In a transparent bid to defuse the mounting backlash, aviation's trade lobby, the International Air Transport Association, pledged beforehand to reduce emissions to half of 2005 levels by 2050. It would also accept a $5 billion penalty as the price of admission to a global cap-and-trade scheme. Greenpeace denounced the plan as "greenwashing." Even neutral observers found it self-serving.

In Copenhagen, Branson called for binding reduction targets but decried a tax on emissions. "It could be that governments may decide the world is such a catastrophe, they're going to impose measures that will cost the industry money, and we're going to be faced with a balancing act," he told me. "We're suggesting reducing CO_2 emissions from the airline industry from 2 percent to more like 1.5 percent. At the same time, the airline industry produces 8 percent of the GDP of the world. And I suspect that's a fair balance. International airlines are the only way of traveling overseas, but we've got to build cleaner planes and do everything we can."

He has leaned on both Airbus and Boeing to create all-composite planes, and has made it clear to them that fuel efficiency is Virgin Atlantic's overriding concern. But fuel efficiency will take Branson and his peers only so far. If passenger growth resumes its previous 5 percent pace for the next twenty years, as Boeing predicts (much faster than world population growth or GDP), then his best intentions will be undone by golfing jaunts to Hainan.

That's not worth worrying about, however, if oil production peaks and there's no Virgin Fuel on the shelves to replace it. "The next five years will see us face another crunch—the oil crunch," Branson warned U.K. ministers last year. "This time, we do have the chance to prepare. The challenge is to use that time well. Don't let the oil crunch catch us out in the way that the credit crunch did."

The race to build the perfect biofuel is being run by small teams of biochemists and molecular engineers lured from their ivory towers by the promise of saving the world and owning the basic patents. There are as many approaches to cracking the nut as there are companies, although so-called first-generation fuels like corn ethanol or biodiesel are already considered a bust—the farmland required is needed more for food than for fuel. The next step down the food chain is oils derived from inedible plants, like babassu palms or the nuts of a bush named *jatropha curcas*.

In February 2008, Virgin Atlantic tested a babassu–coconut oil blend aboard one of its 747s flying from London to Amsterdam. The flight was a success in that the biofuel (mixed with kerosene) didn't freeze. Afterward, Branson was photographed sipping the concoction from a coconut shell like a piña colada, gamely choking it down. He was quick to admit, however, that babassu oil wasn't the answer, or even the beginning of one. He had thought the *jatropha*, which needs neither care nor feeding, might be promising, but this hope ran smack into the law of large numbers. Growing enough *jatropha* to replace five million barrels of jet fuel each day would require hedgerows twice the size of France. So he'd scratched that one too.

"The flight proved we can run biofuels without modifying the engines," Branson told me later. "Up until two years ago, the engineers we'd spoken to had sworn it was impossible. Having proved that, we now believe the real breakthrough will be algae." Better known as pond scum or seaweed, algae grows quickly—thirty times faster than terrestrial plants—and lives on a diet of sunlight, CO_2, and salt water. Sharing Branson's enthusiasm, Boeing believes all the jet fuel in the world could be wrung from one big pond the size of Belgium—an area a little larger than the seven-million-acre palm oil plantation China is building in the Congo, on top of the five million acres it's leased in Zambia.

There may be a better solution closer to home. Branson has placed a personal bet on San Francisco's Solazyme, whose genetically tailored strains of algae act like factories, digesting sugars and cellulose into oil. Harvesting that oil is a bit like brewing beer, which is why doing so on an industrial scale requires simple stainless-steel fermenters instead of a lake next to a refinery. The resulting fuel smells like paraffin wax instead of gasoline, because they're both composed of the same long molecular chains of hydrocarbons.

It's the only fuel of its kind, the company boasts, that can be dropped into a diesel tank unblended. The U.S. Navy has ordered thousands of gallons of jet fuel. But Solazyme is waiting for further refinements to bring the price of its oil down to between $60 and $80 per barrel before ramping up to commercial scale, which president and chief technology officer Harrison Dillon expects will happen within two years. In the meantime, rivals like Amyris and Sapphire Energy have announced ambitious timetables of their own.

"What we have here is a platform for making oil," Harrison told me at their labs. "We can take basically any plant material—miscanthus, sugarcane, switchgrass, even sawdust—and put it through a fermentation process to produce not just fuel, but food." (Think canola instead of crude.) "There needs to be enough feedstock to produce billions of gallons, and the Department of Energy estimates that there are *fifty billion* gallons of feedstock in the U.S. alone." Solazyme has dibs after the DOE awarded it a $21.8 million grant to build its first test refinery in Pennsylvania.

If algae oil sounds like a deus ex machina—the impossible quick fix allowing us to carry on as if the sky weren't falling—then remember we've been here before. Another contender to produce green crude is

Craig Venter, whose company, Synthetic Genomics, has partnered with ExxonMobil to build an oil-sweating microorganism from the DNA up. Venter is the geneticist who beat all of his peers to the punch a decade ago when he first sequenced the human genome, and for a fraction of the Human Genome Project's $3 billion budget. When sequencing the genome was first floated in 1985, many thought it was impossible, or would cost as much as the Manhattan Project. Yet Venter managed the feat in just two years, for a tenth of the anticipated cost. Computing power had caught up in the meantime because of Moore's law—which dictates that computing power halves in price every eighteen months—transforming what had been a slog at the beginning into a wind-aided sprint.

Last May, Venter pulled off the inarguably greater trick of synthesizing a living cell from chemicals in a lab. "Synthia," as it was called, is "the first self-replicating species we've had on the planet whose parent is a computer," Venter crowed. And its parent is growing smarter every day. The cost of sequencing a human genome is falling tenfold annually; IBM plans to bring the price down to as little as $100 apiece. There are good reasons to believe Kasarda's insistence that human ingenuity will prove equal to the obstacles standing between us and our desire—our necessity—to range across earth at near-supersonic speeds. We have the technology: cleaner, farther, faster.

Planes, Trains, and the High-Speed Rail Fallacy

We forget all too soon and too easily that flight itself is arguably the farthest quantum leap in human history. For the first two hundred thousand years of *Homo sapiens'* existence, we were earthbound; for barely a hundred have we owned the sky. Only a century ago, on September 29, 1909, Wilbur Wright was at the controls of the Wright Brothers' Flier, circling the Statue of Liberty and swooping up and down the Hudson River above a million cheering New Yorkers.

Airports have also been with us for most of a century, but it's getting harder to find anyone who cheers them on. Most of us consider even G. M. Rao's Vatican of the skies an ecological nightmare, a concrete wasteland of runways, parking lots, and cloverleafs, ear-splitting shrieks, and a noxious mix of Jet A and diesel fumes. We worry the same goes for the aerotropolis.

Airports have always been noisy and filthy: this we know. They make it impossible to forget they're really factories minting connectivity, ones we can't just tuck away behind the tallest hill on the edge of town. That's what led us to the current mess—the tangled highways, the decaying sprawl—as cities tried to pair like with like, dumping one LULU after another on its edges, as if the airport were urban planning's answer to landfill.

We're still paying for these mistakes, which did as much damage to the environment as they did to our landscapes. But if we accept the idea that aerotropoli are the urban crucibles of our era—the places where new wealth and new walks of life will be created—then they are the ne plus ultra of fixer-uppers. We need not only cleaner airplanes to carry nine billion people and cleaner airports to fly from but cleaner *cities* as well. Aerotropoli are where we start to build and rebuild cities anew— cities that are greener, denser, and more sustainable than anything in orbit around them now. "There's nothing inconsistent with a smart-growth aerotropolis," Kasarda stresses. "The two can and should go hand in hand."

But there's still the problem of the airports themselves. They will always be stuck doing a dirty job, but they can be scrubbed and muffled somewhat. Improvements in engine design since the dawn of the Jet Age have shaved about thirty decibels off the din of an airliner at takeoff, the difference between a jackhammer starting outside your window on a Sunday morning and the hum of traffic on a city street. Given enough runways and enough forethought, it is entirely possible to reconcile tranquillity and approach paths. Some of the busiest airports are pulling their noise contours *in*, not pushing them out.

As for fumes, Richard Branson may have hit upon the obvious solution: keep the engines off until takeoff. But Virgin had to give up this plan of towing its planes to and from the runways when airports resisted and tests showed signs of stress on the landing gears. "For this to work, you would have to redevelop the airport holding bays and make other changes," Virgin Atlantic's COO explained. "We tried it and showed that the emissions reductions could be enormous," as much as the 90 percent Branson had originally promised. Burning biofuel may be net carbon-negative in the long run, because the algae it came from digested more CO_2 than it released, but that's little consolation to the person you're burning it next to. Resurrecting Virgin's so-called starting grid in some form is a must if airports are to make for greener, better neighbors.

They're trying their best. San Francisco's is installing solar panels on the roof, while O'Hare is recycling 90 percent of the debris from its runway expansion. Thirty-one European hubs, including those in Paris, Frankfurt, Amsterdam, Milan, and Dublin, have vowed to become carbon neutral. None currently holds a candle to Stockholm's airport, whose terminals are heated by burning wood chips, shrinking its prior carbon footprint by 94 percent. The airport's cab stands are manned by hybrids and its buses run on locally produced biodiesel.

Even better are trains, which raises a separate question: Why not replace planes with trains? High-speed rail is a mainstay of Japan and Europe, shuttling more intercity commuters between Tokyo and Osaka or Paris and Lyon than the Delta Shuttle does between New York and Boston, and with a vastly lower carbon footprint. The Obama administration has made HSR in America a priority, assigning $8 billion in stimulus funds to exploring ten potential corridors in the Midwest and South, and along the coasts. "Investing in a high-speed rail system will lower our dependence on foreign oil and the bill for a tank of gas," Vice President Joe Biden explained, "loosen the congestion suffocating our highways and skyways, and significantly reduce the damage we do to our planet." Not all at once, however. The $8 billion is just a "down payment" on marginally faster trains. Building a domestic Shinkansen network will require many billions more.

While there are at least as many arguments against high-speed rail in America as there are for it—the vast distances, the cost overruns, the potential for unchecked sprawl around stations, and the carbon footprint of forging all that steel and pushing it with coal-fired electricity—the bigger issue is how planes and trains are entwined in their own version of the Jevons Paradox. Trains won't replace planes, but they will make it easier than ever to fly. Trains are more efficient only across short distances—anything farther still requires a flight. This means high-speed trains act more like an intercity subway than do aircraft, carrying commuters to cities hundreds of miles away. Trains also connect people to airports. Bullet trains running through Illinois or California would mean fewer flights from Springfield or Fresno but more passengers leaving O'Hare or LAX for London and Tokyo.

If it sounds counterintuitive, it is. Just ask the Brits, who became embroiled in the same debate at Heathrow. All three major political parties support high-speed rail to all points from London, but Heathrow's owner has pointed out that a stop at the airport would increase demand for a third runway. Why? Because thousands of people would rather jump on a train from Glasgow to Heathrow for a flight to America than brave a connecting flight through the world's most congested airport. Trains would unleash latent demand for planes. (Or perhaps they're holding out for an easier solution. In a recent study, nearly a third of Britons believed teleportation would be perfected within a decade.)

This argument was dismissed as "propaganda" by those opposed to a third runway, but it is exactly what happened in Spain, which is caught up in an orgy of track laying—another five thousand miles over the next decade, all of it high speed. Air traffic between Madrid and Barcelona fell 40 percent in the first two years of the bullet trains' operation, with no bottom in sight. But both cities' airports have expanded. Madrid has become Europe's front door to Latin America, displacing Schiphol as one of the Continent's busiest hubs. Barcelona recently opened a new terminal, doubled the number of long-haul routes (including Buenos Aires and Singapore), and even bought one of the country's largest airlines. Not content to be Spain's second city, it's making a bid to be a global one.

Four of the five busiest hubs in Europe sit astride high-speed rail lines (Heathrow is the exception), and all four have seen drops in domestic passengers paired with an increase in international ones. Schiphol, for instance, has become the gateway for ten million people living within a hundred miles. Before we lay a high-speed rail network radiating from Chicago, we might want to finish expanding O'Hare.

And given Kasarda's claim that airports are the competitive edge of cities, regions, and even nations in the Instant Age, perhaps the Obama administration should rethink its neglect of the country's aerial infrastructure. The congestion the vice president railed against is due to an air traffic control system created in the 1930s. The annual cost of delays at the gate or in the air at the hands of air traffic controllers is $8.3 billion, according to researchers at MIT—more than all of the industry's losses combined. The cost to passengers is twice that. It will cost only $15 billion to replace the system with an umbrella of satellites, GPS, and cockpit computers plotting the shortest distance between two points—a vastly more efficient system known as NextGen. It is fifteen years behind schedule and another fifteen years away, with no plans or guaranteed funds set aside to speed up its deployment. Obama has pledged a "robust investment" in NextGen as part of his $50 billion infrastructure plan, but it remains to be seen what form it will take. The original stimulus package awarding $26 billion for highway maintenance and $8 billion for high(er)-speed rail included only $1 billion for aviation. In a similar vein, the Department of Energy has made $25 billion in loans available to electric-auto makers and battery manufacturers, and less than a billion dollars for biofuels. Tests by Alaska Airlines, among others, suggest that deploying NextGen could cut fuel burn and thus carbon emissions by 35 percent. Before dismissing air travel as hopelessly dirty and delayed, we might make an honest effort to clean and fix it.

But the need for greener airports pales next to the need for greener cities, and the aerotropolis straddles both. The world's urban population is poised to nearly double by 2050, adding another three billion people to places like Chongqing. We will build more cities (and slums) in the next forty years than we did in the first nine thousand years of civilized existence. The United Nations predicts the vast majority will flood cities in Africa and Asia, especially China.

While the developing world wrestles with this population boom, the developed one struggles with reinventing itself in the face of climate change. The battle against global warming will ultimately be fought in the streets. The world's twenty largest megacities consume a staggering 75 percent of Earth's energy. Buildings alone contribute 15 percent of all greenhouse gases, more than all forms of transportation combined.

Flying's carbon footprint is a pointless indicator if we don't fix cities first. How do you build green ones from scratch at the mind-boggling pace of a Philadelphia-size city per week—for *forty years*?

Our past attempts to build instant cities produced a litany of planning disasters including Brasília and Chandigarh, where human scale took a backseat to barren plazas and impassable boulevards. But a team of American architects, developers, technologists, and engineers are convinced they've cracked the code, creating a template for cities that are green, humane, dense, smart, and able to be cloned. Their prototype is Stan Gale's $35 billion aerotropolis rising from the Yellow Sea: New Songdo City.

Instant Cities

New Songdo didn't set out to be green. Its original purpose was one John Kasarda would have applauded: a weapon for fighting trade wars.

In the aftermath of the Asian financial crisis, the International

Monetary Fund handed South Korea a $58 billion bailout, with condi-
tions. One was a command to seek foreign investment. By then, however,
its manufacturing base was decamping to China—70 percent of its factories left over the next decade. Trade between the two countries didn't
exist in 1980, but twenty-five years later China would be its largest trading partner. Eager to follow the flying geese once more as its factories
vanished into China, Korean leaders resolved to make Seoul the financial and creative hub of northeast Asia—a title for which there was no
end of contenders. In this competition, New Songdo would be its blunt
instrument, its sharp edge.

South Korea's capital is the archetypal twentieth-century megacity,
doubling in size every decade or so since 1950 to twenty-four million
inhabitants—the second most populous on earth after greater Tokyo.
But badly scarred by the Korean War, Seoul buried its landscape under
mammoth apartment blocks and epic traffic jams. There's nothing sustainable about it. As an aspiring cool city, it offered little to card-carrying
members of the creative class, and less than Hong Kong or Singapore—
the preferred postings of Western expatriates. So Korea would have to
build a new city up to their standards.

Where? Hemmed in by mountains on two sides, a demilitarized zone
on a third, and the Yellow Sea on another, Seoul had reached the limits
to expansion. But as Dubai would prove, coastline can be manufactured.
In the 1990s, the decision was made to build a new international airport
on landfill off the coast of Incheon, the neighboring port where General
Douglas MacArthur and the marines had stormed ashore. Not stopping
there, engineers raised thousands of additional acres for future development. The airport opened in 2001; reclamation continues to this day.

That same year, the government went looking for some Americans to
build the cool city it couldn't. Its agent stumbled across Stan Gale on the
Web; his partner tried to blow the man off, saying he was in the middle
of a really big deal. "You don't know what big is," he was told. Seduced by
the possibilities, Gale would eventually commit to building a pocket
Manhattan on fifteen hundred acres of mud, with a daytime population
of three hundred thousand and sixty-five thousand permanent residents.
It was scheduled to take fifteen years.

The master plan was finished in 2003. What Gale envisioned—
although he didn't know it at the time—was a textbook aerotropolis.

Designed to compete for the hearts and minds (and direct investments) of foreign multinationals, New Songdo promises to be more American than any of its neighbors—an English-speaking island stocked with prep schools from Boston, malls from Beverly Hills, and a golf course designed by Jack Nicklaus. In exchange for moving knowledge workers to a literal backwater instead of Shanghai or Beijing, they could fly on a moment's notice to any of a hundred cities within a four-hour flight and be home in time for supper. This would be made possible by the twelve-mile-long, billion-dollar bridge connecting New Songdo to the airport, which cut the commute to fifteen minutes when it opened in 2009.

The task of designing an instant city fell to Gale's architects at Kohn Pedersen Fox, whose lengthy résumé includes supertall skyscrapers and dozens of corporate headquarters, but nothing on the order of New Songdo. The principal in charge of the project is Jamie von Klemperer, whose willingness to explain himself in simple English runs counter to flashier "starchitects."

Previous attempts at conceiving instant cities had been hobbled by their own utopianism, he explained one afternoon at KPF's Manhattan offices, as we watched his assistants carve matchstick skyscrapers out of Styrofoam. In trying to draft the perfect city, he said, architects had produced inhuman ones. "Renaissance planners would take a circle and decide what geometry of roads, what uses, and what utopian order would be given to that circle," he said. This thinking still lurks behind the layouts of built-to-order capitals like Washington, D.C., or Brasília. "They weren't particularly pleasant places to live. And so we made a point to avoid abstraction, choosing collage instead."

New Songdo cherry-picks the signatures of universally beloved cities and recycles them as building blocks. The city trumpets itself as an amalgam of New York, Venice, and Savannah. In practice, this means its streets and Central Park are modeled on Manhattan's, its canal is inspired by Venice, and its gardens are borrowed from Savannah's. The product is an eerily familiar mix tailor-made for a homesick "global business class with a morning meeting in Seoul and an afternoon one in Beijing," as von Klemperer described its intended residents.

On my first visit to New Songdo in 2007, the city was still a mud pile. Roaming the floodplain where Central Park would be, I stumbled over clamshells—a stark reminder this had all been underwater. Two years later, on the park's opening day, I closed my eyes in an ersatz teahouse along the water's edge, listening to cicadas in the saplings and children whizzing by on bicycles, their laughter interrupted by the percussion of pile drivers. The park itself was a manicured landscape of pine forests, boulders, and flower beds—an obvious fake. Then again, so were the original Central Park's hills, lakes, and ice-skating rinks. Like any perfect knockoff, it had obliterated the distinction between the counterfeit and the real.

New Songdo has also been designed to be the greenest, most energy-efficient city in the world. Just as it copied great cities' best features, it's rounding up the state of the art in sustainable technologies and taking them to scale the way only an instant city can. All of its water and waste will be recycled, for instance. Rainwater and graywater will be collected for cooling and irrigation, while solid waste will be burned for heat and electricity. These will in turn be recycled to warm New Songdo's buildings, using a centralized approach known as district heating. The goal is to use 30 percent less water than other cities its size, and save 75 percent of its trash from landfills.

The buildings will boast solar panels and sod on their roofs, specially glazed windows, and superefficient fixtures for heating, cooling, and ventilation. Even their concrete will be green by using 20 percent less cement, which means 20 percent less electricity used to make it. And because New Songdo had the opportunity to install all of its infrastructure first, three stops on the Seoul/Incheon subway were running before the city even opened.

On top of that, New Songdo will be intrinsically green for the same reason Manhattan is: density. Calculated by the square foot, the original "Terminal City" looks like an environmental Chernobyl of greenhouse gases, garbage, noise, and traffic. But rerun the numbers by resident or by household, and the city is practically Eden. Manhattanites consume gasoline at a rate the United States hasn't seen since the 1920s, and 82 percent of its residents commute via public transit, by bicycle, or on foot. If all Americans lived like New Yorkers do, our carbon emissions would drop 71 percent. We wouldn't need a cap on carbon; we would have already done it on our own.

Green Metropolis author David Owen argues, "Dense urban centers offer one of the few plausible remedies for some of the world's most discouraging environmental ills. To borrow a term from the jargon of computer systems, dense cities are scalable, while sprawling suburbs are not . . . The environmental challenge we face, at the current stage of our assault on the world's nonrenewable resources, is not how to make our teeming cities more like the pristine countryside. The challenge is how to make other settled places more like Manhattan." By cramming its sixty-five thousand eventual residents into two and a half square miles, New Songdo has done exactly that—their densities are almost identical.

The results are eye-opening. If all goes according to plan, New Songdo's carbon footprint will be a third of a city its size—a big step toward the reductions needed to halt global warming. There is, of course, the environmental absurdity of erecting a sustainable city on former wetlands, but Jamie von Klemperer would counter it's a better alternative than clear-cutting mountains.

Not content to be green and an aerotropolis, it's meant to be a "smart city" too. As preached by technology companies such as IBM and Cisco, the Internet will be the next big utility, tying the others together. If you hook cities up to the right mix of sensors and software, their thinking goes, who knows what efficiencies might be revealed? When buildings, power lines, gas lines, roadways, cell phones, residential systems, and so on are able to talk to one another, that information can expose hidden patterns of waste and ways to avoid it. Just as wiring made corporations leaner and meaner, wiring cities may be one way to tease efficiency out of dumb networks like the power grid. New Songdo will be the first citywide experiment.

While still a long way from being finished, this new pocket city is arguably the nicest in Korea. The Koreans themselves seem to think so—even during a housing bust, New Songdo's apartment blocks have all been instant sellouts. As population pressure mounts not just on Seoul but on cities across Asia, New Songdo's pragmatic pastiche may become the template for all the instant cities to come. Stan Gale has assembled a dream team of architects and technologists to make sure it does. Paired with Cisco's smarts, 3M's green materials, United Technologies' engineers, and KPF's blueprints, Gale won't be content until he can mass-produce cities in half the time it takes China to do it.

Indeed, New Songdo's first clone may break ground this year on the outskirts of Chongqing, a city in western China growing at superhuman speed. It would be twice as large as its parent but just as dense, smart, and green. It's no coincidence that Gale's following the airports. These and every subsequent city will be standardized around his partners' products: the same light fixtures, traffic signals, elevators, fuel cells, air conditioners, and sensors. It's the only way to build them in time for the tidal wave of new inhabitants.

"We're trying to replicate cities," said Cisco's chief globalization officer Wim Elfrink, but "we have no standards. Every city is a new project, a new process, a new interface," he told me in New Songdo, marveling at the inefficiency of it all. "You shouldn't spend time on an elevator. You shouldn't spend time on lighting." You should spend time planning the next one. Gale's timetable is, if anything, too slow for Cisco, which has signed deals for additional instant cities in Saudi Arabia, India, and Qatar—all of which will also be aerotropoli.

"Everything can be connected and everything can be green," Elfrink promises, and his customers are dying to believe him. The implicit promise of a sustainable world is one in which six and a half billion people—or, in forty years, *nine* billion—live like Americans, only with no penalty to the planet. It's the promise of taking the definition of an unsustainable way of life to global scale without deprivation and without poisoning ourselves. Stan Gale and Kasarda both propose matching scale with scale, cloning cities—one green and one connected—that reflect the competing needs of the Instant Age, walking a tightrope between delivering prosperity and triggering peak oil, peak food, and peak *everything*. At a time when many of us are calling for simplicity—a way of life that is more local and thus buffered against peak oil and climate change—they are building just the opposite in the place that needs them most: China.

11

GO WEST. GO OUT. GO.

China's current success is built on its huge volume of exports—which it sends to the rest of the world on fully loaded 747s. Now the Chinese middle class is ready to follow Chinese-made products abroad, and China is building hundreds of new airports to send them. Is this progress, or the beginning of the end?

The Chinese may or may not have a saying: "China makes, the world takes." But they have run their economy this way for thirty years. China makes an inexhaustible supply of ever better, ever cheaper goods, and we take them. If there is a cause of the global financial crisis, it's that China made too much and we took too much, with ruinous consequences for only one side (so far). Explanations why China will alternately rule the world or wreck it have understandably focused on what it makes and how—on its factories. Collectively, the country employs 140 million migrant workers—ten times the number of manufacturing jobs in the entire United States. They helped lift six hundred million peasants out of absolute poverty, creating the largest burgeoning middle class in history.

But we should have paid closer attention to the taking. China's climb to become the world's top exporter was unimaginable until recently, not because of poverty or politics, but because the infrastructure needed to create the "world's factory" didn't exist. Its ports could handle bulky, inexpensive goods such as clothes or toys or steel, but as China's sweatshops grew in sophistication, their products gained in worth and urgency that demanded they go by air. Years before laying tracks for the high-speed trains that are the envy of America, China built record-setting airports; before connecting its cities to each other, it connected its factories to the world. It takes forty-eight hours at most for an iPod to travel eight thousand miles via Hong Kong to America; it often takes longer for assembly-line workers to travel to their hometowns a few hundred miles inland.

China is ready to remedy that. In addition to paving thousands of miles of highway and laying thousand of miles of track, it is building hundreds of airports and dozens of aerotropoli. Together, they compose a map of China's future—the literally hundreds of unbuilt cities (so far) designed to house another four hundred million peasants leaving the countryside for factories—and will offer even the most remote backwaters an open window on the world. China is taking Kasarda's logic of the aerotropolis—an urban machine not for living but for competition—to global scale. Not content to build airports at home, Chinese construction crews are hard at work on them across Africa and Pakistan too, planting waypoints along a New Silk Road that will carry oil and mineral wealth back to China, where they'll be transmuted into goods. So while we fret about the making—about exchange rates and spare factory capacity and a real estate bubble threatening to dwarf our own—China is quietly preparing to set loose its people on the world. It's there for the taking.

Inside the "World's Factory"

Crossing the border from Hong Kong means passing from the developed world to the developing one, from a city of skyscrapers to a sprawl of factory towns on a scale Henry Ford could not have foreseen. Beyond lies the Pearl River Delta, stretching for a hundred miles inland. For Liam Casey this chasm is his commute.

Twice, his driver handed over our passports at checkpoints, opening the van doors so the attendants could match the names to our faces. "You're going to love this," Casey said, just when I thought we were in the clear. A few seconds later, my door was opened again, this time by a guardsman in the People's Liberation Army. Without a sound, he shot me between the eyes with a laser, did the same to Casey, and closed the door in one fluid motion.

"What was that?" I asked, trembling. "A retina scan?"

Casey shook his head. "He was taking our temperature." In case we were carrying SARS. The mysterious disease swept through the Delta and then vanished without a trace in 2003.

Casey was dubbed "Mr. China" by *The Atlantic*'s James Fallows in a cover story, and Fallows's word was enough to make it so. Casey was the first Westerner to insinuate himself into Delta's willfully anonymous factories. He and his company, PCH International, were unknown to the Western public when Fallows wrote about him, but you undoubtedly know his clients—a few of the companies that sell laptops, MP3 players, cell phones, cameras, servers, and just about anything else with a chip in it—none of which he'll name out loud. Fallows called it outsourcing, but the term doesn't do Casey justice. I had just booked a ticket to China when the *Atlantic* piece came out, and I immediately got in touch with Casey myself. Touring his factory in Shenzhen, I saw the birthplace of some of my most prized possessions. Casey and his competitors are the headwaters of an Amazon's worth of goods leaving China for Los Angeles, Memphis, and Louisville.

We had barely crossed the border before he opened his laptop and began walking me through the true costs of those shipments. He'd built a widget calculating every conceivable variable: the weight, volume, value, and quantity of the products in question; the lead times for sourcing and building them; time spent in transit; their shelf life; the spread between paying his vendors and being paid himself; the cost of money in the meantime; and the cost of returns. An entire calculus, in other words, underlies the pivotal question of our era: *What is the price of speed?*

The widget's answer: slow is more expensive. The only thing faster than a FedEx 777 Freighter out of Hong Kong is the velocity of money, and the last thing Casey wants to pay for are the days his parcels are stuck on a boat. Obsolescence sets in the moment they leave the factory. "Revenue evaporation," he calls it. "Air freight is key," he muttered while running the numbers. "We like to work with products that can go by air. We build them in Shenzhen, and they're in New York two days later. Time is often our number one currency, and the dollar is second."

The story of China over the last two decades is really the story of second-day air. At that speed, and for the right price at retail, you could build everything of anything here—every flat-screen television, every PC—and fly it to customers anywhere. You'd need only one factory, or one person like Casey to orchestrate all the others. The story of China in the coming decades is where they will fly once their top export is ideas, like our own. This transformation has been hastened by the global downturn. Abandoned by many of their shadowy clients, ambitious companies like Casey's are learning to innovate instead.

Both stories begin in Shenzhen. Liam Casey arrived in 1996, a few years after paramount leader Deng Xiaoping declared "to get rich is glorious" while passing through the city on his farewell tour. Deng is the father of Shenzhen, having chosen this sleepy fishing village as the first of China's "special economic zones" in 1980. Foreign firms were invited to open shop here with few constraints or taxes, triggering the transformation of the Pearl River Delta into "the factory of the world" and Shenzhen into the "Overnight City," having grown two-hundred-fold since then. While Shanghai's *Blade Runner* landscape symbolizes China's future, Shenzhen is the template for its instant cities.

Until the crisis, the Delta was the world's biggest boomtown, crowding 5 percent of China's population into less than 1 percent of its land, where they produced 20 percent of the country's GDP and 40 percent of its exports. A single factory—Foxconn's forbidden city on the edge of Shenzhen—was responsible for all of the world's iPhones and most of its iPads, iPods, PlayStations, Nintendos, and Kindles. For obvious reasons, all involved would rather you didn't know. At its peak, some 320,000 workers toiled on its assembly lines and slept in its dormitories.

To a relatively small outfit like Casey's, a titan like Foxconn is "a competitor, a customer, and a supplier," assembling finished goods for some of its clients while buying and selling pieces of others. These tangled webs are typical. But unlike the gatekeepers of what Apple's engineers call Mordor (the forbidden kingdom of *The Lord of the Rings*), Casey was happy to show me the inner workings of his factory and to explain how and why all the world's ended up here.

His own path is no less remarkable. Now in his forties, Casey was raised on a farm near Cork, and after finishing high school he went to work in the garment trade, first in Cork and then in Dublin. A trader by instinct, he eventually left Ireland for a brief stint in Orange County.

(PCH is named for the Pacific Coast Highway.) He discovered China while visiting Taiwan for an electronics show. Spotting his opening on the mainland, Casey moved to Shenzhen some months later. Boyish looking with a perpetually sly grin, Casey surrounded himself with Irish expats. His brogue is as thick as ever.

Our first stop was his warehouse, where the night shift was nearing its 8:00 a.m. crescendo. The scene was familiar to anyone who's ever seen a pick-and-ship operation in Memphis: women in their late teens and early twenties scanned and packed orders originating from the website of a well-known American brand. What was different this time is that they were arriving live from Boston, Boulder, and San Francisco— twelve, fourteen, and fifteen time zones away. Sealed boxes awaited FedEx pickup a few hours later. Barring any snafus at customs, they would catch the nightly flight to Anchorage, and onward to domestic hubs. As promised, Casey's customers would sign for them forty-eight hours after the first click.

Casey was a middleman during his early years in China, battling with all the others for the rights to match factories' output with buyers overseas. Business depended on making the process as opaque as possible. "Confusion was their competitive advantage," he said. But it wasn't his. By 2003, just as China's export-driven boom was cranking into its highest gear, Casey decided his only hope of success was to climb higher up the value chain. He opened his own factory and began hiring engineers.

Today, PCH has around nine hundred employees, revenues of $220 million, and a loose network of several hundred factories taking orders. Casey's workers still don't make anything in any traditional sense. They pack, "postpone," and "flavor" them. One of the company's specialties is what he calls "OOBE," the "out-of-box experience." It means he doesn't only ship products for the brand mentioned above but also oversees their packaging. Millions of unsuspecting Americans have ripped through boxes of his design.

"Postponement" is how the Delta's factories and their customers reconcile competing economies of scale and speed. It's in the former's best interests to run their assembly lines flat out, earning the highest return on their investments. But the brand names are loath to carry inventory, so they postpone these decisions, manufacturing goods halfway but leaving them in a malleable shape. When it's finally time to ship, Casey finishes them.

Women arriving for the morning shift took their stations alongside a conveyor belt. Laptops commissioned by another household name began rolling down the line. "These are bare computers," practically generic, Casey said. They had been flown in from Japan. "We don't make them here, we flavor them." The women were soon busy adding extra memory and installing Windows, matching each machine to someone's personal specifications. They typically finish two thousand a day, a pace of fifty thousand per month. "North Carolina is an expensive place to touch a computer; Austin is too," Casey noted. They happened to be home to Dell's domestic factories, the first of which is set to close; the other has already been shuttered.

His larger point isn't that China is cheaper than anywhere else—Hanoi and Saigon offer even lower wages—but that its pools of labor and raw materials are so much vaster. This size has given cities like Shenzhen a metabolism no other manufacturing hub can match. You can see it in places like the SEG Electronics Market, which has eclipsed Tokyo's Aki-habara district as nirvana for hardware geeks. On a recent trip, the top engineer for one of Casey's customers was stunned to discover a section he had never seen before. "Imagine a market, the acreage of two gymna-siums, but four stories tall, packed with nothing but mobile phone bits and pieces (and finished phones too)," he wrote on his blog. "You hear numbers like 500 million phones being made in China per year, but you don't actually get to feel it until you walk this market. There is literally everything in there to make phones, from blank PCBs, to intermediate assemblies, to shells, testing equipment, raw chips, batteries, LCDs, bro-ken down parts, you name it."

The combination of these clusters and air cargo created a feedback loop carpeting the Delta with factories capable of supplying the entire world. Nearly a third of all the magnetic recording heads at the heart of your hard drive and a sixth of all keyboards are made in the city of Dong-guan, just up the road from Shenzhen. Twenty years ago, it was another fishing village; today it's larger than Chicago.

These instant megacities were inevitable. They didn't have to happen here—they did because Deng and his successors willed them to—but they would have sprouted somewhere. The economics make too much sense. Research by the World Bank suggests the reason China's mega-cities have grown so big, so fast is that the returns to scale have grown so massive. What has made this growth possible, the bank argued, is cheap transportation. The catalyst is the jet engine, "perhaps the most significant innovation in long-distance transport ever," in the bank's estimation.

You already know what happened next: cities began to specialize in pieces of supply chains, clusters formed, and these clusters got bigger—in China's case, *a lot* bigger. "A decline in transport costs—with increasing returns to scale—generally means more spatial concentration of production," the report's authors deduced. In essence, the jet invented the Pearl River Delta. How? The bank suggested a formula: supply chains + clustering + air power = higher productivity the bigger cities get. How big is *too* big isn't clear; the bank wasn't sure there's an upper limit. One thing is certain: the bigger they are, the smaller the world.

For example, one of Liam Casey's big ideas is running fulfillment for all of his American customers from China. And not just individual orders arriving over the Web, either, but the entire tail of their supply chains. He'll ship inventory straight to their stores, no warehouses necessary. Why tie up capital if they didn't have to? He'd replace Memphis with Shenzhen, eight thousand miles away. "It's much cheaper to do it here than in Memphis," he said with a shrug. He has the technology—his own home-brewed tracking software that deftly melds GPS data and bar code scans into a real-time look inside every plane, ship, and truck carrying his shipments.

"The world is very small," he explained. "When the A380 arrives, there will be excess capacity, and we're going to take up a lot of it." He didn't have to wait long. Some months later the stock markets crashed, and factories began closing up shop as maxed-out Americans lost their homes. China's exports fell 25 percent during the darkest days of the crisis, and freighters across Asia were flying half full. While many worried that the world's factory was seizing up, Casey saw an opportunity.

He's still keen to take the *Fortune* 500's money, but his sympathies lie with the garage entrepreneurs who have an idea but no factory—nor any idea of what to do with one. For every Bill Hewlett and David Packard, who built a giant to last (and invented Silicon Valley to boot), there's a Preston Tucker. Tucker was the quixotic automaker whose 1948 Tucker Torpedo Sedan offered an engine and safety features decades ahead of their time. To build it, he leased the world's biggest factory (a converted B-29 bomber plant in Chicago) but was crushed by the Big Three before he could start production. Tucker could invent a better car than Henry Ford, but he couldn't invent a better assembly line. With Liam Casey in his corner, he wouldn't have had to.

Our next stop was Casey's office, where he clicked on a map of the nine hundred factories he keeps tabs on. Tell him what you want—a smartphone or a gadget you haven't invented yet—and he'll find the ones who can make it. The Delta is more than an agglomeration of factories; it's a gigantic black box capable of producing anything you ask, in any quantity, at prices a fraction of what they would be anywhere else. Two days later, the product is in your customers' hands, and you don't have to think twice about it.

"If you have a concept for a product and you have your funding in place, we'll find a factory to manufacture it," he explained. "We'll put our engineering team working on it, and they'll develop the product with the right factory—a best-in-class factory—to your spec. You'll approve the product, you'll place the orders to us, we'll start bringing it into our facility, we'll package it, and we'll ship it to your consumers. So the good thing for you is you don't need to have a distribution company. You don't need to have anything other than our facilities in China. And we call this 'disruptive commerce.' *You* have a disruptive technology, *we* have a disruptive supply chain. Put them together, you get disruptive commerce. We work with start-ups that didn't exist a year ago, and they'll have products out in the fall. It's how you use air freight to form your business that's new."

The one customer he'll admit to having is chumby industries, the San Diego–based maker of digital widgets. It's a software and media start-up masquerading as a gadget one. Its eponymous device resembles an iPod mounted in a sleek clock radio, only one that broadcasts Facebook feeds and Twitter tweets instead of Howard Stern. The chumby's guts are nothing special, filled with off-the-shelf parts. It's a red herring and loss leader for the company's actual business plan, which is to own the network delivering those tweets. Rather than waste time and money stamping radios—let Liam Casey handle that—chumby wants to own the WiFi airwaves instead. (Its ambitions are similar to Amazon's for the Kindle, which isn't about selling electronic books so much as patenting Paper 2.0.) Here's the story behind its latest version, the chumby one, as told by the company's one and only hardware engineer, Bunnie Huang, on his blog:

> The idea sort of slow-rolled through the first few months of 2009, and after chinese new years, I taped out the first prototype board in late March. Around May we contracted an industrial designer to do some sketches, and by June we had a near-final [design]; our first 3D printed prototypes were made around then . . . In July, we inked a PO for steel tooling and by August we had first-shot plastics. September was spent refining and de-bugging the design, and October was spent doing more testing, refining, and ramping up mass production. And, here we are now, in November. When I wrote this, the first shipment of chumby Ones were somewhere 35,000 feet above the Pacific Ocean en route to LAX.

"If you're a start-up with only so many millions in funding and you're trying to break into a market," Casey asked rhetorically as we admired a prototype, "is it better to have it tied up in a factory or a warehouse, or in your designers? Or in new technology?"

You don't need millions to get started; sometimes all it takes is a credit card. An old coworker of mine, a former *Time* magazine editor named Nathaniel Wice, resurfaced a few years ago running a two-man outfit named miShare. Their bright idea was a device for sharing music between two iPods, no computers necessary. They tried selling the idea but found no takers. So they hired a factory in the Delta instead. Wice paid with plastic.

"China is nice in the same way it's nice to live in a neighborhood with a lot of Kinko's," he told me. "You don't have to be an expert on bind-ing a presentation; there's a place on the corner that can do that for you. It's just that in China, the place on the corner prints circuit boards." The fastest way to find one is through Alibaba.com, the country's largest one-stop shop for factories and wholesalers. Search the site (in English) for someone who makes what you're looking for and fire off an instant mes-sage asking for a quote. Alibaba's chat program translates Chinese into English (and vice versa), so the language barrier isn't an issue. Replies come in minutes.

In miShare's case, the cost of the circuit boards, battery, and spare parts in each unit added up to about $35. The device wholesales for $65 and retails for $99.95, meaning only a third of its theoretical value is derived from China, while another third accrues to retailers like SkyMall. What's left is pure profit for miShare's pair of inventors, whose personal contribution is a secret sauce of software.

In that respect, miShare is a textbook example of the smiley curve. It's what you get when you graph the value (and thus the profits) added throughout the life cycle of a made-in-China product. In the beginning is the brand (e.g., Apple), followed by the idea (the iPad), look-and-feel ("there's an app for that"), and industrial design. Next come the components, manufacturing, and assembly (in this case by Foxconn), then shipping and handling. It ends with the sale and customer service (by Apple again, or AT&T). If you follow the money, it starts high, dips low, and rises again at the end—hence the smile. The Delta is the toothy grin while American firms perch in the dimples. Remember "designed in California, assembled in China"? Where would you rather be?

What's interesting about both start-ups is that neither has anything to do with outsourcing. No American manufacturing jobs were harmed during the making of these gadgets. They are pure creation. Ideas that might never have found expression otherwise were given form by a combination of entrepreneurial pluck, the Delta's black box, and an air bridge between the two. The factories minted wealth from nothing, although two-thirds of it flew back to the United States.

Some have hailed this development as a "new Industrial Revolution" propelled by seemingly invisible assembly lines set into motion with a few keystrokes. But it's really the culmination of the old one's economies of scale, blown out to global proportions. There is no law stating China will remain at the bottom of the smiley curve forever. In fact, its long-term goal—as well as stated government policy—is to climb higher up both ends of the curve by nurturing its own entrepreneurs and brands. This was always the point of its joint ventures with Western firms and why it turned a blind eye to the inevitable counterfeits and knockoffs that followed. It explains Lenovo's purchase of IBM's PC division in North Carolina, and why Chinese automakers like BYD are hiring Detroit's engineers by the bushel. On the Boston Consulting Group's list of "100 New Global Challengers," thirty-six are Chinese, more than any other nationality.

Shortly before the crisis hit, China's leaders passed new labor laws designed to force the Delta's worst sweatshops out of business. Many were destined to leave even before Premier Wen Jiabao declared the sweatshop model "unsteady, unbalanced, uncoordinated, and unsustainable" in 2007. Local politicians referred to this policy as "emptying the cage for the new birds." The downturn scattered many more to the winds.

Anyone tracing the smiley curve over Raymond Vernon's classical notion of the product cycle would find the same lesson underneath: it's not *what* you make that's important, but *where* you fall along the curve. China is big enough to have it all—ideas, factories, and consumers—balanced between its rich cities on the coast and poor ones in the interior.

How exactly will it manage this? As usual, Liam Casey has a few ideas. While sitting in his office on a high floor in one of downtown's many towers, I flipped through a presentation for one of the world's largest cell-phone brands. It opened with a trend forecast of hot styles and colors, followed by sketches of new phones. The finale was an entire lineup of cases and accessories with an "urban sportswear" or "1950s revival" theme. In essence, he was asking this prospect to hand over its design and marketing to him . . . in China. Everything on the table—including sample cases and packaging—was conjured in ten days. "This is adding the smarts to the process," he said. "It's actually faster to get these products to the market from *here* than over *there*."

His aims are modest compared to what some Chinese firms have planned. The crisis is their opportunity to go toe-to-toe with Western brands. While in the Delta, I toured a factory belonging to MiTAC, one of the many Taiwanese firms manufacturing large chunks of the world's PCs. The assembly line I saw belonged to its bread-and-butter business, which is soldering motherboards for Dell. (At the time, they were bound for Austin.) But MiTAC has another factory near Shanghai, where it produces portable GPS devices sold under its own brand, Mio. It has sold enough already to be considered the second-largest supplier of PDAs in the world (behind only the maker of the BlackBerry). Mio's latest hit is the Knight Rider, which issues directions in the voice of KITT. You too can own a talking car.

MiTAC rebelled against the smiley curve in the early 1990s with a doomed campaign to market its own PCs. Chastened, it went back to making pieces of IBMs and Apples instead. But it never stopped looking for an escape hatch. "We realized there is no Microsoft in the digital map business," its president explained. Ergo the Mio, for now, at least. MiTAC is only a bit player by Taiwan's standards. Besides Foxconn, for example, five firms produce 90 percent of the world's laptops, none of which you've probably ever heard of: Quanta, Compal, Inventec, Wistron, and one formerly known as ASUSTeK.

That began to change a few years ago, when Quanta won the contract for the so-called $100 laptop commissioned by the nonprofit One Laptop per Child. Its design was radically different, running lightweight software on a hyperefficient machine. Inspired, or maybe terrified, Quanta's archrival ASUSTeK devised a laptop along similar lines, albeit with a sleeker look-and-feel and a price tag of $349. Instead of children, its intended audience was families in China and India. When the first batch of Eee PCs hit Taipei's shopping malls in 2007, however, they sold out in thirty minutes. Europeans and Americans snatched up the rest by Christmas.

In creating a computer for Chinese tastes at China-friendly prices, ASUSTeK had stumbled onto netbooks, those practically disposable laptops perfect for e-mail, Google Docs, and surfing the Web. Without meaning to, it had tapped into the unconscious desires of Western customers who had subliminally wondered why their bulky laptops cost as much as a used car. It turned out they didn't have to. A year later, the brand names rushed their own netbooks to market, undercutting only themselves in the process while perversely creating more business for their upstart competitors. By the end of 2008, ASUSTeK had sold five million under its own name, a third of the total. In a single year, netbooks captured 7 percent of the world's entire laptop market; the next year they doubled that, as laptops outsold desktops for the first time ever. In Europe, wireless carriers began giving them away for free to lure new customers. Without meaning to, netbooks had paved the way for the PC's extinction.

ASUSTeK didn't take it upon itself to invent just a new product; they invented a new category. It's a classic example of the disruptive innovations Clayton Christensen describes in *The Innovator's Dilemma*—a cheap, seemingly inferior imitator appears to gut the incumbents' business models. In this case, their only response was to hire the insurgents to slap their names on the same models. Suddenly, the Taiwanese firms and their mainland factories were dictating terms to the rest of the industry.

Netbooks are old hat—tablets are where the action is. By one estimate, tablets will outsell netbooks as early as next year, and desktop computers the year after that, rising to twenty million a year by 2015. Before Apple introduced the iPad in 2010, Foxconn's iWonder was already on sale in China—for just $100. Another manufacturer with a tablet and nothing to lose threatened to sue Steve Jobs for patent infringement despite its own being an obvious knockoff. (Which raises an existential question: Can something be a knockoff if an original doesn't exist? China seems determined to find out.) ASUSTeK split itself in two, the better to make and sell cell phones, Kindle killers, and video games under its own name—now simply ASUS—while honoring its old contracts. Foxconn intends to open ten thousand stores across China, where its products will share shelf space with Apple's and other customers'. It's even investing millions of dollars in Silicon Valley start-ups in search of an edge against its own clients.

"What ASUSTeK proved is that the companies with real leverage are the ones that actually *make* desirable products," Clive Thompson argued in *Wired.* "The Taiwanese laptop builders possess the atom-hacking smarts that once defined America but which have atrophied here along with our industrial base." A $28 billion high-tech trade surplus to China ten years ago had withered into a $54 billion deficit by 2007. They'd successfully inverted the smiley curve. American firms unwittingly do their bidding, instead of the other way around.

"When I talk to them now," says Willy Shih, a Harvard Business School professor who's studied them closely, "they say, 'We outsource our branding and sales to *them*.'"

It's taken us twenty-five years to turn on a billion PCs every morning, but it will require only seven to add the next billion, this time as tablets and their ilk. As big as the Delta's black box is, it's not big enough to sustain that pace. For one thing, it's running out of roads. Shenzhen alone is adding seven hundred cars each day to its beltways, where they jockey for lanes with eighteen-wheelers racing against FedEx deadlines.

From the bottom of his bag of tricks, Liam Casey produced a map plotting every factory in his database against the Delta's sclerotic traffic patterns. He chose two at random. "Back in '96, it used to take four hours to get from here to here," he said, pointing to a tangle of roads around Dongguan. With a click, a highway appeared. "In 2001, it was forty-five minutes." But traffic clotted faster than they could add stents. "In 2003, it was two hours again. Now there's a new highway, and it takes twenty minutes." For how long, he couldn't say.

Across the river, MiTAC had given up on the bridges and turned to ferries instead, floating shipments down the Delta to the airport at its mouth. Hong Kong International cost $20 billion to build (still the all-time record), most of it on a man-made island and the tunnels, bridges, highways, and railways connecting it to Kowloon. Until the credit crisis knocked the wind out of China's exports, it was within a few thousand tons of dethroning Memphis as the world's busiest cargo airport. (Shanghai's Pudong isn't far behind.) But unlike the home of FedEx, Hong Kong's airport lacks a nightly sort. Its tonnage more or less flows in only one direction: west.

During construction, HKIA was seen by mainland politicians as a final binge by the colonial government to practically bankrupt the city ahead of the handover in 1997. The truth was the opposite: the most ambitious public works project in Hong Kong's history was their last chance to install the infrastructure that would guarantee its continued prominence. It still wasn't enough—barely ten years after opening in 1998, it was bumping up against its limits. Airports come in two sizes, remember—too big and too small.

There is talk of dumping enough landfill into the sea for a third runway, but that will likely take a dozen years at least. "As an export gateway, Hong Kong will eventually decline because of capacity issues and cost," a local FedEx executive told me. Officials at China's all-powerful Civil Aviation Administration (CAAC) echo this view, not least because they have a vested interest in seeing the mainland's airports take off at Hong Kong's expense.

Determined to hurry the process along, they agreed in 2005 to plant a FedEx hub at the opposite end of the Delta, at Baiyun International outside Guangzhou. Opened last February, it is the common carrier's largest abroad, replacing its hub at Subic Bay. I saw it in its skeletal stages, all steel beams and rebar. But its engineers had been busy. First, they drained the pond covering the site—the only reason urban scrubland hadn't subsumed it already. Then they diverted a river, paved over its marshes, and pumped concrete into caves underneath. FedEx had sought equally drastic changes to China's legal code, rewriting customs and aviation statutes to grant itself an unlimited number of flights. (Kasarda coauthored the study used to make its case.) True to form, doing so required a year of tortuous negotiations with more than a hundred agencies and bureaucracies. Once given the green light, construction of the six-lane highway linking the hub to the Delta's factories had taken all of six months.

The up-front costs totaled $300 million, a steal for what is supposed to be the centerpiece of a satellite city carved from wheat fields twenty-five miles north of Guangzhou. It is zoned to be larger than Hong Kong and Macau put together; the first signs are visible from the airport freeway, long stretches of which resemble the Dulles Toll Road. "There are two ways to build an aviation city," a CAAC official told me in Guangzhou. "One is natural growth—as long as the airport attracts passengers, it will grow. The other is to plan it, and we're in the midst of planning one right now," an aerotropolis with Chinese characteristics.

The Store Versus the Factory

The sociologist Fei Xiaotong described the Delta as "a store at the front and a factory in the back." Hong Kong is the store; Shenzhen and Guangzhou are the factory. But the dynamic is changing. It's now the store *versus* the factory, with the winner claiming a starring role on the world stage. For the moment, the store has the upper hand.

The urban fabric of modern Hong Kong was knit following the end of China's civil war in 1949, which sent two million refugees streaming across its border with little more than the shirts on their backs— appropriate, considering Shanghai's fleeing capitalists underwrote its first textile factories. Textiles are the bottom rung of industrial economies. Britain's woolen mills were the first to be mechanized in the eighteenth century by the flying shuttle and spinning jenny, and the first to be copied on cut-rate American looms. Hong Kong followed in their footsteps until Deng's Reform and Opening in 1978, when its reservoir of cheap labor was undercut by the bottomless one pooling in Shenzhen.

The Delta was built with Hong Kong's jobs and Hong Kong's dollars. By the early 1990s, the territory's budding industrialists had spent $40 billion in China, two-thirds of its total foreign investment. Drawing on family and village connections, they hired six million workers for twenty thousand new factories—more than the entirety of Hong Kong. The city underwent its own transformation, shedding half of its factory jobs in a five-year stretch and replacing them with an equal number in trading, banking, and assorted commercial services.

Little is made in Hong Kong anymore besides money. The city is composed of middlemen like Liam Casey, who weave the strands of capital, components, and customers into finished goods—the warp and weft of the Delta. The result is unlike any megalopolis we have seen before: a tapestry of cities, each with its own role—storefront, factory, or casino (Macau)—as opposed to the distinctly autonomous ones found in the Rhine and Silicon valleys. Hong Kong orchestrates the others in much the same way Casey conducts his network of factories, and he would be the first to tell you this arrangement is nothing new here. His method of farming out production to his partners was invented by another all but invisible middleman, Li & Fung.

Li & Fung is a pure product of the Delta. Founded a century ago, the family-run firm was among the first Chinese merchants to operate overseas. From Guangzhou—formerly Canton, one of the treaty ports opened by the British—the founders exported porcelain, silks, and tea. It wasn't until the war (and a move to Hong Kong) that the next generation entered the garment trade. The third set of Fungs, brothers William and Victor, took the reins in the early 1970s, after the global quota system had fractured the industry along national borders. Their competition began leaving town for Taiwan shortly thereafter.

These days, the brothers work from the top of the Li & Fung Tower, a converted factory in one of the densest quarters of Kowloon. Downstairs are showrooms attesting to the firm's full line of offerings—not just clothing and linens, but glassware, luggage, furniture, and toys. Scattered throughout are tableaux devoted to the likes of Target, Disney, and Coca-Cola. Li & Fung is responsible for all of the latter's latter-day memorabilia—the invariably plastic knickknacks hoarded by collectors and showcased under glass at the Coca-Cola "museum" in Atlanta.

The floor is a successor to the vanished Toy Center on lower Fifth

Avenue in Manhattan, where the entire industry gathered each spring. (The Toy Center was converted into condos in 2005.) But the transfer of power wasn't total. The epicenter of the toy business isn't here in Kowloon any more than fashion's is still on Seventh Avenue. "There is no new Garment District or Toy Center," the Fungs wrote in their contribution to management literature, *Competing in a Flat World*. "You might not be able to corner the market on expertise or pin it down to a few buildings in New York. But you can find it all around the world. You can hire it. You can orchestrate it." And this is what Li & Fung does.

Its revenues are greater than those of Toys "R" Us or Gap without owning either a single brand or factory. "Orchestration" means micromanaging eight thousand factories from seventy offices in forty countries. The company employs an estimated two million textile workers worldwide—a workforce the size of Walmart's—only ten thousand of whom are actually on payroll.

On another floor are the creative teams handling the same tasks for their Seventh Avenue clients that Liam Casey hopes to win from his Silicon Valley ones. Their cubicles are knee-deep in the debris of Polaroids, tear sheets, and fabric swatches you'd find cluttering a designer's atelier. Each team frantically oversees creation, production, and distribution for brands like Juicy Couture and Tommy Hilfiger, without ever laying a hand on the merchandise. A jacket might be designed in New York, its cloth woven in Thailand, the zippers found around the Delta, and finally sewn in Shenzhen, with each step conducted from Hong Kong.

As the consummate middlemen, the Fung brothers insist that the fundamental clash in business—company versus company, grappling mano a mano—is an illusion. The real competition, as Kasarda continually stresses, is supply chains versus supply chains, networks against networks. Even in textiles, the most ruthless and primitive industry, the lowest costs matter less than speed, smarts, and resilience. It typically takes a year for a mainstream brand to design a line, source it, make it, and literally ship it to its stores. Li & Fung does it for them in six weeks with its massively parallel network of factories. Fashion has been superseded by the "fast-fashion" labels of H&M, Zara, Uniqlo, and Topshop, all of which restock their shelves from the Delta via air, often courtesy of Li & Fung. As a report by the American Chamber of Commerce in Hong Kong put it: "Clothing is increasingly considered a perishable good."

Or a disposable one. Either way, the fact remains that the Delta is once again stuck at the bottom of the smiley curve, while this time Hong Kong profits at both ends. There's a reason why it let the mainland have its factories in the first place—they didn't pay. This is galling to China's policy makers, who are accustomed to picking winners.

Decreeing a long march up the smiley curve, they began by hiking taxes in 2008. The rate for foreign companies will climb from 15 to 25 percent by 2012, while taxes for homegrown ones will fall to match it. The only exceptions will reside within tax-free zones specializing in high-tech, higher-paying work. A new labor law aimed at cleaning up the sweatshops required bosses to sign written contracts, limit overtime, and offer severance pay. Unnerved by the speed and severity of the recession, Beijing rolled back some of these reforms, while many factory bosses simply chose to ignore them. But the Delta's upward trajectory is set.

As exports were falling off a cliff at the end of 2008, China's highest-ranking think tank unveiled plans for the "reform and development" of the Delta through 2020. Their wish list included a new Big Three of "superautomakers" led by the electrified BYD. The Delta would also dominate wind power, "environmental protection," stem-cell research, "bio-breeding," and a grab bag of electronics, including the shining symbol of Americans' home equity hangover: the flat-screen TV. Not by coincidence, their list matches one by Harvard's Willy Shih of the bleeding-edge technologies America is most at risk of losing, which also includes "electronic ink," LEDs, and thin-film solar cells. If they get their way, a decade from now there will be twenty more companies the size of Li & Fung, only they'll be "globally recognized brands" instead of hiding in the shadows.

The central government intends to do this by "phasing out a number of backward enterprises, relocating a batch of labor-intensive ones, uplifting those with advantages, and fostering some with potentials." Such strident intervention was once incomprehensible to Western free marketeers, but that was before GM and AIG. For obvious reasons, China has more policy levers to pull than most, including a $586 billion stimulus and an open spigot of borrowed cash. Tax breaks, nationalized banks, and bureaucratic prodding can do wonders, but China has turned once again to what it does best: paving tarmac. The bulk of the stimulus has already been spent on highways, high-speed railways, and a hundred new airports. (America's own stimulus paid for only two out of three.)

Guangzhou and Shenzhen have been designated as all-around hubs. The expansion of Baiyun Airport and FedEx "will be quickened to reinforce its pivotal status and strengthen its international competitiveness." Hong Kong's historical advantage as a free port has always been its infrastructure—its harbor and its airport—an advantage the central government is now trying desperately to erase.

The endgame, as far as anyone can tell, is to supplant Hong Kong. The roles have been cast. Shanghai will replace it as China's financial hub (a plan ratified in 2010), while "Guangzhou will be developed into the 'Best District'" as "an international metropolis that embraces the world and serves the whole country. Shenzhen will continue to play its role as the window of the special economic zones" and fulfill its destiny as "a city exemplifying socialism with Chinese characteristics." But the Overnight City and Hong Kong had other ideas.

The morning I arrived in Kowloon, its citizens were shocked to learn that their government was plotting an outright merger with Shenzhen. A think tank backed by the city's chief executive had concluded Hong Kong was barely punching above its weight. As big as it is—with seven million inhabitants, it's around the size of Greater London—it can't hope to keep up with the megacities next door. Presaging the World Bank's findings, they determined Hong Kong didn't have the scale to go it alone—it would eventually be surpassed by the Delta's exponentially accelerating metabolism. Together, however, they would pull ahead of Guangzhou economically (and Shanghai and Beijing) to trail only the global city trinity of New York, Tokyo, and London. The one stumbling block—and it will likely be their undoing—is Hong Kong's political autonomy, as codified in the "one country, two systems" edict guaranteeing its freedoms through 2047. In an editorial supporting the plan, the voice of the city's establishment, the *South China Morning Post*, argued this was a "straitjacket" that, "but for history," was holding Hong Kong back. For fifty years, its biggest problem was its proximity to China; now it seemed it couldn't get close enough.

Overheated rhetoric aside, the think tank's top priority for merging the pair into a megacity of twenty million was to combine their airports, "creating a Hong Kong–Shenzhen super air hub that would be the focus of global attention." Shenzhen is mimicking its neighbor once again by planning to pave what is essentially a new airport into the Delta, then connecting it to Hong Kong's via high-speed rail. Hong Kong's is already an aerotropolis, by their own admission: "Hong Kong airport is the heart of Hong Kong."

"It's a defensive gesture for both," Victor Sit expounded over breakfast at the University of Hong Kong, as clouds swirled by our window on the mountainside. "Shenzhen also needs Hong Kong as a counterweight to Guangzhou." An economic geographer, Sit has been tracing the Delta's evolution for thirty years. The airports receive top billing, he said, because they are the best proxies for the region's balance of power.

"The airport people have been trying to sell the idea of linking all five." Hong Kong's standing as the first among equals would be cemented in a Delta-wide aerotropolis. "It would remain the international hub, while the other four would play their parts—a division of labor," he said. "Guangzhou would be a feeder into Hong Kong, while Macau specialized in tourism and Zhuhai in cargo." Hong Kong would separate the Delta into its constituent parts, keeping the plum roles for itself and away from Guangzhou.

While it chases the City and Wall Street, Macau has been thoroughly colonized by Las Vegas. The former Portuguese possession has been China's gambling hub for half a century—a mecca for the mainland's day-tripping, chain-smoking baccarat addicts. In the bad old days a decade ago, Macau's rackets recalled the nadir of Vegas in the eighties, between the Rat Pack's heyday and Cirque du Soleil's, when the city made its money from the RVs camped in front of Circus Circus, then the most profitable casino in the world. Things began to change after Steve Wynn opened the Mirage in 1989, ushering in the current age of spectacles in which the Strip has been imploded block by block and rebuilt with self-contained resorts drawing a convention crowd via air.

As with everyplace else in China, Macau is baldly copying the American model at warp speed. The first concessions to foreign casinos were granted in 2002. Five years later, it had overtaken Sin City as the globe's gambling capital. Not content with opening the world's biggest casino, the Venetian Macao, its billionaire owner Sheldon Adelson announced plans for a dozen others on the "Cotai Strip™" ("Asia's Las Vegas™"), built atop landfill adjacent to the airport. The Great Recession nearly sank the project, pushing Adelson to the brink of insolvency as he raced to cover his bets.

If the Cotai Strip is to live up to its billing, let alone its budget, Macau must attract a different breed of gambler than the factory workers of the Delta, for whom a night at the Venetian costs half a year's pay. Adelson and his rivals will have to fly them in by the tens of millions—from Mumbai to Manila and all points in between. More than slot machines, the casinos aspire to export a distinctly American brand of hedonism—chaste but chasing a glint of danger, fueled by equal parts shopping, eating, relaxing, and gambling, in that order.

(Ironically, Adelson's desperate lieutenants in Vegas have taken to importing Chinese high rollers—the last whales still gambling—aboard private jumbo jets outfitted with baccarat tables to while away the fourteen-hour flights. Winnings above international waters are tax free.)

Bordering Macau to the north is Zhuhai, the younger brother of Shenzhen. Founded around another special economic zone, the city never really took off by China's standards, topping out at about the size of Philadelphia. But it was blessed with an airport that was a tabula rasa, gleaming and empty. Victor Sit brought it to John Kasarda's attention more than a decade ago, inspiring him to recycle the blueprints of the Global TransPark. As a man in good standing with Beijing, Sit pressed their plan on party leaders, who nodded their approval and then were never heard from again. Consensus had already settled on Guangzhou. A new airport five times the size of the old one opened there in 2004 and is now in the midst of its second expansion (to a capacity exceeding O'Hare's). It isn't deserted, either. The hub of China Southern Airlines, the largest carrier in Asia, is also one of the busiest.

Sit made his case again for cooperation over competition during breakfast, but he was philosophical. What else could one expect from the Middle Kingdom's five-thousand-year legacy of command and control (to say nothing of Mao's). You can still see it clearly in Beijing, where the ring roads radiate outward from the Forbidden City. Hidden within his hub, the emperor received word from earth and instructions from heaven, replying via a network of couriers who relayed his divine orders to every corner of *tianxia*, all under the sky. Now a network of planes and hubs is being built to ferry their descendants, but the ancient need for hierarchies still applies.

The Space of Flow

"Guangzhou is trying to catch up, but I wouldn't say it's a 'threat,'" said Stanley Hui, drawing out his distaste for the word. Hui is Hong Kong's dapper airport chief and the former head of Dragonair, one of the dozens of airlines now flying around China. We were sipping tea that afternoon atop the Li & Fung Tower, waiting for Victor Fung.

The older brother long ago relinquished his daily duties to act as the Delta's economic czar instead. Picture Steve Jobs advising Obama; that's Victor Fung. He was chairman of the Airport Authority during the Delta's long boom, until he was tapped by the city's chief executive to somehow make the meltdown work for Hong Kong.

It was tempting to see the pair, Victor and Stanley, as the ghosts of Hong Kong's past and present. Although both men are Chinese, Stanley's clipped speech and reticence seemed quintessentially British, while baby-faced Victor struck me as a laissez-faire American—the result of time spent as a teacher and student at Harvard Business School.

He wanted to send the message that Hong Kong would steer the Delta rather than the other way around, and that this would keep both entities in touch with the financial realities of trade. "We kept the front end and the back end in Hong Kong, and the labor-intensive middle moved across the border," he said, recapping the smiley curve. "Then we consolidated what was left into what we call 'producer services,'" the orchestration Li & Fung does so well. "The U.S. is very service-intensive too, but it's all about McBurgers," he said pointedly. "Retail, real estate, and consumers."

"Our economy is sustained by the efficient movement of people," said Fung. "You should think of it like this: if you want to manufacture things, go to China. If you want to orchestrate the flow of goods, do it in Hong Kong. We want the *flow*; the rest can go to China. We should have a big sign over the airport's marquee: '*Flow*.' Flows of goods, flows of people . . ."

". . . Logistics, in a way," Hui interrupted. "Supply chains . . ."

". . . Anything to do with flow. We orchestrate it; we remove the constraints holding it back . . ."

". . . Traders who come and go . . ."

". . . The more flow we have, the better, and it's all made possible by the airport, of course. If you want to stow something, stow it in China. Our valuable land should be dedicated to flow."

Their banter reminded me of "the space of flows," the shadowy plane of existence where globalization lives. Coined by the sociologist Manuel Castells in his epic *The Rise of the Network Society* (a *Das Kapital* for the Instant Age), the space of flows is like the Matrix—it is all around us, everywhere, even now in this very room.

"Our society is constructed around flows," he wrote. "Flows of capital, flows of information, flows of technology, flows of organizational interaction, flows of images, sounds and symbols . . . *The space of flows is the material organization of time-sharing social practices that work through flows*" (the frantic italics are his). In English, the space of flows is a way of mapping the social and other networks, which play a bigger role in defining who we are and how we live than the patches of physical space we happen to call home. Think of it as a flowchart for understanding globalization.

John Kasarda teaches us that people have always sought to cover as much ground and forge as many bonds as possible, and that each new form of transportation explodes the previous scope of daily life and with it our communities. But it was Castells who first saw the shape of the Instant Age—the network as metaphor. His theory explains why we have aerotropoli, because "the space of flows is constituted by its nodes and hubs," the places where the spectral becomes corporeal—where globalization is made flesh in the form of cities. Castells identifies a "new spatial form" emerging: the megacity. His textbook example is the Delta, which he tellingly diagrams with Hong Kong on the edge and Guangzhou at its core. The most striking thing about such cities is that they are "*globally connected and locally disconnected.*" The Delta may be the world's factory, but nothing it makes is within reach of the peasants past its fringes, who are uprooting seventy generations of history to find their fortunes here. An estimated 140 million farmers have already left their homes, and the gap between rich and poor, urban and rural, is widening. China's solution is to build megacities in its interior, like Chongqing, which is officially three times the size of New Jersey and equally dense. China's biggest challenge in the Instant Age will be linking its hinterlands to the world—and dialing them into the space of flows.

Hong Kong is already there. Before the crash, *Time* splashed a story on its cover praising New York, London, and Hong Kong as the world's tripartite financial capital. "Connected by long-haul jets and fiber-optic cable, and spaced neatly around the globe, the three cities have (by accident—nobody planned this) created a financial network that has been able to lubricate the global economy, and, critically, ease the entry into the modern world of China, the giant child of our century. Understand this network of cities—Nylonkong, we call it—and you understand our time."

Something Victor said snapped me back to attention: *Our valuable land should be dedicated to flow.* This was the logic of the aerotropolis in a sentence; Hong Kong International and its $20 billion island is literally a space of flows. SkyCity, as it's called, combines the city's largest expo hall and hotel with the world's biggest cargo terminal—the local beginning and end of the smiley curve. He credits Kasarda with giving him the idea for it. "From the showrooms at the exhibition hall to the freight forwarders—of whom we have more than anyone else—it's everyone in the chain," Fung said. "That's a pretty crisp description of an aerotropolis."

When its plans were drafted, the airport lay on the far western edge of the territory, across from verdant wilderness. The city landed on its doorstep in the form of Tung Chung, a "new town" intended to be larger than Orlando. Its skyline is a score of seventy-story apartment towers standing shoulder to shoulder, each with spectacular views of the airfield. Farther up the coast is Hong Kong Disneyland, a shrunken facsimile of Walt Disney World's Magic Kingdom, although its neighbor fulfills Walt's dream of a Disney World International Airport.

Pan back far enough, and you'll see that rather than bobbing on the rim of Hong Kong, the airport floats at the center of the Delta. Especially now that construction has begun on the Zhuhai–Macau Bridge, an eighteen-mile, $5.5 billion causeway spanning the mouth of the Delta and landing on Hong Kong's doorstep at SkyCity. Kasarda is in awe of the airport's "quadramodality"—its combination of planes, trains, automobiles, and ferries running between all points upstream—and it's not hard to imagine it as the core of a galactic mega-aerotropolis of more than 140 million people. What would it take to make the Delta's magnetic poles reverse? How do you divert the space of flows?

Tea Leaves and Factories

Ask Kasarda about the origin of the word "aerotropolis," and he'll readily admit he first heard it in Zhuhai. Rem Koolhaas overheard it too, while on one of his periodic quests for urban dystopia. The master builder was the first to notice the predatory planning practiced in the Delta. Dueling municipalities had abandoned solving common problems to prey on one another instead, building bridges to nowhere or, in Zhuhai's case, waiting to see whether it was worth building to Shenzhen or Hong Kong. (Who would win?)

"So here we are facing a new concept of infrastructure," Koolhaas noted dryly. "Infrastructures that were mutually reinforcing and totalizing are becoming more and more competitive and local . . . This enormous system only exists to trigger off a future urban situation. Infrastructures no longer pretend to create functioning wholes but now spin off functional entities," aerotropoli being some of them. "Zhuhai is a failure," he added, but "even though the city is a failure, it is very adamant about being a success in the future." Not so. Disobeying Beijing's orders, it built a gleaming airport of its own. Its punishment was a permanent ban on international flights—and any hopes of tourism. Overruled by Beijing, the theater of operations has shifted to Guangzhou.

The receding wheat fields outside city limits will become an aerotropolis because the government said so. Not that there were better options. The largest city in southern China is still growing steadily and is busy arranging a metropolitan merger of its own with Foshan, yet another factory town of seven million. Naturally, the area around the airport is growing faster, and the results haven't been pretty.

The aerotropolis zone is tabletop flat, supposedly empty land, and this is the essence of its appeal. "The land is very smooth," one of its caretakers rhapsodized. "It's easy to plan, to build, and to use." Its perimeters are sketchy, its cartography minimal: thirty-four square miles of open land, a blank slate broader than Hong Kong Island. Having conceded that Memphis's sprawl is a lost cause, FedEx is keen not to repeat any of its mistakes at "America's Aerotropolis™" or around its European hub outside Paris at Charles de Gaulle. "Aerotropolis Europe™" is envisioned as part of French president Nicolas Sarkozy's plan to create a Grand Paris twice the size of Hong Kong.

Guided once again by Kasarda, FedEx is determined to take a more active role at its Pacific hub in China, at "Asia's Aerotropolis™" in Guangzhou. The aerotropolis's borders are zealously guarded by city planners, who have forbidden anyone to build without permission. But it's hardly vacant.

On the short drive over the gravel back roads between the FedEx hub and terminal, I passed tin shacks and stunted orchards, deserted apartment blocks, and cement mixers pouring concrete for new ones next door. Schoolgirls on bicycles wheeled circles around me like a school of curious fish. All of this exurban scrub would be cleared—to date eight thousand families have been evicted—but left to its own devices it would cover the site like kudzu (a species native to the Delta). The only way to preserve the land was to declare a city on the spot—to defer its use by fiat until they figured out a use for it.

Until then, the layout is hazy and the figures are rounded. The impact of the FedEx hub and its customers in orbit is officially pegged at $63 billion by 2020, compounded by billions more once the battery makers and windmill fabricators envisioned by Beijing are compelled to set up shop around it. Adjacent to the hub is an industrial park modeled on the Guangzhou Economic and Technological Development Zone, one of the first commissioned by Deng Xiaoping. Factory zones are to China's instant cities what the exurbs were to American ones—the simplest formula for propelling growth. A common strategy is to clear the land, flip it to factory owners at below-market rates, and subsidize their investors with tax breaks. The GETDZ pioneered this approach to become the world's factory for chewing gum, toothpaste, and artificial flavors. The aerotropolis is aiming higher, at the microchip and motherboard makers stranded around FedEx's abandoned hub in Subic Bay. The attempted theft of a national industry is not something anyone here wants to talk about, considering the British did the same once to Guangzhou.

The first factories had appeared along the Delta's banks three hundred years before, in the 1680s, when the city was still known as Canton. The Thirteen Factories were stores in the front with a warehouse in the back, named for the foreign agents, or "factors," within. In 1757, Emperor Qianlong closed all of China's ports to barbarian influence except for one, an arrangement called the Canton System. Overnight, its docks became the single hub for all the porcelain, silk, and tea in China.

Just as his successors developed a taste for Treasury bills, the emperor demanded New World silver. Then as now, the ensuing trade imbalance drained the British treasury. Unable to just print money, the Crown's agents had a better idea: opium. If the emperor would not accept textiles, they would trade one addiction for another. When he tried to ban the drug, Britain went to war for its habit. The Treaty of Nanking, signed in 1842, ceded Hong Kong outright and lifted Canton's restrictions. The Thirteen Factories burned later, after which China agreed to open additional ports. Once and future capitalist experiments, they were among the earliest cities reformed and reopened by Deng.

The liberation of the tea trade triggered the last, fullest flowering of the Age of Sail: clipper ships. With their tall masts, narrow hulls, and sharply raked bows, they were designed to outrun blockades but were quickly repurposed for running tea. The all-time sailing record between New York and Canton was set by the *Sea Witch*: seventy-four days, fourteen hours—shaving more than a month off the route. America experienced its first glut of cheap imports. By 1850, a fifth of all household goods in Salem, Massachusetts, were made in China.

Tea leaves are the definition of a perishable good, vulnerable to mold in the damp sea air. A long voyage home ran the risk of spoilage or staleness. The prospect of writing off seventeen million rotting pounds had forced the British East India Company to ask for a bailout in 1773. Parliament relented, paying for it with a tax that touched off the Boston Tea Party. The first American clipper to run the London route was *The Oriental*, arriving after ninety-seven days—half the time it took lumbering "East Indiamen" to make the trip.

Anticipating our manias for the newest thing—whether iPads or Mios or miShares—serving the first tea of the season became all the rage in London. In lieu of brands or blends, they were named for the ships they came in on—the faster and more famous, the better. The competition soon grew so fierce that all that mattered was being first—crowds slept on the docks in anticipation. Their desire drove the tea clippers from Canton up to Fuzhou, a treaty port closer to the tea-growing regions. The premium on speed sparked a twenty-year run of clipper races culminating in the Great Tea Race of 1866, in which a field of forty ships sprinted for sixteen thousand miles and ninety-nine days, ending with a photo finish on the Thames.

The races ended a few years later. The opening of the Suez Canal in 1869 and the arrival of steamships on the route spelled the end for clippers, as their combined speed once again redrew the maps. Still, when FedEx founder Fred Smith describes his fleet of Boeing 777s as "clipper ships," he isn't trying to be poetic. He's drawing a line between the Qing dynasty and the current one, in which the Delta's preeminent port is again Canton, and everything made in China is as fresh and fleeting as tea.

One Hundred Airports

I first landed in Beijing exactly a year before the Olympics, when it still felt necessary to see the place before China turned on the pivot of the Games. Hindsight being what it is, the opening ceremonies—a $300 million spectacle of human synchrony—have since been recast as the last bender on America's tab. Lehman Brothers imploded a month later, and for the second September in a decade, recent history was divided into Before and After. The Olympics (along with the empty Bird's Nest) were relegated to the irrelevant Before.

The Delta's export machinery worked well enough before the crisis, but the deleveraging of America's household debt meant the end, at least temporarily, of the outflow of flat-screen TVs. Without missing a beat, the Politburo gave a green light to every shovel-ready scheme once put on hold to prevent the economy from overheating. China began ramping up for the greatest infrastructure spending spree any economy had ever seen. What happened next belongs to the After.

I had the misfortune of arriving ahead of Terminal 3, Norman Foster's updated take on his vaulted glass cathedral for Hong Kong. As I emerged from the depths of the dour Terminal 2, my first sight of China was a Starbucks. The writer Kurt Andersen later made a similar mistake, one he quickly rectified. "Taking the shuttle from Terminal 2 to Terminal 3 is like going on a theme-park time-travel ride," he wrote, "whisked from grotty old Communist China to the bright, shimmering World of Tomorrow in 15 minutes flat. And it's a perfect illustration of the speed with which history and architecture are moving in China, since the 'old' terminal opened only in 1999."

Foster's mile-long, dragon-headed concourse could accommodate all five of Heathrow's terminals, with enough room left over for a sixth. (It was the world's largest building under one roof before surrendering the title to Dubai's own Terminal 3.) As impressive as it is—and architecture critics swooned—it's arguably the least ambitious piece of the airport's master plan. The dragon is an ornament on "Beijing Capital Airport City," John Kasarda's latest brainchild. Lying northwest of the ring roads encircling the Forbidden City, the aerotropolis will be larger than Guangzhou's, with an "inland free port" and special zones for one hundred thousand workers and three hundred thousand residents. The renderings bear a familial resemblance to Suvarnabhumi's but are otherwise generic, which is the point. Beijing's aerotropolis is the template for dozens under construction, including the capital's second hub, due in 2015.

China is placing the single biggest bet on aviation of any country, ever. Even before the crisis and China's subsequent stimulus, the central government announced as part of its Eleventh Five-Year Plan that it would build a hundred new airports by 2020, at a cost of $62 billion. The first forty were ready last year. The vast majority lie inland, hugging provincial capitals and secondary cities bigger than any in the States. Full-scale aerotropoli are planned for China's western hubs, Chongqing and Chengdu, and its ancient capital in the northwest, Xi'an. The others are slated for a mix of historic cities and outsourcing hubs like Changsha, Kunming, Hangzhou, Shenyang, and Dalian. Shanghai built two for the crowds headed to Expo 2010, expected to be the best-attended World's Fair in history.

Besides airports, China laid as many miles of high-speed railroad track in the last five years as Europe did in the last two decades. The trains, in turn, are meant to keep people off the highways, to which China's adding thirty thousand miles—enough to eclipse the American interstate highway system. China's planners have internalized the lessons of America's Eisenhower-era infrastructure boom, designing a world-class system for moving people and goods quickly, cheaply, and reliably across any distance, whether locally by highway, regionally by rail, or globally by air. The plan is to pick up and move large swaths of the Delta hundreds or even thousands of miles inland. There is nothing to stop them.

If China's leaders want to do something, they just do it. This is as true for local party secretaries as it is in Beijing. The dirty secret of

China's breakneck growth is the ruthless competition between cities to attract business, because land sales comprise as much as a quarter of their budgets. As the Hong Kong economist Steven Cheung once explained their attitude, "You want a business license? The locality will assign someone to do the walking and talking for you. Want a building permit? They will give you one with money-back guarantees. Unhappy about that dirty creek passing through the site? They may offer to build a small lake for you . . . They sell their cheap electricity, sell their parks and entertainment, sell their easy transportation, sell their water supply, sell their glorious history and even sell how good-looking their girls are—no exaggeration!" This is both their greatest strength and in the long run their greatest weakness. Remember what they said about democracy? *It just gets in the way.* This is how Foster's dragon was built in five years flat, at a cost of ten thousand flattened homes. Multiply that by a hundred, and you have the initial human cost of China's aerotropoli.

This has not gone unnoticed in the United States. President Obama first sounded the alarm on the campaign trail. "Think about the amount of money that China has spent on infrastructure," he said at one stop. "Their ports, their train systems, their airports are all vastly the superior to us now, which means if you are a corporation deciding where to do business, you're starting to think, 'Beijing looks like a pretty good option.'" He was wrong about one thing: corporations are looking much, much farther afield than Beijing.

General Electric's CEO, Jeff Immelt, talks openly about using China's airports as a treasure map pointing the way to hundreds of billions of dollars in power, water, and rail projects to follow. "The Chinese are beginning to shift growth out of the major metropolitan cities like Shanghai and Beijing and move into tier-two cities," explained GE's point man in China, Steve Bertamini. "We figure in the next five-year period, the Chinese government is going to spend two trillion dollars on infrastructure projects. We think there's probably a good chunk of that, let's say at least half, that has some GE opportunity."

China's airport strategy has even thawed relations with Taiwan. Their first step to rapprochement was the resumption of regularly scheduled flights in 2009, after a sixty-year freeze. Taiwan's president, Ma Ying-jeou, marked the occasion by unveiling Taipei's own aerotropolis—a ten-year, $13 billion project copied from Kasarda's handbook effectively doubling the capital in size. A free-trade agreement with the mainland followed in the summer of 2010, providing Taiwan's economy with a much-needed jolt. Its future hinges on rerouting the flows of talent and capital currently skipping it for Shanghai and the Delta.

Twenty-five years ago, China's airlines carried 7 million passengers annually—as many as America's handle every few days. Twelve months ago, it was 230 million, and the goal is to match America's 725 million passengers a year by 2020. While trains connect its coastal megacities, China is counting on its airports to bind east and west together, and then tie them all to the world. Or so explained Sha Hongjiang, deputy director of planning for the aviation ministry. "In addition to the hubs in Beijing, Shanghai, and Guangzhou," he said, "we're trying to turn cities in the south and northwest into international ones. Just as a place like Dubai is building a new airport to connect itself to the world, so are we." He didn't think China was overdoing it. "We'll have two hundred and fifty airports when we're finished with these, but America has five hundred," he reasoned. The dilemma he faced everywhere was, "Should we expand the old airport, or just abandon it and build a new one?" It was usually the latter. "In the past, we always underestimated the growth of the economy. We would build a new one, and as soon as we were done, it was full. Now we're trying to overestimate and see where we are five years from now."

Finding another five hundred million passengers should be easy. China has anywhere between 125 and 150 cities with populations greater than a million. The United States has nine; Europe, thirty-six. When the first phase of China's airport-building boom is complete, the number of hubs handling thirty million passengers annually—more than Boston's Logan or Washington's Dulles—will have risen from three to thirteen, all of which will be the host of aerotropoli. By the time they're finished in 2020, 82 percent of the population—1.5 billion people—will live within a ninety-minute drive of an airport, nearly twice the number today.

But how many can afford to fly? You may recall that travel invariably rises with income. Since Deng's Reform and Opening, the average Chinese person's has risen nearly sevenfold. Martin Ravallion, the World Bank's head of research, defines the planet's emerging middle class as earning between $2 and $13 a day—the gap between absolute destitution and America's poverty line. Using this range as his benchmark, he found China's middle class added 600 million members in fifteen years, rising from 174 million in 1990 to a staggering 806 million in 2005. Who knows how much bigger and richer it will be a decade from now.

What sets cities such as Changsha and Kunming apart from Hong Kong and Guangzhou is that they have never had a window on the world. With the exception of Xi'an, the terminus of the Silk Road, China's heartland cities have been isolated for millennia. The nation's first—and last—foreign expeditions were the treasure fleets of Zheng He, the admiral who cruised the Indian Ocean nearly a century before the Portuguese. His nine-masted junks were the jumbo jets of their era, outclassing anything Europe could put in the water. Following his seventh, final voyage in 1433, the Ming emperor abruptly halted the expeditions and turned his back on trade. His mandate was buttressed by later emperors who banned oceangoing vessels and made it a crime to go to sea. When the Qings came to power in 1644, they took the extreme measure of torching a seven-hundred-mile strip of coastline. These sanctions had the intended effect of putting the Middle Kingdom into a coma.

"Let China sleep," Napoleon famously admonished, "for when she awakes, she will shake the world." The sleeper awakened in 1979 and had started shaking twenty years later when president Jiang Zemin urged factory owners to "Go West." He hoped to drive growth toward China's impoverished interior provinces, narrowing the noxious inequality between them and the coast. In 2001, on the eve of joining the WTO, Jiang instructed his own people to "Go Out" into the world. What began as a race to lock up natural resources has evolved into a mass migration of traders and tourists to the Middle East and sub-Saharan Africa, where there are as many as a million Chinese on the ground in mining, construction, farming, and any other sector they can dominate.

So what will China do with hundreds of new airports and dozens of aerotropoli? It will go west, go out, and go global. More than any other nation, China grasps that the aerotropolis is a weapon, a well-oiled piece of urban machinery that recasts cities as competitive engines. It will use them to unleash China's greatest competitive advantage on the world: its people.

China has arbitraged its labor all along by keeping exchange rates artificially low, studding the countryside with frictionless zones, and turning a blind eye to the 140 million illegal immigrants flooding the coast. All so it can keep growing 8 percent per year—the minimum speed before the wheels start to come off from unemployment and unrest. Until now its people have been largely immobile, confined to the countryside or the factory towns of the Delta, scrimping and saving. All of this will change as the Chinese begin to leave the west for the West, streaming into Africa and Detroit, or places like Prato, the center of Italy's textile industry.

As James Kynge tells the story in *China Shakes the World*, Prato became a magnet for illegal immigrants smuggled out of China in the 1990s. "A Chinese cloth and garment cutter could expect to take home about 1,000 euros for a month of six-day weeks at fifteen hours a day," enough to save up until he quit and started a competing factory the next day. The number of Chinese-run companies in Prato rose from 212 in 1992 to 1,753 a decade later, and to more than 3,000 today. More and more of the Italian firms' spinning, weaving, cutting, and sewing left for China as their new rivals unraveled trade secrets and passed them back home. Before long, the Chinese were putting their former employers out of business. Of the six thousand or so Italian firms in Prato circa 2000, less than half remained in 2005. In roughly twenty years, through hard work and sheer will, the immigrants had thoroughly beaten them at their own game. So it goes. And so go the Chinese.

Go West

China was woken from its slumber by a wedge of "flying geese." The Japanese economist Kaname Akamatsu conjured this image in the 1930s to explain the development of Asia's economies. Innovations trickled down from the leader of the flock to the next wave of geese, and then to a third tier and a fourth. Japan was out in front, of course, and for decades the model held up. The Asian Tigers were next in line for its hand-me-downs—textiles and toys in Hong Kong, for instance.

The Tigers gradually climbed from clothes to cars to computing, shedding unprofitable industries along the way. Rising wages were the sign of when it was time for them to go—sooner or later, they would be priced out, as when Hong Kong's factories decamped en masse for Shenzhen. Where they would end up wasn't always clear—someplace cheaper, for sure, but also one equipped with the prerequisite infrastructure. This is how the world's factory ended up in the Delta—no one builds highways, ports, and airports faster or more furiously than China. According to the Chinese National Bureau of Statistics, China's GDP more than tripled and its exports quadrupled during the long boom between 9/11 and the crash; the real figures are likely much higher.

Could they have caused the crisis? The Great Recession's roots have proved impossible to trace, but at the macro level there's consensus that "global economic imbalances" were to blame. China's factory workers had produced too much and consumed too little—what future Federal Reserve chairman Ben Bernanke had blithely referred to in 2005 as a "global savings glut"—while Americans had done the opposite. The historian Niall Ferguson dubbed their codependency "Chimerica" to underscore how dangerously they'd become entwined, with China's savings financing America's debt in order to keep its factories humming.

In the aftermath, Ferguson led a chorus of critics calling for the dismantling of Chimerica. A "rebalancing" was necessary; Chinese consumers needed to pick up the slack, buying more of their own goods instead of sending them abroad. To speed things along, he asserted, the government must allow the yuan to rise against the dollar, instantly increasing its citizens' wealth by making imports less expensive. The world could then pull itself out of its rut by selling to China. But this would put a crimp in China's own exports as they grew more expensive. Its economy would cool until homegrown firms learned to climb the smiley curve just as Japan's and the Tigers' had done before them. In the meantime, textiles and toys would leave for Vietnam and Bangladesh, taking low-paying jobs with them. The flying geese would be sprung from their cages to make way for new birds.

Party leaders demurred. Faced with twenty million angry, idled peasants in the Delta alone, they kicked the factories back into high gear. "China is heading in the opposite direction of 'rebalancing,'" warned former U.S. labor secretary Robert Reich. "China wants to become the world's pre-eminent producer nation. It also wants to take the lead in the production of advanced technologies . . . China's export policy is really a social policy, designed to maintain order." The goal wasn't rebalancing but something more like full employment.

Determined to create jobs in the teeth of the recession, China exploited its cost advantage to the hilt. As the dollar sank against the euro, the yuan sank with it, making exports cheaper than ever. French president Nicolas Sarkozy accused the government of "monetary dumping," while the Nobel laureate economist Paul Krugman denounced its mercantilist approach as "a beggar-thy-neighbor policy—or, more accurately, a beggar-everyone-but-yourself policy." He estimated that China cost Americans 1.4 million jobs during the recession, many of them the green ones President Obama had promised "can't be outsourced." In just two years, it had leapfrogged the West to become the world's largest manufacturer of wind turbines and solar panels, employing a million workers and adding a hundred thousand annually. Ninety-five percent of the panels made by its flagship company were bound for overseas.

China's GDP growth resumed its double-digit pace, while developed nations stumbled from one crisis to the next. It overtook Germany as the world's top exporter and became America's largest trading partner, supplying a staggering 19 percent of imports—and a tenth of all goods traded worldwide. Its strategy was the same as Japan's in the 1970s: while America reeled from stagflation, it went for the jugular with a massive export blitz. It worked now as then, but like Japan, China was only eating a larger piece of its partners' shrinking pies.

To make up the difference, its state-owned banks dispensed $1.4 trillion in no-strings-attached loans on top of the stimulus. With $2 trillion in fiscal adrenaline hitting circulation at once, credit bubbles were a given. Billions found their way into real estate—land prices in China doubled that year, rising 200 percent in Shanghai and 400 percent in Guangzhou. "Both China and America are addressing bubbles by creating more bubbles and we're just taking advantage of that," explained the chairman of the People's Republic's $300 billion sovereign wealth fund. "So we can't lose."

But the vast majority was spent on yet another upgrade to the world's factory: more steel mills than the EU, Japan, the United States, and Russia combined, built with more cement than the rest of the *planet* combined. At this moment, China is spending a higher percentage of its GDP on infrastructure—planes, trains, and power plants—than any nation in history, close to half of its total output. Even Germany and Japan spent less on reconstruction following the atomic bomb and the blitz.

The sums being invested in the pursuit of exports—which all but guarantee China will chase them even harder, in an increasingly vicious cycle—have spooked analysts tallying numbers so large they can't possibly add up. The longest any country maintained a ratio as high as China's was Thailand's nine-year run until the baht crashed, taking most of Asia along with it. By that standard, China's time is just about up.

The most prominent skeptic is Jim Chanos, a billionaire investor who made his fortune spotting companies too good to be true and betting heavily they were a lie. Enron and the housing bust were his biggest scores. Now he's set his sights on China, recognizing signs of another massive property bubble ready to burst, "Dubai times one thousand—or worse," as he put it. In a speech last year at Oxford, he noted that China had thirty billion square feet of office space on the drawing boards, "which would work out to a five-by-five cubicle for every man, woman and child in the country. It's a frightening statistic." Chanos wagered they would never fill it.

He compared China to the Asian Tigers of the 1990s—high-flying geese that failed to evolve. They threw money and factories at their declining growth rates instead, working harder instead of smarter and never ascending the smiley curve. Inevitably, they smashed face-first into the wall of diminishing returns. The harder they come, the harder they fall.

Is Chanos right? There's smart money on both sides. It's too early to tell whether the central bank will succeed in deflating bubbles (or deferring them into the future), although one thing is certain: if beggaring the world is what it takes to raise a billion of its own people out of poverty, China is determined to try.

Maybe the most notable feature of its record-breaking build-out is where it's taking place: in the west. Only a few years ago, government investment was still focused along the coast, especially in the Delta, Shanghai, and Beijing. "Let some get rich first," Deng Xiaoping had ordained, which meant life expectancy in Guizhou province is a decade shorter than in the Delta, only a few hundred miles away.

Such massive inequality is the primary source of China's unrest—an estimated eighty thousand protests each year in rural towns and villages, suppressed and kept (mostly) out of sight. Despite the size of its coastal megacities, China is less urbanized than its peers. Barely half its citizens live in one, far below the developed world's 80 to 90 percent. The State Council expects another four hundred million peasants—the second wave in the largest migration in history—to move to cities in the next twenty years. In obeisance to Jiang's edict to "Go West," they are being herded away from the coast toward new megacities rising inland. The fear of this influx and the slums it might create underlies China's resolve to export its way out of poverty. The flying geese are migrating again.

It used to be that companies like Walmart or Intel outsourced to China; now they're outsourcing *within* China, keeping their headquarters and R & D in the Delta while shipping the rest westward as new airports come online. This is where the aerotropoli come in—they make it possible for a company like Siemens to invest billions in former backwaters like Wuhan, Chongqing, and Chengdu.

Li & Fung can feel it too. "The big shift in China is that the southern region that was really the heart of our industry is no longer the focus," its American president explained. "It is very clearly moving as quickly as it can to the other regions. [The Delta] will become the Silicon Valley of China, and everything else will move significantly inland."

"The factories are moving what we call 'more north,'" explained Munir Mashooqullah, a McKinsey alumnus who counts Zara among his clients. He tells them where to go. "The industrial areas have already been identified," he told me, "and the factories are being moved. The only problem used to be you had to drive three or four hours from the nearest airport to the factories; now they're putting the airports next to industrial hubs. The ones they're building are as nice as anything in Frankfurt or New York, but it takes a lot of courage for most people to leave Hong Kong. It isn't until they arrive in a place like Nanjing or Changsha that they realize these aren't bad places, that there are five-star hotels going up, and the airports are easy to use."

No place embodies China's inland megacity strategy quite like Chongqing. One of the master planners of its aerotropolis, a Dutchman, compares it to "Pittsburgh on steroids"; both cities perch above a confluence of rivers (in this case, the Yangtze and the Jialing), and both know what it's like to choke on acrid smog. But a more accurate comparison is Chicago at the peak of its vertical boom. "Chicago, then known as the fastest city on earth, took fifty years, until 1900, to increase its population by 1.7 million people," wrote James Kynge. "Chongqing is growing at *eight times* that speed," adding a city the size of Pittsburgh to its outskirts this year, and every year—year after year.

The central government has vowed to transform Chongqing into a city of twelve million—the "Chicago of the East"—by 2020, investing $147 billion to double its population between now and then. But the Dutchman couldn't figure out how. "No one knows what the economy is all about," he confessed. "They're building one ring road after another here, and trains, and even when they finish the whole shebang at the airport, they'll still have huge tracts for development. But when you stand on a lookout and look over the city at dusk, all you can see are high-rises, and the lights are off. It feels like an empty shell to me, but then again, there are a lot of companies moving to the southeast." Companies like HP. In 2009, the city signed a deal with the world's biggest seller of PCs to build laptops, notebooks, netbooks, tablets, and whatever's next here for export, as many as thirty million per year. Although technically speaking, HP wouldn't make them; Foxconn would.

China's factory owners might as well wear bracelets emblazoned "WWTGD." *What would Terry Gou do?* The mercurial founder of Foxconn and its parent, Hon Hai Precision Industry, is a legend in manufacturing circles, and, until recently, totally unknown in the West. He started out making plastic knobs for television sets, borrowing the money from his parents in Taiwan. After twenty years in Shenzhen, he'd built his monster factory there and a dozen smaller ones across China. Hon Hai is bigger than most of its customers, including Apple, Microsoft, and Dell. It is bigger than its ten closest competitors combined. It's the largest exporter in the world's largest exporting country. By one estimate, it produces half of all the electronics on earth. Gou's zeal for cost cutting is such that one of his lieutenants once quipped he was "worth about $2 billion in nickels and dimes."

His worst nightmare came true last summer when a spate of employee suicides at his Shenzhen plant caught the world's attention. The man who had always prided himself on being invisible stood accused of running the world's biggest sweatshop. Seeing no other way out, he promised to double wages and dismantle the factory-town model that had served him so well. "Today we are going a bit quickly and moving ahead of everyone else," he said, but when wages begin to rise across the Delta, "its speed and ferocity will be greater than you can imagine," he promised.

But Gou had no intention of passing higher costs along to Apple, which would probably laugh at such a request. He began dismantling his Shenzhen fortress instead. He wasn't giving up on China; in fact, just the opposite. "In the next twenty years, China won't have a competitor" as the world's factory, he told reporters. He planned to more than double his workforce, hiring 1.5 million new employees—all of them inland. In the weeks following the pay increase, Gou signed a flurry of deals to expand or open new factories north of the Delta, in Tianjin and Zhengzhou— where he planned to hire three hundred thousand workers—and in Chengdu, where he would invest $10 billion and hire a hundred thousand more. The Delta had at last grown too rich for his blood, so he was headed west too.

But he had saved his most audacious plans for Chongqing. Eventually, he told reporters, 80 percent of Foxconn's basic components would be assembled here, and in the meantime he and his partner—the former president of Google in China—would sift through the city's software outfits in hopes of finding a Facebook or Twitter killer.

Gou's old rivals, Quanta and Inventec, swiftly followed in his footsteps, each making its first foray into the hinterlands. If all goes as planned, a year from now computers will have overtaken cars as the largest industry in a city bigger than its Windy City namesake, gainfully employing seven hundred thousand new arrivals from the countryside. Three years after that, Chongqing aims to achieve its stated goal of becoming "Asia's biggest production center for laptops," minting eighty million a year, currently half the worldwide market.

In the beginning at least, they will all go by air. The architect of its cargo strategy is, of course, Kasarda, who has quietly advised all involved on the lift needed to ship three hundred thousand tons of batteries, screens, and circuitry a year from a former backwater lying a thousand miles upriver from Shanghai. The answer: ten fully loaded 747s a day, every day, forever. And that's just for laptops; they're expecting much more to be made there. There's a reason why Terry Gou has reportedly considered starting his own airline.

The Dutchman was right: the city *is* an empty shell, ready and waiting to be filled by peasants pouring in and companies alighting from the east. All of Chongqing, and all of its highways, high-rises, and ten thousand acres of pavement absorbed annually, has been prepared like a virgin bride for its union with Kasarda's aerotropolis.

Go Out

There was a hitch in China's plans to make more and sell more than ever before: Americans had stopped buying. The world's consumers of last resort had hit their credit limits. In polls, they swore to spend less and save more—to act Chinese, in other words—and the sales numbers bore out their resolve. By early 2009, Chimerica was unraveling. "Americans cannot—and will not—borrow and buy the world's way to lasting prosperity," President Obama declared. "No nation should assume its path to prosperity is simply paved with exports to the United States." The Politburo was unfazed; if Americans won't buy their goods, they reasoned, they would find someone who would. They would reopen the Silk Road. And not just to Dubai; the number of visitors to China from the Middle East, Africa, and Latin America quintupled between 2000 and 2007.

"If we can take the Congo," Mao said, "we can have all of Africa." He was talking about hearts and minds, but today's party leaders want what's in the ground. To feed both its export machine and rising standards of living, China needs not just oil and coal but also vast quantities of lumber, land, and minerals—all of which the Congo has in spades. China is already the world's biggest importer of copper, aluminum, nickel, and iron ore, but to reach South Korea's standards, "Chinese consumption of aluminum and iron ore will increase fivefold; oil, eightfold; and copper, ninefold," calculated the journalist Richard Behar. A Greek chorus of climatologists foretells disaster if this continues, but once again, China is determined to try.

No one knows how many Chinese are already on the ground there—a million is merely the most widely quoted estimate—engaged in what Behar has described in harrowing detail as "one of the most sweeping, bare-knuckled, and ingenious resource grabs the world has ever seen." Trade between the Continent and China has skyrocketed from $2 billion to $100 billion in the last decade, dwarfing the latter's trade with the Middle East.

Whether it's copper in Zambia, oil in Angola, or rare minerals in Congo, China wants it. Its agents are eight hundred or so state firms backed up by tens of thousands of private entrepreneurs. The Politburo softens up Africa's leaders with offers of cash, easy credit, investment, and aid, usually packaged as infrastructure, and always no questions asked. Armies of

Chinese laborers are as busy laying tracks and paving highways here as their countrymen are at home, in addition to the stadiums, pipelines, palaces, and parliaments they're building. Oil-rich Equatorial Guinea will receive a whole new capital. And then there are the airports.

A complete list is hard to come by, but China appears to be building one everywhere it deems strategic. Khartoum's opened last year, followed by Luanda's. The capital of Angola has surpassed the Saudis in Riyadh as China's largest source of crude. Nonstop flights arrive daily from Brussels, Moscow, Houston, and Beijing, filled with oilmen and bureaucrats ready to cut deals.

China's airlines began flying to Africa only in 2006, after President Hu Jintao personally instructed China Southern to open routes anywhere it saw fit. Its Dubai branch manager Jiang Nan chose Lagos, Nigeria—the largest city in what was then Africa's largest oil producer—upon discovering fifty thousand Chinese living there. There are more in Nigeria at this moment than there were Britons when it was still a colony.

They're in Africa because there aren't yet enough jobs for twelve million reformed peasants in Chongqing, so the government is sending them overseas. Chongqing's airport is pumping out settlers even faster than it's pumping investment in. "To convince the farmers to become landlords abroad," the head of China's Export-Import Bank told Behar, he's supplying them with sales leads, capital, and expertise. Thirteen thousand Chinese have landed in Africa from Chongqing alone; around 750,000 laborers in all shipped out just in 2009. They too are leaving by air. As Jiang Nan boasted to *China Safari* authors Serge Michel and Michel Beuret, "As a Chinese company we have a huge competitive edge shipping the Chinese to Africa, and you can't imagine how much the Chinese want to come."

As Americans grudgingly learned to make do with less, China looked to the Middle East and Africa to expand. Rather than wait for developed nations to come around, the economist Xu Shanda called for a Chinese "Marshall Plan" to build demand in developing ones instead. People's Bank of China governor Zhou Xiaochuan suggested using some of his $2 trillion in foreign currency reserves as a down payment. Officially, their ideas went nowhere; unofficially, both are being put into practice.

In November 2009, at a summit in the Egyptian resort town of Sharm el-Sheikh, Chinese premier Wen Jiabao pledged to double aid to

Africa to $10 billion while forgiving the debt from previous loans. He promised leaders from the forty-nine nations present that this "represents a new stage of development in relations with Africa." A month later, World Bank president Robert Zoellick told the *Financial Times* that he and Chinese commerce minister Chen Deming had discussed outsourcing some of China's dirtiest work to the continent—like smelting the copper mined there. But Chen had other things in mind.

China is creating seven special economic zones across Africa: in Nigeria (two), Egypt, Ethiopia, Mauritius, Zambia, and possibly Algeria. At least one will be anchored by an aerotropolis. Zambia's Lusaka New Airport City will be home to one hundred thousand residents, many of them Chinese. The same entities in charge of the Delta's export zones will manage these, while the China-Africa Development Fund will own stakes in at least three. Africa's rulers recognize the pattern. "When we look at the reality on the ground we find that there is something akin to a Chinese invasion of the African continent," Libyan foreign minister Musa Kusa noted darkly.

It's not just Africa, but anyplace vital to China's influx of raw materials and outflow of finished goods. An army of Chinese laborers is paving an aerotropolis near the newly built port of Gwadar in southwest Pakistan, where Chinese tankers will fill up on Iraqi oil and Afghanistan's minerals. The prospect of a "Chinese Dubai" has set off a land rush among the locals, but as the head of the Gwadar Development Authority told them, "By the time it's developed you might just need a visa to get here."

China is taking the New Silk Road as far as Australia. A free-trade agreement signed in 2002 with the Association of Southeast Asian Nations (ASEAN) finally took effect last year, eliminating tariffs on 90 percent of all goods traded with Thailand, Indonesia, Malaysia, Singapore, the Philippines, and Vietnam. Trade between both sides tripled in anticipation, climbing from $59.6 billion in 2003 to $192.5 billion by 2008. While China's total exports tumbled during the financial crisis, exports to ASEAN rose an eye-opening 21 percent. Combine the two, and you have a trading bloc of 1.9 billion people—the largest in the world by population and trailing only the EU and NAFTA in volume. But China's leaders are thinking still bigger: integration with the "global south" of India, Australia, and Latin America. China is already Brazil's largest target market; Australia's too. Barely a year after the crisis began, China's trade with ASEAN and Africa alone matched its trade with America. China was indeed "rebalancing," albeit toward the global south instead of the United States.

What trade statistics cannot predict is if and when China will at last come into its own—when its companies climb into the dimples of the smiley curve, and its top export becomes ideas. (Or whether its economy will melt down between now and then.) If Liam Casey, Terry Gou, and the brains at ASUS have their way, the back of your next smartphone may read "Designed in Shenzhen; assembled in Chongqing" or "Designed in Taipei; assembled in Wuhan." Once all of China is a store at the front and a factory in the back, what's left for us? China is building a hundred airports and aerotropoli to this end.

The problem with this vision, as Krugman and others have pointed out, is that in the long run China will have succeeded only in beggaring its neighbors along with the United States. All that would be left for poorer nations are its toxic scraps, of which there would be no shortage. As Jared Diamond underscored in *Collapse*, in order for 1.5 billion Chinese to live like Americans do, we will need a second Earth just to clear-cut and strip-mine. Chimerica is giving way to ChiWorld.

The New Silk Road has become a conduit for people as well as goods. International travel has exploded from China in recent years, tripling between 2000 and 2006, when thirty-four million Chinese headed abroad, and surpassing the number of visitors for the first time in 2009. That last fact is worth repeating: more Chinese are leaving to see the world than foreigners are arriving to see China. Their numbers are expected to triple again by 2020 to 115 million, rising in lockstep with incomes. Picture, twenty years from now, a Chinese middle class—a real one, with a 45 percent savings rate and twice the size of America's—set loose upon the world. Where will they go? And more important: What will they buy?

One hint was the Great Recession's "foreclosure tours," packs of millionaires (China has four hundred thousand) picking over the carcass of the American housing market. One such tourist, a real estate developer in Changsha, bought a million-dollar home in Silicon Valley for his daughter, on the assumption she would be attending Stanford. It was originally priced at $1.3 million. "The price is low now," the buyer admitted, "but it's in a good neighborhood with breathtaking views, so it will definitely appreciate." America's next Chinatowns may be made of McMansions.

Just as Japan's tourists defined the 1980s (remember tripping over salarymen and their families, Nikons clicking away?), China's will be the next to gawk at Times and Trafalgar squares, Notre-Dame and Niagara Falls, taking in the scenery through their cell phones. Wait until a hundred million people are in line ahead of you at Disneyland—you'll see it's a small world after all.

Millions more may never leave China, and they won't have to. The government is commissioning pleasure domes as fast as factories. On Hainan Island in the South China Sea—an island the size of Belgium with the climate of Hawaii—the State Council has decreed a "test case" in developing an "internationally competitive tourist destination," which developers have taken as their cue to build Miami by way of Macau. One is single-handedly building twenty-two golf courses—from links to desert to one modeled on Augusta National—lined with shopping malls and luxury villas. Who needs Malibu when this is all an hour's flight from Hong Kong? But if you insist, Hainan Airlines offers nonstop flights from Beijing to Honolulu.

Before long, China's tourists will outnumber their goods. Asia has nudged ahead of North America as the world's largest aviation market, led once again by China. Analysts predict its airlines' fleets will be more numerous than Europe's a decade from now and poised to overtake America's. This is why Airbus has built its first factory outside of Europe here, and why China is building its own rival to Airbus and Boeing. The majority of these planes will shuttle passengers within Asia as their middle classes take to the skies, binding China more tightly to its neighbors than even its exports could.

Immediately after its trade agreement with ASEAN took effect last year, the two sides began hammering out the final details of Open Skies. Roughly defined as the right of an airline to fly wherever and whenever it pleases between two nations, the advent of Open Skies agreements in the 1990s may rank as the most important milestone in aviation since the jet engine. It's the international equivalent of America's own 1970s deregulation, albeit on a much grander scale. By eliminating barriers to competition, Open Skies increases flights and lowers prices. Open Skies in Europe led directly to the rock-bottom fares of easyJet and Ryanair (and in turn to an invisible London suburb of more than a million). ASEAN and China intend to do the same within five years, and ASEAN is pushing similar deals with India and Japan. The latter signed one with the United States last year.

Japan in particular is searching for salvation through the air. Facing the prospect of a third "lost decade," Prime Minister Yukio Hatoyama has made trade and tourism the central planks in turning around his country's stagnant economy. Positioning Japan as the "bridge nation to Asia," Hatoyama has called for a pan-Pacific free-trade zone before this decade is out in a bid to hitch its fate to China's. His first moves: bailing out Japan Airlines and transforming Tokyo's formerly all-domestic Haneda Airport into a round-the-clock international hub.

Will it work? Kasarda once wondered how tightly Open Skies and economic growth are coupled. The short answer is: very. As seen in Europe, deregulation releases pent-up demand, which in turn bolsters new connections. This makes a place hospitable for investment, creating jobs. Maps are thrown out and economic geography is rewritten. For this reason, "countries should view air routes as highways in the sky," he wrote, a "public good whose capacity is limited only by the number of routes and the seats or tonnage traveling on them."

A simulation sponsored by Boeing went further, asking what would happen if the skies were to open on some of the most lucrative off-limits routes, China's among them. The results were unequivocal: traffic would soar 63 percent, and the trickle-down effects would create twenty-four million jobs in tourism and trade. They would add $490 billion to the global economy—the equivalent of dropping another Thailand on the map. If Japan needs another stimulus, this could be it.

China already treats its airlines as a public good, to a fault. Deng's reforms somehow missed aviation, as it wasn't until 2005 that China's first privately owned airline, Okay Airways, started flying. The rest are state-owned or controlled at the national, provincial, and even municipal level. In China, if you're a city with an airport in search of airlines to serve it, you can always roll your own. Chongqing did it (Chongqing Airlines, established 2007), and Shanghai, Chengdu, and Kunming have all done it too. (Chongqing is considering starting another just to move all of those laptops.) The central government owns three carriers—Air China, China Southern, and China Eastern—and runs each about as well as the capitalists in the United States. Which is to say they've collectively lost billions of dollars to date.

If there's one thing Chinese aviation is missing, it's the maverick who makes flying accessible to the regular Joe (or Qiáo). Every major market has one, whether it's Southwest Airlines's whiskey-slamming Herb Kelleher or Ryanair's voluble Michael O'Leary. JetBlue's David Neeleman is trying to do the same for Brazil. Even India had Captain Gopinath spotting silver aerials below. There were still no signs of their counterpart in China, but not much time had passed since Okay Airways had gotten off the ground. Curious to see where it might take me, I bought the first ticket I found heading west.

I'm Okay, You're Okay

Okay's maiden voyage left Tianjin, a city of twelve million a ninety-minute drive from Beijing, for Changsha, the capital of Hunan province several hours south. As it turned out, I had booked myself on the same route. The day before departure, the airline's founder and chairman, Liu Jieyin, invited me over for tea.

Okay has its hub in Tianjin but keeps its headquarters in an industrial district of Beijing. The chairman's office occupied a corner of what resembled a dilapidated bank lobby, propped up by fake marble columns. The space was bare of decoration save for a handful of maps that might have been recycled from a second-grade classroom. Liu wore a short-sleeve shirt and dark trousers—the business casual that has replaced the Mao jacket in bureaucratic circles. The way his glasses kept slipping off his nose underscored his professorial air. He was hardly the hard-charging salesman I'd been expecting.

Liu is an old hand in Chinese aviation, having served two tours of duty at the Civil Aviation Administration, with a stint abroad at Swissair in between. Okay was his third airline. The first, China United, started flying in 1986 as the official carrier of the People's Liberation Army. (Back then, the army was run like a conglomerate, with stakes in hotels and karaoke bars along with civilian airlines.) His second had been combined at the government's insistence with Shanghai Airlines, which has since vanished inside China Eastern. This was his last chance, he told me, to be remembered as a pioneer.

There was nothing pioneering about his business model, though, which he had copied from Southwest and planned to roll out in China. He was working at a disadvantage, having been forbidden to fly on the heavily trafficked trunk routes like Beijng–Shanghai or Beijing–Guangzhou. So he had bypassed Beijing for Tianjin, aping Southwest's original strategy of flying where the big carriers weren't. This is how Okay had ended up in a smoggy backwater bigger than Bangkok or Teh-ran. From there he started flying to second-tier provincial capitals like Changsha and Kunming. His planes were the same make as Southwest's, and so were his passengers—a sprinkling of road warriors among virgins.

All that matters to them, Liu said, is arriving on time. If you don't, there could be hell to pay. Irate passengers have been known to stage ri-ots and sit-ins during delays. "They're peasants!" he exclaimed. "They've never flown before and have no earthly idea what to expect." Their na-ïveté is his niche. He told me a joke. "A woman on board is so excited, she says, 'Golly, this flight is so smooth and so good. You fly so high, people on the ground look just like ants!' So the passenger next to her says, 'Sit down, lady, the flight hasn't taken off yet.'" The punch line is that she's flying his airline.

There are millions just like her, he explained, but what was holding him back—and by extension, all of China's airlines—was government interference. The market was growing so fast that CAAC was trying to rein them in. As the first and still one of China's only private carriers, Okay was last in line for permission to do anything. Growth might be high, but it could be a lot higher if they'd only take off his restraints. He believed the Chinese had not yet begun to fly. "The great majority have never been to the United States, but that's not because they don't want to. For one thing, the U.S. isn't necessarily open to Chinese travel these days, and for another, they can't find the flights."

The deck was stacked against him. Like good Socialists, government policy is to prop up the state carriers, no matter how many billions it costs. Raising cash and storming the market—as JetBlue did in the United States ten years ago—is impossible. "When the banks hear you're a *pri-vate* airline, they just deny your application," Liu said. There was no chance of foreign investment, and no hope of floating shares in an IPO. He was making it up as he went along, starting routes when he could scrounge up the planes. Okay had seven 737s but needed twenty or thirty to turn a profit on economies of scale. He figured he was three or four years away from retiring with his legacy intact. It might take longer. Desperate to raise cash, he sold a controlling stake to a competing private airline in equally dire straits. He immediately clashed with his new investors, who couldn't afford losses of $10 million a year. They ousted him at the end of 2008, a few weeks before the government announced its latest billion-dollar bailout of China Eastern. Yet another change in ownership brought him back two years later.

Outward Bound

The road between Tianjin and Beijing—linking cities of twelve and fifteen million—is three lanes in each direction, packed bumper to bumper by knockoff Jettas, monster trucks, and black government sedans. Running alongside for stretches was the new Intercity Railway, the world's fastest bullet train (top speed 217 mph) connecting the pair in time for the Summer Olympics. The goal is to create a megacity in the north that can hold its own with the others around Shanghai and the Delta.

Tianjin is larger than any city in America, and yet its airport was the size of Tupelo, Mississippi's. As late as 2001, there were only eleven flights a day. Okay Airways had since muscled in on a quarter of its traffic, roughly a million passengers a year. The airport was a fragment of an aerotropolis zoned around an Airbus plant on the edge of the airfield. The factory is capable of producing fifty A320s a year (the workhorse jet Captain Sully landed in the Hudson), or half of how many Airbus expects to sell in China. It's a joint venture with the government's aircraft manufacturer, Comac, whose executives can't be bothered to conceal their glee about the technology transfer that will inevitably follow. (Airbus accepts this slow leak of know-how as the cost of doing business.) Their answer to the A320 is the C919, a jet with a range of 3,450 miles—far enough to connect any two points in China.

The old terminal had six gates (one for every two million residents) and a single check-in counter, above which hung a departure board lit with the dull red glow reminiscent of ancient calculators. At the gates, boarding times were scrawled on whiteboards erased and rewritten whenever flights left for Shenzhen, Qingdao, Hefei, and Dalian. The new terminal confronted us through the windows—a steel-and-glass mountain three times larger than the one we were standing in, designed to gracefully quadruple in size again. Traffic in Tianjin is climbing 20 percent annually, one of the fastest rates in the country, but still trailing Chengdu and Chongqing.

There was no pretense of boarding by zones or even of forming a line, just the mad scrum indigenous to China. But the passengers were familiar—families who had obviously never flown together before and road warriors in their uniforms of polos and pressed khakis. We could have been flying to Tampa.

And in a way, we were. After I disembarked in Changsha, the flight continued onward to Kunming, a city in the Himalayan foothills popular with tourists drawn to its eternal sunshine. As the capital of the province bordering Indochina, Kunming is strategically important to China's plans of running highways and pipelines from a second port like Gwadar through Myanmar, and as such, it is yet another of the designated aerotropoli. Its new hub opens this year with the capacity of Schiphol.

As it happens, Kunming's climate is also perfect for growing roses. Its sunshine and high altitude compare favorably with Colombia's and Kenya's. The city is famous across China for its camellias, lilies, orchids, and azaleas but has a new cash crop. Searching for work for tens of millions of impoverished farmers, Beijing has ordered the construction of gigantic greenhouses on the hillsides. Growers in Africa and South America can look forward to the brutality of the "China price" being brought to bear on roses; wages in the province start at $25 a month, a third of Ethiopia's and an eighth of Ecuador's. Depending on the time of year, its stems might cost half of anything you'd find from Kenya. The plan is to be the world's second-largest exporter after Holland.

About the name Okay Airways. The chairman had argued that "Okay" stood for exuberance, not ambivalence, although I could see the value in preemptively lowering expectations. On board, Okay was better than okay—a brand-new Boeing with leather seats, hot meals, and cold beer for free. I haven't flown better in coach since.

In the row behind me were two girls barely out of their teens; one was still wearing braces. They were students on summer break from Tianjin University (majoring in environmental science) on their way to Kunming. This was their first flight anywhere and only their second trip away from home. The first, three years ago, had taken two days to reach

Changsha by train; our flying time today was two hours. The girl with the braces confessed to being scared. "I thought the plane would be bigger—it's much bigger on TV," she said. But by the end of the flight, they had their next flight planned—a postgraduation shopping spree in Hong Kong.

Across the aisle was a road warrior who worked for a maker of wigs. His job was procuring human hair. This was his first time on Okay Airways, and it was okay. Coming from him, he said, this was high praise. After eight years on the road, he hated every airline he'd ever flown. His hometown carrier in Qingdao had been the worst, staffed by "farmers from the north: unfriendly, aloof, and not very intelligent." Things had gotten better since. When he started, "There were fewer flights, the airports were often several hours away from the cities, and many smaller ones still didn't have an airport. But it's easier now we're rich, so we can afford to fly."

Down the aisle, an older man offered a second opinion. A professor on his way to see colleagues in Changsha, he's been making this monthly trip for twenty years. What was it like when he started? "It was very underserved," he replied. "Less passengers, less flights, and the planes were terrible. It's better now, but with so many people flying, it takes more time to get on, and it's more troublesome to get through the airport— security is that much stricter. But this is still better than anything in the States, where you have to pay for everything you eat." He assumed the Chinese would ruin flying just as the Americans had. "More and more will fly, and we'll have to bear it. There will only be more competition, and things will get worse." As China will discover, both men are right.

Window on the World

Final approach to Changsha skims miles of rice paddies and ramshackle farmhouses, giving way to warehouses and hangars only at the last seconds. The terminal was half the size of Tianjin's, which is proportional considering it's a city of six million residents instead of twelve. A new terminal five times its size opened last year as the centerpiece of Changsha Airport City, which will in turn be the core of a proposed eight-city megalopolis of forty million—the mind-boggling size of greater Tokyo. And I had never even *heard* of Changsha until I booked my ticket.

Mao got his start here as a student and a teacher at the Hunan Number 1 Teachers' Training School, destroyed during China's civil war. The rest of the city followed during the subsequent Japanese invasion. Rebuilt in 1949, Changsha appeared to still be under construction—the city center was a forest of cranes interrupted by car dealerships.

Changsha is exactly the sort of provincial city Beijing had in mind when it ordered manufacturing inland. Admittedly second rank, the capital of Hunan province is larger than Dallas–Fort Worth. Labor costs a third less here than on the coast, and manufacturers are beginning to take advantage. Foreign investment is climbing 30 percent annually, at nearly four times the national pace. City officials dream of even higher multiples. Plans call for a local auto industry twenty times larger in 2015 than in 2007, helped along by a Fiat factory with capacity for 250,000 vehicles a year. BYD is producing electric buses there. It has become a hot spot for companies manufacturing green tech such as batteries and windmills, while the two-year-old Hunan Sunzone Optoelectronics builds solar panels and ships nearly all of them to Europe. The city's newest technology zone is closer to the airport than it is to downtown. Cartons of iPads departing for California could arrive in three days.

During my daylong layover, I paid my respects to the mummified Marquis of Dai and his wife, Lady Xinzhui. The city's most popular tourist attractions, their tombs had been excavated intact from the surrounding hillsides. The marquis had been chancellor of the Kingdom of Changsha by order of the Emperor Gaozu in the second century B.C. One of the emperor's successors dispatched the envoy Zhang Qian to the West a few generations later in search of civilization beyond the neighboring barbarians. Zhang returned with news of India and Persia, and emboldened by these reports, the emperor marched his armies westward, clearing the first leg of what would become the Silk Road. Lady Xinzhui was buried in the silks that gave the road its name. Her burial shroud, preserved for two thousand years and now under glass, depicts the journey of her soul from earth through the afterlife to the heavens.

I stopped again on the way to the airport, willing to risk missing my flight to see Window on the World. Its ecstatically pink, life-size replica of the long since vanished Lighthouse of Alexandria is visible for miles.

Window on the World is a theme park in EPCOT's mold, although the world monuments on display are less than faithfully reproduced. It's a counterfeit knockoff of a knockoff of the world. Above the entrance is the Louvre's glass pyramid, flanked by the Winged Victory and the Venus de Milo, both eroded from acid rain. Inside on Civilization Hill are scale models of the U.S. Capitol, the Taj Mahal, and the Leaning Tower of Pisa—none more than twenty feet tall. Instead of a Hall of Presidents, there's an animatronic Mao. In the center of the park is a lagoon in which the Pyramids, the sphinx, and Easter Island's moai statues have been dumped. A bulldozer sluggishly dredged the pond while I watched—this was peak season, and the park was still open. It was dusk by now, and it occurred to me I hadn't seen anyone in nearly an hour. They'd already left.

EPILOGUE: OPENING DAY

The consultants with their wheelie bags are already gone. Now it's my turn. The first pitch of the season at Wrigley Field is eight hours and seven hundred miles away—still plenty of time, not that catching a flight to see my family ever feels that way. Adrenaline and the road warrior's routine kick in: yank the MacBook from its socket, slide the aluminum slab into the bag, stow my Chicago Cubs cap and plane ticket, shower and dress, kiss my wife good-bye. Half asleep, she murmurs, "Have a fun trip. See you tonight."

The first shift of schnauzers and their bleary owners rule Brooklyn's sidewalks. I hail a cab and we swing onto the expressway, heading east into daybreak and then north past cemeteries and drowsing Williamsburg hipsters. LaGuardia Airport is closer to my doorstep than Seoul's airport is to New Songdo. A year ago the flight paths changed, and I looked up one morning to see a 737 soaring a few hundred feet above my apartment.

The driver misses the exit and doubles back past the Art Deco hangars to a half-forgotten corner of the airfield, dropping me at the Marine Air Terminal. It was built along the water's edge in 1939 for Pan Am's flying boats. A fossil now, it predates LaGuardia's runways; it is the oldest terminal still in service—the missing link to aviation's golden age.

A few years ago Delta stuck some gates on the end for hourly shuttles to Boston, Washington, and Chicago. I go inside. The rotunda is as hushed as any cathedral's. At the top of the wall is an answer to the Sistine Chapel's ceiling: *Flight*, a Depression-era mural 12 feet tall, circling the room for 235 feet in the styles of Miró and Masaccio, Picasso and Michelangelo. *Flight* follows Icarus to the Wright Brothers to those flying boats, which are what we imagine the aircraft of the golden age to be: yachts piloted by captains in full naval regalia; private sleeping bunks; five- and six-course meals served in dining rooms by white-jacketed stewards, and separate men's and women's dressing rooms where passengers changed from sharp suits and smart dresses into black tie and evening gowns. Flights from New York to Southampton took eighteen hours, with stops in New Brunswick, Newfoundland, and Ireland each way. A round-trip ticket cost $675 ($10,000 in today's dollars).

A handful of flying boats flew out of LaGuardia for only three years before World War II put a stop to transoceanic service. By war's end, larger and faster planes were rolling off the assembly lines of the Warfare State. Airlines faced a choice: "to carry the well-to-do at high prices—or to carry the average man at what he can afford to pay," the chairman of Pan Am said. He chose the latter. Luxury had been rendered obsolete by speed. From then on, speed itself was the luxury. Measured in these terms, the golden age of aviation is a golden age that never was; the golden age is now, when a plane can get you to Chicago in time for the first pitch and back to New York in time for *The Daily Show*.

Still, we are up in the air. At thirty thousand feet, the sky is clear, the weather perfect; sunlight suffuses the cabin with vitamin D. The flight to Chicago is as boring as any train or bus ride, as it should be—it's mass transit. More people will fly this year than flew in the entirety of the 1960s.

John Kasarda predicts air travel will dramatically change the way we live in the next twenty years as it did in the time from flying boats to the Delta Shuttle. If he's right, I'll remember this flight the way some remember America's roads before the interstates—before vast concrete ribbons flattened the landscape and tilted us south toward the Sun Belt, a development unimaginable only fifty years ago. Does the future look like Dallas or Dubai? Or both?

"As aviation increasingly connects the world's people and places, we will simultaneously observe *global homogenization* and *local diversification*," Kasarda promises. "Fashion, food, entertainment, gadgets, families, and work will diffuse even more rapidly throughout the world, creating strikingly observable commonalities among widely dispersed places while enriching the variety of products and services in those places."

The future he envisions is one of nearly limitless choices—where to live, whom to love, what to eat, how to act—even if the total effect of those choices is to erase our differences. It's a world in which all of our leaders' promises have been kept, in which we are fitter, happier, more productive. Everyone will be connected—by plane, by WiFi, by high-speed rail. Everyone will visit Disneyland and the Louvre. Everyone will roam farther, work harder, go faster. No one will be shackled by the circumstances of birth or upbringing.

And the common denominator is aviation. Just as jets made it possible for the Brooklyn Dodgers to hop a flight for Los Angeles, he reminded me, sooner or later the World Series will live up to its name. Someday, major league teams shuttling among Tokyo, Havana, and Mexico City at near-supersonic speed will remind us that the national pastime is no longer ours alone.

It's hard to imagine Kasarda's vision while watching the Cubs take the field at Wrigley as they have every April since 1916, when the Wright Brothers were still a novelty. The ivy and scoreboard followed in 1937, and the lights fifty years after that. Everything else is more or less unchanged, with the conspicuous exception of the 747s overhead and the subliminal hum of jet wash we notice only in its absence, as if a machine had been switched off.

That machine is called globalization. It's run on jet engines, which began flattening the world thirty-five years before anyone had even heard of the Internet. Today, we measure distances in terms of flying times and bind economies together with the cargo carried in the bellies of 747s. We also wonder if this machine will soon be switched off for good, willingly or not, by some combination of financial collapse, peak oil, and climate change. Whereas Kasarda's unwavering vision is that of global efficiency in the name of growth, there is a craving in some quarters (often the most affluent) for its antidote—local resiliency in service of sustainability. His rejoinder, in so many words, might be, "So what?" The decision is no longer ours to make.

"Each form of transportation began with only a minuscule portion of the population being able to afford it, and then it slowly diffused to the masses," he says. "So it will be with aviation. When that proportion changes from minuscule, as it is now, to a small but significant minority of the world population, its economic and social impacts on people and places will be immense. There's an invasion of Asian tourists coming, and it cannot be stopped."

He's doing his best to see it goes smoothly. When I last saw him, his eyes were cloudy with jet lag and his spine crumpled from shuttling among meetings in Beijing, Taipei, and Bangalore. All parties present had invited him to sketch the world as he sees it—a world of convention center complexes and luxury hotels linked via a series of tubes—the city-as-terminal. The question posed by Rem Koolhaas, "Is the contemporary city like the contemporary airport—all the same?" is moot. The city *is* the airport.

"I always tell my students that those companies, communities, and countries that can read the handwriting on the wall will catapult to commercial success," Kasarda told me. China and India have seen the writing on the wall—written in his hand—and the word is "aerotropolis." "This is why they're building so many," he said, "treating their airports and cities and their primary infrastructure to compete in the twenty-first century. Meanwhile, we see them as nuisances or toxic threats. If we don't realize that city plus airport equals the future, the game will be over. In some ways, we've already surrendered."

He might be right, but sitting in the grandstand at Wrigley Field with my mother and brother, I feel triumphant. Everything seems possible. No distance is insurmountable. Even if flying can be agony with security and delays and cattle-car conditions in coach, it's worth it if I can occasionally be in two places at once, leading my own life in New York and staying close to my family in the Midwest. These bonds will only become stronger in the Instant Age, as we invent new ways to find each other, follow each other, and come together. Today, it's opening day at Wrigley, and tomorrow it will be spring break for Chinese students in Hong Kong, Iranian reunions in Dubai, and breadwinners flying home on weekends to Mumbai.

The aerotropolis is a time machine. Time is the ultimately finite commodity setting the exchange rates for all the choices we make.

Monstrous in size, infinitely scalable, and endlessly repetitive—machines for living with interchangeable parts—Kasarda's aerotropoli are as foreign to us as O'Hare or Heathrow would have been to a passenger aboard a clipper ship. But they may be necessary to make these occasions as common and as memorable for families in Chennai as in Chicago, and they won't be denied.

Cubs win! The song "Go Cubs Go" echoes off the scoreboard as my mother and I sway back and forth, singing along. An hour later, I'm on a plane bound for New York. An hour after that, we're at cruising altitude. Drifting off to sleep, I hear echoes of a song about a similar vista outside my window: moving toward the farmlands, out of the grid, the plan of a city was all I could see.

NOTES

SELECTED BIBLIOGRAPHY

ACKNOWLEDGMENTS

INDEX

NOTES

Just as this book is a collaboration between myself and John Kasarda, its contents are a fusion of John Kasarda's scholarly research and my on-the-ground reporting in each of these places (save India, where Kasarda supplied the pair of eyes), producing thousands of pages of notes and hundreds of interviews. These have been supplemented by innumerable books, newspaper articles, magazine stories, government statistics, e-mails, blog posts, and even tweets. Most of the facts in this book can be Googled or found in Wikipedia, if you feel so inclined.

Kasarda's decades of conversations with airport executives and government officials in places like Dubai, China, Thailand, India, Memphis, Detroit, and North Carolina provide another layer of insights, even if their contents cannot be reproduced verbatim here (owing to confidentiality). In all instances, except where stated below, facts, quotes, and statistics draw upon this mosaic of research.

Kasarda didn't coin the word "aerotropolis"; he first heard it in the mid-1990s in the Chinese city of Zhuhai. The word described an airport city (never built) a quarter of a mile north of its airport. Kasarda's repurposed use of the word debuted in 2000 in *Urban Land*, the house magazine of the Urban Land Institute. Since then, he has refined the idea dozens of times in journals such as *Airport World*, *Real Estate Issues*, *Just-in-Time Real Estate*, *Next American City*, and *Global Airport Cities*. The seed of this book was my profile of Kasarda in *Fast Company* (July/August 2006). I have drawn from all of them too.

Aerotropolis is both an attempt to document something categorically new—cities rising out of whole cloth from farmland, sand, and mudflats—and to identify a phenomenon that has been hiding in plain sight in front of us all along. Kasarda and I are convinced that any distaste you might feel toward flying is the consequence of it having first become so commonplace and then so critical to our everyday lives we no longer recognize the miracle as such—until it disappeared in the days following 9/11, or under a volcanic ash cloud.

Introduction

The opening scene with Stan Gale took place at New Songdo in August 2009. It is the slightly modified lead to a story I wrote for *Fast Company* called "The New New Urbanism" (February 2010). I drew upon source materials provided by Gale International, Kohn Pedersen Fox Associates, and interviews with Gale International's Stan Gale and John Hynes, KPF's Jamie von Klemper, and Cisco's Wim Elfrink.

Figures on the scope and scale of urbanization are drawn from published reports by the United Nations Human Settlements Programme (UN-HABITAT), including *State of the World's Cities 2010/2011*.

Lewis Mumford's quote is from *The City in History*. Marx's "annihilation of space by time" appears in the *Grundrisse* (1857), and Melvin Webber's notion of the "elastic mile" appears in his essay "Culture, Territoriality, and the Elastic Mile."

Joel Garreau's *Edge City* was a particular inspiration; his transportation-determinist view toward cities is a foundational principle of this book. His quotes are from chapter 2 of his book and an interview, respectively.

The World's Unofficial Longest Line is on YouTube: www.youtube.com/watch?v=f4xba_YFHj8.

The science-fiction author J. G. Ballard lived in the Thames Valley town of Shepperton from 1960 until his death in 2009. His quote (and also his epigraph) appeared "The Ultimate Departure Lounge," first published in the magazine *Blueprint* (1997) and republished in Steven Bode and Jeremy Millar's *Airport*, from which I have drawn it.

Statistics on global GDP, world trade, and air cargo value between 1975 and 2005 are from the World Bank and the International Air Transport Association.

The impact of volcanic ash on European aviation April 19–26, 2010, merited headlines the world over. My capsule summary is drawn primarily from *The New York Times*, although the plight of Kenyan rose farmers was covered by the BBC, and estimates of airline losses and the number of stranded passengers were provided by the Centre for Asia Pacific Aviation.

"The airport leaves the city . . ." was given to me by Maurits Schaafsma, a senior planner at Schiphol Real Estate. The best account of "Terminal City" is found in Kurt C. Schlichting's *Grand Central Terminal*.

Statistics on the energy use and carbon emissions of the built environment are taken from Linda Tischler's "The Green Housing Boom" (*Fast Company*, July/August 2008). Figures on aviation's declining share of carbon emissions are from the Air Transport Association, an airline industry lobbying group, and from *Climate Change 2007: Mitigation*, a report by the Intergovernment Panel on Climate Change (IPCC). Richard Branson's commitment to devote his transportation businesses's profits to biofuel research was made at the Clinton Global Initiative conference in September 2006.

1: A Tale of Three Cities

The early history of Los Angeles International Airport and its first incarnation as Mines Field was drawn from notes taken during a trip to the airport's Flight Path Learning Center, which has kept Ford A. Carpenter's original field notes and report to the Chamber of Commerce, along with plans for the LAX II at Palmdale that never was.

The origins of the Warfare State are succinctly told by Manuel Castells and Peter Hall in *Technopoles of the World*. I also found inspiration in Joan Didion's account of

Lakewood's creation in *Where I Was From.* Aerospace's impact on Silicon Valley was measured by the economist Kenneth Flamm in *Creating the Computer.* Carey McWilliams mentioned the overnight invention of Westchester in *California.*

The smiley curve was added to the lexicon by James Fallows in "China Makes, the World Takes" (*The Atlantic,* July/August 2007). The breakdown of the Apple iPod's value chain comes from a widely quoted May 2007 study by the Personal Computing Industry Center in Irvine, California.

Details on the freight dogs and what they're hauling are drawn from two articles worth mentioning: Michael Walker's "Anything, Anywhere, Anytime (*Men's Vogue,* March 2008) and Barry Lopez's "On the Wings of Commerce" (*Harper's Magazine,* October 1995).

The Battle of El Toro was ably told by the University of California at San Diego's Steven P. Erie in his book *Globalizing L.A.* He and Kasarda coauthored a series of reports documenting the economic benefits of an Orange County International Airport.

The invasion of northern Virginia by defense contractors—and why they needed Dulles International Airport—was explained to me by Stephen Fuller, public policy professor and director of the Center for Regional Analysis at George Mason University. He also provided the numbers for what a single flight to Beijing can do for a region's economy. Thomas Frank's disgust at the results is borrowed from *The Wrecking Crew.*

Joel Garreau mentions Sears's decision to decamp from the (former) Sears Tower in *Edge City.* (In a nice bit of irony, United Airlines recently moved its headquarters from O'Hare to Willis Tower.) Unless otherwise noted, all commercial real estate statistics—and comparisons made with other cities—are drawn from regular, freely available reports published by Grubb & Ellis.

The history of Chicago's airports is mostly drawn from the *Chicago Tribune*'s Pulitzer Prize–winning report published in November 2000. The newspaper was also my primary source about the battles over St. Johannes and Rest Haven, although *Chicago* magazine's "Dead Reckoning" (October 2009) was a big help too. The paper was also the first to break the news about Governor Rod Blagojevich's December 2008 indictment. The notion of Chicago becoming a global city is taken from *Crain's Chicago Business,* "Mayor Daley Runs Up Big Debts Building His Global City: What About the Rest of Chicago?" (June 14, 2010).

2: Just in Time

The Memphis Cotton Museum taught me much about the city's original commodity; my capsule history is taken from its exhibits. The best history of FedEx is Roger Frock's *Changing How the World Does Business.* FedEx Corporation founder and chief executive Fred Smith was kind enough to debunk a few myths.

Many of the sources in this chapter stem from two people in particular—Dexter Muller at the Greater Memphis Chamber of Commerce and Daryl Snyder at Greater Louisville Inc. Both were instrumental in explaining the roots of each city, supplying source materials, and arranging a series of interviews with local leaders, including Arnold Perl, John Moore, and Larry Cox in Memphis, and Mayor Jerry Abramson, Burt Deutsch, and UPS's Mark Giuffre in Louisville. They also opened the doors to Geek Squad City, Genentech, and the National Eyebank Center. FedEx's Jo Ferreira arranged my tour of the world's largest painkiller stockpile at excelleRx.

It was Giuffre who booked my tours of both the UPS Worldport and UPS Supply

Chain Solutions. He had done so before for John McPhee, whose descriptions of both in *Uncommon Carriers* are still the gold standard.

The section on Zappos.com's warehouse is based on interviews with both Craig Adkins and Tony Hsieh, supplemented with SEC filings after its purchase by Amazon, analysts' reports, *The New Yorker* stories (both about the company and Malcolm Gladwell's contrarian take on e-commerce), and Peter Drucker's "Beyond the Information Revolution" (*The Atlantic*, October 1999). Amazon Prime numbers are hard to come by; many thanks to ChannelAdvisor CEO Scot Wingo for publishing some on his blog Amazonstrategies.com. E-commerce statistics are from Forrester Research. The impact on booksellers is taken from the paper "E-commerce and the Market Structure of Retail Industries." And all the talk about long tails comes, of course, from Chris Anderson's *The Long Tail*.

Dexter Muller and Commercial Advisors CEO Larry Jensen gave me a crash course in distribution and the effect that the proliferation of warehouses has had on Memphis in particular. The plight of Whitehaven residents was detailed by *The New York Times* in "Blacks in Memphis Lose Decades of Economic Gains" (May 30, 2010). And it was Mayor Abramson and Burt Deutsch who made it clear to me how far they were prepared to go to keep UPS in Louisville—even if that meant bulldozing the neighborhoods around the airport and building Heritage Creek.

3: Up in the Air

I owe the description of Euless Trinity High School's performance of the *haka* to *The Wall Street Journal* and to YouTube, although it was Ilaiasi Ofa who filled me in on the Tongans who came to be in Euless.

Robert Smithson's unrealized artwork for DFW and his meditations on the site were published in his essay "Towards the Development of an Air Terminal Site" (*Artforum*, June 1967). The thinking behind DFW's terminal layout and the statistics on hijackings are taken from Alastair Gordon's indispensible *Naked Airport*.

The transformation of hubs into some of the world's highest-grossing shopping malls has been well documented in periodic reports of the International Council of Shopping Centers.

Douglas Coupland's "Hubs" originally ran online at *HotWired* in 1996. Walter Kirn coined the term "Airworld" in *Up in the Air*. And I met "Sir, Alfred" Mehran Nasseri at Charles de Gaulle in September 2005, an encounter described in *Advertising Age*.

Passenger numbers are from the International Air Transport Association and the U.S. Department of Transportation's Bureau of Transportation Statistics. "The Arbitron Airport Advertising Study" of 2004 remains a valuable source of frequent-flier demographics, although IHS Global Insight's August 2009 analysis yielded the most up-to-date research on the habits of business travelers. The value of their time is courtesy the Brookings Institution's Steven A. Morrison and Clifford Winston and their paper "The Effect of FAA Expenditures on Air Travel Delays" (March 2008).

Fortune chronicled "The Strange Existence of Ram Charan" (April 30, 2007). *BusinessWeek* captured the not-so-strange lifestyles of Dallas–Ft. Worth's frequent fliers in "Home Is Where the Airport Is" (August 20, 2007). And it was Peter T. Kilborn who popularized the word "relo" to describe America's ten million road-warriors-for-life in *Next Stop, Reloville*.

The website of the Las Vegas Convention and Visitors Authority (www.lvcva.com) is the definitive source for charting the impact meetings, incentives, conventions, and exhibitions (MICE) have on the city, including a complete calendar of events. (The National Hardware Show, with thirty thousand attendees, is starting as I write this.) Likewise, the Dallas Market Center supplied me with visitor statistics, while *The Wall Street Journal* ably covered Trammel Crow's exploits in the 1970s and '80s.

A version of John Kasarda's Law of Connectivity appears in Warren Berger's "Life Sucks and Then You Fly" (*Wired*, August 1999) as "Saffo's Law," after the futurist Paul Saffo. Except Saffo already has a law named after him, and that isn't it. Berger's story also tells of how the Nerd Birds came to be. Kenneth Button and Roger Stough's analysis of technology workers' travel habits appeared in their book *Air Transport Networks*.

Melvin Webber's concept of "community without propinquity" is best explained in his essay "Order in Diversity: Community Without Propinquity," which was collected in *Cities and Space: The Future Use of Urban Space*. His quotation is lifted from the same.

Marchetti's Constant is derived from Cesare Marchetti's paper "Anthropological Invariants in Travel Behavior" (*Technological Forecasting and Social Change*, vol. 47, 1994). His maglev thought experiment appears in "The Evolution of Transport," by Jesse H. Ausubel and Cesare Marchetti (*Industrial Physicist*, April/May 2001). The Future Forum report was published by the British travel firm Thomson in 2006. The University of California sociologist Claude Fischer wrote about Americans' itinerancy (or increasing lack thereof) in "Ever More Rooted Americans" (*City & Community*, June 2002). And Kasarda's formula for calculating the real estate worth of proximity to a hub comes from his M.B.A. Business Demographics course at the University of North Carolina.

The story of Las Colinas is drawn from newspaper reports, interviews with tenants, and the Greater Irving–Las Colinas Chamber of Commerce, and Joel Garreau's gimlet-eyed take on the place in *Edge City*.

Kasarda's research on job growth around airports and route networks is drawn from such papers as his "Air Routes as Economic Development Levers," and Kenneth Button and Somik Lall's "The Economics of Being an Airport Hub City." Jan Brueckner's findings were published in "Airline Traffic and Urban Economic Development" (*Urban Studies*, vol. 40, 2003).

The notion of "companies without propinquity" was informed by interviews with Lenovo's Gerry Smith and SAP's Scott Lutz, along with Barry C. Lynn's *End of the Line*, which in the course of arguing why multinationals are doomed offers the most cogent explanation of how we ended up with them in the first place.

DFW's relationship to its owners, Dallas and Ft. Worth, and to its neighbors Euless, Grapevine, Irving, and Coppell was explained by CEO Jeff Fegan and vice president of commercial development John Terrell, who is also the mayor of Southlake.

4: Welcome Home to the Airport

Brian Tellinghuisen patiently told me the stories of his childhood and his eventual return to Stapleton in a series of e-mails and phone interviews. My best resource for the history of Stapleton and its galvanizing effect on Aurora was Owen D. Gutfreund's *Twentieth-Century Sprawl*. He is unequivocal about the effect of Denver's airports on the suburb: "The main catalysts were the growth (and eventual relocation) of the Denver airport," he wrote, and the interstates serving them.

Richard Florida introduced me to the economic geographer David Harvey and Harvey's notion of the "spatial fix." Florida uses the term in his own *The Great Reset* to describe the transformations of urban landscapes from one economic era to the next. He believes the next spatial fix will involve concentration into denser cities and suburbs connected via mass transit and high-speed rail.

Mary Rose Loney, then president of the DIA Partnership (now part of the Metro Denver Economic Development Corporation) introduced me to Cal Fulenwider, who in turn told me the story of DIA's genesis and his plans for Reunion. William H. Whyte's map plotting the relationship between corporate relocations and the CEO's country club is found in *City*.

For an introduction to New Urbanism and the ideas of Andres Duany and Elizabeth Plater-Zyberk, I recommend *Suburban Nation*.

The notion of Denver and the Front Range as a "megapolitan" and one of several "mountain megas" including Phoenix, Las Vegas, and northern New Mexico was advanced by Robert E. Lang and Mark Muro of the Brookings Institution in their 2008 report "Mountain Megas: America's Newest Metropolitan Places and a Federal Partnership to Help Them Prosper." David Brooks reflected on the exurban fringe of Arapahoe County in *On Paradise Drive*.

A copy of the Stapleton "Green Book" was given to me by Forest City Stapleton's Tom Gleason. Gleason, who was once Mayor Federico Peña's press secretary, also supplied background on Peña's decision to shutter the airport in the first place. For details on the LEED certification program and all it entails, visit the U.S. Green Building Council's website, www.usgbc.org/. Jim Jacoby and the Jacoby Group provided details on the ambitiously green credentials of Atlantic Station and the recycling of a former Ford automotive plant into Aerotropolis Atlanta.

Forest City's plans for Mesa del Sol in Albuquerque are quoted at length from *BusinessWeek*'s "The Easiest Commute of All" (December 12, 2005). It remains to be seen when and in what form the aerotropolis will be realized—the recession has forced the project into hibernation. Planning for the Mesa, Arizona, aerotropolis continues, however. The *Economist* story that name-checked Kasarda as the plan's architect was "City of the Future" (December 4, 2008).

Details on Ørestad are mostly drawn from the Port & City Development Corporation's report "Urban Development—in Ørestad and in the Harbour Areas of Copenhagen."

5: *The Aerotropolist*

John Kasarda most closely identifies with the intellectual tradition of the University of Chicago's urban sociologists. Influential figures of the Chicago School include Robert E. Park and Ernest Burgess, who developed the concentric ring model of urban growth in such works as "The Growth of the City" in *The City*. One of their intellectual heirs was Roderick D. McKenzie, who studied metropolitan growth and urban hierarchies in *The Metropolitan Community*. McKenzie's student, in turn, was Amos Hawley, who was Kasarda's own mentor and the author of *Human Ecology*. Other works by University of North Carolina professors during Kasarda's time as a Ph.D. student include Gerhard

Lenski's *Human Societies* and *Power and Privilege*, and Hubert M. Blalock's *Causal Inferences in Nonexperimental Research.*

The interview with Amos Hawley was conducted at his home in March 2008. He died August 31, 2009. Marshall McLuhan's quote is taken from the first chapter of *Understanding Media.* The Ed Glaeser reference is to the working paper "Did the Death of Distance Hurt Detroit and Help New York?" by Edward L. Glaeser and Giacomo A. M. Ponzetto. Jane Jacobs's recollection of Scranton and Wilkes-Barre is taken from *Cities and the Wealth of Nations.*

Raymond Vernon introduced the product cycle in "International Investment and International Trade in the Product Cycle." Vernon's quotes are taken from the essay "Economic Sovereignty at Bay" (*Foreign Affairs*, October 1968). The line "Democracy sacrifices efficiency" appeared in the story "China's Infrastructure Splurge" (*The Economist*, February 14, 2008).

Kasarda developed the Global TransPark model at length in such papers as "An Industrial/Aviation Complex for the Future" and, with Dennis A. Rondinelli, "Innovative Infrastructure for Agile Manufacturers." Background on the North Carolina Global TransPark was obtained from interviews with Kasarda and former governor James G. Martin, and from a visit to the TransPark in March 2008.

Kasarda and David L. Sullivan outlined the success of Subic Bay in "Air Cargo, Liberalization, and Economic Development." The history of Research Triangle Park was provided by the RTP itself on its website, www.rtp.org/.

"Envisioning a Truly Great Philadelphia International Airport" was held November 24, 2008. Kasarda credits Art Pappas of the Pappas Consulting Group for his quote on "Transformation."

6: Aerotropolis or Bust

The histories of Ford Airlines, Ford Airport, and Willow Run were gleaned from a number of online resources; the common thread was Wikipedia, with backup from Alastair Gordon's *Naked Airport.* Ford's proclamation "We shall solve the City Problem by eliminating the City" appears in *Ford Ideals.*

The Detroit delegation's trip to Amsterdam and Schiphol occurred in March 2007. Detroit Metropolitan Wayne County Airport was recognized by J. D. Power and Associates as having the highest overall customer satisfaction among large airports in its "2010 North America Airport Satisfaction Study." The single best source of information on the Detroit Regional Aerotropolis plan is its website, http://detroitaerotropolis.com, which includes the Strategic Development Master Plan prepared by the commercial real estate firm Jones Lang LaSalle and a summary of Kasarda and Stephen J. Appold's benchmarking study.

The decline and fall of Detroit is a sad tale often told. For recent history, I drew most heavily upon James Howard Kunstler's *The Geography of Nowhere* and Matt Labash's "The City Where the Sirens Never Sleep" (*The Weekly Standard*, December 29, 2008), from which L. Brooks Patterson's quote is taken.

The assessment that Detroit died the moment Henry Ford perfected the moving assembly line is Jane Jacobs's from *The Economy of Cities*, as is the capsule history of Detroit industry. The snapshot of the city's transportation history is from *Edge City.* Christopher Leinberger's suggestion that the auto industry and its subsidiaries composed as much as a third of GDP is found in *The Option of Urbanism*. Lester Brown's assertion that we have reached peak auto ownership is found online at www.earth-policy.org/index.php?/plan_b_updates/2010/update87.

Statistics on Pittsburgh's steel industry employment are borrowed from Jeffrey Rothfeder's "The Doomsday Scenario" (*Condé Nast Portfolio*, May 2008). The visitor who prophesied a "Utopia of the Machine" was R. L. Duffus in "Detroit: Utopia on Wheels" (*Harper's Magazine*, December 1930).

The stories of Schiphol, Schiphol Real Estate, SADC, and the Zuidas are drawn from interviews, documents, and presentations provided by Maurits Schaafsma and other airport executives. Michel van Wijk's *Airports as Cityports in the City-Region* was also quite helpful.

My interview with Robert Ficano took place in his old office at the Wayne County Building. The comparison to Fiorello La Guardia is courtesy of *Naked Airport*. Statistics on tax rates and the number of college students in greater Detroit are taken from Detroit Renaissance's "Assessing Regional Competitiveness: Benchmarks" report published in August 2008. A full list of taxes and incentives in the "Aerotropolis Zones" can be found on the Detroit Aerotropolis website.

Maps and proposals presented during the University of Michigan's Detroit Design Charrette in 2006 were later published as a report titled "Aerotropolis. A New City Willow Run to Detroit." The backstory of Visteon Village was gleaned from materials provided by the company and interviews with executives. Its R & D spending figures are from "Beyond Borders: The Global Innovation 1000" (*Strategy + Business*, Winter 2008).

The full text of Jeff Immelt's speech to the Detroit Economic Club on June 26, 2009, is available on General Electric's website. Richard Florida's suggestion that Detroit residents may need to become aerial commuters is taken from "The Ruse of the Creative Class" (*The American Prospect*, January/February 2010). James Fallows's interview with BYD's chairman, Wang Chuanfu, ran in "China's Way Forward" (*The Atlantic*, April 2009). The projections on the global growth of auto ownership are from "The Best Years of the Auto Industry Are Still to Come," by Ronald Haddock and John Jullens (*Strategy + Business*, July 29, 2009). The Tempo Group's plans for Detroit are from an interview with the general manager Jeff Zhao and stories in *Crain's Detroit Business*.

7: The Cool Chain
The migration of the tulip from the steppes of Central Asia to Holland in the saddlebags of Carolus Clusius is best told by Mike Dash in *Tulipomania*. The history and details of the Dutch East India Company are drawn from a number of sources found through Wikipedia. The idea that all financial bubbles are bets on globalization is suggested in Michael Pettis's *The Volatility Machine* and Peter Thiel's "The Optimistic Thought Experiment" (*Policy Review*, February and March 2008).

The early history of floral logistics is found in *From Green to Gold: An Illustrated History of the Aalsmeer Flower Auction*, a book commissioned by the Aalsmeer. The scenes detailing how the auctions work are taken from interviews and tours with auction officials (including Henk de Groot), interviews with the staff of Hilverda De Boer (including Aard de Boer), and Amy Stewart's invaluable *Flower Confidential*, from which I also gleaned innumerable details about the history of Dutch floriculture and the globalization of the floral industry. Additional details on Kenyan rose farms and the loss of business to Ethiopia were found in "Roses Are Red" (*The Economist*, February 9, 2008). The path my tulips took through the auctions was explained in an e-mail from Hilverda De Boer's Chicago representative Susan Tock. And plans for the futuristic Aalsmeer appeared in *From Green to Gold*.

Japan Airlines sent me Akira Okazaki's final report on the events leading up to "the day of the flying fish," which also appears in Sasha Issenberg's *The Sushi Economy*. Tom Asakawa of NOAA's Fisheries Service was kind enough to lead me on a tour of Tsukiji. Dane Klinger and Kimiko Narita explained why the Atlantic bluefin tuna is likely doomed in their article "Peak Tuna" (ForeignPolicy.com, February 12, 2010). The combination of the cool chain and everyday low prices willed Chilean farmed salmon into being. Charles Fishman explored the unintended consequences of this in *The Wal-Mart Effect*.

The New Yorker's Michael Specter chose to open his critique of the food miles movement with Sir Terry Leahy's speech to the Forum of the Future, and I chose to do the same. Leahy's speech (the full text of which is available on the forum's website) was simply too good a setup to pass up. Specter's story "Big Foot" (February 25, 2008) introduced me to Cranfield University's Adrian Williams, who conducted the study demonstrating that Kenyan roses have less of a carbon footprint than Dutch ones. I also borrowed his quote by Iowa State University's Rich Pirog, whose study on how far American produce typically travels by truck is often used to bolster locavore arguments.

The study comparing New Zealand lamb and milk with their British counterparts is "Food Miles—Comparative Energy/Emissions Performance of New Zealand's Agriculture Industry," a research report published by Lincoln University's Agribusiness & Economics Research Unit in July 2006, written by director Caroline Saunders, Andrew Barber, and Greg Taylor. The breakdown of a Big Mac's carbon footprint is courtesy of Jamais Cascio's "The Cheeseburger Footprint" (http://openthefuture.com/cheeseburger _CF.html). Christoper L. Weber and H. Scott Matthews argued for substitution in "Food-Miles and the Relative Climate Impacts of Food Choices in the United States" (*Environmental Science & Technology*, vol. 42, no. 10, 2008).

Michael Pollan's prescription for increased organic farming appeared in "Farmer in Chief" (*The New York Times Magazine*, October 9, 2008). Paul Collier's sustained argument against it originally appeared as "The Politics of Hunger" (*Foreign Affairs*, November/December 2008), from which many of his quotes were taken; the piece became the basis of his book *The Plundered Planet,* which expands upon many of his points. I interviewed him in January 2009.

Bangor University's Gareth Edwards-Jones sent me two papers of which he was the lead author: "Testing the Assertion That 'Local Food Is Best': The Challenges of an Evidence-Based Approach" (*Food Science & Technology*, vol. 18, 2008) and "Vulnerability of Exporting Nations to the Development of a Carbon Label in the United Kingdom" (*Environmental Science & Policy*, 2008).

The best introduction to the trend of Asian and Middle Eastern nations buying and developing farmland in African ones is Andrew Rice's "Is There Such a Thing as Agro-Imperialism?" (*The New York Times Magazine*, November 16, 2009). The leaked World Bank report "The Global Land Rush" was obtained by the *Financial Times* ("World Bank Warns on 'Farmland Grab,'" July 27, 2010). *The Economist* saw the trend as "Outsourcing's Third Wave" (May 21, 2009). The Oxfam report cited is "Fair Miles: Recharting the Food Miles Map," by Kelly Rae Chi, James MacGregor, and Richard King, published by the International Institute for Environment and Development.

James E. McWilliams's vision of global food hubs and spokes appears in *Just Food*. Carlo Petrini advanced his idea of food communities in *Terra Madre*. And Walmart's sustainability index was introduced in *The New York Times* ("At Wal-Mart, Labeling to Reflect Green Intent," July 15, 2009).

8: The Big Bangs

The phrase "unsinkable aircraft carrier" was used by General Douglas MacArthur to describe Taiwan; the details of its mini–Marshall Plan are from Barry C. Lynn's *End of the Line*.

Pasuk Phongpaichit supplied me with an English translation of her research team's history of what would become Suvarnabhumi. John Kasarda provided a copy of the "Suvarnabhumi Aerotropolis Development Plan" and his personal history in Thailand. The Asian financial crisis was covered everywhere; I found the best overview to be Paul Krugman's *The Return of Depression Economics*.

The recap of Thaksin Shinawatra's first term as prime minister is drawn from *Thaksin*. The long and twisting story of Thaksin's intentions toward the airport is drawn from numerous off-the-record interviews with government officials, airport executives and consultants, international news reports (especially from *The New York Times* and *The Economist*), and daily coverage of his downfall, coup, and exile in Bangkok's two daily English-language newspapers, *The Nation* and the *Bangkok Post*. Human Rights Watch published "Not Enough Graves: The War on Drugs, HIV/AIDS, and Violations of Human Rights" in June 2004.

The effects of PAD's airport shutdown of November 2008 were covered extensively in the *Bangkok Post*, from which the details on the damage to the tourism and computer industries were taken. Past examples of supply chain disruptions are from Lynn's *End of the Line*. Adam Przeworski's link between the resiliency of democracies and per capita incomes is from "What Makes Democracies Endure?" (*Journal of Democracy*, 1996) by Adam Przeworski, Michael M. Alvarez, Jose Antonio Cheibub, Fernando Papaterra, and Limongi Neto. The comments by Pacific Asia Travel Association president Greg Duffell appeared in "Bangkok Loses 30 Per Cent Air Capacity Since Airport Closures" (*Deutsche Presse-Agentur*, March 18, 2009). And the confrontation between red shirts and the army was witnessed by a correspondent for *The Economist* ("Thailand's Ugly Crisis," April 13, 2009).

"The touching thing about monumental architecture is its awkward betrayal of its own purposes," begins Benjamin Moser's condemnation of Brasília, "Cemetery of Hope: Brasília at Fifty" (*Harper's Magazine*, January 2008). Mahathir Mohamad's hopes for Malaysia's "Multimedia Super Corridor" are best captured by Jeff Greenwald's "Thinking Big" (*Wired*, August 1997), and his post–Asian financial crisis comedown is documented in "Mahathir's High-Tech Folly" (*BusinessWeek*, March 22, 1999).

Statistics for the worldwide growth in tourism are taken from the *OECD Environmental Outlook to 2030*. Tourism's contributions to worldwide GDP appeared in the U.N. World Tourism Organization's paper *Aviation, Tourism and Poverty* (2005). Kofi Annan made his comments at the World Bank/ICAO/ATAG conference in 2005. UNWTO assistant secretary-general Geoffrey Lipman described tourism as "the best foreign direct investment system ever invented" at the UK Tourism Society annual meeting in 2008. And the World Economic Forum report is *The Travel & Tourism*

Competitiveness Report 2007: Furthering the Process of Economic Development, edited by Jennifer Blanke and Thea Chiesa.

The section "Medical Leave" is adapted from a story of the same name I published in *Fast Company* (May 2008). The itemized cost of coronary bypass surgery at Bumrungrad was provided on request by the hospital. Ruben Toral's presentation on the Toyotaization of health care can be found on his website at http://mednetasia.com/. My initial conversation with Fortis Hospitals' Vishal Bali took place at the Healthcare Globalization Summit, held in May 2008 at the Venetian in Las Vegas.

My portrait of GMR and G. M. Rao is primarily drawn from Marcus Gee's profile "Paving Bedlam" (*The Globe and Mail,* April 9, 2008). The story of Air Deccan's Captain Gopinath is from *The Economist* ("The Flying Elephant," March 11, 2007). Statistics on the increase in middle-class Indians' incomes and travel budgets are from "India's Rising Middle Class Wants a Better Life" (*McKinsey Quarterly,* 2008). India's crying need for infrastructure was covered well by *The Economist* in three stories: "The Insidious Charms of Foreign Investment" (May 3, 2005), "Building Blocks" (June 3, 2006), and "The Bangalore Paradox" (April 23, 2005). The opening-day chaos of Bengaluru International was documented in "Bumpy Landing for Bangalore's Airport Dream" (Silicon.com, July 30, 2008). Praful Patel's overhaul of Indian aviation and his plans for adding fifty airports are taken from news reports and Kasarda's private briefings. Opening day at New Delhi's Terminal 3 was described by the *Financial Times* ("Delhi Gets Better Flying, but Mumbai Stuck in Holding Pattern," July 5, 2010). The most comprehensive overview of the rocky recent past and bright future of Indian aviation is the Centre for Asia Pacific Aviation India's report "Indian Aviation: A Review of 2009 and Outlook for 2010." Also helpful was Kasarda and Rambabu Vankayalapati's "Indian Aviation Sector."

9: The Aerotropolis Emirates

Dubai changes so quickly that it's nearly impossible to keep up with it in print. I followed its fortunes from boom to bust to bottoming out in the *Financial Times,* the *National, Gulf News, Emirates Business 24/7,* Zawya Dow Jones, and *MEED,* by listening to commentators such as Mishaal Al Gergawi, and in blogs such as "Secret Dubai" (http://secretdubai.blogspot.com/), "The Emirates Economist" (http://emirateseconomist.blogspot.com/), and "Suq Al Mal" (http://suqalmal.blogspot.com/).

The evolution of Dubai from backwater to entrepôt to kingdom of bling is traced in Chrisopher M. Davidson's *Dubai* and Jim Krane's more accessible *City of Gold.* I also drew upon a pair of more recent additions to the emirate's history, Raymond Barrett's *Dubai Dreams* and Syed Ali's *Dubai.*

The hallucinatory architecture of the Gulf is best captured in *Al Manakh* (2007) and *Al Manakh 2: Gulf Continued* (2010). Rem Koolhaas's quote about Dubai's virtual density is taken from the first. Lee Smith compared Dubai to Baghdad in "The Road to Tech Mecca" (*Wired,* July 2004).

The history of Dubai International Airport, Open Skies, and Emirates is told in Krane's *City of Gold,* Graeme Wilson's *Emirates,* and Matthew Maier's "Rise of the Emirates Empire" (*Business 2.0,* October 2005). An early take on the dark side of Dubai was Mike Davis's "Sand, Fear, and Money in Dubai," which appears in *Evil Paradises,* edited by Mike Davis and Daniel Bertrand Monk. The definitive piece of postcrash schadenfreude was Johann Hari's "The Dark Side of Dubai" (*The Independent*, April 7, 2009). Human Rights Watch investigated the treatment of the UAE's "guest workers" in "Building Towers, Cheating Workers: Exploitation of Migrant Construction Workers in the United Arab Emirates," published in November 2006.

In addition to his history of Dubai up until the crash, Christopher Davidson has written a comprehensive book about its older brother, *Abu Dhabi*. The Guggenheim's Thomas Krens was interviewed by Rem Koolhaas in *Al Manakh*. The emirate's plan to clone NYU was detailed in "The Emir of NYU" (*New York*, April 13, 2008), from which NYU president John Sexton's quotes are taken.

My road trip to the site of Dubai World Central occurred in June 2007. Kasarda's ill-fated audience with its various executives occurred a year earlier. His subsequent meetings to plan a "Dubai Aerotropolis" took place between March 2009 and April 2010. Sheikh Ahmed's comments on Dubai going back to trading roots were made in an interview with Zawya Dow Jones on March 16, 2010.

RBS's chief China economist Ben Simpfendorfer wrote *The New Silk Road*. He talked up Dubai's potential as a hub for Africa in an interview. Issa Baluch described the Sea Air Model in his book *Transport Logistics*.

10: The Sustainable Aerotropolis?

The "peak whale" notes are taken from David Owen's *Green Metropolis* and from Peter Applebome's "They Used to Say Whale Oil Was Indispensible, Too" (*The New York Times*, August 3, 2008). The full text of William Stanley Jevons's *The Coal Question* is available online at www.econlib.org/library/YPDBooks/Jevons/jvnCQ.html. The Rocky Mountain Institute's Amory Lovins made his comments about whales during his talk at TED in February 2005 about his cowritten book *Winning the Oil Endgame*.

Once a fringe topic, peak oil is now the subject of intense mainstream discussion. Perhaps the most searingly honest look at life after peak oil is James Howard Kunstler's *The Long Emergency*, which imagines America's future as a sort of Antebellum Dark Ages. Two books arguing that peak oil will be good for us are Christopher Steiner's *$20 Per Gallon* and Jeff Rubin's *Why Your World Is About to Get a Whole Lot Smaller*. Online, "The Oil Drum" (www.theoildrum.com/) offers daily discussion and dissection of oil prices and production; the website of the Association for the Study of Peak Oil and Gas (ASPO) is also worth visiting at (www.peakoil.net). How permanent triple-digit oil prices could affect aviation was best described in Bradford Plumer's "The End of Aviation" (*The New Republic*, August 27, 2008). Plumer's story mentions Richard Gilbert and Anthony Perl's *Transport Revolutions*. And the definitive history of oil is Daniel Yergin's *The Prize*.

Jeff Rubin's reports for CIBC World Markets were "Soaring Oil Prices Will Make the World Rounder" (Jeff Rubin and Benjamin Tal, October 19, 2005) and "The New Inflation" (May 27, 2008). Rubin continues to comment on oil prices at www.jeffrubinssmallerworld.com/.

The Travel Foundation–commissioned study asking Britons about aviation's carbon footprint was published as "The Travel Foundation Consumer Research" and was prepared by Nunwood in 2007 at www.thetravelfoundation.org.uk/index.php?id=91. The Ryanair effect's impact on Murcia, Spain, and its carbon footprint are from Elisabeth

Rosenthal's "Low-Cost Airfares, Big-Time Carbon Footprint" (*The New York Times*, May 30, 2008). The details of Carcassonne, France, are borrowed from Anthony Lane's "High and Low" (*The New Yorker*, April 26, 2006), as is Michael O'Leary's "bollocks" quote. Plane Stupid's website is http://planestupid.com/.

The carbon footprint of housing is taken from "The Green Housing Boom" (*Fast Company*, July/August 2008). The carbon footprint of cattle is from the UN Food and Agriculture Organization's report "Livestock's Long Shadow" (2006), available online at www.fao.org/docrep/010/a0701e/a0701e00.HTM. And the carbon footprint of driving is taken from the World Resources Institute's "Navigating the Numbers: Greenhouse Gas Data and International Climate Policy" by Kevin A. Baumert, Tim Herzog, and Jonathan Pershing (December 2005). The data showing that U.S. airlines' carbon emissions actually fell from 2000 to 2007 are from the Air Transport Association of America's 2008 Economic Report.

China's looming environmental catastrophe was foreshadowed by Elizabeth C. Economy in "The Great Leap Backward?" (*Foreign Affairs*, September/October 2007). The note on the real versus ad valorem costs of air transport is taken from David Hummels's "Transportation Costs and International Trade in the Second Era of Globalization" (*Journal of Economic Perspectives*, 2007).

The best introduction to Julian Simon and his heresies is Ed Regis's "The Doomslayer" (*Wired*, February 2007), from which the Simon quote is taken. (Simon died a year later.) Researchers at the Santa Fe Institute led by the physicist Geoffrey West have published a number of papers on the metabolism of cities. An introduction to their work is Jonah Lehrer's "The Living City" (*Seed*, July 2007). The statistics on oil demand destruction are taken from Jad Mouawad's "Wondering if Crude Could Fall Even More" (*The New York Times*, March 9, 2009). The International Energy Agency's predictions are taken from its *World Energy Outlook 2009*.

James Hansen's refusal to aid Heathrow protesters appeared in the *London Observer* ("Climate Expert Snubs Heathrow Protesters," February 1, 2009). His subsequent e-mail was published widely, including at www.columbia.edu/%7Ejeh1/mailings/2009/20090203_CoalRiverMountain.pdf.

The IEA's chief economist Fatih Birol has said that if no big new discoveries are made, "the output of conventional oil will peak in 2020 if oil demand grows on a business-as-usual basis" ("20/20 Vision," *The Economist*, December 10, 2009). Sir David King's belief that OPEC has exaggerated reserves appeared in many news outlets, including *The Daily Telegraph* (March 22, 2010). The Kuwaiti researchers made their prediction in "Forecasting World Crude Oil Production Using Multicyclic Hubbert Model" by Ibrahim Sami Nashawi, Adel Malallah, and Mohammed Al-Bisharah (*Energy Fuels*, 2010). The McKinsey Global Institute's scenario was published as "How High Will It Go?" (*Foreign Policy*, September/October 2009).

Richard Branson's conversion from climate change skeptic to prominent environmentalist was profiled by Michael Specter in "Branson's Luck" (*The New Yorker*, May 14, 2007). I was present at the Clinton Global Initiative when he made his R & D commitment, at the follow-up press conference a week later, and at a third press conference in 2008 where I asked him about the biofuels test. I made a pilgrimage to Solazyme's headquarters in South San Francisco (barely a mile from San Francisco International Airport) in October 2009, where I met with cofounders Harrison Dillon and Jonathan Wolfson and toured their labs. Craig Venter detailed the creation of "Synthia" in *Science* ("Creation of a Bacterial Cell Controlled by a Chemically Synthesized Genome" (May 2010).

On the subject of high-speed rail (HSR) in America, the U.S. High Speed Rail Association is pushing for a seventeen-thousand-mile national network of bullet trains— essentially every credible project under review. The estimated price tag is $600 billion ("High-Speed Rail Advocates Say $8B Is Just a Start," Associated Press, October 23, 2009). The sprawl issue of HSR in California's Central Valley was raised by *Wired News's* Jason Kambitsis ("High-Speed Rail as a Conduit of Sprawl," March 16, 2010).

As for the Jevons Paradox aspect, this was noted in the debate over HSR connecting to Heathrow. The British Airport Authority said a stop on the proposed line could lead to increased air traffic by releasing latent demand ("Pollution Fears Over High-Speed Rail Link," *The London Evening Standard*, August 12, 2009). Britons' belief in teleportation was discovered in a survey conducted by Cisco and covered by *The Daily Telegraph* ("Britons Expect to Be Teleporting in the Next Ten Years" (July 11, 2010).

Airline Network News & Analysis (www.anna.aero) noted the 40 percent drop in Madrid–Barcelona air passenger traffic in a story posted February 9, 2010 ("Madrid Air Traffic to Barcelona (Down 40%), Malaga (Down 50%) Impacted by Expanding AVE High-Speed Rail Network"). The details from the section on NextGen and its endless delays are taken from my *Fast Company* story "Ground Control" (May 2009).

As in the introduction of this book, urbanization statistics are drawn from reports by UN-HABITAT, while the New Songdo section is derived from source materials and interviews supplied by Gale International, KPF, and Cisco.

11: Go West. Go Out. Go.

PCH International founder Liam Casey was the main subject of James Fallows's "China Makes, the World Takes" for *The Atlantic*. I was fortunate to be leaving for China a few weeks after the story was published. I e-mailed Casey immediately, who graciously invited me to Shenzhen. Casey's quotes and passages are derived from our time together and an interview with the BBC's Peter Day. Fallows's story is the definitive take on how China's factories actually work.

Foxconn/Hon Hai 517 is unknown to most Americans, and founder Terry Gou would prefer to keep it that way. But its clients are open secrets on technology blogs. *The Wall Street Journal's* Jason Dean was once invited inside ("The Forbidden City of Terry Gou," August 11, 2007). The World Bank's findings on agglomeration economies were published in the *World Development Report 2009: Reshaping Economic Geography*. Bunnie Huang's blog post is at www.bunniestudios.com/blog/?p=611. Clive Thompson wrote about the origins of the netbook craze (now the tablet craze) in "The Netbook Effect: How Cheap Little Laptops Hit the Big Time" (*Wired*, March 2009). The triumph of the tablet over the netbook by 2012 was predicted by Forrester Research and covered by Erick Schonfeld for the blog *CrunchGear* at www.crunchgear.com.

My histories of Li & Fung and Hong Kong are primarily drawn from interviews with Hong Kong University's Victor Sit and the brothers Victor and William Fung, and from the latter's book (with Jerry Wind) *Competing in a Flat World*. The sociologist Manuel Castells also discusses the Delta at some length in *The Rise of the Network Society*, along with "the space of flows."

Beijing's vision for the Delta was spelled out in the National Development and

Reform Commission's "Outline of the Plan for the Reform and Development of the Pearl River Delta (2008–2020)."

Rem Koolhaas's comments on Zhuhai's failure were published in *Mutations*, while his mention of its aerotropolis appears in *Great Leap Forward*. I visited the FedEx hub at Guangzhou while it was still under construction in August 2007. My favorite history of the tea trade, clipper ships, and the Great Tea Race of 1866 is in Sarah Murray's *Moveable Feasts*.

Steven Cheung's explanation of Chinese cities' cutthroat development tactics is taken from a paper titled "The Economic System of China," delivered at the Forum on Thirty Years of Marketization in August 2008 in Beijing. The English translation of his quotes is taken from Richard McGregor's *The Party*, as no complete translation exists. China's airport strategy is laid out in the Eleventh Five-Year Plan, available on the government's website, www.gov.cn/english/special/115y_index.htm. GE's plans to capitalize on this strategy are found in Mark Borden's "All Systems Go" (*Fast Company*, May 2008).

Harvard's Niall Ferguson and Moritz Schularick called for "The End of Chimerica" in their working paper of the same name published in October 2009. Former labor secretary Robert Reich's warning appeared as "China and the American Jobs Machine" (*The Wall Street Journal*, November 16, 2009). Paul Krugman's denunciation of China's "beggar-everyone-but-yourself policy" appeared on his blog on the *New York Times* website on December 31, 2009. China Investment Corp. chairman Lou Jiwei told a reporter from Reuters "we can't lose" on August 28, 2009. And Jim Chanos explained his bet against China in a lecture at Oxford University titled "The China Syndrome: Warning Signs Ahead for the Global Economy," delivered January 28, 2010.

Terry Gou's maneuvers in China were covered extensively by the *Financial Times* and *People's Daily*. China's plans to make Chongqing the global capital of laptop production have been covered extensively in *DigiTimes*, a daily newspaper for the computing industry published from Taipei. Lyn Wu, a professor at the Chongqing University of Technology, collaborated with Kasarda on a study of Chongqing's air logistics platform.

The economist Ben Simpfendorfer and the journalist Richard Behar have been the best at describing the implications of China's "Go Out" policy. Simpfendorfer's *The New Silk Road* covers the Middle East, while Behar's "China in Africa" (*Fast Company*, June 2008) not only documents China's strip-mining of the continent but also makes clear that China is doing it to keep its exports rising. Also helpful was Serge Michel and Michel Beuret's *China Safari*. China's presence in Gwadar, Pakistan, was described in Shahan Mufti's "Persian Gulf View" (*Harper's Magazine*, February 2010).

John Kasarda's analysis of Open Skies appeared in "Air Cargo, Liberalization, and Economic Development." The Boeing-sponsored study was "The Economic Impact of Air Service Liberalization" (2006), conducted by the consulting firm InterVISTAS. The U.S. National Committee for Pacific Economic Cooperation–sponsored study "An Analysis of the Economic Benefits From Full Liberalization of Integrated Air Express Services in the Asia-Pacific Region" was conducted by the Campbell-Hill Aviation Group with Kasarda's assistance.

SELECTED BIBLIOGRAPHY

Al Manakh 1. Vol. 12, no. 2. New York: Columbia University GSAPP, 2007.

Al Manakh 2: Gulf Continued. Vol. 23, no. 1. Amsterdam: Archis Publishers, 2010.

Ali, Syed. *Dubai: Gilded Cage.* New Haven: Yale University Press, 2010.

Altshuler, Alan, and David Luberoff. *Mega-Projects: The Changing Politics of Urban Public Investment.* Washington, D.C.: Brookings Institution Press, 2003.

Anderson, Chris. *The Long Tail: Why the Future of Business Is Selling Less of More.* New York: Hyperion, 2006.

Baluch, Issa. *Transport Logistics: Past, Present and Predictions.* Dubai: Winning Books, 2005.

Barrett, Raymond. *Dubai Dreams: Inside the Kingdom of Bling.* London: Nicholas Brealey Publishing, 2010.

Berry, Brian J. L., and John D. Kasarda. *Contemporary Urban Ecology.* New York: Macmillan, 1977.

Bidwell, Charles E., and John D. Kasarda. *The Organization and Its Ecosystem: A Theory of Structuring in Organizations.* Greenwich, CT: JAI Press, 1985.

Blalock, Hubert M., Jr. *Causal Inferences in Nonexperimental Research.* Chapel Hill: University of North Carolina Press, 1964.

Bode, Steven, and Jeremy Millar, eds. *Airport: The Most Important New Buildings of the Twentieth Century.* London: Photographers' Gallery, 1997.

Borsook, Paulina. *Cyberselfish: A Critical Romp Through the World of High-Tech.* New York: Public Affairs, 2000.

Brooks, David. *On Paradise Drive: How We Live Now (and Always Have) in the Future Tense.* New York: Simon & Schuster, 2004.

Burdett, Ricky, and Deyan Sudjic. *The Endless City: The Urban Age Project by the London School of Economics and Deutsche Bank's Alfred Herrhausen Society.* London: Phaidon, 2008.

Burgess, Ernest Watson. "The Growth of the City: An Introduction to a Research Project." In *The City*, edited by Robert E. Park, Ernest W. Burgess, and Roderick D. McKenzie, 47–62. Chicago: University of Chicago Press, 1925.

Button, Kenneth, and Somik Lall. "The Economics of Being an Airport Hub City." *Research in Transportation Economics* 5 (1999): 75–105.

Button, Kenneth, and Roger Stough. *Air Transport Networks: Theory and Policy Implications*. Northampton, MA: Edward Elgar, 2000.

Caro, Robert A. *The Power Broker: Robert Moses and the Fall of New York*. New York: Vintage Books, 1975.

Castells, Manuel, ed. *High Technology, Space, and Society*. Beverly Hills, CA: Sage Publications, 1985.

———. *The Rise of the Network Society*. 2nd ed. Malden, MA: Wiley-Blackwell, 2010.

Castells, Manuel, and Peter Hall. *Technopoles of the World: The Making of Twenty-First-Century Industrial Complexes*. New York: Routledge, 1994.

Ceruzzi, Paul E. *Internet Alley: High Technology in Tysons Corner, 1945–2005*. Cambridge, MA: MIT Press, 2008.

Chanda, Nayan. *Bound Together: How Traders, Preachers, Adventurers, and Warriors Shaped Globalization*. New Haven: Yale University Press, 2007.

Chung, Chuihua Judy, Jeffrey Inaba, Rem Koolhaas, and Sze Tsung Leong, *Great Leap Forward*. Cambridge, MA: Harvard Design School, 2001.

Cobb, James C., and William Stueck, eds. *Globalization and the American South*. Athens: University of Georgia Press, 2005.

Collier, Paul. *The Bottom Billion: Why the Poorest Countries Are Failing and What Can Be Done About It*. New York: Oxford University Press, 2007.

———. *The Plundered Planet: Why We Must—and How We Can—Manage Nature for Global Prosperity*. New York: Oxford University Press, 2010.

Conway, H. McKinley. *The Airport City and the Future Intermodal Transportation System*. Atlanta: Conway Publications, 1977.

———. *The Airport City: Development Concepts for the 21st Century*. Rev. ed. Atlanta: Conway Publications, 1980.

Cooley, Charles H. "The Theory of Transportation." *Publications of the American Economic Association* 9, no. 3 (May 1894): 13–148.

Corn, Joseph J. *The Winged Gospel: America's Romance with Aviation, 1900–1950*. New York: Oxford University Press, 1983.

Cwerner, Saulo, Sven Kesselring, and John Urry, eds. *Aeromobilities*. New York: Routledge, 2009.

Dash, Mike. *Tulipomania: The Story of the World's Most Coveted Flower and the Extraordinary Passions It Aroused*. New York: Crown, 1999.

Davidson, Christopher M. *Abu Dhabi: Oil and Beyond*. New York: Columbia University Press, 2009.

———. *Dubai: The Vulnerability of Success*. New York: Columbia University Press, 2008.

Davis, Mike. *City of Quartz: Excavating the Future in Los Angeles*. New York: Vintage Books, 1992.

———. *Planet of Slums*. New York: Verso, 2006.

Davis, Mike, and Daniel Bertrand Monk, eds. *Evil Paradises: Dreamworlds of Neoliberalism*. New York: New Press, 2007.

Dempsey, Paul Stephen, Andrew R. Goetz, and Joseph S. Szyliowicz. *Denver International Airport: Lessons Learned*. New York: McGraw-Hill, 1997.

Diamond, Jared. *Collapse: How Societies Choose to Fail or Succeed*. New York: Viking, 2005.

Didion, Joan. *Where I Was From*. New York: Knopf, 2003.

Dierikx, Marc. *Clipping the Clouds: How Air Travel Changed the World*. Westport, CT: Praeger, 2008.

Dogan, Mattei, and John D. Kasarda, eds. *The Metropolis Era*. Newbury Park, CA: Sage Publications, 1988.

Doganis, Rigas. *The Airport Business*. New York: Routledge, 1992.

Duncan, Otis Dudley. *Metropolis and Region*. Baltimore: Johns Hopkins Press, 1960.

———. "Social Organization and the Ecosystem." In *Handbook of Modern Sociology*, edited by Robert E. Lee Faris, 37–82. Chicago: Rand McNally, 1964.

Erie, Steven P. *Globalizing L.A.: Trade, Infrastructure, and Regional Development*. Stanford: Stanford University Press, 2004.

Erie, Steven P., John D. Kasarda, and Andrew M. McKenzie. *A New Orange County Airport at El Toro: An Economic Benefits Study*. Orange County, CA: Orange County Business Council, 1998.

Erie, Steven P., John D. Kasarda, Andrew M. McKenzie, and Michael A. Molloy. *A New Orange County Airport at El Toro: Catalyst for High-Wage, High-Tech Economic Development*. Orange County, CA: Orange County Business Council, 1999.

Fagan, Brian M. *The Great Warming: Climate Change and the Rise and Fall of Civilizations*. New York: Bloomsbury, 2008.

Fallows, James. *Postcards from Tomorrow Square: Reports from China*. New York: Vintage Books, 2009.

Fishman, Charles. *The Wal-Mart Effect: How the World's Most Powerful Company Really Works—and How It's Transforming the American Economy*. New York: Penguin Press, 2006.

Fishman, Ted C. *China Inc.: How the Rise of the Next Superpower Challenges America and the World*. New York: Scribner, 2005.

Flamm, Kenneth. *Creating the Computer: Government, Industry, and High Technology*. Washington, D.C.: Brookings Institution Press, 1988.

Florida, Richard. *The Great Reset: How New Ways of Living and Working Drive Post-Crash Prosperity*. New York: Harper, 2010.

———. *The Rise of the Creative Class: And How It's Transforming Work, Leisure, Community and Everyday Life*. New York: Basic Books, 2004.

Flyvbjerg, Bent, Nils Bruzelius, and Werner Rothengatter. *Megaprojects and Risk: An Anatomy of Ambition*. New York: Cambridge University Press, 2003.

Ford, Henry. *Ford Ideals*. Dearborn, MI: Dearborn Publishing Company, 1922.

Frank, Thomas. *The Wrecking Crew: How Conservatives Rule*. New York: Metropolitan Books, 2008.

Friedman, Thomas L. *Hot, Flat, and Crowded: Why We Need a Green Revolution, and How It Can Renew America*. New York: Farrar, Straus and Giroux, 2008.

————. *The World Is Flat: A Brief History of the Twenty-first Century.* 1st updated and expanded ed. New York: Farrar, Straus and Giroux, 2006.

Friedmann, John. "The World City Hypothesis." *Development and Change* 17, no. 1 (January 1986): 69–83.

Fröbel, Folker, Jürgen Heinrichs, and Otto Kreye. *The New International Division of Labour: Structural Unemployment in Industrialised Countries and Industrialisation in Developing Countries.* New York: Cambridge University Press, 1980.

Frock, Roger. *Changing How the World Does Business: FedEx's Incredible Journey to Success—the Inside Story.* San Francisco: Berrett-Koehler, 2006.

Fung, Victor K., William K. Fung, and Yoram (Jerry) Wind. *Competing in a Flat World: Building Enterprises for a Borderless World.* Upper Saddle River, NJ: Wharton School Pub., 2008.

Gans, Herbert J. *People and Plans: Essays on Urban Problems and Solutions.* New York: Basic Books, 1968.

Garreau, Joel. *Edge City: Life on the New Frontier.* New York: Anchor Books, 1992.

Gilbert, Richard, and Anthony Perl. *Transport Revolutions: Moving People and Freight Without Oil.* Washington, D.C.: Earthscan, 2010.

Gleick, James. *Faster: The Acceleration of Just About Everything.* New York: Pantheon, 1999.

Goldmanis, Maris, Ali Hortacsu, Chad Syverson, and Önsel Emre. "E-Commerce and the Market Structure of Retail Industries." *The Economic Journal* 120, no. 545, (June 2010): 651–82.

Gordon, Alastair. *Naked Airport: A Cultural History of the World's Most Revolutionary Structure.* New York: Holt, 2004.

Gottdiener, Mark. *Life in the Air: Surviving the New Culture of Air Travel.* Lanham, MD: Rowman & Littlefield, 2001.

Gras, N.S.B. *An Introduction to Economic History.* New York: Harper, 1922.

Greis, Noel P., and John D. Kasarda. "Enterprise Logistics in the Information Era." *California Management Review* 39, no. 4 (Summer 1997): 55–78.

Greis, Noel P., Jack G. Olin, and John D. Kasarda. "The Intelligent Future." *Supply Chain Management Review* 7, no. 3 (May 2003): 18–23.

Güller, Mathis, and Michael Güller. *From Airport to Airport City.* Barcelona: Editorial Gustavo Gili, 2003.

Gutfreund, Owen D. *Twentieth-Century Sprawl: Highways and the Reshaping of the American Landscape.* New York: Oxford University Press, 2004.

Hall, Edward N. "The Air City." *Traffic Quarterly* 26, no. 1 (1972): 15–31.

Hall, Peter. *The World Cities.* 3rd ed. New York: St. Martin's Press, 1984.

Harvey, David. *A Brief History of Neoliberalism.* New York: Oxford University Press, 2005.

Hawley, Amos Henry. "Human Ecology." In *International Encyclopedia of the Social Sciences,* edited by David L. Sills and Robert K. Merton, 323–32. New York: Macmillan, 1968.

————. *Human Ecology: A Theoretical Essay.* Chicago: University of Chicago Press, 1986.

————. *Human Ecology: A Theory of Community Structure.* New York: Ronald Press, 1950.

————. *Urban Society: An Ecological Approach.* New York: Ronald Press, 1971.

Hoover, Edgar Malone. *The Location of Economic Activity.* New York: McGraw-Hill, 1948.

Hurd, Richard M. *Principles of City and Land Values.* New York: The Record and Guide, 1903.

Irwin, Michael D., and John D. Kasarda. "Air Passenger Linkages and Employment Growth in U.S. Metropolitan Areas." *American Sociological Review* 56, no. 4 (August 1991): 524–37.

Isard, Walter. *Location and Space-Economy: A General Theory Relating to Industrial Location, Market Areas, Land Use, Trade, and Urban Structure.* New York: Wiley, 1956.

Issenberg, Sasha. *The Sushi Economy: Globalization and the Making of a Modern Delicacy.* New York: Gotham Books, 2007.

Jacobs, Jane. *Cities and the Wealth of Nations.* New York: Vintage Books, 1985.

————. *The Death and Life of Great American Cities.* New York: Modern Library, 1993.

————. *The Economy of Cities.* New York: Random House, 1969.

Jevons, William Stanley. *The Coal Question: An Enquiry Concerning the Progress of the Nation, and the Probable Exhaustion of Our Coal-Mines.* 2nd ed. London: Macmillan, 1866.

Kasarda, John D. "Aerotropolis: Airport-Driven Urban Development." In *ULI on the Future: Cities in the 21st Century*, 32–41. Washington, D.C.: Urban Land Institute, 2000.

————. Aerotropolism.com website, 2011.

————. "Air Routes as Economic Development Levers." *Global Airport Cities* 2, no. 3 (2008): 32–33.

————. "Airport Cities." *Urban Land* 68, no. 4 (April 2009): 56–60.

————. "Airport-Related Industrial Development." *Urban Land* 55, no. 6 (June 1996): 54–55.

————. "Aviation Infrastructure, Competitiveness, and Aerotropolis Development in the Global Economy: Making Shanghai China's True Gateway City." In *Shanghai Rising: State Power and Local Transformations in a Global Megacity*, edited by Xiangming Chen, 15: 49–72. Minneapolis: University of Minnesota Press, 2009.

————. "From Airport City to Aerotropolis." *Airport World* 6, no. 4 (August–September 2001): 42–45.

————. "Global Air Cargo–Industrial Complexes as Development Tools." *Economic Development Quarterly* 5, no. 3 (August 1, 1991): 187–96.

————. "The Global TransPark: Logistical Infrastructure for Industrial Advantage." *Urban Land* 57, no. 4 (April, 1998): 107–10.

————. "The Implications of Contemporary Distribution Trends for National Urban Policy." *Social Science Quarterly* 61, no. 3/4 (December 1980): 373–400.

————. "An Industrial/Aviation Complex for the Future." *Urban Land* 50, no. 8 (August 1991): 16–20.

————. "Logistics & the Rise of Aerotropolis." *Real Estate Issues* 25, no. 4 (Winter 2000): 43.

————. "Planning the Aerotropolis." *Airport World* 5, no. 5 (October/November, 2000): 52–53.

———. "The Theory of Ecological Expansion: An Empirical Test." *Social Forces* 51, no. 2 (December 1972): 165–75.

———. "Time-Based Competition & Industrial Location in the Fast Century." *Real Estate Issues* 23, no. 4 (Winter 1998): 24–29.

———. "Transportation Infrastructure for Competitive Success." *Transportation Quarterly* 50, no. 1 (Winter 1996): 35–50.

Kasarda, John D., ed. *Global Airport Cities.* London: Insight Media, 2010.

Kasarda, John D., and Charles E. Bidwell. "An Ecological Theory of Organizational Structuring." In *Continuities in Sociological Human Ecology,* edited by Michael Micklin and Dudley L. Poston, Jr., 85–116. New York: Plenum Press, 1998.

Kasarda, John D., and W. Parker Frisbie. "Spatial Processes." In *Handbook of Modern Sociology,* edited by Neil J. Smelser, 629–66. Beverly Hills, CA: Sage Publications, 1988.

Kasarda, John D., and Michael D. Irwin. "National Business Cycles and Community Competition for Jobs." *Social Forces* 69, no. 3 (March 1991): 733–61.

———. "Trade, Transportation, and Spatial Distribution." In *The Handbook of Economic Sociology,* edited by Neil J. Smelser and Richard Swedberg, 342–67. Princeton: Princeton University Press, 1994.

Kasarda, John D., and Dennis A. Rondinelli. "Innovative Infrastructure for Agile Manufacturers." *Sloan Management Review* 39, no. 2 (Winter 1998): 73–82.

Kasarda, John D., Dennis A. Rondinelli, and John W. Ward. "The Global TransPark Network: Creating an Infrastructure Support System for Agile Manufacturing." *National Productivity Review* 16, no. 1 (1996): 33–41.

Kasarda, John D., and David Sullivan. "Air Cargo, Liberalization, and Economic Development." *Annals of Air and Space Law* 31 (May 2006): 167–84.

Kasarda, John D., and Rambabu Vankayalapati. "India's Aviation Sector: Dynamic Transformation." In *Indian Economic Super Power: Fiction or Future?* edited by Jayashankar M. Swaminathan, 135–60. Hackensack, NJ: World Scientific, 2009.

Kilborn, Peter T. *Next Stop, Reloville: Life Inside America's New Rootless Professional Class.* New York: Times Books, 2009.

Kirn, Walter. *Up in the Air.* New York: Doubleday, 2001.

Koolhaas, Rem, Stefano Boeri, Sanford Kwinter, Nadia Tazi, and Hans Ulrich Obrist. *Mutations: Rem Koolhaas, Harvard Project on the City.* Barcelona: Actar, 2001.

Koolhaas, Rem, and Bruce Mau. *Small, Medium, Large, Extra-Large.* 2nd ed. New York: Monacelli Press, 1997.

Krane, Jim. *City of Gold: Dubai and the Dream of Capitalism.* New York: St. Martin's Press, 2009.

Krugman, Paul. *The Return of Depression Economics.* New York: Norton, 1999.

Kunstler, James Howard. *The Geography of Nowhere: The Rise and Decline of America's Man-Made Landscape.* New York: Simon & Schuster, 1993.

———. *The Long Emergency: Surviving the Converging Catastrophes of the Twenty-first Century.* New York: Atlantic Monthly Press, 2005.

Kynge, James. *China Shakes the World: A Titan's Breakneck Rise and Troubled Future— and the Challenge for America.* Boston: Houghton Mifflin, 2006.

Lang, Robert E. *Edgeless Cities: Exploring the Elusive Metropolis.* Washington, D.C.: Brookings Institution Press, 2003.

Le Corbusier. *The City of Tomorrow and Its Planning.* Trans. Frederick Etchells. Cambridge, MA: MIT Press, 1971.

Leinberger, Christopher B. *The Option of Urbanism: Investing in a New American Dream.* Washington, D.C.: Island Press, 2008.

Lenski, Gerhard. *Human Societies: A Macrolevel Introduction to Sociology.* New York: McGraw-Hill, 1970.

———. *Power and Privilege: A Theory of Social Stratification.* New York: McGraw-Hill, 1966.

Leontief, Wassily. "A Multiregional Input-Output Model of the World Economy." In *The International Allocation of Economic Activity: Proceedings of a Nobel Symposium Held at Stockholm,* edited by Bertil Gotthard Ohlin, Per-Ove Hesselborn, and Per Magnus Wijkman, 507–30. New York: Holmes & Meier, 1977.

Logan, John R., and Harvey L. Molotch. *Urban Fortunes: The Political Economy of Place.* Berkeley: University of California Press, 1987.

Lovins, Amory B., et al. *Winning the Oil Endgame: Innovation for Profits, Jobs and Security.* Snowmass, CO: Rocky Mountain Institute, 2004.

Lynn, Barry C. *End of the Line: The Rise and Coming Fall of the Global Corporation.* New York: Doubleday, 2005.

Markusen, Ann R. *Profit Cycles, Oligopoly, and Regional Development.* Cambridge, MA: MIT Press, 1985.

McGregor, Richard. *The Party: The Secret World of China's Communist Rulers.* New York: HarperCollins, 2010.

McKenzie, Roderick Duncan. "The Concept of Dominance and World-Organization." *American Journal of Sociology* 33, no. 1 (July 1927): 28–42.

———. "Industrial Expansion and the Interrelations of Peoples." In *Race and Cultural Contacts,* edited by E. B. Reuter, 19–33. New York: McGraw-Hill, 1934.

———. *The Metropolitan Community.* New York: McGraw-Hill, 1933.

———. *Roderick D. McKenzie on Human Ecology: Selected Writings.* Ed. Amos H. Hawley. Chicago: University of Chicago Press, 1968.

McLuhan, Marshall. *Understanding Media: The Extensions of Man.* Corte Madera, CA: Gingko Press, 2003.

McPhee, John. *Uncommon Carriers.* New York: Farrar, Straus and Giroux, 2006.

McWilliams, Carey. *California: The Great Exception.* Berkeley: University of California Press, 1999.

McWilliams, James E. *Just Food: Where Locavores Get It Wrong and How We Can Truly Eat Responsibly.* New York: Little, Brown, 2009.

Michel, Serge, and Michel Beuret. *China Safari: On the Trail of Beijing's Expansion in Africa.* New York: Nation Books, 2009.

Morrison, Steven A., and Clifford Winston. "The Effect of FAA Expenditures on Air Travel Delays." *Journal of Urban Economics* 63, no. 2 (March 2008): 669–78.

Mumford, Lewis. *The City in History: Its Origins, Its Transformations, and Its Prospects.* New York: Harcourt, 1961.

Murray, Sarah. *Moveable Feasts: From Ancient Rome to the 21st Century, the Incredible Journeys of the Food We Eat.* New York: St. Martin's Press, 2007.

Niemann, Greg. *Big Brown: The Untold Story of UPS.* San Francisco: Jossey-Bass, 2007.

Norton, R. D., and J. Rees. "The Product Cycle and the Spatial Decentralization of American Manufacturing." *Regional Studies* 13, no. 2 (April 1979): 141–51.

Ogburn, William Fielding. *Inventions of Local Transportation and the Patterns of Cities.* Indianapolis: Bobbs-Merrill, 1960.

———. *The Social Effects of Aviation.* Boston: Houghton Mifflin, 1946.

Owen, David. *Green Metropolis: Why Living Smaller, Living Closer, and Driving Less Are the Keys to Sustainability.* New York: Riverhead, 2009.

Pascoe, David. *Airspaces.* London: Reaktion Books, 2001.

Park, Robert Ezra. "The City: Suggestions for the Investigation of Human Behavior in the City Environment." *American Journal of Sociology* 20, no. 5 (March 1915): 577–612.

———. "Human Ecology." *American Journal of Sociology* 42, no. 1 (July 1936): 1–15.

Park, Robert E., Ernest W. Burgess, and Roderick D. McKenzie. *The City.* Chicago: University of Chicago Press, 1925.

Pasuk, Phongpaichit, and Chris Baker. *Thaksin: The Business of Politics in Thailand.* 2nd ed. Seattle: University of Washington Press, 2010.

Perloff, Harvey S., et al. *Regions, Resources, and Economic Growth.* Baltimore: Johns Hopkins Press, 1960.

Petrini, Carlo. *Terra Madre: Forging a New Global Network of Sustainable Food Communities.* White River Junction, VT: Chelsea Green, 2010.

Pettis, Michael. *The Volatility Machine: Emerging Economies and the Threat of Financial Collapse.* New York: Oxford University Press, 2001.

Porter, Michael E. *The Competitive Advantage of Nations.* New York: Free Press, 1990.

Pred, Allan. *City-Systems in Advanced Economies: Past Growth, Present Processes, and Future Development Options.* New York: Wiley, 1977.

Reshaping Economic Geography. Washington, D.C.: World Bank, 2009.

Rubin, Jeff. *Why Your World Is About to Get a Whole Lot Smaller: Oil and the End of Globalization.* New York: Random House, 2009.

Sachs, Jeffrey. *Common Wealth: Economics for a Crowded Planet.* New York: Penguin Press, 2008.

Sassen, Saskia. *The Global City: New York, London, Tokyo.* 2nd ed. Princeton, NJ: Princeton University Press, 2001.

Schaafsma, Maurits, Joop Amkreutz, and Mathis Güller. *Airport and City: Airport Corridors: Drivers of Economic Development.* Amsterdam: Schiphol Real Estate, 2008.

Schafer, Andreas, and David G. Victor. "The Future Mobility of the World Population." *Transportation Research*, Part A: Policy and Practice 34, no. 3 (April 2000): 171–205.

Schlichting, Kurt C. *Grand Central Terminal: Railroads, Engineering, and Architecture in New York City.* Baltimore: Johns Hopkins Press, 2001.

Simpfendorfer, Ben. *The New Silk Road: How a Rising Arab World Is Turning Away from the West and Rediscovering China.* New York: Palgrave Macmillan, 2009.

Specter, Michael. "Big Foot." *New Yorker*, February 25, 2008.

———. *Denialism: How Irrational Thinking Hinders Scientific Progress, Harms the Planet, and Threatens Our Lives.* New York: Penguin Press, 2009.

Starr, Kevin. *Golden Dreams: California in an Age of Abundance, 1950–1963.* New York: Oxford University Press, 2009.

Steiner, Christopher. *$20 Per Gallon: How the Inevitable Rise in the Price of Gasoline Will Change Our Lives for the Better.* New York: Grand Central Publishing, 2009.

Stewart, Amy. *Flower Confidential: The Good, the Bad, and the Beautiful in the Business of Flowers.* Chapel Hill, NC: Algonquin Books, 2007.

Stock, Gregory N., John D. Kasarda, and Noel P. Greis. "Logistics, Strategy and Structure: A Conceptual Framework." *International Journal of Operations & Production Management* 18, no. 1–2 (January 1998): 37–52.

Thompson, D'Arcy Wentworth. *On Growth and Form.* Cambridge: Cambridge University Press, 1917.

Thompson, Wilbur R. *A Preface to Urban Economics.* Baltimore: Johns Hopkins Press, 1965.

Toffler, Alvin. *Future Shock.* New York: Random House, 1970.

———. *PowerShift: Knowledge, Wealth, and Violence at the Edge of the 21st Century.* New York: Bantam Books, 1990.

Tomkins, J., N. Topham, J. Twomey, and R. Ward. "Noise versus Access: The Impact of an Airport in an Urban Property Market." *Urban Studies* 35, no. 2 (1998): 243–56.

Turner, Chris. *The Geography of Hope: A Tour of the World We Need.* Toronto: Random House Canada, 2007.

Ullman, Edward. "A Theory of Location for Cities." *American Journal of Sociology* 46, no. 6 (May 1941): 853–64.

United Nations Human Settlements Programme. *State of the World's Cities 2010/2011: Bridging the Urban Divide.* London: Earthscan, 2010.

van Lier, Bas. *From Green to Gold: An Illustrated History of the Aalsmeer Flower Auction.* Amsterdam: Meteor Press, 2005.

Vanderbilt, Tom. *Traffic: Why We Drive the Way We Do (and What It Says About Us).* New York: Knopf, 2008.

Vernon, Raymond. "International Investment and International Trade in the Product Cycle." *Quarterly Journal of Economics* 80, no. 2 (May 1966): 190–207.

———. *Metropolis 1985: Interpretation of the Findings of the New York Metropolitan Region Study.* Cambridge, MA: Harvard University Press, 1960.

Webber, Melvin M. "Culture, Territoriality, and the Elastic Mile." *Papers in Regional Science* 13, no. 1 (December 1964): 58–69.

Whyte, William H. *City: Rediscovering the Center.* New York: Anchor Books, 1990.

Wijk, Michel van. *Airports as Cityports in the City-Region: Spatial-Economic and Institutional Positions and Institutional Learning in Randstad-Schiphol (AMS), Frankfurt Rhein-Main (FRA), Tokyo Haneda (HND) and Narita (NRT).* Utrecht: Koninklijk Nederlands Aardrijkskundig Genootschap, 2007.

Wilson, Graeme. *Emirates: The Airline of the Future.* London: Media Prima, 2005.

Wingo, Lowdon, Jr., ed. *Cities and Space: The Future Use of Urban Land.* Baltimore: Johns Hopkins Press, 1963.

World Energy Outlook 2009. Paris: International Energy Agency, 2009.

Yergin, Daniel. *The Prize: The Epic Quest for Oil, Money & Power.* New York: Free Press, 2008.

Zakaria, Fareed. *The Post-American World.* New York: Norton, 2008.

ACKNOWLEDGMENTS

No two collaborations are alike, and it gives us pleasure, having completed this one, to acknowledge each other's efforts and to express the satisfaction we have taken in working together. It has been an education for us both—an education in how the world works, and an education in the nature of joint effort across borders of time and space that the aerotropolis makes possible. We are both thankful for the guidance and support of Jonathan Galassi, Paul Elie, Jeff Seroy, Sarita Varma, Jennifer Carrow, Stephen Weil, Marion Duvert, and Karen Maine.

John D. Kasarda | Greg Lindsay
January 2011

John Kasarda
To all those at the Kenan-Flagler Business School, the Frank Hawkins Kenan Institute of Private Enterprise, and the William Rand Kenan Jr. Fund who provided constant encouragement to reach for the sky. Especially Cynthia Reifsnider, the Kenan Institute Director of Research Services and Knowledge Management, who gathered a monumental amount of information for the book and superbly supervised those who worked with her: Donna Polat, for providing daily research and knowledge management; the intern Allyson Dyer, who developed our subject wiki; the intern Lizzy Hogenson for obtaining images and copyright permissions; the intern Brian A. Schneider, who worked long hours researching various environmental topics under a tight deadline; and the interns Betsy Ronan Herzog, Gretchen Ptacek, and Qianqian Rui for their substantial background research. Dr. Steve Appold, research assistant professor, who compiled data and consistently provided me with excellent critiques and insights as we drafted the book; Ronda Ragan, executive assistant, for coordinating all aspects of manuscript preparation; Jack Walker, director of information systems, for keeping our technology running

smoothly; and Raymond Farrow, executive director, who provided valuable feedback on several of the book's drafts.

And then there are those who offered their personal ingenuity and ideas—friends and colleagues from around the world who gave their time to be interviewed by my coauthor, Greg Lindsay.

My deepest gratitude to Greg, as well, for effectively challenging me on a number of ideas I have put forth on the aerotropolis. His critical engagement and questioning substantially extended my thoughts, greatly contributing to this book.

And special thanks to my wife, Mary Ann, who, although not quite the saint most authors seem to marry, has been the bedrock of my life since our teenage years. This book is thus dedicated to her.

Greg Lindsay

This book wouldn't have a home were it not for David Kuhn, who knew a perfect match when he saw one. I am also grateful for the help and friendship of Billy Kingsland and Jessi Cimafonte.

Many of the best passages bear the invisible signature of Will Bourne, who initiated me into *Fast Company* and edited the features several chapters are based on. I'm proud to share a masthead with such talented journalists, and thank Bob Safian, Noah Robischon, and Rick Tetzeli for that. I owe a special debt of gratitude to Charles Fishman, who introduced me to the man behind the aerotropolis and graciously stepped aside when I asked to borrow his subject.

Jack Kasarda himself enthusiastically agreed to my suggestion that we join forces and then entrusted me with his life's work. He has been everything I could have asked for in a collaborator, lending me his voice and encouraging me to use my own.

Eric Gillin's ideas, suggestions, and enthusiasm were crucial to the early drafts. Many others read all or part of the manuscript and offered useful advice: Paul Ingrassia, Daniel Safarik, Will Leitch, Douglas Kelbaugh, Paulina Kubiak, David Beeman, Emily Griffin, Melissa Junttila, Andrew Blum, Laura Sullivan, Erin Collier, Rachel De Nys, and Lorelei Nikkola. John Mantia, Drake Baer, Amber Greviskes, Erin Renzas, and Claire Feeney also provided invaluable help.

Writing is the hard part; the fun is in the reporting. Some of the people who made it fun are: Frederick W. Smith, Daryl Snyder, the Louisville mayor Jerry Abramson, Mark Giuffre, Burt Deutsch, Linda Solley-Kanipe, Ilaiasi Ofa, "Sir, Alfred" Mehran Nasseri, Matthew and Jennifer Kelly, Jon Fine and Laurel Touby, Cal Fulenwider, Brian Tellinghuisen, Tom Gleason, Jon Ratner, Elizabeth Plater-Zyberk, Moshe Safdie, the late Amos Hawley, Dave Tyler, the Wayne County executive Robert Ficano, Maurits Schaafsma, Henk de Groot, Aard de Boer, Paul Collier, Adrian Williams, Gareth Edwards-Jones, Suwat Wanisubut, Ruben Toral, Vishal Bali, Phil McArthur, Assem and Dina Hamzeh, Marwan Bibi, Ram Menen, Geert Boven, Issa Baluch, Behram Baluch, Shaju Unnithan, Sir Richard Branson, Jonathan Wolfson, Harrison Dillon, Genet Garamendi, Stan Gale, Jamie von Klemperer, Wim Elfrink, Mary Lou DiNardo, Liam "Mr. China" Casey, Victor Fung, William Fung, Stanley Hui, Michael Pettis, Ching Wang, Dennice Wilson, Eddy Chan, Liu Jie Yin, and Richard Behar.

I'd like to thank Skip Barrie, both for being my mom and for explaining how the conference business works, and my brother, Todd, for scoring Chicago Cubs season tickets. And most of all, I'd like to thank my wife, Sophie Donelson, for her patience, copyediting skills, and love. I wouldn't have made it through this ordeal without her, and for that reason this book is dedicated to her.

INDEX